The Development of the Liturgical Reform

As Seen by
Cardinal Ferdinando Antonelli
from 1948 to 1970

The Development of the Liturgical Reform

As Seen by
Cardinal Ferdinando Antonelli
from 1948 to 1970

Msgr. Nicola Giampietro

Foreword by Archbishop Albert Malcolm Ranjith

Printed in the United States of America

ISBN 978-1-934888-12-4

Contents

Preface

This book was born of an urgent need to evaluate Cardinal Giuseppe Ferdinando Antonelli's contribution to the science of liturgy. It hopes to give due prominence to a man who made an important contribution to the history of the liturgical reform but, somewhat surprisingly, whose name is not mentioned even in the most recent histories of the liturgical reform.

Studying liturgy at the Pontifical Liturgical Institute of St. Anselm has afforded me a particular direction in my liturgical formation and has introduced me especially to the history of the liturgy which has conditioned a true theoretical, spiritual, and pastoral renewal of the liturgy. Symptomatic of that training is the research I have undertaken so as to discover and understand the initial promoters and pioneers of the liturgical reform up to Second Vatican Council. This was the context and the origin of Cardinal Antonelli's liturgical work. An analysis of his published and unpublished writings, and of his thoughts on the reform conducted by Pius XII, and on that of the Council (1948-1970) allows us to give historical recognition to one of the architects of the initial liturgical reform who was a notable research scholar, pastor, and promoter of the ideas of the liturgical movement of the 20th century.

His liturgical writings, which have not yet been studied, were inspired by the broad magisterial lines set out by Pius X, Pius XI, and Pius XII. In this initial liturgical reform, he found the theological acumen and the necessary pastoral insights to spark a long personal theologico-pastoral reflection which matured during his service in the Historical Section of the Sacred Congregation of Rites, in his teaching career at the *Antonianum*, and in his pastoral work. All of this ultimately made him an architect of the liturgical reform and a passionate promoter of the liturgy as theology and spirituality in the service of the Christian life.

This work happily coincides with the centenary of Antonelli's birth which is a propitious opportunity to reflect on his contribution to the liturgy and to the Church.

I wish to dedicate this work of mine to the Second Vatican Council and to the liturgical reform initiated by the Council. Its fruits are "the result of the preparations laid by the liturgical movement and the fulfillment of expectations for which many ecclesiastics and scholars have worked and prayed".[1] Among these, we wish to give special consideration to Cardinal Antonelli. It is our hope to be able to make this figure of our times better known since he strove to impress on the liturgy that form by which it is defined in the contemporary Church.

I wish to thank all those who assisted me in this work: my Superiors, the President and Professors of the Pontifical Liturgical Institute, the archival staff at the Congregation for the Causes of Saints and La Verna who oriented and facilitated my work, Father Francesco Antonelli, OFM, the Cardinal's nephew, Msgr. Sandro Corradini, Promotor General of the Faith, and the Superiors at La Verna. I owe particular thanks to Professors Matias Augé, Rinaldo Falsini, and Domenico Sartore for their wise counsel, direction, and for their patience throughout this work. I also owe a special thanks to Msgr. Martimort, one of the greatest liturgical experts behind the liturgical reform of the Second Vatican Council and a close friend of Cardinal Antonelli, for his help and his suggestions in better presenting Antonelli's thought and the history of the liturgical reform. Finally, I wish to thank my parents who, with faith and the simplicity of their lives, guided me towards the prayer of the Church since childhood.

Nicola Giampietro

[1] Paul VI, *Discorso al Concistoro per la creazione di quattro Cardinali*, in *Insegnamenti di Paolo VI*, vol. XV, Vatican City 1977, p. 662.

Presentation

Dear Father,

You wish me to present your book to the public because I am not only a witness to the role played by Cardinal Antonelli in the great task of the reform of the liturgy in our times, but also because of the friendship with which he honored me right up to the time of his death. I first met him in June 1947 at a reception in the Abbey of San Girolamo in Rome. His intuition of the problems posed for our age by pastoral liturgy and his knowledge of the history of divine worship surprised me.

In secrecy together with a small number of collaborators he drew up the *Memoria sulla Riforma Liturgica* as we later discovered in 1962. The successive and sensational decisions concerning the reform of the Easter Vigil and Holy Week as well as the Decree for the Simplification of the Rubrics began to appear in 1951. During this time his role in these initiatives remained unknown to the commentators because he remained silent and always emphasized that the initiative for them came from Pius XII.

His position in the Congregation for Rites did not allow him to be part of the Council's Preparatory Commission on the Liturgy. In compensation, he was named Secretary of the Conciliar Commission on the Liturgy. Here too his work and influence were exercised with great discretion. The application of the Constitution *Sacrosanctum Concilium* on December 4, 1963 had many reverberations, among them the erection of the *Consilium ad exsequendam Constitutionem de Sacra Liturgia* which went to work with vitality. Antonelli played his part in this work: but again, always with great discretion.

It has to be recognized, however, that it was with difficulty that Antonelli entered the new phase of the liturgical reform that was ushered in with the promulgation of *Sacrosanctum Concilium*. In the Consilium he was often ill at ease but never expressed it. For good reason, he felt bitter towards Paul VI's decision in 1969 to suppress the Congregation for Rites in which he had served since 1930. There are always pioneers: but these are overtaken by others traveling the roads which they opened up.

Antonelli kept a diary of his activities and of the meetings which he attended. It extends from 1915 to his death in 1993. This diary and the numerous texts which he wrote are conserved in the archives at La Verna. You have been able to study them and to use them so as to present in this book not only an account of his achievements, but also his personal convictions, his emotions, and his intimate thoughts. Your book, therefore, is an important contribution to the history of the liturgical reform. In some respects, it completes and corrects Msgr. Bugnini's book.

Ferdinando Antonelli was created Cardinal in 1973. On some of my frequent

Roman sojourns I would visit him, and I would be invited to dine with him in Piazza San Calisto. On these occasions, I can assure you that he spoke of past controversies as though they were faded memories and that he regarded the liturgical reform that had been effected as the ideal which he cherished.

Msgr. Aimé Georges Martimort

Monsignor Aimé Georges Martimort was a liturgist who was peritus *to the Preparatory Commission during the Second Vatican Council and a consultor to the Congregation for Divine Worship.*

Foreword

How much of the post-conciliar liturgical reform truly reflects *"Sacrosanctum Concilium"*, the Second Vatican Council's Constitution on Sacred Liturgy, is a question that has often been debated in ecclesial circles ever since the *Consilium ad exsequendam Constitutionem de Sacra Liturgia* finished its work. It has been debated with even greater intensity in the last couple of decades. And while some have argued that what was done by the Consilium was indeed in line with that great document, others have totally disagreed.

In the search for an answer to this question we ought to take into account the turbulent mood of the years that immediately followed the Council. In his decision to convoke the Council, Pope John XXIII had wished the Church to be prepared for the new world that was emerging in the aftermath of the disastrous events of the Second World War. He would have prophetically foreseen the emergence of a strong current of materialism and secularism from the core orientations of the preceding era which had been marked by the spirit of the Enlightenment and in which the traditional values of the old worldview had already begun to be shaken. The Industrial Revolution along with its strongly anthropocentric and subjectivist philosophical trends, especially those resulting from the influences of Kant, Hume and Hegel, led to the emergence also of Marxism and Positivism. It also led to the ascendance of biblical criticism relativizing, to a certain extent, the veracity of the Holy Scriptures, which in turn had its negative influences on theology, generating a questioning attitude vis-à-vis the objectivity of established truth and of the usefulness of defending ecclesial traditions and institutions. Some schools of theology were bold enough even to question basic doctrines of the Church. In fact, modernism had earlier been seen as a source of danger for the faith. It is in this background that Pope John XXIII had felt that more convincing answers needed to be found.

The call for *aggiornamento* by the Pope thus assumed the character of a search for a fortification of the faith in order to render the mission of the Church more effective and able to respond to these challenges convincingly. It was certainly not a call to go along with the spirit of the times, a sort of drifting passively along, nor was it a call to effect a new start to the Church as much as to render the message of the gospel even more responsive to the difficult questions mankind would face in the post-modern era. The Pope explained the ethos behind his decision when he stated, "today the Church is witnessing a crisis under way within society. While humanity is on the edge of a new era, tasks of immense gravity and amplitude await the Church, as in the most tragic periods of its history. It is a question in fact of bringing the modern world into contact with the vivifying and perennial energies of the Gospel ... in the face of this twofold spectacle – a world which reveals a grave state of spiritual poverty and the Church of Christ, which is still so vibrant with vitality – we ... have felt immediately the urgency of the duty to call our sons together to give the Church the possibility to contribute more efficaciously to the solution of the problems of the modern age" [Apostolic Constitution *Humanae Salutis* of 25th December 1961]. The Pope went on, "the forthcoming Council will meet therefore at a moment in which the Church finds very alive the desire to fortify its faith, and to contemplate itself in its own awe-inspiring unity. In the same way, it feels urgent the duty to give greater efficiency to its sound vitality and to promote the sanctification of its members, the diffusion of revealed truth, the consolidation of its agencies" [*ibid*].

Thus the Council was basically a call for a fortification of the Church from within in order to make it better prepared for its mission amidst the realities of the modern world. Underlying these words was also the sense of appreciation the Pope felt towards what the Church indeed already was. The words, "vibrant with vitality" used by Pope John XXIII to define the status of the Church at that moment, surely do not betray any sense of pessimism, as though the Pope looked down upon the past or what the Church had achieved up until then. Hence one cannot justifiably think that with the Council the Pope called for a new beginning. Neither was it a call to the Church to "de-classify" itself, changing or giving up totally its age-old traditions, getting itself, so to say, absorbed into the reality of the world around. In no way was change to be made for the sake of change but only in order to make the Church stronger and better prepared to face new challenges. In short, the Council was never to be an aimless adventure. It was intended to be a truly Pentecostal experience.

Yet, however much the popes who guided this event insisted upon the need for a true spirit of reform, faithful to the essential nature of the Church, and even if the Council itself had produced such beautiful theological and pastoral reflections as **Lumen Gentium**, **Dei Verbum**, **Gaudium et Spes** and **Sacrosanctum Concilium**, what happened outside the Council – especially both within the society at large and within the circle of its philosophical and cultural leadership – began to influence it negatively, creating tendencies that were harmful to its life and mission. These tendencies, which at times were even more virulently represented by certain circles within the Church, were not necessarily connected to the orientations or recommendations of the documents of Vatican II. Yet they were able to shake the foundations of ecclesial teaching and faith to a surprising extent. Society's fascination with an exaggerated sense of individual freedom and its penchant for the rejection of anything permanent, absolute or other worldly had its influence on the Church and often was justified in the name of the Council.

This view also relativized tradition, the veracity of evolved doctrine, and tended to idolize anything new. It contained within itself strong tendencies favorable to relativism and religious syncretism. For them, the Council had to be a sort of a new beginning for the Church. The past had overrun its course. Basic concepts and themes like sacrifice and redemption, mission, proclamation and conversion, adoration as an integral element of communion, and the need of the Church for salvation – all were sidelined, while dialogue, inculturation, ecumenism, Eucharist as banquet, evangelization as witness, etc., became more important. Absolute values were disdained.

Cardinal Joseph Ratzinger had this to say on this ever increasing spirit of relativism, for him, the true Council "already during its sessions and then increasingly in the subsequent period, was opposed by a self-styled 'Spirit of the Council', which in reality is a true 'anti-spirit' of the Council. According to this pernicious anti-spirit [*Konzils–Ungeist* in German], everything that is 'new' ... is always and in every case better than what has been or what is. It is the anti-spirit according to which the history of the Church would first begin with Vatican II, viewed as a kind of point zero" [*The Ratzinger Report*, Ignatius Press, San Francisco 1985, pp. 34-35]. The Cardinal discounted this view as untrue for "Vatican II surely did not want 'to change' the faith but to represent it in a more effective way" [*ibid*]. Actually, the Cardinal affirmed that in fact "the Council did not take the turn that John XXIII had expected". He further stated, "It must also be admitted that, in respect to the whole Church, the prayer of Pope John that the Council signify a new leap forward for the Church, to renewed life and unity, has not – at least not yet – been granted" [*ibid*, p. 42]. These are hard words indeed, yet I would say very true, for, that spirit of exaggerated theological freedom indeed hijacked, so to say, the very Council itself away from its declared goals.

The *Consilium ad exsequendam Constitutionem de Sacra Liturgia* too was not exempt from being influenced by this overwhelming tidal wave of a so-called desire for "change" and "openness". Possibly some of the above mentioned relativizing tendencies influenced the liturgy too, undermining the centrality, the sacredness, sense of mystery as well as the value of what the continuous action of the Holy Spirit in the bi-millennial history of the Church had helped ecclesial liturgical life to grow into. An exaggerated sense of antiquarianism, anthropologism, confusion of roles between the ordained and the non-ordained, a limitless provision of space for experimentation – and, indeed, the tendency to look down upon some aspects of the development of the liturgy in the second millennium – were increasingly visible among certain liturgical schools. Liturgists had also tended to pick and choose sections of *Sacrosanctum Concilium* which seemed to be more accommodating to change or novelty while ignoring others. Besides, there was a great sense of hurry to effect and legalize changes. Much space tended to be provided for a rather horizontalist way of looking at the liturgy. Norms of the Council that tended to restrict such creativity or were favorable to "the traditional way" seemed to be ignored. Worse still, some practices which *Sacrosanctum Concilium* had never even contemplated were allowed into the liturgy, like Mass *"versus populum"*, Holy Communion on the hand, altogether giving up on the Latin and Gregorian Chant in favor of the vernacular and songs and hymns without much space for God, and extension beyond any reasonable limits of the faculty to concelebrate at Holy Mass. There was also the gross misinterpretation of the principle of "active participation" (*actuosa participatio*).

All of that had its effect on the work of the Consilium. Those who guided the process of change both within the Consilium and later in the Sacred Congregation of Rites were certainly being influenced by all these novel tendencies. Not everything they introduced was negative. Much of the work done was praiseworthy. But much room was also left for experimentation and arbitrary interpretation. These "freedoms" were exploited to their fullest extent by some liturgical "experts" leading to too much confusion. Cardinal Ratzinger explains how "one shudders at the lackluster face of the post-conciliar liturgy as it has become, or one is bored with its banality and its lack of artistic standards ...." [*The Feast of Faith*, Ignatius Press, San Francisco 1986, p. 100]. This is not to lay the responsibility for what happened solely on the members of the Consilium. But some of their approaches were "weak." There indeed was a general spirit of uncritical "giving in" on certain matters to the rabble rousing spirit of the era, even within the Church, most visibly in some sectors and geographic regions. Some of those in authority at the level of the Sacred Congregation of Rites too did show signs of weakness in this matter. Too many indults had been given on certain requirements of the norms.

Naturally the "spirit of freedom" which some of these powerful sectors within the Church unleashed in the name of the Council, even leading the important decision makers to vacillate, led to much disorder and confusion, something which the Council never intended, nor did the popes who guided it. The sad comment made by Pope Paul VI during the troubled seventies that "the smoke of Satan has entered the Church," [Homily on 29th June 1972, Feast of Sts. Peter and Paul] or his comment on the excuses made by some to impede evangelization "on the basis of such and such a teaching of the Council" [*Evangelii Nuntiandi* 80], show how this anti-spirit of the Council render his labors most painful.

In the light of all of this and of some of their troublesome consequences for the Church today, it is necessary to find out how the post-conciliar liturgical reform did emerge and which figures or attitudes caused the present situation. It is a need which, in the name of truth, we cannot abandon. Cardinal Joseph Ratzinger analyzed the situation thus: "I am convinced that the crisis in the Church that we are experiencing is to a large extent due to the disintegration of the Liturgy .... when the community of faith, the worldwide unity of the Church and her history and the mystery of the living Christ are no longer visible in the Liturgy, where else, then is the Church to become visible in her spiritual essence? Then the community is celebrating only itself, an activity that is utterly fruitless" [*Milestones*, Ignatius Press, San Francisco 1998, pp. 148-149]. As we saw above, certain weaknesses of those responsible and the stormy atmosphere of theological relativism, coupled with that sense of fascination with novelty, change, man-centeredness, accent on subjectivity and moral relativism, as well as on individual freedom which characterized the society at large, undermined the fixed values of the faith and caused this slide into liturgical anarchy about which the Cardinal spoke above. The penned notes of Cardinal Ferdinando Antonelli take on new significance. One of the most eminent and closely involved members of the Consilium which supervised the reform process, Cardinal Antonelli can help us to understand the inner polarizations that influenced the different decisions of the reform and help us to be courageous in improving or changing that which was erroneously introduced and which appears to be incompatible with the true dignity of the liturgy. Actually, Father Antonelli was already a member of the Pontifical Commission for the Reform of the Liturgy appointed by Pope Pius XII on 28th May 1948. It was this commission that worked on the reform of the Liturgy of Holy Week and of the Easter Vigil, which reforms were handled with much care by the same. That very commission was then reconstituted by Pope John XXIII in May 1960 and, later on, Father Antonelli was also part of the inner group that worked on the redaction of *Sacrosanctum Concilium*, the Conciliar Constitution on the Sacred Liturgy. Thus he indeed was very closely involved in the work of the reform from its very inception.

Yet, his role in the reform movement seems to have been largely unknown until the author of this book, *The Development of the Liturgical Reform As Seen by Cardinal Ferdinando Antonelli from 1948 to 1970*, Msgr. Nicola Giampietro, had come across his personal agenda notes and decided to present them in a study. This study, which was also the doctoral dissertation of Msgr. Giampietro at the Pontifical Liturgical Institute of St. Anselm in Rome, helps us to understand the complex inner workings of the liturgical reform prior to and immediately following the Council. Cardinal Antonelli's notes reveal a great man of faith and of the Church struggling to come to terms with some of the inner currents which influenced the work involving the *Consilium ad exsequendam Constitutionem de Sacra Liturgia*. What he wrote in these diaries reveal quite candidly his feelings of joy as well as of sorrow and at times of fear at the way things were being made to move along, the attitudes of some of the key players and the sense of adventurism which had characterized some of the changes that had been introduced. The book is well done. Indeed, it has also been quoted by Cardinal Joseph Ratzinger himself in an article he wrote in the well-known liturgical review *La Maison-Dieu*, entitled *"Réponse du Cardinal Ratzinger au Père Gy"* [*La Maison-Dieu*, 230, 2002/2, p. 116]. Above all it is a timely study which would help us to see another side of the otherwise over-euphoric presentations of the conciliar reform by other contemporary authors.

The publication in English of this interesting study would, I am sure, contribute greatly to the ongoing debate on the post-conciliar liturgical reforms. What is most clear to any reader of this study is that as Cardinal Joseph Ratzinger stated, "the true time of Vatican II has not yet come" [*The Ratzinger Report*, Ignatius Press, San Francisco 1985, p. 40]. The reform has to go on. The immediate need seems to be that of a reform of the reformed Missal of 1969, for, quite a number of changes originating within the post-conciliar reform seem to have been introduced somewhat hastily and unreflectively, as Cardinal Antonelli himself repeatedly stated. One needs to correct the direction so that changes are indeed made to fall in line with *Sacrosanctum Concilium* itself and it must indeed go even further, keeping along with the spirit of our own times. And what urges such changes is not merely a desire to correct past mistakes but much more the need to be true to what liturgy in fact is and means to us, and what the Council itself defined it to be. For, indeed, as Cardinal Ratzinger stated: "the question of liturgy is not peripheral: the Council itself reminded us that we are dealing here with the very core of Christian faith" [*ibid*, p. 120]. What we need today is to not only engage ourselves in an honest appraisal of what happened but also to take bold and courageous decisions in moving the process along. We need to identify and correct the erroneous orientations and decisions made, appreciate the liturgical tradition of the past courageously, and ensure that the Church is made to rediscover the true roots of its spiritual wealth and grandeur even if that means reforming the reform itself, thereby ensuring that liturgy truly becomes the "sublime expression of God's glory and, in a certain sense, a glimpse of heaven on Earth" [Benedict XVI, Post-Synodal Apostolic Exhortation *Sacramentum Caritatis* of 22nd February 2007, 35].

Archbishop Albert Malcolm Ranjith

8th December 2008
Feast of the Immaculate Conception of Mary

Abbreviations

AAS = *Acta Apostolicae Sedis*, Vatican City 1909 ff.

AA.VV. = Various authors.

ALV = Archives of La Verna, the Antonelli Deposit [*Fondo Antonelli*], 1896 ff.

ANSA = Agenzia Nazionale Stampa Associata.

art. c. = cited article.

col., coll. = column, columns.

Consilium = *Consilium ad exsequendam Constitutionem de Sacra Liturgia* (1964).

CPRL = *Commissione Pontificia per la Riforma Liturgica*, Rome 1948.

Diario/i = Diary [or Diaries] of Antonelli, 1915-1993.

DPIL = A. BUGNINI, *Documenta Pontificia ad Instaurationem Liturgicam spectantia, I (1903-1953), II (1953-1959)*, Rome 1953-59.

ed., edd. = *editor, editors*.

EncC = *Enciclopedia Cattolica*, Vatican City 1949-1954.

EL = *Ephemerides Liturgicae*, Rome 1827 ff.

EV = *Enchiridion Vaticanum*, Documenti ufficiali del Concilio Vaticano II e della Santa Sede, voll. 1-13, Bologna 1962-1993.

GFAC = *Gioventù Femminile Azione Cattolica*.

IGMR = *Institutio Generalis Missalis Romani*, Vatican City 1969.

LJ = *Liturgisches Jahrbuch*, Münster-Trier 1951 ff.

LMD = *La Maison Dieu*, Paris 1945 ff.

Mem. = *Memoria sulla Riforma Liturgica*, Vatican City 1948.

ms = manuscript.

n., nn. = number, numbers.

OFM = *Ordinis Fratrum Minorum*.

OM = *Ordo Missae*.

OR = *Opera della Regalità di NSGC [Nostro Signore Gesù Cristo]*, Milan.

PAA.OrPr = *Pontificium Athenaeum Antonianum ab origine ad praesens*, Rome 1969.

RAC = *Rivista di Archeologia Cristiana*, Rome 1924 ff.

RAI = *Radio Televisione Italiana*.

RCI	= *Rivista del Clero italiano,* Milan 1920 ff.
RL	= *Rivista Liturgica,* Finalpia/Torino-Leumann 1914 ff.
RPL	= *Rivista di Pastorale Liturgica,* Brescia 1963.
SC	= *Sacrosanctum Concilium,* Constitution on the Liturgy the Second Vatican Council: *AAS,* 56 (1964), pp. 97-134.
SCCS	= *Sacra Congregazione per le Cause dei Santi,* Vatican City.
sd	= undated.
Sect. Hist.	= *Sezione Storica della Sacra Congregazione dei Riti,* Vatican City.
SRC	= *Sacra Rituum Congregatio,* Vatican City.
VeP	= *Vita e Pensiero,* Milan 1917 ff.
VV.AA.	= Various authors.

Introduction

There has been a realization, in recent times, of an increasing need to revisit many aspects of the liturgy from a perspective above or beyond the conventional manner in which it has been considered. Our concern to explore various aspects of the liturgical reform instituted by Pius XII up to the Second Vatican Council can be situated within that general context. This study is based on particular sources, personalities, concrete situations, and their consequent results.

In particular, we wish to devote special attention to Cardinal Giuseppe Ferdinando Antonelli and, assessing his contribution to the liturgical sciences, thereby afford proper significance to someone who played such an important role in the liturgical reform, firstly under Pius XII and subsequently under the Council (1948-1970), but, somewhat surprisingly, whose name never appears even in the most recent historical studies on the liturgy.

Antonelli's liturgical writings have not yet been studied. These were inspired by the broad magisterial lines set out by Pius X, Pius XI, and Pius XII. In this initial liturgical reform, he found the theological acumen and the necessary pastoral insights to spark a long personal theologico-pastoral reflection which matured during his service in the Historical Section of the Congregation for Rites, in his teaching career at the *Antonianum*, and in his pastoral work. All of this ultimately made him an architect of the liturgical reform and a passionate promoter of the liturgy as theology and spirituality in the service of the Christian life.

The completion of this work happily coincides with the centenary of Antonelli's birth which is a propitious opportunity to reflect on his contribution to the liturgy and to the Church.

We shall present a biographical profile of Cardinal Antonelli which allows us to see just how much his life was characterized by his relationship with the liturgy, with its problems and with its renewal.

At a more analytical level, we sought to identify the main liturgical themes that emerge from some of his more significant writings. These were not solely restricted to academic study. Rather, they were translated into an active commitment which resulted in the great fruits of the first and second part of the liturgical renewal. These we can attribute in large measure to Antonelli.

Our work was not exempt from various types of difficulty. The first was the obvious problem of attempting to order Antonelli's liturgical thought according to the norms of a scientific method. There was the difficulty of identifying the various sources which lay behind Antonelli's liturgical formation. Moreover, Antonelli's papers have not yet been definitively catalogued – indeed, the collection of his unpublished writings is still in progress. As a result of this situation, the *modus citandi* employed here is provisional and concords with the archives of the Sacred Congregation of the Causes of Saints and with those at La Verna.

The sources which have been used and assessed in our study have been numerous and significant. It would perhaps have been better to classify them according to the diversity of their nature and scope – especially in view of the personal nature of many of them. Thus, we are aware that some references to persons and things might seem too marked by a historical reality which demands greater reflection and more objective distance. However, we believe that these texts are also useful when read with the necessary equilibrium and due attention.

Notwithstanding these limitations, we hope to lift the veil covering Cardinal Antonelli and to break a certain silence which, unjustly, surrounds his work and his contribution, especially, to the renewal of the liturgy in its first and second phases.

Chapter 1

Giuseppe Ferdinando Antonelli: A Biographical Profile

For any understanding of the events and questions that inspired Antonelli's contribution to the various phases of the reform of the liturgy, a brief glance into his life, such as this, is necessary. It serves to highlight the multiplicity of his interests and commitments, among which precedence must be given to his absorption with matters liturgical.

Giuseppe Ferdinando Antonelli was born to a good, simple family on July 14, 1896 at Rassina, in the district of Vallebona on the outer confines of the municipality of Chiusi della Verna. He was baptized in the parish of Rassina.[1]

His birth had been preceded by those of an elder sister and brother, and followed by those of two other brothers (one of whom died at Piave during the First World War) and a sister. When he was three months old, his parents, Ferdinando Antonelli and Francesca Angioloni, moved to Poggio D'Acona, a district in the municipality of Subbiano (Arezzo). Here the future Cardinal began his elementary education. The local Parish Priest, Reverend Antonio Miglioni, introduced him to the study of Latin and to a delight for poetry, especially that of Pascoli and Zanella.

Noticing Giuseppe's fine voice, Miglioni encouraged him at an early age to use this talent in church, and he did so, singing things such as the "*pastorelle*" at Christmas and lamentations during Holy Week. The friars at La Verna often came to the parish to preach, hear confessions, and to sing on the great feasts. They fascinated the young Giuseppe.

In 1909, at the age of 13, having finished elementary school, he entered San Romolo, the junior seminary of the Friars Minor at Figline. He was vested with the Franciscan habit on July 25, 1925 and began his novitiate in the Order.

His first experience of Franciscan life took place at La Verna, the austere hermitage where St. Francis had received the Stigmata. La Verna remained one of his favorite places both for its inherent qualities and for his personal memories of it.

Throughout his life, Antonelli would recall both the solemn ceremonies savored at La Verna during his novitiate and the Gregorian chant of the Friars, some of whom (such as Fr. Urbano Martini) had been to the famous Swiss abbey of Einsiedeln to learn Gregorian chant. Of all of the music he encountered there, in a particular way he always remembered the hymns, especially the *Veni Sancte Spiritus, Sanctitatis Nova Signa*, and the *Canticle of Creation*.

Following his novitiate, the young Antonelli began to study classics and philosophy at the Convent of San Francesco in Fiesole (Florence). At the close of the First World War, he began a four year period of military service as a Sergeant. Because of his fine script he was assigned to military records at Frosinone. While a student at Sargiano (Arezzo) Antonelli attended a drawing school and even in his old age he still preferred to write by hand rather than use a typewriter.

At the end of his military service, Giuseppe was admitted to the study of theology at the Convent of Sargiano. His Excellency Emanuele Mignone, Bishop of Arezzo, conferred him with minor orders on February 13, 1921.

Cardinal Achille Ratti was elected Pope on February 6, 1922 and took the name of Pius XI. He would be an important figure in Antonelli's life. On April 7, 1922 Antonelli made his final profession, and less than two weeks later on the 15th, he was ordained to the sub-diaconate. Ordained deacon on July 4, 1922, Giuseppe Ferdinando Antonelli was ordained to the priesthood on July 25, 1922.[2]

In 1923 he began higher studies in ecclesiastical history at the International College of San Antonio in Rome[3], eventually obtaining the degree of *Lector Generalis* which permitted him to teach ecclesiastical history throughout the entire Order of the Friars Minor.

Simultaneously, he followed a course in palaeography and diplomatics conducted by the School of Palaeography of the Vatican Archive.[4] He was among the first students inscribed at the Pontifical Institute of Christian Archaeology which had been erected by Pius XI on December 28, 1925 on the Via Napoleon III in Rome. Of his professors, Antonelli frequently recalled Professors Josi and Silvagni, Msgr. Kirsch, and the Abbot Quentin who, in 1930, proposed his name to Pius XI for the post of assistant in the recently founded Historical Section. At the conclusion of his studies in 1928 he was awarded the License in Christian Archaeology (*honoris causa*), and in December of 1938, he would receive the doctorate in Archaeology (*honoris causa*).

When the College of San Antonio was erected as a Pontifical Athenaeum (the *Antonianum*), the future Cardinal Antonelli was appointed Professor of Ancient Ecclesiastical History and of Archaeology. He was also professor of Liturgy at the *Antonianum* which was near both the International Institute of the Discalced Carmelites and the *Apostolicum*. During these years he gained valuable experience, devoting much effort and study to make the liturgy known and loved. This idea occurs frequently in the dispensa that Antonelli prepared for his students. This period established his intellectual stature in liturgy and history.

His research deepened his knowledge of western monasticism and eventually led to the publication of his thesis: *I primi monasteri di monaci orientali in Roma*. The manuscript, containing plans drawn by himself, is conserved in the archive of La Verna.[5] Much of his early research concentrated on the study of western monasticism and on the great masters of the patristic tradition. Fr. Tomás Larrañaga, on the occasion of Cardinal Antonelli's 90th birthday, paid homage to him in the following terms:

> I can personally testify, remembering as I do, the tremendous impression made by his lectures in Christian Archaeology in the license course in theology, and by his lectures on liturgical formation for the students at the *Collegio di San Antonio*: for example those on the reform of Holy Week during the 1950s, a reform which, under Pius XII, had Fr. Antonelli for one of its principal architects.[6]

Antonelli was Rector of the *Atheneo* for twelve years (1937-1943; 1953-1959). During the intervening years, he was involved in the government of the Order of the Friars Minor as Definitor General for Italian affairs during the fateful years of the Second World War.[7] At that time the General Curia of the Friars was located in the *Collegio di San Antonio*.

Within the vast Franciscan movement, Ferdinando Antonelli was particularly supportive of the intuition of his friend and confrere Fr. Agostino Gemelli,[8] the founder of the Catholic University of the *Sacro Cuore*. Fr. Gemelli was an exceptional assistant and especially effective in the area of the spiritual promotion of committed laity in the secular circumstances of the modern world.

It came as no surprise, therefore, when Antonelli was nominated Assistant General of the Secular Institute of the Missionaries of the Kingship of Our Lord Jesus Christ[9] by the Congregation for Religious following Gemelli's death in 1959.

Cardinal Antonelli's life and his many activities are characterized significantly by an unconditional and zealous service to the Roman Curia "where he had been able to dedicate himself all the more to an area which eventually absorbed the greater part of his time: namely, the liturgy".[10]

On February 22, 1930 Antonelli was appointed *Consultor* for the Historical Section of the Sacred Congregation for Rites. In March of the same year he became *Vice-Relator* for the Historical Section and eventually *Relator-Generalis* of the same section in 1935.

In 1936 he became a corresponding member of the Pontifical Roman Academy of Archaeology. In 1943 he was designated *Consultor* of the Sacred Congregation for Ceremonies and a *Commissarius* of the Sacred Congregation for Religious.

Antonelli was appointed to the Pontifical Commission for the Reform of the Liturgy in 1948. He continued in this capacity until 1960, the eve of the Council.

In 1954 he was nominated to the Pontifical Commission for the Historical Sciences and a *Consultor* of the Sacred Congregation for Religious in 1956. In 1959 he was nominated Promotor General of the Faith in the Congregation for Rites.

During the Second Vatican Council he acted as a *peritus* and secretary for the Conciliar Commission for the Sacred Liturgy having been appointed as such on October 4, 1962. On February 26, 1964 he was nominated a member of the *Consilium ad exsequendam Constitutionem de S. Liturgia*. On January 26, 1965 his appointment as Secretary to the Sacred Congregation was published. When, in 1969, this Dicastery was divided into the Sacred Congregation for Divine Worship and the Sacred Congregation of the Causes of Saints, Antonelli became secretary of the latter. He discharged this office with great earnestness and with indefatigable dedication to the service of the Church, especially in promoting the liturgy, a task to which he had completely dedicated himself.

A bibliography of Antonelli's written works reveals his many contributions in the area of liturgical studies, as well as two manuals on the liturgy compiled for student use. Fr. Tomás Larrañaga, on this subject, testifies to the greatness of this man who completely dedicated himself to that study of the liturgy which was necessary for the Church's great liturgical reform:

> Allow me to mention a personal recollection: as a student in the now long distant mid 1950s, I enjoyed going to Fr. Antonelli's rooms on certain afternoons when he was to be found a little freer from his many official duties and taking advantage of the cordiality with which he always received me. During our talks, he told me that he had prepared a great deal of material for a manual on the liturgy. However, the heavy demands of his office prevented him from finishing the project and publishing the manual.[11]

Nominated titular bishop of Idicra on February 21, 1966,[12] he was consecrated by Pope Paul VI on the following March 19 in St. Peter's Basilica. Seven years later, he was created Cardinal by Paul VI with the diaconal *titulus* of San Sebastiano al Palatino in the Consistory of March 5, 1973.

During his years of service in the Roman Curia, Cardinal Antonelli committed himself to a very impressive level of work. He contributed to over eighty hagiographical publications while Vice-Postulator and *Relator-Generalis* of the Sacred Congregation of Rites. He wrote some noteworthy entries for several dictionaries and encyclopedias, and was also the author of many significant articles which were published in the *Osservatore Romano*.[13]

In its initial phase, Antonelli was one of the principal architects of the reform of Holy Week which had been desired and activated by Pius XII:

> Antonelli's most important fields of activity, and for which he will be remembered in Church's history, were in the Causes of Saints, the liturgical reform initiated by the Council and its implementation in the post-conciliar period.[14]

He remained lucid and independent until the final years of his life. His greatest joy was to celebrate Mass every morning and to participate in the solemn ceremonies of St. Peter's (vespers, beatifications, canonizations, and other papal ceremonies).

Comforted by the presence of his nephew, a Franciscan priest, and of his niece, a Franciscan nursing sister, Antonelli died peacefully at 2:45 a.m. on July

12, 1993. In accordance with his wishes, he was buried in the Chapel of the Pietà in the basilica at La Verna on July 14, 1993, which would have been his 97th birthday.

[1] Biographical details have been extracted from *Acta Ordinis Fratrum Minorum*, 84 (1965), p. 107; and from *Pontificium Athenaeum Antonianum ab origine ad praesens* [= PAA.OrPr], Rome 1969, pp. 398-400, 447 and following. In the Archive of the *Antonianum*, documents relating to Father Antonelli are to be found in folder n. 1 in the deposit relating to Professors.

[2] Cf. F. ANTONELLI, *Diario* n. 1 for 1922 in *ALV*, pp. 20-35.

[3] Cf. PAA.OrPr, p. 699.

[4] Cf. *Ibidem*, p. 699.

[5] Cf. F. ANTONELLI, *Diario* for December 17, 1938. An extract of the thesis was published in *Revista di Archeologia cristiana*, 5 (1928), pp. 105-121.

[6] T. LARRAÑAGA, "Omaggio a S. Em. Card. Ferdinando Giuseppe Antonelli" in *Antonianum*, 61 (1986), p. 510.

[7] Cf. *Acta Capituli Generalis totius OFM in Protocoenobio S. Mariae Angelorum de Portiuncula (Assisii) die 19 Maii usque ad diem 3 Iunii 1939 celebrati*, Rome 1939, pp. 21 and 29.

[8] Cf. F. ANTONELLI, "La spiritualità di Padre Gemelli" in *Vita e Pensiero*, 42 (1959), pp. 561-572.

[9] Cf. F. ANTONELLI, *Consacrazione e Missione negli Istituti Secolari*, Milan 1979, p. 144.

[10] T. LARRAÑAGA, *Omaggio*, p. 512.

[11] *Ibidem*, p. 513.

[12] Cf. *La scomparsa del Card. Ferdinando Giuseppe Antonelli: L'Osservatore Romano*, July 18, 1993, p. 3.

[13] Cfr. *PAA. OrPr, p. 447* and folder n. 1 in the Archive of the *Antonianum*.

[14] T. LARRAÑAGA, *Omaggio*, cit., p. 517.

Chapter 2

Antonelli's Academic and Liturgical Formation

As already mentioned, Antonelli was a member of the Family of the Friars Minor. He studied classics and philosophy at the Convent of San Francesco in Fiesole near Florence. His military service was discharged in Rome at the Policlinico Hospital where, under the direction of Dr. Arturo Petacci (1915-1919), he was assigned many arduous duties as administrator of the entire first medical section. While at the Policlinico he was promoted to Corporal and Sergeant.[1]

In 1920, following his military service, he returned to the Convent at Sargiano and to his theological studies which had been interrupted by the outbreak of war.

It is interesting to quote a significant extract from his diary which is prescient of his future archaeological research and of his love for the liturgy. The young Antonelli wrote: "While going up to the Cathedral, which emerged mysteriously from the morning penumbra, I sensed a tremor of love and veneration for Mother Church, so solemn in her portals and rites".[2]

On September 28, 1923 he departed for Rome and the International College, the *Antonianum*, where he was to commence his studies in ecclesiastical history. Less than two months later, on November 12, he began a course of studies in palaeography, diplomatics, and archival procedure in the Vatican. The course was conducted by Professor Bruno Kallerbach, OFM. Of some twenty students admitted to the course in this school, six were in Antonelli's class. The school was situated on the via della Fondamenta, beneath the Vatican Museums.[3] Fr. Antonelli derived great satisfaction from these courses and noted that:

> It was a consolation to touch, see, and leaf through the famous Codex *Virgilius Vaticanus* from the beginning of the 4th century. So many thoughts came flooding to my mind at the sight of this antiquity which had seen the history of so many centuries and so many generations.[4]

While following this course in palaeography, he was fortunate, he recounts, to have seen and handled several Codexes: the *Exsultet Beneventani* from the 9th, 10th, and 11th centuries, *The Winchester Psalter* from the 11th century, *The Farfa Bible*, *The Register of Gregory VII* (1873-85), *The Tivoli Register,* and a 14th century *Franciscan Breviary*.

The Development of the Liturgical Reform

On June 12, 1924 he received his certificate of attendance at the Sacred Congregation's school for studies in archival method, paleology, and jurisprudential history. The certificate bore the seal of the Vatican Archive and was signed by Professors Fr. Bruno Katterbach, OFM, and Fr. Giustiniano Sederi, OSB.[6]

That same year on the 9th of November he was informed that Msgr. Kirsch held a course in archaeology in the *Camposanto Teutonico*, close to the Vatican. The course was open to only five students, three of whom were foreign students, the other two being Antonelli and one of his confreres. He enthusiastically agreed to enroll and began the course just days later on the 11th.[7]

The course consisted of lectures *in loco*. As is clear from his writings, Antonelli was avid to explore such an important complex of historical buildings and to analyze their every vestige and monument, revealing the joy and love he had for archaeology. Professor Kirsch soon proposed a theme for his final thesis: *I Monasteri di Roma ai tempi di S. Gregorio Magno*. The sources for such a dissertation were the writings of St. Gregory and the *Liber Pontificalis*. He found a bibliography in Keher and Grisar's *I Papi del Medioevo*.[8]

At the beginning, the professorial staff consisted of the following: Msgr. Belvederi as the secretary, Msgr. Respighi, Dr. Iosi, and Dr. Kolsbach.

On December 28, 1925 the *AAS* published the *motu proprio* of His Holiness Pius XI by which the new Institute of Archaeology was created. Antonelli noted, "I had the honor to be among its first eight students".[9]

The following are its first four professors: *Msgr. Johannes Kirsch*[10] of the University of Freiburg, for General Christian Archaeology and for the Topography of Christian Rome (churches and catacombs); *Msgr. Joseph Wilpert*,[11] Protonotary Apostolic, for Ancient Christian Iconography (paintings and sculpture); *Professor Angelo Silvagni*, for Christian Epigraphy; *Professor Enrico Quentin, OSB*, for Liturgy, Hagiography, and Ancient Ecclesiastical Institutions.[12]

Antonelli simultaneously attended the Pontifical School for Higher Musical Studies and the lectures of Professor Paolo Ferretti, OSB on Gregorian Chant as well as those of maestro R. Casimiri on Polyphonic Music.[13]

Through his frequent contact with Professor Kirsch at the *Camposanto Teutonico*, he also came into contact with Fr. L.C. Mohlberg, OSB.[14]

Through the flattering gesture of Abbot Quentin, he was put into contact with Abbot Schuster at San Paolo whom he then visited. Of this encounter Antonelli noted:

> Abbot Schuster received me very well and we spoke for about half an hour on the ancient monks of Rome. He told me that he was very pleased to see that someone had undertaken this subject. On the whole, he gave me the impression of being a very good and thoughtful person.[15]

After one of his examinations with Abbot Quentin, Antonelli noted:

> He is always most kind. We spoke a little about my work, then I asked him some

questions about the *Liber Pontificalis*. He wished me all the best and said that he had great hopes for my scientific work.

Concerning my doctoral examination, he said that he would provide me with a kind of program which would concentrate on the historical martyrologies, the Hieronymian Martyrology, the Sacramentaries, and on some hagiographical questions.[16]

Shortly afterwards, Dom Enrico Quentin was appointed *Relator-Generalis* of the Historical Section of the Sacred Congregation of Rites. Then, on March 19, 1930 the Holy Father added a *Vice-Relator* to the section, chosing Father Antonelli for the post since "he was well known for his special competence in this area".[17]

Both would work together closely. Notwithstanding some initial difficulties experienced from the outset by the Historical Section, they carried forward much work and won the esteem of both the whole Section and the Pontiff himself. On March 12, 1934 Quentin was nominated Abbot of San Girolamo in Rome which had been established by Pius XI for the revision of the Vulgate. Following Abbot Quentin's unexpected death on February 4, 1935, Fr. Antonelli was nominated *Relator-Generalis* of the Historical Section just days later on the 16th.

Antonelli's nomination created the difficulty of finding another *Vice-Relator*. After several suggestions and various presentations, Antonelli proposed the name of Fr. Joseph Löw.

With professional competence and a great work capacity, Antonelli expended much study and historical research on the causes of saints, and subsequently on the liturgical reform desired by Pius XII. His training was similar to that of A.G. Martimort, E. Bourque, and other liturgists who had begun their liturgical studies at the Institute of Christian Archaeology. With regard to Antonelli's liturgical expertise, his advanced historical training must always be born in mind, since this drew him to explore the liturgical sources in depth. From thence he proceeded to the reform's liturgical application.[18]

Antonelli habitually referred to sources and to studies such as those of P. De Puniet,[19] M. Andrieu,[20] H. Grisar,[21] F.G. Holweck,[22] S. Bäumer,[23] K. Kastner,[24] K.A.H. Kellner,[25] A.I. Schuster,[26] P. Alfonso,[27] P. Albrigi,[28] P. Batiffol,[29] F. Cabrol and H. Leclercq,[30] L. Duchesne,[31] L. Eisenhofer,[32] O. Rousseau,[33] P.S. Syxto,[34] J. Wilpert,[35] M. Righetti,[36] A. Olivar,[37] J.M. Hanssens,[38] P. Bruylants,[39] L. Bouyer,[40] and G. Baudot.[41]

Fr. Antonelli had many contacts with Italian and foreign liturgists, among whom mention can be made of Father B. Botte of Rome, J.A. Jungmann of Innsbruck, Professor B. Fischer of Trier, Dom B. Capelle of Louvain, Father L.C. Mohlberg of Rome, Abbot I. Schuster, Msgr. M. Righetti,[42] and Msgr. A.G. Martimort.

It is also worth noting Antonelli's friendship with Martimort. The archive at La Verna contains all of the letters written or received by Antonelli. Antonelli's preface to a *Festschrift* in honor of Msgr. Martimort is also significant.[43]

Other famous liturgists corresponded with Antonelli offering him advice, especially during the experimental period of the reform of the Easter Vigil and Holy Week. At this time, both liturgists and Ordinaries were invited by the Historical Section to forward their comments on the liturgical reform then in progress.

Antonelli knew and appreciated the writings of other great figures such as the Belgian Benedictine, Fr. Lambert Beauduin who emphasised the importance of the liturgy at a pastoral level; Fr. Odo Casel, OSB, of Maria Laach, to whom we owe much of the twentieth century's theology of the liturgy; Msgr. Moglia of Genoa who was a conspicuous figure in the Italian liturgical movement; Abbot Emmanuele Caronti, OSB,[44] who was an emblematic figure for the numerous liturgical-pastoral initiatives promoted in Italy which tried to emphasize the close relationship between liturgy and Christian piety.

From the outset of Antonelli's stay in Rome at the *Antonianum*, he maintained close contact with Fr. Agostino Gemelli. They met frequently and informally discussed the possibility of Fr. Antonelli's teaching in Milan.

Father Gemelli later turned to Antonelli for assistance in guiding the *Missionarie della Regalità*. Antonelli became one of their most intrepid formators and a great promoter of the ideals and charitable works of the *Opera della Regalità*. From the moment that the Missionaries undertook the promotion of a liturgical apostolate among the Italian people, Antonelli held frequent meditations on the liturgy for them. By means of courses, study weeks, conventions, periodicals, and other initiatives, the Missionaries set out to bring the liturgy to people of every class and condition.[45]

Mention must also be made of the conventions on pastoral liturgy promoted by the Missionaries which began in 1958 and were initially open only to the priests working in collaboration with them. Later, they were made available to all priests and eventually to the laity who desired to be formed in the area of liturgy. Antonelli promoted and organized these conventions and remained their president until 1988:

> He favored them and closely followed their organizational phase, informing himself of their themes, titles, and lecturers. He presided over their executive phase for as long as he was physically able to do so, trusting but never totally delegating to the undersigned who was his immediate assistant, always vigilant, discreet, and benevolent.[46]

These conventions, which sought to form both clergy and laity in the liturgy, multiplied in number according to the wishes of Fr. Agostino Gemelli, the founder of the *Opera della Regalità*. Here we reproduce Antonelli's opinion of Gemelli:

> We cannot call Fr. Gemelli a liturgist in the full sense of the term. He has written very little about the liturgy: a couple of articles and a few prefaces for booklets produced by the *Opera della Regalità*. On the other hand, his spiritual formation is that of the Franciscan Order which emphasizes meditation and the practice of asceticism rather than liturgical piety.[47]

Fr. Gemelli, however, was much concerned with the liturgical revival and became the inspiration for and promoter of an active participation in the liturgical ceremonies. Gemelli wrote:

> It is sufficient to remember that we are priests so as to desire and procure that many live the life of the Church with us. Nothing is more painful for me than to celebrate Mass alone, with no one other than the altar server. Nothing is more consoling for me than giving the peace, the greeting of God, the blessing, the very flesh of God himself to the faithful when they attend in great numbers for the great and truly consoling moment of the Sacrifice of the Mass so as to enjoy the fruits of this same sacrifice.[48]

Fr. R. Falsini writes, "With great ardor Father Gemelli always inculcated a solid piety, derived from the Church's true sources, especially from the Sacred Scripture and from the liturgy".[49] Fr. Gemelli firmly believed that the faithful should freely express their piety by approaching the liturgy, and from it they would receive rich nourishment.

The Development of the Liturgical Reform

[1] Cf. F. ANTONELLI, *Diario n. 1, "Vita Militare"* in ALV, pp. 1-11.

[2] *Ibidem*, p. 15.

[3] Cf. *ibidem*, pp. 48-49 and 53-54.

[4] *Ibidem*, p. 55.

[5] Cf. *ibidem*, pp. 78-91 and *Diario n. 2*, in ALV, p. 5.

[6] Cf. F. ANTONELLI, *Diario n. 2*, pp. 13-14; AA. VV. "A. Anselmo. Saggi storici e di attualità" in *Studia Anselmiana* 97 (1988), p. 311.

[7] Cf. *Diario n. 2*, pp. 59-60.

[8] Cf. *ibidem*, pp. 62-63. Such were his studies and research that he published several articles on oriental monasticism: cf. F. ANTONELLI, *"De re monastica in Dialogis Sancti Gregorii Magni"* in *Antonianum* 2 (1927), pp. 401-436; IDEM, *"I primi monasteri di monaci orientali in Roma"* in *Rivista di Archeologia cristiana*, 5 (1928), pp. 105-121; IDEM, *"Monachesimo Occidentale"* in *Enciclopedia Cattolica Italiana*, Città del Vaticano, 1952, vol. VIII, coll. 1246-1256.

[9] F. ANTONELLI, *Diario no. 1*, in *ALV*, p. 1. For further information on the erection of the Institute cf. SRC, *I professori e i corsi nel Pontificio Istituto di Archeologia Cristiano: Corriere d'Italia*, April 21, 1926, p 6. This article describes the composition and work of the Institute as well as the preparations that had to be made to accomodate the Institute in the former monastery of Sant'Antonio at Santa Maria Maggiore. The Holy Father wished that the Institute would begin its scientific work as quickly as possible. Indeed, he directed that courses should start in the Autumn of 1929. As organized, the Institute covered the following disciplines: 1. Christian archaeology in general: a methodic introduction to archaeological studies; bibliography; 2. The topography of Christian Rome *a*) Cemeteries, *b*) ancient churches; 3. Christian iconography, painting, sculpture, mosaic, and other minor arts; 4. Christian epigraphy; 5. Specialized history of the early Church as well as liturgy, hagiography, and Christian institutions; 6. Practical instruction in directing excavations, the custody of monuments, precious artistic objects and literary works, drawings, etc.; R. JACQUARD, *L'Institut pontifical d'archéologie chrétienne. Journal de cinquante années (1925-1975)*, Rome 1975.

[10] Cf. E. IOSI, *"Istituto Pontificio di Archeologia cristiana"* in *Enciclopedia Cattolica*, Città del Vaticano, vol. VII, coll. 351-352.

[11] Cf. E. CATTANEO, *Il culto cristiano nel occidente. Note storiche*, Rome 1992, p. 486.

[12] Cf. *ibidem*, p. 8; F. ANTONELLI, *Communication au Cinquantenaire de l'Institut d'archéologie chrétienne*, in *Atti del IX Congresso internazionale di archeologia cristiana*, Vol. I, Città del Vaticano, 1978 (*Studi di antichità cristiana*, 32), pp. 87-91.

[13] Cf. F. ANTONELLI, *Diario n. 4*, cit., p.127; E. CATTANEO, *Il culto cristiano in occidente,* Rome 1992, p. 499. Bibliographical references to the work of Prof. R. Casimiri can be found in this work on p. 487, note 2.

[14] Cf. F. ANTONELLI, *Diario n. 4*, cit., p. 134; AA.VV., *Miscellenea liturgica in honorem L.C. Mohlberg,* Rome 1948, I-II.

[15] Cf. F. ANTONELLI, *Diario n. 4*, cit., p. 171; P. BORELLA, *Il Card. I. Schuster,* in AA.VV., *Profili di Liturgisti*, Rome 1970, pp. 111-145.

[16] Cf. F. ANTONELLI, *Diario n. 4*, cit., p. 214-215.

[17] SRC, *Il nuovo Vice-Relatore della Sezione Storica della Sacra Congregazione dei Riti: Messaggero* March 21, 1930, p. 4.

[18] Cf. F. ANTONELLI, *Diario n. 4*, cit., pp. 217-219.

[19] Cf. P. DE PUNIET, *Le Pontifical Romain*, 2 vols., Louvain 1930.

[20] Cf. M. ANDRIEU (edt.), *Le Pontifical Romain au Moyen Age*, 4 vols. [Studies and Theses, nn. 86, 87, 88, and 99], Vatican City 1938, 1940-1941; *idem, Les Ordines Romani du Haut Moyen Age*, vol. 1, Louvain 1931.

[21] H. GRISAR, *Roma alla fine del mondo antico*, 3rd Italian edition, Rome 1930.

[22] Cf. F.G. HOLWECK, *Calendarium liturgicum festorum Dei et Matris Dei*, Philadelphia 1925.

[23] Cf. S. BÄUMER, *Geschichte des Breviers*, 2 vols., Freiburg 1893.

[24] Cf. K. KASTNER, *Praktischer Brevierkommentar*, 2 vols., Freiburg 1923-1924.

[25] Cf. K.A.H. KELLNER, *L'anno ecclesiastico e le feste dei santi nel loro svolgimento storico*, German language version of A. Mercati, 2nd edition, Rome 1914.

[26] Cf. A.I. SCHUSTER, *Liber Sacramentorum. Note storiche e liturgiche sul Missale Romano*, Turin 1933.

[27] Cf. P. ALFONSO, *I riti della chiesa. La S. Messa*, Rome 1945.

[28] Cfr. P. ALBRIGI, *Sacra Liturgia. Il Sacrificio cristiano*, Vicenza 1943.

[29] Cf. P. BATIFFOL, *Lecons sur la Messe*, Paris 1923.

[30] Cf. F. CABROL – H. LECLERCQ, *Dictionnaire d'archaéologie chrétienne et de liturgie*, Paris 1909-1915.

[31] Cf. L. DUCHESNE, *Origines du culte chrétien. Etude sur la liturgie latine avant Charlemagne*, 5th edition, Paris 1925.

[32] Cf. L. EISENHOFER, *Compendio di liturgia*, Turin 1944.

[33] Cf. O. ROUSSEAU, *Histoire du mouvement liturgique*, Paris 1945.

[34] Cf. P.S. SYXTO, *Notiones archaeologiae christianae disciplinis theologicis coordinatae*, 2 vols., Rome 1909-1911.

[35] Cf. G. WILPERT, *La fede della Chiesa nascente secondo i monumenti dell'arte funeraria antica*, Vatican City 1938.

[36] Cf. M. RIGHETTI, *Manuale di storia liturgica*, 4 vols., Milan 1946.

[37] Cf. A. OLIVAR, *El Sacramentario di Vich*, Estudio y edición por Dom A. Olivar, *Monumenta Hispanica sacra*, vols. I-IV, Barcelona 1953.

[38] Cf. J. M. HANSSENS, *Amalarii Episcopi opera liturgica omnia*, tomes I-III, Vatican City 1948.

39 Cf. P. BRUYLANTS, *Les oraisons du Missel Romain. Tabulae synopticae fontium Missalis Romani*, Indices tomorum I-II, Louvain 1952.

[40] Cf. L. BOUYER, *Il Mistero Pasquale*, trans. by L. Migliorini, Florence 1955.

[41] Cf. G. BAUDOT, *Il Breviario Romano, Origini e storia*. Roma 1909.

[42] Cf. B. BOTTE, *Le mouvement liturgique. Témoignages et souvenirs*, Paris 1973. Also cf. *Notitiae*, 164 (1980), pp. 123-124; *Maison Dieu*, 141 (1980), pp. 167-172; B. BAROFFIO, *Mons. Mario Righetti (1882-1975). Un'esemia figura del clero e della cultura italiana* in *RL*, 61 (1975), pp. 597-606; IDEM, *L'Osservatore Romano* August 8, 1975, p. 7; *ibidem*, August 9, 1975, p. 7.

[43] *Prefazione* by Cardinal Antonelli, in AA.VV., *Mens concordet voci* pour Mgr. A.G. Martimort à l'occasion de ses 40 années d'enseignement et des 20 ans de la Constitution *Sacrosanctum Concilium*, Paris 1983, pp. 9-12.

[44] On Dom Lambert Beauduin cf. A. HAQUIN, *Dom L. Beauduin et le renouveau liturgique*, Gembloux 1970. On Abbot E. Caronti cf. E. DE VINCENTIIS, *Ricordo dell'abate E. Caronti* edited by M. BALLATORI and A. GALLETTI (pp. 245-264). On Msgr. Moglia cf. L. ADRIANOPOLI, *Liturgia e pastoralità nella figura di Mons. Moglia: L'Osservatore Romano*, August 19, 1966, p. 6.

[45] Cf. OR Archive, Milan, letter 44. For further information on Fr. Agostino Gemelli cf. R. FALSINI, *P. Gemelli e la rinascita liturgica in Italia*, Milan 1961. IDEM, *Profili*, cit., Rome 1970, pp. 175-180. For further information on the promotional work of the Opera della Regalità in the field of liturgy, see A. LAMERI, *L'attività di promozione liturgica dell'Opera della Regalità (1931-1945)*, Milan 1992.

[46] R. FALSINI, *Una pagina di storia. Il Card. Antonelli e la riforma liturgica*, in AA. VV., *Il mistero cristiano e la sua celebrazione*, Milan 1994, p. 177. Further documentation may be found in P. SORCI, *Una pagina di storia del movimento liturgico in Italia: i trenta convegni nazionali di liturgia dell'Opera della Regalità* in *Rivista di Pastorale Liturgica*, 150 (1988), pp. 69-76. Further historical information may be had in R. FALSINI, *I convegni liturgico-pastorali dell'Opera della Regalità di NSGC* in *Notitiae*, 270-271 (1989), pp. 195-202.

[47] Cf. F. ANTONELLI, *La Spiritualità di P. Gemelli* in *Vita e Pensiero*, 42 (1959), pp. 561-572.

[48] A. GEMELLI, "*Liturgia e 'liturgismo'*" in *Revista del Clero*, 14 (1933), pp. 491-494.

[49] R. FALSINI, *P. Gemelli e la rinascita liturgica in Italia*, Milan 1961, p. 15.

Chapter 3

Preparatory Studies and Partial Attempts at a General Reform of the Liturgy Under Pius XII

The Genesis of the Liturgical Reform

In the previous chapters we examined Antonelli's liturgical formation and the influence of other liturgists, Italian and foreign, upon him. Now we wish to turn to the most sensitive and demanding period of his life during which he became a pioneer and organizer of the reform of the liturgy. He discharged this task with the utmost dedication to the delicate responsibilities entrusted to him.

Reading through Antonelli's published and unpublished writings it is easy to identify his contribution to the liturgical reform, especially in its initial phase. He was very conscious of the momentous times which the Church was then experiencing in the field of liturgy. The fruits of the liturgical movement had reached maturity. Antonelli presented them to his students saying:

> Thus was born the so-called liturgical movement, which contributed in an ever increasing and impelling way to the realization of the need for a general reform of the liturgy. As was erroneously believed and sometimes said, the movement was not concerned simply with the creation of a decorative liturgical facade, nor with the external solemn celebration, nor a liturgical aestheticism which moved the senses but not the heart. Rather, it was a true liturgical movement, concerned above all to promote a solid knowledge of the liturgy itself, to conduct and live the liturgy, in other words, with promoting a true liturgical education.
>
> It was not something extrinsic or superimposed. Rather, it was concerned to bring every Christian to live his own life with a heightened, personal spirituality in a union of faith and charity with God, and at the same time to nourish that strength which was necessary for the liturgy, true teacher of the *plebs Dei*, with Sacred Scripture, the Sacraments, the Sacrifice of the Mass, and the Collects. [...] In short, the liturgical movement, properly understood, is a sign of the same vitality of the Church which adapts to the times, to present circumstances, and which, under the direct impulse of the Holy Spirit, always favors the most opportune and necessary remedies for the ailments of every age.[1]

Having seen some of Antonelli's views on the liturgical movement, we now wish to consider the historical period in which the liturgical movement came to function. In particular, we shall deepen our knowledge of the three Popes who were active in this area of the Church's life from 1903 to the Second Vatican Council.

Saint Pius X and Pius XI

Saint Pius X's contribution to liturgical renewal began with the *motu proprio "Tra le Sollecitudini"* of November 22, 1903. The Pope recalled that the Christian spirit has its primary and indispensable source in "the participation of the faithful" in the most sacred mysteries and in the Church's public and solemn prayer.

As Antonelli recognized, Saint Pius X made a notably important contribution to the reform of that prayer:

> With the publication of the Apostolic Constitution *Divino afflatu* of November 1, 1911, a new arrangement of the Psalter was introduced to the Breviary. The *motu proprio "Abhinc duos annos"* of October 23, 1913 promised a general reform of the Breviary.[2]

This reform called for *labores cum magnos, tum diuturnos*. Before this *aedificium liturgicum* could be restored, a *longa annorum series* would be necessary to free it from the *squalor vetustatis*.[3] "With the outbreak of war, the liturgical reform remained but a desire of the liturgists".[4] Later, Pius XI:

> with his *motu proprio "Già da Qualche Tempo"* of February 6, 1930 created a section in the Sacred Congregation for Rites called the "Historical" Section, for the critical study of the Causes of the Saints and for the "reform, emendations, and preparation of new editions of the liturgical texts". In fact, this liturgical competence was used immediately to initiate a study for the reform of the *Pontificale Romanum*.[5]

So great was the desire for a major reform that "this event rekindled the hopes of liturgists for the promised liturgical reform".[6] Studies continued in these decades and some notable progress became evident, "the pastoral liturgical movement had developed by vast proportions. And thus, the call to take the desired liturgical reform in hand began to be increasingly heard, and felt almost everywhere".[7]

Unfortunately, the work begun under Pius XI also ground to a halt. Meanwhile, the liturgical movement continued to grow, and became a movement of vast proportion and "it was really Pius XII, ascending the throne of Peter in March of 1939, who seriously concerned himself with the problem of a true general reform of the liturgy".[8]

The Liturgical Work of Pius XII

Pius XII was one of the great Popes of the liturgical reform. The reform had become increasingly necessary and the revision and updating of the liturgy of the Church more urgent. Pius XII's contribution to the liturgy can be summed up in five documents which clearly demonstrate the interest in the liturgy of this great Pope, as well as his strong desire to bring Christians to the life of the Church through the liturgy. Perusal of any basic text will give an idea of all the liturgical documents published by this Pope.[9] Here we shall present these documents in chronological order.

The *motu proprio "In Cotidianis Precibus"* of March 24, 1945 was the first document published by Pius XII on the liturgy. It established the use of the new critical version of the Psalter, prepared by the Pontifical Biblical Institute, for both public and private recital of the Breviary. Pius XII, from the outset of his Pontificate, desired the use of this version of the Psalter because the version in use up to that point was so defective that it often made fluent reading of the Breviary impossible and obscured the correct meaning of the Sacred Text. This new translation proved very useful for it enabled priests to read the Psalter devoutly and consciously.[10] It also gave rise to some difficulties, especially in relation to the liturgical tradition.

The Encyclical Letter *Mediator Dei* of November 20, 1947 is another important document for the liturgy published by Pius XII. Antonelli describes it as follows:

> This is a true monument which defines an epoch in the history of the liturgy. As far as I am aware, it is the first time that a Supreme Pontiff has systematically dealt with this matter which is so important. It is a magisterial and complete treatment of the subject. Above all, it spells out the doctrinal principles at the base of the liturgy. There follow some pastoral directives. It subsequently identifies and reproves certain extremist tendencies, calling on the Sacred Pastors to direct their attention and vigilance to them. *Mediator Dei*, in short, will be from now on the *magna carta* of the true liturgical movement. It will be a point of departure, a true renaissance of the liturgical piety which is so desired and hoped for by all who see the urgency of bringing the faithful to live the life of grace with the Church.[11]

The Apostolic Constitution *Christus Dominus* published on January 6, 1953 with an *Appendix of the Holy Office* is the third document published by Pius XII. It introduced a new discipline with regard to the Eucharistic fast and granted the faculty to celebrate Mass in the evening in certain specific circumstances.

> These are questions of a disciplinary nature in sacramental matters. It is easy, however, to see their practical interest and also their importance for the liturgical life. The concession of the so-called evening Mass has opened up new horizons for the apostolate, especially with regard to those groups of people who ordinarily, and in good faith, cannot attend morning Mass.[12]

A fourth document is a Decree of the Sacred Congregation of Rites published on March 23, 1955 concerning the *simplification of the rubrics*:[13]

> The general public hardly noticed it because it was concerned almost exclusively with the rubrics for the recitation of the Breviary. The priests, however, who are the true jury of this vein, from the 1st of January this year, are bound to recite the Breviary in accordance with the new disposition, are aware of its contents and the implications of the decree. They will certainly be grateful to the Holy Father. This is not a reform of the Breviary, but it is a very significant event.[14]

The fifth and most important document is the Decree *Maxima Redemptionis Nostrae Mysteria*. It was published by the Sacred Congregation of Rites on

The Development of the Liturgical Reform

November 16, 1955 with an annexed *Instruction* saying, "With this Decree the sacred ceremonies of Holy Week, precisely those of Holy Thursday, Good Friday and Holy Saturday, are being moved back to their more ancient placement in the evening hours".[15]

But, in order to understand developments that followed, one important matter must be clarified:

> These two elements of the liturgical reform, first the Easter Vigil and then the *Novus Ordo* for Holy Week, objectively were two typical examples of how the entire reform would be carried through. Encouraged by the success of these first experiments, the Commission created by Pius XII continued its work quickly. Supplement IV of the *Memoria sulla Riforma Liturgica* (Sacred Congregation of Rites, Historical Section, No. 97), a volume of 139 pages, makes this clear. It was drawn up at the suggestion of Pius XII and contained the results of the consultation carried out among the hierarchy on the reform of the Breviary. It was entitled, *Consultazione dell'Episcopato intorno alla Riforma del Breviario Romano (1956-1957). Risultati e Conclusioni.*[16]

The Origin and Work on the Pontifical Commission for the Reform of the Liturgy

Having seen the importance given to the liturgy by the Pope of the period, we shall now consider the work of the Historical Section instituted by Pius XI. The Historical Section set about its work with such zeal that it was able to present a memorandum in 1946 entitled *Promemoria intorno alla Riforma liturgica*:

> Cardinal Salotti, Prefect of the Sacred Congregation of Rites, gave a report on it to the Holy Father at an Audience on May 10, 1946. The Holy Father ordered that a concrete project be drawn up for a general reform of the liturgy.[17]

These preparations implied a great amount of research for the Historical Section, which was competent to carry out this type of work. The section gathered the documented material, which would eventually serve as a basis for discussion, and they drew up criteria and concrete norms for the reform. But, "while this great project was being carried out, the Lord called Cardinal Salotti to Himself on October 24, 1947. He was succeeded as Prefect by Cardinal Micara".[18]

The new Prefect reported the work being carried out during the audience of May 28, 1948. The Holy Father nominated a Pontifical Commission and designated it to examine the proposed plan for the reform.

> By a *biglietto di nomina* signed by Cardinal Micara, Prefect, the following persons were called to form the Commission, with Micara presiding:
>
> 1. His Excellency Msgr. Carinci, Secretary of the Sacred Congregation of Rites;
>
> 2. The Very Reverend Fr. Ferdinando Antonelli, *Relator-Generalis* of the Historical Section of the S.R.C.;
>
> 3. The Very Reverend Fr. Joseph Löw, *Vice Relator-Generalis* of the same Historical Section;
>
> 4. The Very Reverend Fr. Anselmo Albareda, OSB, Prefect of Apostolic Library of the Vatican;

5. The Very Reverend Fr. Augustin Bea, SJ, Rector of the Pontifical Biblical Institute;

6. The Very Reverend Fr. Annibale Bugnini of the Congregation of the Mission, editor of *Ephemerides Liturgicae.*[19]

At a later date a further three persons were nominated Consultors for the Liturgical Section of the Sacred Congregation of Rites:

These were distinguished liturgists living outside of Rome: one German speaker, Father Joseph Jungmann, SJ, of the University of Innsbruck, one French speaker, Dom Capelle, Abbot of Mont César and Professor of Liturgy at the University of Louvain, and one Italian, Monsignor Mario Righetti of Genoa, author of an excellent manual of the history of the Liturgy, which had been recently published.[20]

Subsequently, the Holy Father nominated another member, Monsignor Enrico Dante, *Sostituto* in the Sacred Congregation of Rites and Prefect of Papal Ceremonies.[21]

As with all commissions, the group which had been formed to work on the liturgical reform was bound to abide by certain norms: "It must be noted that from the outset all members of the Commission were asked to observe the strictest secrecy with regard to their work, and to treat all publications about it as absolutely confidential".[22]

The Commission met for the first time on June 22, 1948 in Cardinal Micara's apartments: "There was an initial exchange of views and it was decided to await the publication of the *Memoria sulla Riforma Liturgica*, which had been prepared by the Historical Section and was already at the printers".[23]

The *Memoria sulla Riforma Liturgica* was signed by Fr. Ferdinando Antonelli who diplomatically concluded the volume thus:

Before passing on from the awaited *Memoria*, may I say that it is the product of a close collaboration between the *Relator-Generalis* and *Vice Relator* of the Historical Section; Father Joseph Löw, CSSR, who is particularly expert in the history of the liturgy, bore the main burden of the work with great dedication, since he drew up the original plan. After many discussions and revisions, especially with regard to the more difficult and delicate points, it has reached its final form.

I have to add that the definitive manuscript, before going to print, was assiduously read by Monsignor Carinci, Secretary of the Sacred Congregation for Rites, who modestly conceals his vast knowledge of liturgical matters. We also wish to thank Father Bugnini, CM, of the Commission for his assistance in revising the drafts and above all in compiling an analytical index.[24]

Father Falsini says the following about it:

In the book *La Riforma Liturgica (1948-1975)* of Annibale Bugnini, Antonelli's name is not mentioned and the work is entirely attributed to Fr. J. Löw. Antonelli, however, was not one who signed his name to the work of others. I know this from experience. Neither was he a jealous or ungrateful man. The injustice is all too evident.[25]

The *Memoria sulla Riforma Liturgica*, a volume [printed on *octavo* paper] of some 342 pages plus the indexes, had been drawn up by Father Joseph Löw in collaboration with Antonelli, the then *Relator-Generalis* of the Historical Section. It "saw the light of day in the early months of 1949"[26] and is considered by Fr. Falsini to be the *magna carta* of the reform.[27] This book is divided into four chapters:

1. The Need for a Liturgical Reform;
2. Fundamental Principles for the Liturgical Reform;
3. A Complete Plan for the Reform;
4. Practical Application of the Liturgical Reform.[28]

Antonelli notes:

> In the Congregation of Rites I have been working for several months preparing the *Memoria sulla Riforma Liturgica*. The new Prefect, Cardinal Micara, is interested in the project. I proposed some names to him and he has already spoken to the Pope about establishing a small expert commission to discuss the question.

> This evening (June 22, 1948), the first meeting of the Commission was held in Cardinal Micara's study at his residence in the *Accademia Ecclesiastica* in the Piazza della Minerva. The following were present: Cardinal Micara, Prefect of the Congregation of Rites, Monsignor Carinci, Secretary of the Congregation of Rites, myself, Fr. Joseph Löw, *Vice Relator* of the Historical Section, Fr. Albareda, OSB, Prefect of the Vatican Library, and Father Bea, SJ, President of the Pontifical Biblical Institute. Father A. Bugnini was absent as he was traveling outside of Italy.

> The most important point was this: we are all convinced that a general reform must be undertaken, rather than a piecemeal reform, as had been attempted up to then. It would be necessary to start from a complete, well studied, organic plan which would fix clear limits.[29]

With reference to the *Memoria sulla Riforma Liturgica*, Historical Section, Number 72, Antonelli says:

> The first copies of the *Memoria* were sent to me from the Vatican Press on June 25. On Monday the 27th I gave a copy to His Eminence, the Cardinal Prefect, who was very pleased with it. On July 1st when speaking with the Cardinal in the presence of Monsignor Carinci, he said that by now it was too late to convoke a meeting of the Commission but that it would be useful to distribute copies of the *Memoria* to the members of the Commission so that they might be able to study it during the holidays.[30]

At four o'clock in the afternoon on November 17, 1949 the second meeting of the Commission for the Reform of the Liturgy took place in Cardinal Micara's apartments and from this date until November 27, 1953 they met thirty times: nineteen of which were devoted to examining the *Memoria*.[31]

Bearing in mind the various meetings of the Commission, we shall now turn to the revisions of the *Memoria*. Few know anything of the initial period of the Commission for the Reform of the Liturgy established by Pius XII. Among Antonelli's papers, however, we found the minutes of the Commission which met eighty-two times between 1948 and 1960. Antonelli, as *Relator-Generalis* of the Historical Section, presided at those meetings. The Commission's slow and methodical development is apparent from the minutes.

The Meetings of the Commission for the Reform of the Liturgy and Antonelli's Personal Contributions

> When, under Pius XII, it came to tackling the question of a general liturgical reform, I myself gave an outline of it in a volume published in 1948 by the Historical Section of the Sacred Congregation of Rites: *Memoria sulla Riforma Liturgica*.[32]

At a first glance, the impression could be given that a good liturgical reform was carried out *ex nihilo* in the post-Conciliar period. However, a study of the period and an exploration of experts' opinions on liturgy show that intense theological and liturgical work had been done during the decades preceding the Council. An article by Hans-Erich Jung, entitled "*Die Vorarbeiten zu einer Liturgiereform unter Pius XII*", introduces the *Memoria sulla Riforma Liturgica* as follows:

> The work which had been done up to that point was summarized in the *Memoria sulla Riforma Liturgica*. The fascicle had been researched and published by Ferdinando Antonelli and Joseph Löw. It was dated December 30, 1948. Its printing was completed on June 25, 1949 and it was then presented to the members of the Commission. Formally, it was a masterpiece of diplomatic tact, while materially a practical work - principally concerned with rubrics - rather than a theological work.
>
> During its preparation, Antonelli had spoken of the need for a liturgical reform in a very generic way. He said: "Everywhere and by everyone it is recognized that today in the Catholic world, especially among the clergy, there is a desire, indeed even a conviction of the need for liturgical reform". Specific reasons for this need are cited in the first part of the *Memoria*.[33]

We must also quote Father Bugnini's valuable testimony with regard to Antonelli's personal contribution to the work of the Commission established by Pius XII. It was made by Father Bugnini on the occasion of Antonelli's Episcopal consecration March 19, 1966:

> I first met Your Excellency at the end of 1946 when the work of the general reform of the liturgy was still in its embryonic stage. This work was getting under way, *in silentio et spe*, under the strictest secrecy, almost clandestinely, with a heart swollen with hope. [...] Father Antonelli followed, reviewed, surveyed, led, and refined everything. This was all done with prudence, wisdom, and balance. The works published in those first years bear the unmistakable mark of a generous fraternal collaboration.[34]

On that happy occasion, Fr. Bugnini added:

> Beginnings are always difficult, especially when opening up new trails, and in our case, I would say [this was] a first breach in the walls of a fortress, centuries old, stoutly built, strong and robust, but no longer capable of responding to the spiritual needs of the age, which needed a fresh breath of life. God alone knows

how difficult, psychologically, that first moment was. The difficult part of the Commission's work was always the meetings of the Commission and convincing them to accept proposals and projects [...]. This required all of Father Antonelli's tact, long anonymity, patience, and intelligent discernment. The meetings of the Commission were masterpieces of the art of diplomacy: when the sessions concluded, the proposals in one way or another, had been accepted.[35]

The Discussions and Proposals Concerning the Memoria

What were the reasons which manifested the need for a liturgical reform? The *Memoria* gave the following five:

1. The actual state of the liturgy;

2. The actual state of the science of liturgy;

3. The actual state of the international liturgical movement;

4. The actual state of the clergy;

5. The promises and initiatives of the Holy See for the definitive liturgical reform.[36]

Examination of the minutes of the Commission shows that at its second meeting on November 17, 1949, the *Memoria* was presented as a "basis for discussion".[37] It should be mentioned that when the Historical Section finished the *Memoria*, it had already compiled another fascicle of historical and hagiographical material for *drawing up the calendar*. Antonelli was asked to have it printed and distributed to the members of the Commission by consent of the Holy Father. The *Memoria* was also sent *sub secreto pontificio* to Dom Bernando Capelle, Father Joseph Jungmann, and to Monsignor Mario Righetti, asking them to examine it within two months.

> The Very Reverend Father Antonelli briefly recounts the history of this initiative and the reasons which motivated it. These reasons were set out clearly in Chapter I of the *Memoria*, which need not be mentioned here. Then he moved to Chapter II and read the most important or basic principles which were to guide the reform. These were generally accepted by everyone as adequate to meet the demands and imperatives for a serious and thorough reform.[38]

The minutes of the third meeting of the Commission, held at 4:30 p.m. on December 5, 1949, contain an account of Antonelli's presentation of the headings for the various questions contained in Chapter III:

> General Plan for the Reform (articles 20 ff.). The following points were examined:
>
> Article 28 – Whether it is convenient to ascribe the five principal feasts of redemption to a single supreme category; and
>
> Article 29 – Whether it is convenient to divide all other feasts of the year into three general categories: solemn, ordinary, and minimal. All are in agreement.
>
> Article 30 – Whether it is convenient to subdivide each of these three categories into solemn, ordinary, and minimal, and into major and minor.[39]

This last proposal was discussed but the question had to be deferred to the following meeting. There followed a discussion of the calendar and it was agreed unanimously to ascribe a simple solemn category to the Sundays of Advent (so that the office would never be omitted). It was unanimously agreed to suppress vigils and octaves in Advent.

Articles 42-44 were on the proximate preparation for Christmas, December 17-23. It was proposed to give the preparatory period for Christmas an "ascensional character", such as Lent for Easter. This was commonly agreed.[40]

The question of the liturgical name of the feast was raised. The official name is *Nativitatis Domini*. The early name for the feast was *Natalis Domini*, a name of Roman origin, from which was derived the Italian, *Natale*. Another matter to be discussed was the abolition of the third Gospel at the third Mass [of Christmas Day]. All voted for the restoration of the term *Natalis* in all three cases.[41] The proposed abolition of the third Gospel received majority vote.

All agreed that the Marian character of January 1 should be restored, and all agreed that it would be suitable for the celebration of the feast of the Maternity of Mary.

The question of the feast of the Holy Name of Jesus was discussed and it was agreed that it should be celebrated on January 2 and that of the Holy Family on January 3.

The fifth meeting was held at 4:30 p.m. on January 17, 1950 in Cardinal Micara's apartments to continue the examination of the *Memoria*. The meeting touched on several points concerning the Vigil of the Epiphany, the insertion of the Gospel pericope (Mt 2:1-6), as well as the creation of a proper Mass. Both proposals were unanimously accepted.[42]

> For the Octave of the Epiphany, in a supplement to the *Memoria*, it was proposed to suppress the Octave and celebrate the eighth day only. The Gospel texts would be distributed as follows: January 6: the coming of the Magi; the Sunday of the Octave: The Baptism of Jesus; January 13: the Wedding at Cana.[43]

This proposal caused some perplexity among the Commission but after discussion, the general lines of the proposal were accepted. A theoretical proposal was advanced concerning "the possibility of inserting the feast of Christ the King into this period, since, conceptually, it would complement the Epiphany".[44] Father Bea observed that in fixing the feast of Christ the King on the final Sunday of October account had been taken of the feast of All Saints, so as to glorify the same King together with His heavenly Court. This idea had been clearly expressed in the Encyclical *Quas Primas* of Pope Pius XI published on December 11, 1925.

Father Antonelli underlined the distinction between the transcendental meaning of the actual feast of the kingship and the Kingship of Our Lord as manifested in the mystery of the Epiphany.[45]

The sixth meeting of the Commission took place at 4:30 p.m. on January

27, 1950 at the apartments of Cardinal Micara. After several discussions the conclusions arrived at during the previous meeting were approved, namely that "it would be more logical to begin the proper of Lent on Ash Wednesday".[46]

A discussion ensued on the rite of Holy Week, but we shall not concern ourselves with it since it will be treated in two subsequent chapters. We shall therefore continue examining the chronological order of the meetings and discussions of the Commission.

The 15th meeting of the Commission met at 5 o'clock in the afternoon on January 22, 1952 at the apartments of Cardinal Micara. Father Antonelli presented a short résumé of the Commission's examination of the *Memoria* which had been interrupted because of the consideration of Holy Saturday.[47]

The question of liturgical gradation was much discussed and the minutes of the 16th meeting mention:

> It must be noted, for the chronicle, that the problem of liturgical gradation has proved to be one of the most sensitive problems and also one of the most important for the success of the liturgical reform; the toil expended on this problem has not been in vain because we have opened up a good way, which above all, follows the traditional line of the Church.[48]

The Commission met for the 17th time on February 19, 1952 to recommence examining the *Memoria*.

Several points were discussed at the 19th meeting of the Commission which took place on April 29, 1952. The following conclusions were arrived at unanimously:

> The *litania minor*, the three Rogation days, which was of Gallican origin and was not, as all acknowledged, in harmony with the spirit of Easter, should be eliminated. As was already decided, the *litania maior* should be retained, and detached from the feast of Saint Mark (April 25) which should not be transferred. [The litany] should then be moved to the Saturday of the nearest Quartertense, which would be that of Spring.[49]

After this meeting the problem of the *litania maior* was raised again on May 13, 1952.

On June 10, 1952, having read the minutes, the session opened "with the examination of the rubrical point of the liturgical day and the law of precedence and translation, on the basis of a *pro-memoria* which had been distributed in the days prior to the meeting".[50]

The following meeting took place on Wednesday, June 25, 1952. The *Relator-Generalis* raised several questions concerning the grouping of the Doctors and founders which had been suspended.[51]

At the 23rd meeting, held on July 8 a proposal was made to institute a feast denominated *Omnium Sanctorum Summorum Pontificum*. Antonelli noted

> that the feast could be an act of veneration and of homage to the office of the Supreme Pontiff; that some saints included, even when they did not have an

ancient cult, and on the basis of historical evidence, do not meet the criteria for inclusion in the universal calendar, but who, over the centuries, have a certain cult, and that would be well to continue with a collective feast.[52]

Finally, it was decided to include the feast *Omnium Sanctorum Summorum Pontificum* in the universal calendar, during the Octave of Saint Peter and Saint Paul, and more precisely, on July 3 with a second class rite.[53] The written conclusion of the minutes states:

> This meeting concluded the series of meetings (12 in all) that took place before the holidays of 1951-1952. In conclusion it can be said that the work done so far, especially at the last meetings, which were very constructive, thanks to the material prepared by the Historical Section of the Sacred Congregation of Rites, opens the horizon to the hope that the reform can now proceed more quickly and more surely, thereby satisfying, as soon as possible, the desires of the entire Catholic world which are reiterated and insisted on daily.[54]

The next meeting took place at the beginning of October. In the meanwhile, material relating to the question of Holy Thursday and Good Friday was prepared. Authorization for this had been granted by the Holy Father.

A year later, discussion of the *Memoria* was resumed from October 28, 1952 to November 6, 1953. During 1952-1953 work began on *a project for the reform of Holy Week*. This project will be discussed in a later chapter. At the 29th meeting of the Commission, held on November 6, 1953, discussion centred on the new feasts to be inserted in the calendar: The Most Precious Blood, all the Marian feasts, the Marian month, *Maria Regina Mundi*, etc..

The 31st meeting of the Commission on January 12, 1954 was the first session over which the new Prefect of the Sacred Congregation of Rites, Cardinal Gaetano Cicognani, presided. A long discussion took place on the institution of the feast of *Maria Regina*. It took a further two sessions to arrive at the decision to propose the possible institution of the feast of *Maria Regina* to the Holy Father. [55]

All of the feasts and memorials of the Saints contained in the liturgical calendar were studied during the following meetings of the 33rd to the 49th. The sessions of the Commission held between June 24, 1955 and March 9, 1956 were devoted to a review of the *Positio De Instauratione Liturgica Maioris Hebdomadae*, which had been proposed by the *Relator-Generalis*, Father Antonelli. It had already been sent to the Cardinal Members of the Sacred Congregation of Rites together with the *Instructio de ordine Hebdomadae Sanctae iuxta instauratum ritum peragendo*.

Various projects were examined in the session held between April 6, 1956 and February 20, 1959: *The Reform of the Breviary*, the arrangement of the recurring scripture readings, some *Ordinationes et Declarationes* resolving difficulties that had emerged with the celebration of the reformed Holy Week; questions concerning the new edition of the *Pontificale Romanum*, the *Instructio Musicae Sacrae*, the blessing of ashes, the reformed rite for the consecration of a church, the principal readings of Holy Week in the vernacular, and on the repetition of the liturgical actions on Good Friday.

On May 15, 1959 the agenda included the examination of the reformed rite for some consecrations and blessings contained in the second part of the *Pontificale Romanum*: consecration of a church, consecration of an altar without consecration of a church, blessing of the foundation stone of a new church, blessing of churches, blessing of a portable altar, consecration of bells, blessing of a cemetery, reconciliation of churches, and reconciliation of cemeteries.[56]

Concerning the consecration of an altar, "Fr. Antonelli is of the opinion that the title should be made uniform with others, suggesting for example: *Ordo Consecrationis Altaris sine Ecclesiae Dedicatione*. The proposal was accepted".[57]

On July 10, 1959 the Rites were discussed again. During the course of this meeting the latest drafts of the *Pontificale Romanum* were examined. The minutes of May 27, 1960 record the changes which had occurred in the Commission for the Reform of the Liturgy. Following the elevation of Father Bea to the Cardinalate, of Monsignor Carinci's promotion to Emeritus Secretary, of the nomination of Monsignor Dante as Secretary of the Congregation, of Father Antonelli to *Promotor Fidei*, of Monsignor Frutaz as *Relator-Generalis*, as Father Löw as Adjunct Relator, it was necessary to re-shape the Commission for the Reform of the Liturgy which had been instituted in 1948. This resulted in the Commission being composed as follows under its new president, Cardinal Gaetano Cicognani, Prefect of the Congregation of Rites:

Original members of the Commission:

> Monsignor Dante, Secretary;
>
> The Reverend Father Antonelli, *Promotor Generalis Fidei*;
>
> Abbot Albareda, OSB, Prefect of the Vatican Library and Commission of Rites;
>
> The Reverend Father Löw, CSSR, Adjunct Relator;
>
> The Reverend Father Bugnini, CM, Consultor of the Sacred Congregation of Rites, Secretary of the Commission.

New members:

> Monsignor Cesario D'Amato, OSB, Abbot of St. Paul's;
>
> Monsignor Amato Pietro Frutaz, *Relator-Generalis* of the Historical Section;
>
> The Reverend L. Rovigatti, Parish Priest [Pastor] of the Parish of the Nativity;
>
> The Reverend Father Braga, CM, *Attaché* for the liturgical reform.

It is worthwhile commenting on a letter presenting the subject of one of the sessions of the Commission. Dated May 17, 1960 and written by Joseph Löw, it is entitled "*La Seconda Semplificazione della Rubriche*".

The Decree *De rubricis ad simpliciorem formam redigendis* of March 23, 1955 was universally welcomed. The object is clearly stated within the Decree itself: restore the recital of the Divine Office to that serenity of soul, without which no serious prayer is possible.

The multiple activities which take up much of the priest's day, even that of the religious who are devoted to a more recollected life, together with a decline in vocations, in some regions quite preoccupying, did not resolve the question of the simplification of the rubrics, even after the reduction of the daily *pensum*, in itself partial, which had been effected in 1955.

In 1956, with the approval of Pius XII, a summary consultation of the Episcopate was organized. Its purpose was to clarify the *desiderata* and the needs of the clergy with regard to the Divine Office. Following the consultation, a further and more effective reduction of the daily *pensum* was proposed. Such would necessarily imply a new and more radical simplification of the *Instructus Rubricarum*. While work began almost immediately on this project, it was delayed because other more urgent projects had to be addressed (e.g. the Instruction on Sacred Music and Sacred Liturgy, and the emendation of the *Pontificale Romanum*). Pius XII, who had a lively interest in the liturgical reform which he set in motion, died and was succeeded by John XXIII, who surprised the world by announcing the next Ecumenical Council.

While still the Cardinal Patriarch of Venice, the new Pope had supported the reform of the Liturgy, as he did the reform of Holy Week and of the Breviary. When requested, he confirmed the Commission and directed the continuation of its work, including the "*La Seconda Semplificazione della Rubriche*". The reasons motivating this simplification were:

a) The first simplification had been limited. The "first simplification", in so far as it was "first", was not exhaustive. In the expectation of a general and complete reform of the liturgy being undertaken within a relatively short period of time, only those points most obviously in need of review, were adjusted.

b) The results of the consultation of the Episcopate. While undertaken with a view to obtaining useful material for a general reform, the consultation quickly revealed the need to make some urgent provisions to be immediately implemented so as to meet the more pressing demands, especially by extending the use of offices with three readings.

c) The need for a complete and unified text of the rubrics. Following on the general consultation of the Episcopate, and after it became clear that a general reform would not be immediately implemented, (the indiction of the Second Vatican Council brought further necessary delays), a complete, unified text of the rubrics became necessary. As every person knows, the rubrics for the Missal and the Breviary are to be found in various sources: "*Rubricae generales*", two different texts for the Breviary and the Missal; "*Additiones et Variationes ad rubricas generales*", a further pair of texts for both books; the Decree of 1955, the thousands of "*decreta authentica*", the resolutions of *dubbia*, etc.. These texts had never been collated, or reworked or harmonized. Hence new *dubbia*, difficulties, and discordant interpretations continually arose. With the postponement at least for several years of the general reform, it became absolutely necessary to collate all legislation on the Breviary and of the Missal to one complete single text. The Commission, at this point, took this to be its principal work. After all of this, one further consideration should be added:

d) that of the economic and industrial circumstances of liturgical publishing.

The 1955 Decree forbade liturgical publishing to circulate Breviaries or Missals updated in accordance with the Decree. Its intention was to spare the clergy the cost of new liturgical books, since those in use could well continue until the expected general reform would oblige all to purchase new books. For reasons beyond the control of the Commission, the general reform had been delayed, some publishers, circumventing the Decree, had published Breviaries revised according to their own criteria, thereby compromising other publishers who suffered serious financial losses. The Holy Father desired that work should be given to serious publishers. These were given permission to publish the revised Breviary. The occasion was used to simplify and unify the rubrics, also taking into consideration some of the more pressing recommendations of the Episcopate.

Following these preliminaries, we now present a schema of the project which is taken from the printed drafts circulated to the members of the Commission. The peculiarities of the project can easily be identified. The text was divided into two parts: the first, a general Decree ordering the adoption of the new, complete, single body of rubrics, together with the necessary dispositions; the second the body of rubrics itself, together with a revised calendar. The body of rubrics was divided into four parts:

1. *Rubricae generales*, valid for Mass and Breviary;
2. *Rubricae generales Breviarii Romani*;
3. *Rubricae generales Missalis Romani*, containing the rubrics specific to both liturgical books;
4. *Dispositiones Transitoriae*, containing various dispositions which would be necessary until the publication of the revised editions, and for those who did not intend to buy the revised editions of the Breviary. Clearly, the principle remained that the editions of the breviary in use could continue, albeit with some inconvenience.

As already mentioned, the drafts of the rubrics would be in accordance with the various parts, already outlined, and with their various subdivisions. For the present, we shall restrict ourselves to some observations concerning the preparations for this project.

The plan for the new simplification of the rubrics was drawn up under the directions of Father Joseph Löw, CSSR, Adjunct Relator of the Historical Section, together with the officials assigned to the Historical Section of the Congregation of Rites for the liturgical reform. These included Father Annibale Bugnini, CM, and especially Father Carlo Braga, CM, who was a specialist in historical and practical liturgy.

The text of the plan was first circulated to ten people for their study and examination. It was circulated a second time to the same ten. Later, it was sent to four other specialists, chosen among the most famous rubricists.

The first group consisted of the following persons:

> Antonana, de Gregorio Martinez, CMF, Madrid, Spain;
>
> Bellocchio, Giovanni, CM, Rome;
>
> Dirks, Ansgario, OP, Rome;
>
> Dubois, Marcel, CSSR, Aylmer, Canada;
>
> Förstinger, Karl, Monsignor, Linz, Austria;
>
> Lurz, Wilhelm, Monsignor, Munich, Germany;
>
> Noirot, Marcel, Monsignor, Rome;
>
> O'Connell, John Baptist, Builth Wales, England;
>
> Trimeloni, Ludovico, SDB, Turin;
>
> Wagenhäuser, Erhart, OESA, Regensburg, Germany.

The members of the second group were:

> Capoferri, Salvatore, Monsignor, Rome;
>
> Meerschaut, Prosper, CSSR, Rome;
>
> Tassi, Ildefonso, OSB, Rome;
>
> Zama, Antonio, Monsignor, Rome/Naples.

Several of these (Förstinger, Lurz, Meerschaut, and O'Connell) had edited and continue to edit diocesan or religious directories and well knew the pitfalls involved with rubrics and the possible complications to which these could give rise. Then there were Bellocchio and Wagenhäuser: Bellocchio prepared the general *Ordo* for the universal Church [*Ordo Generalis*], and Wagenhäuser had been the liturgical editor with the famous liturgical publishing house Pustet for many years. Some had been professors of liturgy or directors of liturgical institutes (Antonana, Dirks, Dubois, Trimeloni, Tassi, Zama) and others had been masters of ceremonies (Capoferri, Dubois, Meerschaut). Monsignor Noirot was a noted expert in the Canon Law of the Liturgy. Some had published significant works on the rubrics (Lurz, Dubois, Noirot). Hence the seriousness of the work was guaranteed.[58]

Until its conclusive eighty-second meeting this new Commission pursued its task of discussing the *Calendarium Breviarii et Missalis Romani* and the *Rubricae Generales Breviarii et Missalis et Romani, Pars prima, pars secunda, pars tertia.* This meeting of the Commission was held on Friday, July 8, 1960 at 5:30 p.m.

in the *Sala del Congresso* in the Sacred Congregation of Rites. The Prefect of the Congregation, Cardinal Gaetano Cicognani, presided at the meeting which continued with its examination of the *Rubricae Generales* starting at article 373, where they had finished at the previous meeting. The Commission again revised the 2nd edition of the calendar which had been distributed at the previous meeting.

Finally, the Commission examined a draft of the *Decretum generale* (later changed to a *motu proprio* by disposition of the Holy Father), which was approved with some minor stylistic modification.[59]

> With this meeting the examination of the second simplification of the rubrics came to a close, and with it the work of the Pontifical Commission for the Reform of the Liturgy, before the Ecumenical Council, was practically concluded. After the Angelus, the meeting was dissolved at 7:30 p.m..[60]

As it appears from the minutes kept by Father Bugnini, the 82nd meeting of the Commission was its final session. We must therefore attempt to explain the interruption of the Commission's work. Antonelli writes:

> The interruption of the Commission's work and its eventual dissolution came as a logical consequence of the great novelty of the Second Vatican Council, announced by John XXIII on January 25, 1959. During the preparatory work for the Council, when the topics to be placed before the Conciliar Fathers were being decided, it was clear that a question of such major importance for the Church as a general reform of the liturgy, would have to be included in their deliberations. Thus a conciliar preparatory Commission was constituted and charged with the preparation of the schema for the reform of the liturgy which would be submitted to the Conciliar Fathers. It may also be said that the work of the Commission instituted by Pius XII, has had its influence in the redaction of the Schema that the preconciliar Commission had to prepare. All the more, the Commission was presided over by Cardinal Gaetano Cicognani, with Father Annibale Bugnini as its Secretary, the former having been President and latter Secretary of the Commission created by Pius XII.[61]

After having reviewed the sessions of the Commission, the questions discussed, and the various changes [introduced], the seriousness with which the Commission protracted its work from June 1948 to July 1960 is made clear.

Fortunately, the numerous "preliminary reports", discussions, and the conclusions reached by the Commission were taken up and developed by the Council. This happened, however, only after an intervention made by Cardinal Bea, in response to which, the five fascicles of the *Memoria* along with its various supplements were distributed to all the members and experts of the Conciliar Commission.

Mention should be made of the Commission's courage and its willingness to renew some traditional rites could well have given rise to criticisms and negative reaction. The first of those rites, chronologically, was the Easter Vigil. However, the *Ordo Sabbati Sancti*, published on February 9, 1951, won universal approval. One should also recall the importance of the printed volumes published as annexes of the *Memoria*.[62]

One partial reform that took place was that of the 1955, *De Instauratione*

Liturgica Maioris Hebdomadae. Not only did this document carry the signature of Father Antonelli, but he also signed the first explanatory article published on the subject in the *Osservatore Romano* on March 4, 1951.

Maxima Redemptoris Mysteria, containing a new *Ordo* for Holy Week, was published in November 1955. It contained a total reform of all the rites from Palm Sunday to the Easter Triduum. This reform was guided by the same criteria as had been employed for the reform of the Easter Vigil and which would subsequently form the basis for the Conciliar reform: the authenticity of the celebration and also of their rubrical aspects; fidelity to the genuine tradition; pastoral utility.[63]

The Instruction on Sacred Music and Sacred Liturgy, published September 3, 1958, constitutes a further reform.

> The Instruction, let it be said, should not be seen as a cataract for the so called liturgical movement with a great damper that, while placed firmly in the current of the great principles repeatedly inculcated by the Holy See, it may succeed in bringing to all the faithful that spiritual river, the living water of the Lord, by an ever more active and conscious participation in the liturgical life of the Church.[64]

> An intense effort led to the re-ordering of the calendar and of the Breviary which ended with the decree simplifying the rubrics in 1955 and to the codification of the rubrics in 1960.

> A revised and simplified edition of the second part of the *Pontificale Romanum* was published in 1961: Dedication of Churches and Altars, Consecration of Bells, etc..

> The *Ordo baptismi adultorum per gradus catechumenatus dispositus* was published on the Eve of the Council, April 15, 1962, in response to the needs of missionary countries, and more recently in response to a meeting of liturgists held in the summer of 1958 at Montserrat, at which Father Antonelli attended. Finally, within a few months of the Council, on July 3, 1962, a correct edition of the *Ritus servandis in celebratione missae* was produced.[65]

Father Antonelli's commitment and contribution to the liturgical reform did not cease with the Council.

The Development of the Liturgical Reform

[1] F. ANTONELLI, *Il movimento liturgico. Visione storica. Visione ideale*. Lezioni di Liturgia, in *ALV*, s.d., pp. 1-5.

[2] F. ANTONELLI, *Pio XII e la Riforma Liturgica*, in AA.VV.; *Pio XII. In memoriam*, Rome 1984, p. 139. Cf. A. BUGNINI, *Documenta Pontificia ad instaurationem liturgicam spectantia (1903-1953)*, Rome 1953, pp. 47-51.

[3] Cf. PIUS XII, *motu proprio "Abhinc duos annos"*, n. 10, in A. BUGNINI, *Documenta*, cit., p. 51.

[4] CPRL, *Promemoria sull'origine della Commissione Pontificia per la Riforma liturgica e sul lavoro da essa compiuto negli anni 1948-1953*, in SCCS, *Archivio fondo Antonelli*, folder *"Verbali della Commissione per la Riforma liturgica creata da Pio XII"*, p. 1.

[5] F. ANTONELLI, *Pio XII*, cit., p. 139.

[6] CPRL, *Promemoria*, cit., p. 1.

[7] *Ibidem*, p. 2.

[8] F. ANTONELLI, *Pio XII*, cit., p. 139.

[9] Cf. A. BUGNINI, *Documenta*, cit.; The Monks of Solesmes, *La liturgie*, Paris 1954.

[10] F. ANTONELLI, *Pio XII e la Liturgia*, ms November 10, 1982, in *ALV*, p. 4.

[11] *Ibidem*, p. 5.

[12] *Ibidem*, p. 6.

[13] Cf. *AAS*, 47 (1955), pp. 218-224.

[14] F. ANTONELLI, *Pio XII e la Liturgia*, cit., pp. 6-7.

[15] *Ibidem*, p. 7.

[16] F. ANTONELLI, *Pio XII e la Liturgia*, cit., p. 141.

[17] CPRL, *Promemoria*, cit., p. 2.

[18] *Ibidem*.

[19] *Ibidem*, p. 2-3.

[20] *Ibidem*, p. 3.

[21] Cf. *ibidem*, p. 3.

[22] *Ibidem*, p. 4.

[23] *Ibidem*, p. 4-5.

[24] SRC, *Memoria sulla Riforma Liturgica*, Historical Section, n. 71, Vatican City 1948, p. 318.

[25] R. FALSINI, *Il Card. Antonelli e la riforma liturgica* in *Il mistero cristiano e la sua celebrazione*, Milan 1994, p. 177. A. BUGNINI, in his book, *La riforma liturgica*, p. 20 says nothing of Antonelli's contribution and attributes everything to Fr. Löw.

[26] CPRL, *Promemoria*, cit., p. 5.

[27] R. FALSINI, *Il Card. Antonelli e la riforma liturgica*, in *RPL*, 180 (1993), p. 73.

[28] SRC, *Memoria, cit.*, pp. 337-342.

[29] F. ANTONELLI, *Diario n. 12*, folder *"Riforma Liturgica"*, in *ALV*.

[30] F. ANTONELLI, *Diario n. 13*, folder *"Riforma Liturgica"*, in *ALV*. In addition, we also discovered a manuscript containing an account of the audience of the Holy Father which is entitled *Presentazione della Memoria sulla Riforma Liturgica*. This states: "At the suggestion of Cardinal Micara, the Prefect, I had a copy of the *Memoria sulla Riforma Liturgica* bound in white silk and, on July 22, I accompanied His Eminence who went to present it to the Holy Father. The cardinal wanted me to present it to the Holy Father, but I preferred that he make the presentation, however I was introduced at a certain point during the audience. The Holy Father was leafing through the volume with satisfaction, and while I do not exactly remember what he said, he must have mentioned something to the effect that we were making courageous proposals, to which I more or less replied that if we were making courageous proposals, it was because we could rely on the courage displayed by the Holy Father (in his new version of the Psalms). I remember that he noted that we had taken everything into account and that I had observed that the liturgy was an organic system of which one part could not be touched without repercussion in all the other parts. He said that the liturgy is like a mosaic: if you move one tessera, it affects all the others. In short, the Holy Father appeared pleased and very satisfied".

[31] CPRL, *Promemoria*, cit., p. 5.

[32] F. ANTONELLI, *Pio XII*, cit., p. 140.

[33] V.H.E. JUNG, *Die Vorarbeiten zu einer Liturgiereform unter Pius XII*, in *LJ*, 26 (1976), pp. 165-166.

[34] A. BUGNINI, *Parole dette in occasione della consacrazione episcopale di Mons. Antonelli*, Rome, March 19, 1966, in *ALV*, pp. 2-3.

[35] *Ibidem*, p. 3.

[36] SRC, *Memoria, cit.*, p. 7.

[37] SCCS, *Archivio fondo Antonelli*, folder *Verbali della Commissione per la Riforma liturgica creata da Pio XII*, p. 4.

[38] *Ibidem*, p. 4-5.

[39] Cf. *ibidem*, p. 6.

[40] Cf. *ibidem*, p. 7-8.

[41] Cf. *ibidem*, p. 11.

[42] *Ibidem*, p. 12; 14.

[43] *Ibidem*, p. 15.

[44] *Ibidem*.

[45] *Ibidem*.

[46] *Ibidem*, p. 19.

[47] Cf. *ibidem*, p. 45.

[48] *Ibidem*, p. 49.

[49] *Ibidem*, p. 55.

[50] *Ibidem*, p. 59.

[51] Cf. *ibidem*, pp. 61-62.

[52] *Ibidem*, p. 64.

[53] Cf. *ibidem*.

[54] *Ibidem*, p. 65.

[55] Cf. *ibidem*, pp. 80-96.

[56] Cf. *ibidem*, pp. 96-180.

[57] *Ibidem*, p. 181.

[58] It is to be noted that the preparatory work was officially assigned to the *Historical Section of the Sacred Congregation of Rites*, for which purpose the section has a number of particularly well trained personnel to deal with the tasks specified by the liturgical reform (cf. *Motu proprio* of Pius XI of February 6, 1930 instituting the Historical Section and attributing it specific competences). A. BUGNINI, *Commissione Pontificia per la Riforma liturgica*, dated May 17, 1960, in SCCS, *Archivio fondo Antonelli*, folder *Verbali della Commissione*, p. 2; also folder entitled *Simplificatio Rubricarum*, in SCCS, *Archivio fondo Antonelli*, pp. 3-7.

[59] SCCS, *Archivio fondo Antonelli*, folder *Verbali della Commissione per la Riforma liturgica creata da Pio XII*, pp. 183-194.

[60] *Ibidem*, p. 195.

[61] F. ANTONELLI, *Pio XII, cit.*, p. 142.

[62] SCCS, *Verbali, cit.*, pp. 1-195. These were four *Supplementi* published in the same format: *Supplemento I: Intorno alla graduazione liturgica* (1950, pp. 38); *Supplemento II, Annotazione alla Memoria* containing the responses of the three experts: B. Capelle, J.A. Jungmann, and M. Righetti (1950, pp. 62); *Supplemento III, Materiale Storico, agiografico, liturgico per la riforma del Calendario*, which was a type of dictionary on the various feasts (1951, pp. 203); *Supplemento IV, Consultazione dell'Episcopato intorno alla Riforma del Breviario Romano (1956-1957); Risultati e deduzioni* (1957, pp. 139).

[63] R. FALSINI, *Il Card. Antonelli e la riforma liturgica*, in AA. VV., *Il mistero cristiano e la sua celebrazione*, Milan 1994, p. 179.

[64] F. ANTONELLI, *Importante Istruzione della Sacra Congregazione dei Riti sulla Musica Sacra e la Sacra Liturgia*, p. 2, in SCCS, *Archivio fondo Antonelli*, folder *Riforma liturgica sotto Pio XII*. This article was also published in *L'Osservatore Romano*, October 2, 1958, and as an introduction to the Instruction published by the OR, Milan 1958, pp. 7-20.

[65] A.G. MARTIMORT, *In memoriam. Le Cardinal Antonelli (1896-1993)*, in *Notitiae*, 324 (1993), pp. 432-437.

Chapter 4

The Reform of the Easter Vigil

Thus far we have reviewed the work of the Pontifical Commission for the Reform of the Liturgy from its institution in 1948 by Pius XII up until 1960. Before proceeding to document the developments of the liturgy during the Second Vatican Council and more closely following the activities of Father Antonelli, as documented in his own writings, we should first describe more fully the reform of the Easter Vigil (1951) and of Holy Week (1955). This will be done using the various studies and proposals put forward in the *Memoria sulla Riforma Liturgica* as our guide.

Reasons for the Reform of the Easter Vigil

For some time the Holy See had been petitioned to transfer the ceremonies held on the morning of Holy Saturday to the night or at least to the evening, which was the natural context for these rites. The request for this change had been submitted several times to the Holy See, but initially the requests were archived and subsequently evasive or dilatory replies were given. Despite this, the requests continued for the simple reason that pastoral and liturgical needs continued recommending such a change.

Finally, the delays ended when the German and French Episcopates collectively petitioned the Holy Father towards the end of 1950. The Episcopate was saddened that such important ceremonies were held,

> nullis assistentibus volvantur. Permulti sacerdotes praesertim in urbibus et suburbiis curam animarum gerentes, et etiam non pauci fideles qui in Actione Catholica militant, iterum atque iterum ad Ordinarios suos preces miserunt, ut officium istud sero vesperi vel etiam noctu celebretur ad commoditatem operariorum.[1]

The reasons were not only of a strictly liturgical nature, but above all, they were practical pastoral reasons since the liturgy must take into account the needs of the faithful. The majority of the faithful are obliged to work on the morning of Holy Saturday which renders it a working day. Consequently, most people would be absent from the morning ceremonies, and in order to facilitate the participatory presence of the faithful, these ceremonies would need to be transferred to the evening time. "It was essentially this reason that caused the Holy Father, two years later, to give the noted disposition permitting the celebration of Mass on the evenings of Sundays and Holy Days".[2]

On December 14, 1950, the Secretariat of State transmitted the petitions of the French Episcopate to the Sacred Congregation of Rites, stating explicitly that the Holy Father would favor the concession.

In 1948 the Commission for the Reform of the Liturgy had already examined this problem in its famous *Memoria*. For this reason the dossier was entrusted to the same Commission, which was regarded as the body most competent to examine the question. This was a propitious opportunity for the Commission to offer a foretaste of the liturgical-pastoral reform, then being prepared, that kept in mind the needs of the faithful.

> While the Commission was preparing and discussing this particular project, the Holy Father, in an audience on January 12, 1951, was informed of the progress of the work, and expressed his satisfaction. In a following audience, on February 9, 1951, His Eminence Cardinal Micara presented a definitive project to the Holy Father, explained it, and commented on it. The project was fully approved. (The Decree of the Sacred Congregation of Rites bears the date of February 9).[3]

Finally, in an audience granted on February 16, 1951, the Holy Father gave his approval and authorized the Commission to publish the Decree. Thus the new *Ordo Sabbati Sancti* was drawn up in a definitive form and published in the *Acta Apostolicae Sedis*. "The Holy Father not only carefully read the final drafts which were to be sent to the *Acta*, but he also made one or two corrections".[4] After a period of frantic work, the fascicle of the *Acta*, bearing the date of February 26, was published on the eve of March 1 together with the new *Ordo*, which was followed a few days later by a printing of some twenty-three thousand copies of the liturgical edition. Bearing in mind the short period of time before Easter, which fell on March 25, it was not possible to make the *Ordo* known to all. Consequently, its application was almost exclusively restricted to Europe.

History of the Reform of Holy Saturday

The Commission for the Reform of the Liturgy examined articles 61 through 74 of the *Memoria* on January 27, 1950. A number of general principles accepted by all members of the Commission were established. It was then decided to form a special Sub-commission which would work on the particular modifications and simplifications that would be applied to the complex rites of the Sacred Triduum. Since we will be dealing with the restoration of the celebration of Holy Saturday to the evening, with the necessary adaptations of the rites, it will be useful to bear in mind the various elements of the liturgy of Holy Saturday. This will allow us better to understand the reasons motivating the Commission's decision to restore the ceremonies of Holy Saturday to the evening.[5]

The 9th meeting of the Commission examined the schema contained in article 66 of the *Memoria* which listed the elements comprising the liturgy of Holy Saturday:

1. The minor hours;
2. Blessing of the new fire (three prayers);
3. Blessing of the grains of incense: the prayer *Veniat*, which is the ancient blessing for the candle;
4. The procession: *Lumen Christi*;
5. The Easter *Praeconium*: *Laus cerei*;
6. The twelve prophecies;
7. Blessing of the baptismal font;
8. The solemn Baptism;
9. The procession and the litanies;
10. The solemn Mass;
11. *Pro vesperis.*

Now, bearing these eleven elements in mind, it is clear that at some time in the past, at least some of them must necessarily have been carried out at night or in the evening, such as, the blessing of the new fire, entry into the church with lights, and the festive illumination of the church with new light.[6]

At this point it is important to quote Antonelli's observations on the vigil of Holy Saturday in order to understand the previous structure and how it was reorganized with the reform. Antonelli's history of the Easter Vigil is to be found in a lecture entitled *Il Triduum Sacrum, l'Eucarestia e la pace di Cristo* which he delivered to the International Eucharistic Congress at Barcelona on May 30, 1952 and was published as an article in 1954. Also, we have his heavily annotated manuscript that enables us to obtain the history of the Easter Vigil.

> Here I shall restrict myself to a few observations. It must be remembered above all, that Holy Saturday was always an aliturgical day on which the Eucharistic sacrifice was not celebrated. It was dedicated to the contemplation of Jesus in the tomb, and hence by its very nature it was a day of a mourning, sorrow, and silence.
>
> The liturgical action began in the evening with the celebration of the ancient and solemn Easter Vigil, which ended at dawn. The principal element of the Vigil consisted of the rites of Baptism. Baptism was administered on this night, because, according to apostolic preaching, so vigorously expressed by Saint Paul, the person being baptized and immersed in the water of the sacred font is buried with Christ and rises with Him to new life and to reconciliation which belongs to the restored order and is won by Him through His passion and death.[7]

Then Antonelli presents the development of the rite of light:

> The rites of the *lucernarium* were connected with those of Baptism. This was the so-called liturgical (non-Eucharistic) celebration in the evening at the hour when lamps were lit. From these derive the rites of the fire and of the candle, symbols of the risen Christ, the solemn announcement of the *Lumen Christi*, the *Laus cerei*, which becomes a true *Praeconium paschale*. Together, all this produces a liturgical ensemble, rich with ideas and symbols, that is profoundly effective in moving the soul.[8]

The Development of the Liturgical Reform

The history of this multifaceted liturgy is quite well known. In the absence of adult Baptisms, up to the 6th century, the Vigil was celebrated in the early hours of the night, then later in the afternoon and, in more recent times, in the morning.

> Thus the Vigil celebration of Easter began to occupy the aliturgical day of Holy Saturday with an early anticipation of the Easter joy. With the disfiguration of all the Vigil rites, that no longer took into account the symbolism of the light in the darkness, all of the appeals to the holy night and to the blessed night within in the rites, which were now carried out during the morning hours in a Church inundated with spring sunshine, became contradictory.[9]

A manuscript of Antonelli's, dated March 14, 1951, contains some points on the *Restoration of the Solemn Easter Vigil*. Here Antonelli does not write as a professor delivering a lecture, but as a friend explaining this "liturgical innovation". Here we wish to examine the three points contained in the manuscript since they express Antonelli's mind very clearly. They are the origin of the Decree, the criteria regulating the new rubrics, and a general outline of the new rite.[10]

The Origin of the Decree

Here Antonelli recounts the history of the liturgical movement which sought to carry out various reforms, despite resistance. He emphasizes the importance, for more than a century, given to promoting knowledge of the liturgical movement through the publication of texts and monographs.

> From this emerged an appreciation for the signs of the liturgy and an increasing intolerance for certain liturgical deformations which had been introduced; essentially there was a general desire for revision and it was called for by bishops, better-educated clergy, an informed laity, and liturgical congresses. Thus a double tendency arose:
> a) Conservative, archeological;
> b) Innovative, vital.[11]

Criteria observed

1. Retain everything belonging to the primitive rite or found in the best tradition;
2. Revive important elements, which had been lost or modified, and others which had been deformed;
3. Restore all the liturgical action of the Paschal candle and its position of material and symbolic centrality;
4. Ensure that the people are able to follow the liturgical action consciously and actively rather than as passive spectators.[12]

A Summary Presentation of the Rite
a) *Chronological Innovation*

Antonelli emphasizes the historical development of the Rite:

> By the 9th-10th century, the rite was already anticipated in the evening, and then it was transferred to the morning. This had grave consequences for the symbolism of the fire and the candle. The appeals to the *holy night*, the *blessed night*, and the *splendor of night* became deprived of their meaning.[13]

With regard to reasons motivating the restoration of the Vigil rite to the night, Antonelli writes:

> Neither is it known what grave reason suggested moving this rite to earlier in the day. It is enough, however, to make reference to the contemporary biography of San Giovanni Gualberto (†1073), who restored the nocturnal celebration [of the rite] in Tuscany, because after three in the afternoon the people were given to revelry.[14]

b) *The Divine Office*

The divine office was transferred to the morning of Holy Saturday, since it was an aliturgical day, so that Good Friday evening was free for popular devotions.

> Here someone will ask about communion on Holy Saturday. It has always been an aliturgical day. Christ is in the tomb. Instead, up to the 15th century, the faithful received Holy Communion on Good Friday. Therefore, it would remain as before, the only day without Holy Communion.[15]

c) *The Blessing of the Fire*

With a minor change it would remain as before. "Of the three lessons only the first would be used; the reason: to shorten the rite and because the other lessons were extra parts".[16]

d) *The Blessing of the Candle*

We shall now list all of the ancient elements of this rite, which had been lost:

1. It was a very ancient rite. One of the essential elements was the cross, which was incised in the candle in memory of Christ's death on the cross and his resurrection. When the candle was lit His resurrection was recalled. The tracing of the A (alpha) and the Ω (omega) was also very ancient practice and subsequently the date of the year was added;[17]

2. The lighted candle was carried in procession, Egeria speaks of this already in the 5th century, and the candles of the clergy and the laity were lit from it;

3. With the passage of time, the candle took on such proportions that it could no longer be carried in procession. It was eventually replaced by the arundine lamps. The candle was then lit afterwards.[18]

e) *The Reorganization of the Rite of the Paschal Candle*

1. The candle being the material and symbolic center of the rite, is to return. It is to be prepared by tracing upon it the sign of the cross, together with the A and the Ω, followed by the year;

2. The grains of incense are inserted into the candle;
3. The lighting of the candle is accompanied with a new formula;
4. The blessing will take place with the prayer *Veniat*;
5. The three-fold invocation takes place during the procession, followed by the lighting of candles and the illumination;
6. The *Laus cerei* is only said afterwards.[19]

f) The Prophecies

The rite of the light concludes with the *Praeconium*. The baptismal rite begins with the prophecies, which are the final catechesis in the preparation of the catechumens, and concludes with Mass. The proclamations were reduced to four: the first, fourth, eighth, and the eleventh containing the canticle. These prophecies were chosen with a logical nexus in mind that unifies them. They are:

1. The Creation narrative;
2. The crossing of the Red Sea: symbol of Baptism;
3. The happiness of Isaiah's messianic kingdom, the canticle of the vine;
4. The witness of Moses, which is an admonition of fidelity to Baptism.

During the reading of the prophecies the priest is seated and listens. Antonelli notes in his manuscript that this is a novelty because the liturgical action moves to the lector. In the "Tridentine" Mass, the celebrant would read the readings in a low voice at the altar while the lector proclaimed them at the ambo. Only Saint Pius V had imposed that the priest would read and not the lector.[20]

g) The First Part of the Litanies

Originally, the litanies served the supplemental function of occupying the laity in the absence of the clergy and those being baptized, and they were sometimes repeated as many as seven times.

> When the Baptism of adults ceased, the litanies remained as a transitional element between the blessing of the font and the Mass. Since the *Kyrie* flowed into the Mass it could not be omitted. In the Middle Ages, however, as Durandus mentions in the *Pontificale* (†1296), the practice had developed of splitting the litany, having one part before the blessing of the font, and the other part after. This usage was revived.[21]

h) Blessing of the Font

All remains as before, with the exception that liturgical action no longer takes place near the font in the baptistery at the end of the church but in the sanctuary. This change is for pastoral reasons: namely, to allow the people to follow such a beautiful rite. "It should be noted this is not the blessing of the font, but of the baptismal water".[22]

i) Renewal of Baptismal Promises

Albeit an innovation, this is not arbitrarily introduced. In fact, also in previous times the faithful promised to remain faithful to the demands of their Baptism in daily life.

> The *asperges* or sprinkling of water is a symbol of Baptism, and in many places it is done as though it were something extra-liturgical, however from a pastoral perspective it is highly important. Then follows the priest's speech, and the scrutinies which are contained in the Ritual. The responses are collective, since the entire liturgy is collective. The *Dominus vobiscum* and the *Oremus* of the Baptism follow immediately after the *Pater noster*.[23]

j)   *The Second Part of the Litanies*

The litanies continue with "the only change being the omission of the prostration, which was a late introduction, and borrowed from the rite of ordination".[24]

k)   *The Vigil Mass*

In his manuscript, Antonelli proposes the following schema for the Vigil Mass: the *Kyrie* should be that of the litanies; the omission of both the general preparation for the Mass and the *Pro vesperis,* the latter of which was a late addition; the *Vesperi autem sabbati* remains as the Communion antiphon, and the *Oremus* as a post-communion prayer; the last Gospel is omitted.[25]

In concluding a colloquium he held with the students of the *Antonianum,* Antonelli noted some specific questions in his manuscript:

> Change always gives rise to many questions. Seeing whether these questions are well founded requires a thorough knowledge of the subject. It should be noted that many popular usages, such as the blessing of homes on Holy Saturday, derive from the practice of anticipating the Vigil. A way of accommodating these will have to be found. It must not be forgotten that observations are still expected and following them, the Holy See will do what it believes to be opportune.[26]

After a long exposition, Antonelli concluded affirming that:

> Liturgists and all those concerned for pastoral liturgy will be pleased. I think that we should all be grateful to the Holy Father, Supreme Shepherd of the Church's Flock, for this gesture of his, which will bring the faithful to an ever greater active and conscious participation in the liturgical life of Holy Mother Church.[27]

The Timeliness for a Renewal

It is not necessary at this point to dwell on all of the historical and practical aspects of the Vigil on Holy Saturday contained in the *Memoria sulla Riforma Liturgica.* Rather, we shall limit our focus to a few aspects by way of the notes which Antonelli left us and that deserve our attention. The *Memoria* presents a general picture and essentially gives an affirmative response on one level in view of an eventual renewal of the Holy Saturday Vigil.

The exposition opens with a quotation from Saint Augustine regarding the Easter Vigil: *Mater omnium vigiliarum.* It continues by pointing out that the Oriental Churches have faithfully preserved the practice of celebrating the Vigil at night, and that in the beginning, the Latin Church had also celebrated the Easter Vigil with great solemnity at night, with psalms, canticles, and sacred readings, concluding its night of prayer with the solemn morning Mass, since it was believed that Jesus had risen from the dead in the morning. Only in the 12th century did the Vigil begin to be anticipated in the morning.[28]

The *Memoria*, in explaining the precise value of keeping vigil, refers to the midnight vigil of Christmas as the presumed time of Christ's birth. Hence, from the point of view of its symbolic value, and from a historical perspective, the revival of the practice of celebrating the Vigil at night should not encounter any difficulties.

> Clearly and evidently, all the ceremonies of Holy Saturday, once restored to their original position at night, would in themselves resume all the ancient splendor, as well as all of the liturgical meaning and symbolism they once had. However, in this case, some slight changes must be made so that the ancient Vigil liturgy can be combined with the Office for Easter (Matins and Lauds). On the other hand, if the entire liturgy of Holy Saturday is to be maintained in its current state, some slight changes are almost inevitable.[29]

At this point two possibilities arose, a complete renewal, whereby the Vigil celebration would begin at midnight and end with the dawn Mass, as it was in antiquity; or a partial renewal with the ceremonies beginning late in the evening of Holy Saturday so that Mass is celebrated towards midnight. The latter would seem to be the best way to restore immediate meaning to the celebration of the Vigil.

The *Memoria* continues with an examination of three questions regarding the morning of Holy Saturday which would become an aliturgical day, that is, without any celebration of the Sacrifice of the Mass once the celebration of the Vigil were moved to evening time. It was planned that the celebration of the minor hours would remain intact. However, it envisaged that once Vespers were provided with the same formulas as those of Holy Thursday and Good Friday, it would be necessary to add a new proper antiphon for the *Magnificat*. Compline remained fixed for evening time.

With the transfer of the Vigil to the evening or night, the problem of the absence of Mass and Holy Communion arose. It should be recalled, however, that the absence of Mass and Holy Communion on Holy Saturday is a most ancient characteristic of that day, which is one of liturgical respite in remembrance of Christ's reposing in the tomb.

With the transfer of the Vigil to the evening, and its powerful references to light and to Baptism, a third problem of finding a suitable location for the Matins and Lauds of Easter arose. If Lauds were inserted after the Mass, then what was to become of Matins? Since the first part of the Vigil liturgy celebrates Christ, Light of the World, with the singing of the *Praeconium paschale*, it was suggested that Matins could be integrated into the Vigil liturgy immediately following the canticle. The second part would follow with its reference to Baptism, in which the faithful rise with Christ, and hence to solemn Mass.[30]

Article 69 of the *Memoria* outlines the problems concerning the modification of the Easter Vigil:

1. Blessing of the Easter Candle, the *Praeconium* or the *Veniat*?;
2. Baptism or baptismal font;
3. Number of prophesies, twelve or less?;
4. Renewal of baptismal promises.

All know that in our missals the canticle *Exsultet* is entitled *Benedictio cerei*. Hence the liturgists ask the question of how the deacon can bless the candle. The historian of the liturgy, however, will know that the true prayer of blessing for the candle is the prayer *Veniat*, which today is used for the *Benedictio granorum*, notwithstanding the fact that the prayer refers to the candle and its light.

The *Exsultet* is the true *Praeconium paschale* and should revert to having its ancient name, while the *Veniat* should resume being the *Benedictio cerei*.[31]

Concerning the blessing of the five grains of incense there are the following suggestions: the blessing of the incense could be omitted since the same five grains are blessed every year, resulting in the blessing of something which has been blessed several times.

It was requested that the rite of Baptism be replaced by a new ceremony valid for all churches and for all the faithful participating at the Easter Vigil. It was also proposed that the ceremonies be reduced, especially the prophecies, at least in minor churches.[32]

A further difficulty emerged for those small country places, which do not have baptismal fonts. Without a font the rite of Baptism would lose its significance in the Easter Vigil, especially since it is the most important part of the liturgy, indeed, even the very center of Easter Vigil rites.

Let us first consider the prophecies. [Having] twelve is a very ancient [practice], but it was not always maintained. For many centuries the Roman liturgy in particular used a much smaller number of prophecies, for example, at the time of St. Gregory the Great there were only four.

Perhaps the best thing, therefore, would be a gradual reduction, taking into account the circumstances of various churches, and of the priests who celebrate the rites. In summary, the carrying out of the solemn rite as a whole would be less solemn, that is, still with all of its splendor, but in a less solemn form, and a simple rite, with a reduced number of readings, possibly six or four, as it was from the time of St. Gregory the Great up to the 12th century.[33]

The second point concerns the baptismal font and those to be baptized. With the exception of foreign missions and larger cities, it was proposed to introduce a new element which would take the place of both the rite of Baptism and of the blessing of the font. This would take the form of a solemn renewal of baptismal promises by all the faithful who were present.[34] In light of the ancient tradition and historical development, this element could be introduced into the liturgy of the Easter Vigil instead of the rite of Baptism, which is missing today.

> This would consist of a simple, but striking ceremony, which could take place either immediately after the blessing of the font, when there is a baptismal font, or after the prophecies where there is no font. It would consist of a short but substantial address to the people by the celebrant, the propositions for renunciation of sin, profession of faith, as at Baptism, followed by the response of the people, and ending with a common recital of the creed. Thus, instead of a non-existent Baptism, there would be a true and solemn renovation of the baptismal promises, and the centrality of this part of the liturgy, upon which everything else hinges, would be recovered. The litanies would then follow as a common imploration by the Christian community gathered around for the solemn Mass and the Paschal Light, who is Christ.[35]

Thus, in this way it would be possible to restore and once again to emphasize in the ceremonies of the Easter Vigil the centrality of being buried with Christ and rising with Him through Baptism.

It would also prove necessary to substitute the present set of rites surrounding Baptism with another rite that would be easily and immediately understood by the faithful.[36] The *Memoria* launched a challenge:

> Courageous men must be found, who are well versed in the ancient liturgy and who, today, are able to create a rite, a ceremony, in harmony with both the ancient liturgy and with the spirit of modern life. This is one of the aspects which many await of the much desired liturgical reform.[37]

This is what had been raised so far with regard to the problems and the possibilities for change which the Sacred Congregation of Rites asked of the Holy Father and of the universal Church.

What we have extracted and analyzed is all contained in the *Memoria sulla Riforma Liturgica* of 1948 regarding the subject of the reform of the Easter Vigil. The plan was subsequently studied, developed, and modified by the Liturgical Commission, and the Decree of approval, *De solemni vigilia paschali instauranda*, bears the date of February 9, 1951. It was promulgated first by the Sacred Congregation of Rites and subsequently received the personal approval of Pius XII who promoted it.

For all the above reasons, we can conclude with Antonelli:

> Therefore, all this now makes us think that the Easter Vigil, so ardently desired by all who promote the liturgy, will be celebrated in many churches throughout the Catholic world. May this celebration bring the faithful to a more profound contemplation of the paschal mysteries, which are the foundation of the entire divine economy of redemption, and call them to renew solemnly the sacred promises made by all Christians through Baptism. It will prove an effective element in that renewal of awareness, restoring that coherence of Christian life in the world, to which the Holy Father has called the faithful of Rome, and of the entire world, in his solemn address on the past 10th of February.[38]

[1] F. ANTONELLI, *Sull'aggiornamento della Settimana Santa*, in *SCCS, Archivio fondo Antonelli*, folder *Riforma liturgica sotto Pio XII*, p. 20.

[2] Cf. CPRL, *Verbali*, cit., p. 27.

[3] *Ibidem.*

[4] *Ibidem*, p. 21.

[5] Cf. *Memoria*, cit., nn. 61-74, p. 67.

[6] Cf. *ibidem*; CPRL, *Verbali*, cit., pp. 27-31.

[7] F. ANTONELLI, *Il "Triduum Sacrum", l'Eucaristia, e la pace di Cristo* (manuscript of a paper given at Barcelona in 1952), in *ALV*, p. 10.

[8] *Ibidem*, p. 11.

[9] *Ibidem.*

[10] F. ANTONELLI, *Il ripristino della solenne Veglia Pasquale. Lezioni di Liturgia*, in *ALV*, p. 1.

[11] *Ibidem*, pp. 2-3.

[12] Cf. *ibidem*, p. 5.

[13] *Ibidem*, p. 6.

[14] *Ibidem.*

[15] *Ibidem*, p. 7.

[16] *Ibidem*, p. 8.

[17] *Ibidem*, p. 9.

[18] Cf. *ibidem.*

[19] Cf. *ibidem*, p. 10. The folder with the *Verbali della Commissione per la Riforma liturgica creata da Pio XII*, pp. 27-31, contains everything about the discussions on the reordering of the rite.

[20] Cf. F. ANTONELLI, *Il ripristino*, cit., pp. 11-12.

[21] *Ibidem*, p. 13.

[22] *Ibidem*, p. 14. In the *Verbali* of the Commission for the Reform of the Liturgy to which we have already referred, the CPRL states on p. 34 what the Commission decided with regard to the *blessing of the font*. It agreed that the entire rite should be conducted in the sanctuary, *coram populo*, whether the font be blessed or simply that baptismal promises be renewed. Thus the procession could be avoided and reduced merely to the clergy assembling around the Paschal candle, in front of which would be placed the receptacle for the blessing of water.

[23] *Ibidem*, p. 15.

[24] F. ANTONELLI, *Il ripristino*, cit., p. 16.

[25] *Ibidem*, p. 17.

[26] *Ibidem*, p. 19.

[27] *Ibidem*, p. 20.

[28] Cf. SRC, *Memoria*, cit., p. 70.

[29] *Ibidem*, p. 71.

[30] *Cf. ibidem*, pp. 70-72. In the *Verbali* of the Commission for the Reform of the Liturgy, p. 32, we find that this was proposed for the *Nocturnus*: "The *Relator-Generalis* observed that the Matins of Easter had been introduced here to solve the problem of the *pro vesperis* in whose place it was necessary to substitute something. A *pro laudibus* had been suggested, and this, in turn, supposes Matins."

[31] SRC, *Memoria*, cit., p. 73.

[32] *Cf. ibidem.*

[33] *Ibidem*, p. 74.

[34] *Ibidem*, p. 75.

[35] *Ibidem*, p. 75.

[36] Cf. *ibidem.*

[37] SRC, *Memoria*, cit., p. 75.

[38] F. ANTONELLI, *La Veglia Pasquale. Lezioni di Liturgia*, in *SCCS*, s.d., pp. 17-18.

Chapter 5

The Decree
De Solemni Vigilia Paschali Instauranda

The Renewal of the Solemn Easter Vigil in 1951

In the preceding chapter we explored the reasons which induced the Sacred Congregation of Rites to initiate a renewal of the Easter Vigil. The Decree *De solemni vigilia paschali instauranda* emphasizes those reasons.

The symbolism of the Vigil rite, the blessing of the fire and of the Paschal candle, and the Easter *Praeconium* (which appeals to the "blessed night" and recalls the "nocturnal splendor") had lost their efficacy and meaning. These were the motives, which along with some other pastoral concerns, led the bishops of several countries to petition the Holy See to restore the evening celebration of the ceremonies of Holy Saturday.[1] Antonelli, in this regard, says:

> Hence the desire, expressed several times, of the grandeur of the sacred liturgy and of many liturgical Congresses to return to that Easter Vigil which Augustine called the *Mater omnium vigiliarum* (Serm. 219, PL 38, 1088). To these objective reasons, a further contemporary reason may be added, which is of a practical and pastoral nature, namely, that of permitting all the faithful to participate in the celebration of these rites.[2]

Some historical data must be kept in mind to understand the significance of this last statement. In earlier centuries, Holy Saturday was a holiday, but for more than three centuries, it had become a workday, hence many of the faithful encountered difficulties in attending the sacred functions. That said, let us review quickly the new rubrics so as to understand the criteria on which the reform was based. Fr. Antonelli mentions three:

> In the first place, there was a laudable concern to preserve and scrupulously defend the original liturgical tradition, based on the surest scholarship of historical research on the liturgy. Secondly, care was taken to revive some elements of that tradition which had been lost or eliminated, and to modify others which were late introductions deforming the tradition. Finally, an effort was made to underline the primitive symbolism which is so rich in the rites of Holy Saturday, so as to allow the faithful to follow the sacred function in all their various parts. There was also a lightening of the rites themselves, by shortening them where such was not detrimental, as in the case of the reduction of the prophecies from twelve to four.[3]

Antonelli was concerned that the liturgical experts would accept the reform, and he was even more concerned that the celebration of the mysteries of the passion, death, and resurrection of our Lord would be more imminent and fruitful for the faithful. Let us now consider the changes and innovations that occurred in the sacred rite:

> The first change, the night vigil in expectation of the Lord's resurrection, is chronological and restored the rites to their original time. The ceremonies would begin at about 10 p.m. so that Mass might begin at midnight.
>
> As for the rites themselves, one of the points which has attracted much attention from the outset is the importance which is given to the Easter Candle, which, as a symbol of the Risen Christ, is restored as the material and symbolic center of the entire liturgical action.
>
> Indeed, the candle is prepared using some very ancient and symbolic rites: the etching of the cross, the alpha and the omega, and the date of the current year into the candle while the priest pronounces the words: *Christus heri et hodie, principium et finis, alpha et omega. Ipsius sunt tempora et saecula. Ipsi gloria et imperium per universa aeternitatis saecula. Amen.* The lighted candle, as we have said, is the symbol of Christ, *Lumen de Lumine*, Splendor of the Father, who illumines all things. Thus the priest, while lighting it says: *Lumen Christi gloriose resurgentis, dissipet tenebras cordis et mentis.* It is then acclaimed three times with the *Lumen Christi*. From it, the priest lights his candle, as do the clergy and people. The solemn *Praeconium paschale* is sung before it, which in ancient times was called the *Laus cerei*.[4]

A clarification must be made with regard to the *Praeconium paschale*. The prayer for the emperor was amended because of charged historical circumstances, and a prayer for those who govern the various nations was inserted, the Latin text of which is as follows:

> *Respice etiam ad eos, qui nos in potestate regunt, et ineffabili pietatis et misericordiae tuae munere, dirige cogitationes eorum ad iustitiam et pacem, ut de terrena operositate ad caelestem patriam perveniant cum omni populo tuo.*[5]

Up to now, Antonelli has emphasized those changes that were made so as to revive certain ancient elements which had been lost, or to eliminate others which were later interpolations. However, that which really deserves attention, because it was something genuinely innovative in the vigil rite of Holy Saturday, was the renewal of baptismal promises by all the faithful participating at the ceremony. This, it must be underlined, is something Franciscan, and all who promote the liturgy will acknowledge that it is not an arbitrary innovation:

> This is in accord with the most ancient tradition and the true spirit of one of the most important elements of these rites, namely the blessing of the font, which was followed in antiquity, by baptism. From a litugico-pastoral perspective it is easy to imagine the practical importance of this annual, solemn, public renewal of baptismal promises; of renunciation of the devil and his works and pomps; of the commitment to serve Christ and His Holy Mother, the Catholic Church. The words taken from Saint Augustine and Saint Paul, with which the priest prepares this renewal, are most beautiful. The entire Christian community procedes with

this renewal before the Easter Candle, symbol of Christ, which then concludes with the prayer which He himself has taught us to pray: the *Pater noster.*[6]

Having outlined the reasons, the innovations, and the various criteria behind the reform, an invitation is issued to all to live Lent as a period of commitment and preparation for this solemnity:

> Lenten catechesis should be oriented towards a deepening of knowledge of the supernatural life and to making a richer personal application of the fruits of the redemption. It should be, as they say in modern terminology, a prolonged course of spiritual exercises, in which all Christian communities participate, and conclude with renewal of baptismal promises on the night of the Easter Vigil, and sealed by Easter communion.[7]

Father Antonelli ended his article expressing the hope that this liturgical renewal would be accepted and that thanks would be expressed to Pius XII for this marvelous gift which began with his career as Universal Pastor of the flock of Christ. In a previous article dated March 4, 1954, the Franciscans presented the restoration of the solemn Easter Vigil to the Catholic world, just one month after its promulgation. In his article of February 13, 1952 he speaks of the reception given to the new Vigil.[8] The celebration of the new Vigil had been permitted in 1951 *ad experimentium* and was optional, leaving a decision in its regard to the local Ordinaries who were asked to report on the reception of the new rite by the Christian faithful. In this respect we read:

> News of this innovation, which had been desired and called for by many for a long time, had an immediate and profound echo throughout the Catholic world. Notwithstanding the short period of time between the publication of the decree and Easter, in all about four weeks, the Easter Vigil was in fact celebrated in a great many dioceses and in all of the five continents. It was celebrated not only in the churches of the great and populous cities, but also in rural parish churches, and even in the missionary countries, as is evident from the many thousands of reports which the bishops sent to the Sacred Congregation of Rites.[9]

A year after the experiment there was unanimous gratitude to the Holy Father for this innovation. It had been of great spiritual benefit for the faithful, and it was hoped that the new rite would be adopted for all. Participation at the restored Vigil had been massive, attentive, and devout. Concerning the spiritual fruits deriving from the Vigil, apart from the joy and surprise caused by the restoration, it is sufficient to read the various reports sent by the bishops which are now conserved in Antonelli's papers.[10] As with all things experimental, some difficulties did arise and several bishops wrote to the Holy See requesting instructions on specific points.

The Definitive Reform of 1952

> The new *Ordo Sabbati Sancti* caused quite a stir in the entire world, both Catholic and non-Catholic: in England it was even translated for use in the protestant 'Church.' It tried to eliminate superficiality from the rites and texts, restore the night vigil, from which all of the oldest rites immediately derive their deep meaning and their forceful natural religious efficacy.[11]

The Development of the Liturgical Reform

Antonelli isolates a particularly interesting element in this rediscovery of the ancient liturgical tradition, namely, the renewal of baptismal promises. The baptismal rites were not just for the catechumens but for the entire people of God. This requires a participation in the celebration of baptism that is active rather than one merely of spectators. In this way, everyone can re-live the grace of his own baptism and confirm the commitment he once assumed with Christ. The sprinkling of holy water on the faithful by the priest helps in this.[12]

> The great Vigil concluded in an atmosphere of joy for the Lord's resurrection. This joy continues throughout Easter, a day that is considered the end of the great solemnity, begun on Holy Thursday and continued through Good Friday. The resurrection is inseparable from Christ's death. The Fathers often and rightly speak of a twofold Pasch: the Pasch of the Cross (*Pascha staurosimon*), and the Pasch of the Resurrection (*Pascha anastasimon*).[13]

The Holy Father, bearing in mind both the positive results of the experimental rite of 1951 and the cautions advanced in its regard, requested the liturgical Commission to take due note of the positive reactions to the reform, as well as the difficulties raised by some of the bishops. Antonelli writes:

> The said Commission, following a careful study of the matter which was conducted in the precedence of Cardinal Micara, Pro-Prefect of the Sacred Congregation of Rites, decided to propose continuing the Easter Vigil to the Holy Father, while also proposing for his august approval, some slight modifications of the rhetoric in an audience granted to Cardinal Micara on January 11, 1952. He also confirmed the concession of the Easter Vigil as an option to be used in accordance with the judgment of the local Ordinary for a period of three years. This was the substance of the new decree of the Sacred Congregation of Rites of January 11, 1952 and published in the latest fascicle of the *Acta Apostolicae Sedis* (No. 1, January 25, 1952).[14]

The Directives of January 11, 1952

Let us now turn to the problems addressed by those directives. We shall examine them under seven titles:

1. Preparation of the faithful for the Easter Vigil;
2. The time for the celebration of the Easter Vigil;
3. Shortage of clergy;
4. Prior preparation of the Paschal candle;
5. The Mass, Holy Communion, and the Eucharistic fast;
6. Blessing of homes and confessions;
7. The ringing of bells.

Directives one and two recommend that, during Lent, pastors prepare the faithful to celebrate the Easter Vigil and to renew their baptismal promises. Antonelli comments that, "Nobody can deny the importance of this public and solemn renewal, especially when done responsibly".[15]

The problem of setting a time for the celebration of the Easter Vigil arose. In some places grave reasons would not recommend the celebration of the Vigil at midnight. Directives 3 and 4 granted faculties to local Ordinaries to permit anticipation of the Vigil for just reasons in particular cases. It could not, however, be celebrated before 8 p.m..[16]

Given the richness of the new rite, the possibility of more than one priest attending might cause problems, especially in rural parishes. This difficulty had already been experienced with the old rite. Benedict XIII had attempted to resolve it with the publication of the *Manuale Rituum*, which granted the faculty for a lone priest to celebrate the Vigil, with the assistance of clerics or well prepared altar servers. This same problem arose with the new rite and it was resolved in an identical fashion.[17]

Directives 8 through 12 granted the possibility of preparing the Easter Candle beforehand by etching the sign of the cross, with the A and Ω and the date of the current year into it. It was sufficient for the priest to trace these elements symbolically on the Candle during the celebration of the Vigil. These directives require the faithful to keep their candles lit during the singing of the Easter *Praeconium* and for the renewal of baptismal promises. They further require due decoration of the container holding the water to be blessed for use at baptism.

Directives 13 through 19 address the problems connected with the celebration of Mass, with Holy Communion and the Eucharistic fast. With regard to the priest, it was established that the celebrant of the Easter Vigil could also celebrate Mass on Easter Sunday. For pastoral reasons, and with the necessary indult, the celebrant of the Easter Vigil could binate or even trinate. The faithful who had participated in the celebration of the Vigil Mass, provided this was celebrated after midnight, had satisfied the obligation to attend Mass on Easter Sunday. Concerning the reception of Holy Communion by the faithful, Antonelli writes:

> In accordance with the Code (can. 857), no one may receive Holy Communion twice during the 24 hours of the same day. Hence the faithful who received Holy Communion in the morning, where the celebrations were still held during the morning, may not receive Holy Communion again at the Easter Vigil, should the Vigil, in particular cases, be celebrated before midnight. They may receive, however, when this Mass is celebrated at the proper time, i.e. after midnight. In this case, however, and for the same reason, they may not again receive Holy Communion on Easter Sunday morning, as is the practice at Christmas.[18]

With regard to the Eucharistic fast, directive 18 established that both the celebrant and the faithful, who wished to receive Holy Communion, were to fast from 11 p.m., and when the sacred ceremonies were held at 8 p.m., the fast was to begin an hour before. In cases where, for pastoral reasons, priests who had celebrated the Vigil Mass were obliged to celebrate more than one Mass on Easter Sunday, the directives established that these might take some food per *modum potus* in the interval, since it was regarded as too difficult to have to fast from 10 p.m. in the evening to midday or later on the following day. The fast, however, was to be maintained for at least an hour before celebrating on Easter Sunday. The directives contained no changes with regard to the Lenten fast, which ended at midday on Holy Saturday, as foreseen by the Code.

The directives also examined the problem inherent in the blessing of homes, recommending that Ordinaries should strive to have this blessing imparted not at Easter, but during the Easter season. It was strongly recommended that the blessing be done by priests who had the care of souls, so that they would have an opportunity to visit every family for specifically pastoral reasons.

The Easter confessions also gave rise to some problems, particularly in areas where they were especially popular on Holy Saturday evening and on Easter Sunday morning, with all the implications this brought both for the clergy and for the faithful who found it difficult to prepare to receive the sacrament fruitfully. Directive 23 recommended that parish priests should distribute the hearing of confessions over a number of days so as to avoid the aforementioned difficulties and assure greater spiritual benefit.

Problems concerning the ringing of bells also had to be addressed, especially in relation to the day and time at which they were rung, and to the problem deriving from the close proximity of several churches. As a general norm, directive 22 established that all churches should ring bells in tandem with the principal church. In doubtful cases, recourse should be made to the local Ordinary. It was also established that bells would not be rung from the morning of Holy Thursday until the singing of the *Gloria* at the Mass of Holy Saturday.[19] Antonelli concludes his commentary on these directives, which were designed to resolve problems posed by the various dioceses, saying:

> The rite in itself remains unchanged. As all acknowledge, it is based on the best liturgical tradition and has been shown to be effective in introducing the faithful to an understanding and reliving of the paschal mysteries. It leads them to participate in the sacred rites, not as spectators but as actors. The rubrical modifications therefore are concerned with secondary matters which do not affect the substance of the Vigil rite.[20]

There remained, however, the problem of the Divine Office. Given that Compline is the concluding prayer of the day, it was omitted on Holy Saturday since the celebration of the Vigil replaced it. The same was true for the Office of Readings. Antonelli points out, however, that those who celebrated the Vigil during the morning were bound to celebrate Matins as presented in the Roman Breviary.

With regard to the ceremonies, the most important change concerned the possibility of the celebrant using the simple form rather than the solemn form of the rite, assisted by opportunely trained altar servers, where there was a shortage of priests.

A further modification of the rubrics concerned the blessing of the baptismal water. At the conclusion of the blessing of the water, which was done in the sanctuary so as to enable the faithful to follow the ceremony, the baptismal water was borne in procession to the baptismal font by the clergy. The procession could be accompanied with the singing of the *Sicut cervus*. This was a very suggestive ceremony, designed to awaken among the faithful veneration for that sacred place where, in baptism, supernatural life was dispensed. The litanies then followed, after which the people were sprinkled with holy water. This rite took place where there was a font but nobody for baptism. In places where there was no font, the lustral water served to remind the faithful of their baptism.

Finally, concerning the Vigil Mass, analogously with the *pro vesperis* of the old rite, the prayer *Pro laudibus* was introduced with the proper antiphon of the Lauds of Easter Sunday, and the singing of the *Benedictus*, preceded by the antiphon *Et valde mane* and the incensing of the altar.[21] Antonelli concludes his article hoping that:

> The celebration of the Easter Vigil, together with the solemn renewal of baptismal promises, might be an occasion and a means for all to return to that true and fully consistent Christian life, recently solicited from the faithful of Rome and of the world by the Holy Father.[22]

> This second concession of the revised rites, together with the new directives, has been granted for a further period of three years, in an experimental and optional manner.[23]

From what has already been said, the vast amount of work done for the liturgical reform by the Commission is evident, and even more so, their firm knowledge of the various aspects of the rites. The Commission also expressed the hope that those who disagreed with the reform would note the favorable reception accorded to the reform by the Christian faithful during the previous four years: "The celebration of the Easter Vigil, or rather the concession for the celebration of the restored rite of Holy Saturday, has now had four years of life and experience".[24]

In virtue of the discretional powers conceded to local Ordinaries, both rites coexisted for a certain period. The old rite was celebrated in the morning and the new in the evening or at night. This situation gave rise to criticism and misunderstanding especially among the less educated of the faithful.[25] Notwithstanding some initial resistance, the celebration of the Easter Vigil established itself and was generally accepted as had been hoped by the Ordinaries, priests, religious communities, and by specialist publications. These now called for the reform of the rest of Holy Week by applying the same liturgico-pastoral criteria. They were certain that this would bring abundant spiritual fruits for the good of souls.[26] Antonelli recognized this situation and offered the following explanation:

> The structure of the rites have been made clearer and more straight forward. The rubrics have been carefully drawn up to guarantee an active and lively participation of the faithful. The same structure has received universal approval and praise, as the Ordinaries and the faithful themselves attest.[27]

The Development of the Liturgical Reform

It is undeniable that this partial revision of the rites of Holy Saturday was spiritually beneficial. It set out to make evermore clear the centrality of the Paschal mystery in Christian religion. Fr. Antonelli reflected:

> One thing is certain which should be especially appreciated by priests who have the care of souls: the Paschal mysteries, Holy Thursday, Good Friday, the Easter Vigil, and the Solemnity of Easter are of the greatest importance for the Christian life.[28]

Consequently, it becomes absolutely necessary to bring the faithful back to an active celebration of the Easter rituals which are designed to bring about a renewal of life in each individual that is, "the full, individual fruitfulness of the redemption, which is the true pacification of God with man, and of men with each other".[29]

¹ CPRL, *Verbali*, cit., p. 27.

² F. ANTONELLI, *Il ripristino della Veglia pasquale: L'Osservatore Romano*, March 4, 1951, p. 1.

³ *Ibidem*.

⁴ *Ibidem*.

⁵ *Ibidem*.

⁶ *Ibidem*, p. 1.

⁷ F. ANTONELLI, *Il Triduum Sacrum*, cit., pp. 15-16.

⁸ F. ANTONELLI, *Continuazione della Veglia pasquale: L'Osservatore Romano*, February 13, 1952, p. 1.

⁹ *Ibidem*.

¹⁰ Here we cite a number of illustrative reports contained in F. ANTONELLI, *Sull'aggiornamento liturgico della Settimana Santa*, in SCCS, pp. 22-24. From the Diocese of Gallipoli: "The Cathedral was extraordinarily full of people"; in another report we read: "It was a real triumph of faith and devotion. The Cathedral and the churches were unbelievably full of very devout people. [...] The spectacle of the lighting of the candle was extremely evocative, especially at the blessing of the candle and at the renewal of the baptismal promises. The working class was noticeably present at these ceremonies. [...] The people are especially grateful to the Holy Father, who, inspired by the Lord, has given back to the faithful one of the greatest of liturgical consolations and has allowed them to re-live one of the most beautiful moments of the primitive Church".
An American bishop wrote: "For more than 25 years I have prayed that we should reach this blessed moment. The Lord has listened to the voices of thousands of the faithful who have constantly and devotedly worked throughout the world for the most glorious, the most holy, and the most moving ceremony of the year". (Msgr. Hellriegl, in *Orate Fratres*, now *Worship*, the principle liturgical publication in the U.S.A.). "The Holy Father, with this Decree, has launched the liturgy on a new path". (P. Parsch, in *Bibel und Liturgie*).

¹¹ F. ANTONELLI, *Il Triduum Sacrum*, cit., pp. 11-12.

¹² Cf. F. ANTONELLI, *La veglia pasquale* (manuscript contained in the folder *Riforma Vigilia Pasquale e Settimana Santa*) in SCCS, pp. 11-13.

¹³ F. ANTONELLI, *Il Triduum Sacrum*, cit., p. 1.

¹⁴ F. ANTONELLI, *Continuazione*, cit., p. 1.

¹⁵ *Ibidem*, p. 1.

¹⁶ *Ibidem*.

¹⁷ *Ibidem*.

¹⁸ *Ibidem*, p. 1.

¹⁹ *Ibidem*, p. 4.

²⁰ *Ibidem*.

²¹ Cf. *ibidem*, The Commission decided the following in relation to the *Sistimazione dell'Ufficio Divino (Compieta del Sabato, Mattutino e Lodi del giorno di Pasqua)* and recorded its decision on p. 41 in SCCS, *Verbali della Commissione per la Riforma Liturgica creata da Pio XII*: for Compline, although not unanimous in its deliberations, the Commission finally decided to conserve it. Matins for Easter Sunday could be substituted by the Vigil rites. Lauds, in a reduced form, could be placed after Mass instead of the *pro vesperis* of the old rite and conclude with all singing the *Regina Coeli* (Fr. Albereda) instead of the Last Gospel (Fr. Bea). In the audience of January 8, 1952, p. 43, the following proposal was made: We should adopt as the antiphon *ad benedictus* in the *pro laudibus* at the end of the Vigil Mass, the current antiphon *ad benedictus* in the Lauds of Easter Sunday (proposal of Fr. Albereda). The Commission unanimously adopted the proposal.

²² F. ANTONELLI, *Continuazione*, art. c., p. 4

²³ F. ANTONELLI, *Sull'aggiornamento*, cit., p. 22.

²⁴ *Ibidem*, p. 37.

²⁵ *Ibidem*.

²⁶ In the folder *Verbali della Commissione per la Riforma Liturgica creata da Pio XII*, p. 36, we find a

brief mention by Father Antonelli on the outcome of the of the new Easter Vigil, "So far, 125 official reports have arrived, 63 of which are from Italy, 24 from France, and the other from various other places; all five continents are represented. None is against. The success of the initiative is very consoling and the experiment was a complete success".

[27] F. ANTONELLI, *Sull'aggiornamento,* cit., p. 38.
[28] F. ANTONELLI, *Il Triduum Sacrum,* cit., p. 16.
[29] *Ibidem*, p. 14.

Chapter 6

The Liturgical Reform of Holy Week
and
The *Ordo Hebdomadae Sanctae Instauratus*

History

A lecture on the liturgical reform of Holy Week is contained in a small notebook of Father Antonelli's, the cover of which is marked "Liturgy" and dated February 21, 1956. It is not known where this lecture was delivered[1] but it carries a preface entitled *L'importanza di questa Riforma*[2] and gives a brief historical outline of the reform of Holy Week:

> Holy Week has remained unchanged from 1570 up to the present. If we reflect on the single fact that the restoration of the evening celebration of the sacred rites of the Sacred Triduum from the point of view of their antiquity and liturgical richness, how they constitute the center of the entire ecclesiastical year, it is easy to conclude that the Decree *Maxima Redemptionis Nostrae Mysteria* of November 16, 1955 is the most important event in the history of liturgy since the time of Saint Pius V.[3]

Antonelli then turns to the following points:

    a)   The true reason for the reform and its objective;

    b)   The principal innovations of the reform and their pastoral character;

    c)   Practical difficulties and their solutions;

    d)   Actual progress of the work;

    e)   Conclusion.[4]

The Reason for the Reform and its Objective

Here Antonelli speaks of the reform which began in 1951 with the modification of the Easter Vigil. It had been solicited by the Episcopate so that the faithful, who had to work during the morning, might be able to participate in the celebration of the Vigil. The reform of Holy Week was certainly due to the success of the renewed

Easter Vigil (which was not accepted by two ecclesiastics whose names Antonelli does not mention). The positive reception of the concession of evening Masses contained in *Christus Dominus* of January 6, 1953 should not be overlooked. Account also must be taken of the fact that now the bishops petitioned the Holy See to reform Holy Thursday and Good Friday, as Holy Saturday had been reformed. Their petition was based on two reasons:

a)   Tradition: historical consideration of the Rites favored a return to evening celebrations.

b)   Practical considerations: since 1642 Holy Thursday, Good Friday, and Holy Saturday had no longer been holidays, thereby rendering morning celebration of the rite no longer opportune.[5]

Consequently:

> Once it was decided to return to an evening celebration of the rites, in the context of a general reform, the moment had come to implement the liturgical reform properly speaking. The material had already been prepared by the Historical Section. This work is very delicate and the responsibility for it very heavy. However, it is necessary. At the time of Saint Pius V it was not possible. The work of the Commission should not be forgotten.[6]

By 1954 all was ready. On August 18 the Holy Father decided to place the question before the cardinals. On July 19, 1955 an extraordinary Congregation was held. "The reasons for the reform and its cause, were strictly pastoral and they had a pastoral objective, namely to bring the faithful back to the celebration of these rites. While they were consonant with the history of liturgy, history did not impose the reform".[7]

Pastoral Character and Principal Innovations

The pastoral objective of the reform emerges from many sides. Before this could be applied, the Instruction *Inter Oecumenici* of September 26, 1964, following the first meeting of the Consilium, had to be awaited. In fact "the changes of a pastoral nature are evident in continuous emendation of the texts, and especially of the rites and the ceremonial parts".[8]

A delineation of the pastoral dimension of the reform is to be found in the report of the Pontifical Commission for the Reform of the Liturgy of April 30, 1955, signed by the *Relator-Generalis*, Father Ferdinando Antonelli. He wrote "1954 marks the end of the experimental period for the new *Ordo Sabbati Sancti* which was conceeded in the decree of the Sacred Congregation of Rites of January 11, 1952. Next year, 1955, a decision will have to be taken about it".[9]

The need to make some decision about the *Ordo Sabbati Sancti*, practically opened the way for a complete reform of Holy Week "which, as everyone knows, constitutes a self-standing and central liturgical complex".[10] The idea had been advanced of publishing an *Ordo Hebdomadae Sacrae*, consisting of Palm Sunday, Holy Thursday, Good Friday, and Holy Saturday. The Monday, Tuesday, and Wednesday of Holy Week would remain unaltered *ut in Missali Romano*.[11] The report continues:

> The preparation of an *Ordo Hebdomadae Sacrae* would not require much work. Apart from Holy Saturday which is already in use, Holy Thursday and Good Friday, as will be recalled, have already been prepared and require only to be finally revised. Only Palm Sunday has to be prepared. Given the urgency of the question, since some decision must be taken next year, it has to be published by autumn. With the Cardinal Prefect's consent a study of the liturgical history of Palm Sunday and a concrete plan of reform has been submitted for the deliberation of the Commission.[12]

Holy Week, which converges on the so-called *Triduum Sacrum*, contains the most important day of the liturgical year. This day is one which is "rich with ancient and venerable rites, pregnant with meaning".[13] The successful outcome of the new Easter Vigil encouraged a complete reform of Holy Week which would include all three days of the *Triduum* since they form a liturgical unit.[14] The reports sent to the Sacred Congregation about the experiment with the Easter Vigil recommended that the solemn Mass of Holy Thursday should be celebrated in the evening. On this point Antonelli noted in the report:

> It is therefore licit to ask the Commission for the Reform of the Liturgy whether or not to present the question to the Holy Father for his approval, so as to begin the historical study and prepare the material for discussion immediately after the summer holidays.[15]

In a letter reporting on the progress of the reform of the Easter Triduum, which is among Antonelli's papers in the archive of the Sacred Congregation of Rites, the Commission told the Pope:

> Thus, the Commission for the Reform of the Liturgy requested Your Holiness' authorization to examine in greater detail the question of the reform of these two remaining days of the Sacred Triduum on which the great and fundamental mysteries of the Christian Religion are celebrated. The work of the Commission has been greatly facilitated by important developments in the science of liturgy, in the presentation of original sources, which have been published in important critical editions; in the comparative study of the meaning, significance and subsequent developments of the various ceremonies. With explicit permission obtained from Your Holiness, a detailed study of the question has been undertaken, taking into account what your Holiness has recently approved with regard to Holy Saturday.[16]

The Commission met on October 19, 1954, to discuss the drafts of the *Ordinationes* for the Sacred Triduum. These would be the general norms governing the new liturgical order for this part of Holy Week. The *Relator-Generalis*, Father Antonelli, together with Father Löw, had prepared a *pro-memoria* for the Commission's consideration before eventually submitting it for the Pope's approval.[17]

The Historical Development of Holy Week
according to Antonelli

In order to understand the reasons for the reform of Holy Week, it is necessary to understand the liturgical history of these days. The celebration of the Lord's passion, death, and resurrection is the oldest and most solemn constituent of the liturgical year. From apostolic times, this commemoration was observed every year with great solemnity. The day of the Lord's resurrection became the *dies Domini* or Sunday. The recollection of the resurrection did not stop there. His passion and death were also commemorated,[18] hence the beginnings of the liturgical Triduum, dedicated to Christ, "crucified, buried, and resurrected".[19] The Triduum would subsequently be amplified.

> The memorial of the institution of the Eucharist, which happened on the evening preceding the passion, *pridie quam pateretur*, completed the liturgical celebration of the Paschal Mystery. From the 4th century another celebration had been connected with these mysteries, that of the memorial of the Lord's triumphant entry into the Holy City. This would become our Palm Sunday. Thus Holy Week was constituted of rites and formulae which, even still today, make up the most important part of all of our ancient liturgical patrimony.[20]

From the outset, these sacred rites were celebrated in the evening because they more or less corresponded to the times at which the mysteries they commemorated, actually happened. The solemn Mass, in *Cena Domini*, was celebrated in the late evening on Holy Thursday, and the rites on Good Friday were celebrated in the early afternoon, the time at which Jesus died on the cross. Holy Saturday was considered an aliturgical day, marked by mourning for Christ who laid in the tomb. Towards dark, the solemn Easter Vigil began. It concluded at dawn on Easter Sunday with the singing of the *Alleluia* and was followed by the festive Mass of the Resurrection.[21] With the passage of time, these ceremonies underwent many changes and towards the end of the Middle Ages they were transferred to the morning. In this, however,

> the historical re-evocation of the Easter event undoubtedly lost much of its effect. Holy Saturday was affected the worst. The formulae and the liturgical actions of the Vigil, which had been used during the night, lost their intimate significance and the effectiveness of their symbolism.[22]

The change of times, however, facilitated the participation of the faithful. From the 5th century, Holy Thursday, Good Friday, and Holy Saturday were recognized as holidays, even by the civil authorities. The situation changed with the Apostolic Constitution *Universa per orbem*, published by Urban VIII on September 24, 1642. From then on, these days were no longer considered holidays. This had negative effects, especially with regard to the participation of the faithful at the sacred ceremonies which were often celebrated in almost deserted churches.[23] Such pastoral considerations constrained the Holy See to reconsider the entire Easter Triduum: "In this context those concerned with pastoral liturgy – and thanks be to God, the liturgical movement is operative in all countries – had been hoping for some time that the ceremonies of Holy Thursday, Good Friday, and Holy Saturday, would be restored to evening time".[24]

Particular historical circumstances facilitated this change which was sought everywhere. "After the last war we share in a profound work of reviewing, or updating, as some would have it, of all aspects of social life; in religious life, the liturgy is the social element par excellence".[25] Now, we shall follow our history of the Triduum with an analysis of how the reform was implemented so as to see the changes it introduced. Holy Thursday had three distinct ceremonies which we shall outline, together with Antonelli's reflections on them:

1. The *Reconciliation of public sinners*, with its own rite and proper Mass, was celebrated in the morning so as to allow penitents to participate in the ceremonies with the faithful;

2. The *Consecration of the holy oils*, which would be used at the Easter Vigil for baptism and confirmation;

3. The *Natale Calicis* or the solemn celebration of the institution of the Holy Eucharist, with evening Mass.

Antonelli commented:

Ad 1: Any restoration of the rite for the reconciliation of penitents is to be absolutely excluded because this institution has lapsed for more than a millennium. [26]

Ad 2: The Chrism Mass, whose formulae are known from ancient sacramentaries, should of course be restored, but only for use in Cathedrals on the morning of Holy Thursday. It should be a matter of no more than a few alterations to simplify the very long rites, bearing in mind the ancient formulae.[27]

Ad 3: The principal and most important thing for the Christian faithful is and will be the great solemn Mass in remembrance of the institution of the Eucharist.

The time for the celebration of this Mass suggests itself: the time at which the Last Supper was celebrated, i.e., in the evening. A certain liberty might be permitted in determining the time.[28]

The evening Mass of Holy Thursday was composed of several elements which can be clarified with reference to Antonelli's commentary:

1. Office: Some changes were introduced which were in the spirit of the reform: "For example, Vespers are omitted by those who had participated at the evening ceremonies. Roman discretion forbade accumulating one function on another".[29]

2. Solemn Mass: Two formal items must be noted: "Incense may be used even if the Mass is neither solemn nor sung. The presence of clerics and priests is recommended: priests wearing stoles".[30]

3. Homily: The commentary on the reform refers to its content: "It should be strictly Eucharistic, emphasizing the importance

of the priesthood and stressing charity in as pastoral a manner as possible".[31]

4. *Mandatum*: The washing of the feet should be done after the reading of the Gospel. It is highly recommended because the exterior act has a profound meaning. "It is a very suggestive act but little known. It should be rediscovered and carried out in the sanctuary for all the faithful to see. (It is worth more than a fine sermon.)"[32]

5. Sign of Peace: A change was made for the specific reason that, "At the *Agnus Dei*, the *dona nobis pacem* would be omitted because peace is not given (because of the betrayal of Judas)."[33]

6. Communion of the Clergy and the Faithful: It should be remembered that in the presence of several priests, only one celebrates. The others assist officially, in sacred vestments, and participate actively by reciting in common, some of the prayers of the Mass. They did not however concelebrate.

7. Stripping of the Altar: No modification.

8. Compline: This was recited as usual.

Good Friday was marked by a liturgical ceremony which had a "Collect" but no sacrifice.[34] After the readings and veneration of the cross, the *Pater noster*, originally the preparation for communion, was recited: "It should be recalled that general communion of the faithful was in use up to the 15th century and even later in some places".[35] Here we shall outline the ceremony and note Antonelli's comments on it:

1. Readings and sermon;

2. General intercessions for the needs of the Church and mankind;

3. Veneration of the cross;

4. General communion.

Ad 1.   The readings and the *Passio* need not be changed. The celebrant however should not be obliged to read everything following what has been introduced to the Easter Vigil.[36]

Ad 2.   Substantially, the celebration of the general intercessions can remain unchanged. A slight modification would be easy (*Flectamus genua*..., a prayer for the government, perhaps the insertion of some of the Church's needs.)[37]

Ad 3.   The greatest emphasis should be given to the ceremony of the veneration of the cross. It should be done in such a way that all present may be able to participate in the act of faith.[38]

Ad 4.   Reduce the structural amplification of the Middle Ages, which was derived from the *Mass of the Presanctified*, to the severe and pure original lines of the general communion.[39]

With regard to the beginning of the celebration, the best time is that of the Lord's death. The ceremony and the Vespers should begin before 3 p.m.. It may begin later should local circumstances require it. The recital in choir of Matins or Lauds, where obligatory, should take place in the morning in accordance with the new *Ordo* of Holy Saturday. "Thus the *Sacred Triduum* can appear as a complete liturgical unit with the simple rites accessible to all, framed by the logic of the mysteries which they celebrate".[40]

Palm Sunday

This Sunday derives its name from the blessing and procession of palms. Originally, however, in the Roman Church "...it was considered the gateway to the Week of the Passion and was also known as *Dominica de Passione*, and the Mass, from the earliest of times, is completely centered on the passion, with the solemn reading of the *Passio* according to Saint Matthew".[41] Eventually the procession of palms was introduced from the East, or more precisely from Jerusalem, and at a later stage, a special blessing for the palms.[42]

These two elements, the blessing and procession, required revision of the rite which was too long and unduly conflated. During the blessing of palms the various prayers, which were at one time *ad libitum*, had become obligatory. The rite also had been made equal to a Mass, and various elements associated with Christ the King and the Messiah had been assimilated to it. Thus, the ceremony of blessing was reduced and carried out with solemnity. The procession took on the character of a public demonstration in honor of Christ. "Thus the lost balance was restored, that is, blessing of palms as a preparation for the procession which is the central element (outside of Mass) and a distinctive sign of Palm Sunday".[43] However, notwithstanding this revision of the ceremonies of Palm Sunday, they still continue to be burdened by excessive length and heaviness.

The liturgy of Palm Sunday is divided in two clearly distinct parts: the more ancient, the Mass of Roman origin, and the blessing of palms and procession which is Gallican in origin.[44] We should bear these two elements in mind as we trace the development of the reform.

The Mass

The Mass is the fundamental and primitive part of the ceremony. It is oriented towards the Passion, as its original name suggests: *Dominica de Passione*. Various proposals were made for its reform, but we shall concern ourselves with two: for some it was sufficient to eliminate the first part of the Mass, or better, it was requested that the blessing of palms and the procession would replace the first part of the Mass. The offertory would follow immediately after the procession. Others wished to drop the Passion because it lengthened the ceremony.

The Development of the Liturgical Reform

After serious reflection, the experts came to the conclusion (which was submitted to the Commission) that nothing should be changed. The Mass was better retained in its original form because it was the solemn initiation of Passion Week. However, priests who binated were permitted to limit the Passion at the second Mass, reading in its place the Gospel taken from Mathew 21:1-9.[45] Antonelli's comment on this, written at the foot of a page which was submitted to the Commission reads: "Question: It is asked: (1) Should the Mass remain as it is, or (2) should an insertion be made in the Rubric permitting the omission of the Passion in binated Masses?"[46]

The Blessing of Palms

It seemed convenient to make some variations to the blessing of palms and to the procession. The Roman rite up to the 9th – 10th centuries did not foresee these two ritual elements, of which the procession was more ancient.[47] The procession can be traced to the 4th century, when the Church first enjoyed full liberty to remember the events of Christ's life by processing through the places associated with His passion. Egeria describes the procession around the year 394. The procession passed into all of the Oriental liturgies. There was a preoccupation to reproduce the historical event in all its particularities: the procession, accompanied by hymns and canticles, began outside of the city and proceeded to the city gate and from there to the principal church. Christ was represented by the bishop or by the book of the Gospels, and later by a great cross.[48] This rite entered the West through Spain and France:

> Its first vestiges are conserved in the old Visi-Gothic and Gallican rite, which also fully developed the ceremony. The fundamental element, also in the West, was the procession with palms, or more accurately, with other branches, especially olive branches. By the Carolingian era the procession had reached its fullest development and continued in this form into the first centuries of the Middle Ages, and culminated in its homage to Christ the King.[49]

> The procession underwent much development from the 11th to the 13th centuries and was subsequently simplified: the essential element, the homage to Christ the King, completely disappeared. In many places, popular passion plays evolved which also affected the rite, which was reduced to what remains today.[50]

When did the blessing of palms for the procession begin?

> Its first traces are to be found in the 8th century in a liturgical book from a Gallican background such as the so-called Bobbio Missal, the *Sacramentarium Gallicanum*, the *Sacramentarium Pragense* (10th century) and others. It is completely unknown in liturgical books of Roman origin. Amalarius mentions the procession but not the blessing.

> The complete Rite is to be found in the so-called *Ordo Romanus Antiquus*, published for the first time under this title in 1568 by Hittorp. This *Ordo* is neither Romanus nor Antiquus. It is rather a typical Franco-Germanic *Ordo* of the 10th century with a Gallican base.[51]

The Franco-Germanic liturgy was introduced to Rome during the Ottonian Reform and became that of the Curia and of the Roman liturgy: "In the so called *Pontificale Germanicum* of the 12th century, edited by Andrieu, *Le Pontifical romain au Moyen Âge*, Vol. I. *Le Pontifical romain du 12e siècle* (Città del Vaticano 1938, pp. 210-214), we find a reduced rite which preserves exactly the elements of the earlier one".[52]

The same process is more or less to be found in many other *Ordines*. The definitive arrangement of the blessing of palms is to be found in the *Ordo* of the Missal of the Roman Curia, from the 14th century on. This was subsequently taken as the basis for the missal of Saint Pius V in 1570.[53]

The Reforms of 1955

From the foregoing we can conclude with Antonelli that all was ready for the *Ordo Hebdomadae Sanctae*. It only lacked the approval of the Holy Father. On November 16, 1955 the general Decree *Maxima Redemptionis Nostrae Mysteria* of the Sacred Congregation of Rites was published. With this decree, Pius XII promulgated the liturgical reform of Holy Week.[54] The following is a resumé of the principal changes which were introduced:

> On Palm Sunday the only notable change is that which was made to the blessing of palms. As is known, two elements in this rite precede the Mass: the blessing of the palms and the procession. Of these elements, the older and more important is the procession. The rite of blessing is later and secondary.[55]

In a conversation broadcast by the Italian state radio (RAI) on March 27, 1956, Antonelli presented the reformed *Ordo* for Holy Week to the Italian people. After a brief historical resumé he went on to describe each day of the *Triduum*. He had the following to say about Palm Sunday:

> The ceremony, which, as in the past, is celebrated in the morning, remains practically unchanged. At the beginning for the blessing of the palms, some formularies, which are late and very long, have been omitted. An attempt has been made to restore importance to the procession, which returns to being what it was in the middle ages: a solemn public act of homage to Christ, the Messianic King. To this end, the sacred ministers will return to using red vestments, which correspond to the purple color of regality.[56]

On Holy Thursday, the first day of the *Triduum*, the *Cena Domini* Mass will no longer be said in the morning since it has been restored to its original evening time. It will be forbidden to receive Holy Communion in the morning: "The great solemn Mass of this day and at which all of the faithful participate is the *Cena Domini*. It has been restored to its original evening time and may not be celebrated before 5 p.m. or after 8 p.m.".[57] In the entire liturgical year, if an evening Mass must be celebrated, this is the day on which to celebrate it because of its temporal recollection of the mystery which is celebrated.

The ancient *Missa Chrismatis,* during which the holy oils are blessed and the chrism is consecrated,, will again be celebrated in the morning at the Cathedral church, as in antiquity.

> This Mass will take place in the morning and only at the Cathedral. The clergy especially will participate in the celebration of this Mass whose ancient and beautiful formularies have been preserved in the Sacramentaries. These can easily be used again at this Mass which is reserved to the Cathedral. It is celebrated by the bishop assisted by his clergy.[58]

At the *Cena Domini* Mass the *Mandatum,* or the washing of the feet may be celebrated immediately after the Gospel: "This would also be the opportune time to organize a parish collection for works of Christian charity".[59]

With regard to the so-called Easter Sepulchres, Antonelli makes the following remarks:

> When the decree reforming Holy Week was published many in Italy asked: What is going to happen to the Easter Sepulchres? They have not been suppressed. They have been moved to a different time, beginning after evening Mass and concluding during the afternoon of the following day.[60]

Concerning the name given to the Easter Sepulchres, Antonelli notes:

> Today, after the Mass of Holy Thursday, the Holy Eucharist will be solemnly reserved. Eucharistic reservation derives historically from the communion of the faithful on Good Friday. The Eucharist was reserved in a kind of tabernacle, without public veneration. The solemn veneration of Holy Thursday began after the Council of Trent, but the practice, which had been in use since the 13th – 14th centuries, continued of reposing the Eucharist in a tabernacle, rather than in a monstrance. The practice of exposition of the Blessed Sacrament in a closed tabernacle rather than in a monstrance, it would seem, gave rise to the erroneous popular idea that this exposition represented the tomb of Our Lord despite the fact that on Holy Thursday no reference to a tomb can be made.[61]

Seeing the confusion surrounding the Easter Sepulchres, Antonelli noted in a lecture entitled *Riforma liturgica della Settimana Santa*, given on March 17, 1956 to the Circle of Saint Peter the following:

> As regards to the so-called Sepulchres, this term should be dropped since it creates confusion. The practice has nothing to do with a sepulchre. It is a solemn exposition of Jesus in the Blessed Sacrament, which is a sign of gratitude for the gift of the Eucharist. The exposition has not been suppressed. Rather, it has been moved. Instead of beginning in the morning, it will begin in the evening and continue until Friday afternoon.[62]

Concerning Good Friday, the rite has been preserved in fact throughout the centuries. For this reason very few changes have been made: "The Good Friday ceremony is among the most beautiful and moving of all liturgy. It has been restored to the afternoon, and to the hour at about which Jesus died on the cross. The ceremonies may begin at about 5 p.m. but can also be delayed until about 6 p.m.".[63] As one can see, the ancient liturgical elements of this ceremony remain intact. There have been very few changes, and these for specific reasons:

> An attempt has been made to give greater emphasis to the orientation of the cross, which is the most important element of the original ceremony. A decisive

point was encountered with the so-called Mass of the Presanctified, consisting of many later and unfortunate elements. The Commission for the Reform of the Liturgy, after mature consideration, believed that it would be opportune to reduce the actual formularies to their original nature and function, which was that of a simple communion rite.[64]

The communion of the faithful is a problem with historical implications:

Given that there was no Eucharistic sacrifice on Good Friday, at the beginning of this complex of liturgical rites, there was no communion, neither of the faithful nor of the clergy. At a second stage, sometime before the 8th century, the communion of the faithful began to appear in the Roman liturgy. This became a universal practice and has perdured for centuries. Its cessation is easily understood in the context of the general rarification of communion which had reached such a stage by the 13th century that the Ecumenical Lateran Council of 1215 obliged all the faithful to approach the holy table at least once every year.[65]

After mature and careful consideration, the Commission decided to restore to the faithful the possibility of receiving Holy Communion on Good Friday:

The principal innovation in the ceremonies of Good Friday is that of permitting the faithful to receive Holy Communion. From now on, after having commemorated the passion and death of our Lord, which took place on this day and at this time, and having venerated the cross, the instrument and trophy of our redemption, everyone will be able to render more copiously, in his soul, the fruits of the sacrifice of Calvary by sacramentally sharing in the Divine Victim.[66]

In view of the universal success of the Vigil liturgy, this ceremony remained unchanged. Consequently:

With the suppression of the old rite of Matins, Holy Saturday returns to being an absolutely aliturgical day, taking on again its original character of mourning for Jesus who lays in the tomb. Consequently the Lenten fast, with the explicit approval of the Holy Father, has been brought back to midnight on Holy Saturday, as it had been up to the publication of the 1917 Code which sought to adjust the law to actual practice which, in turn, had derived from the anticipation of the ceremonies of the Easter Vigil.[67]

These, in general terms, were the principal modifications made to ceremonies of the Sacred Triduum. Let us now turn to an appraisal of these days, made by a noted liturgist after the Second Vatican Council so as to show that the post-conciliar reform confirmed the general lines followed by the reforms of 1955, and to allow us to form a clearer picture of the various liturgical questions then current:

Of the texts chosen in 1955 which passed into the Roman Missal, some, such as the Collects, are classical and are excellently composed, others are less fortunate. The general scheme was largely criticized by liturgists. It was pointed out that they suffered from a certain conceptual impoverishment: for example three texts (Epistle, Gospel, and post-communion) are insistent about the oil of the sick which is hierarchically last, and the blessing of which, for centuries, was not even reserved to the bishops, but deputed simply to the priest who blessed it time and time again, as the need arose.[68]

Bugnini continues by referring to the fact that on the morning of Holy Thursday, the diocesan clergy attended with the bishop in the Cathedral, and spent the afternoon and evening in the parishes and other churches celebrating the *Cena Domini* Mass.

The idea of transforming the Chrism Mass into a priestly celebration came from Paul VI who, as Archbishop of Milan, had already stressed this particular aspect of Holy Thursday for his Ambrosian rite clergy. Not all liturgists were convinced of this innovation, especially those anchored in the older liturgical rite which situated the *Missa Chrismatis* in the context of the consecration of the holy oils. This consecration was the basis for every type of consecration in the Church and was seen as an immediate preparation for the baptism of catechumens which took place during the Easter Vigil. Gradually, the benefit of the reform was accepted at the expense of attachment to the previous liturgy.

A further expansive innovation was made in 1965 with the introduction of concelebration of the Mass. This was permitted in every cathedral on Holy Thursday, since on that day the Church celebrates the institution of the Eucharist. For this reason, all of the texts of the Chrism Mass had to be revised: the blessing of the oils, preparation for the celebration of the Sacred Triduum, the exaltation of the priesthood. The texts of the Mass made the need for the revision abundantly clear. The other texts of the Mass remained unchanged including the offertory, during which the hymn *O redemptor sume carmen* accompanied the procession. The versicle *Diligis iustitiam* was moved to the *communio*, and the text slightly modified so that it would correspond with the text. The rites and texts prescribed in the *Pontificale Romanum* for the blessing of the oils continued in use. On March 6, 1970, the Sacred Congregation for Divine Worship published the texts for the renewal of priestly commitment and a proper preface for the Mass. The first consisted of texts for the renewal of priestly commitment in which the priests were addressed by the bishop. The faithful were invited to pray for their priests and for their bishop. Thus, it becomes evident that the *Missa Chrismatis* acquired an altogether different aspect, but one closer to the needs of the contemporary Church.

Concerning Good Friday, no further changes were made apart from a modification of the general intercessions.[69] Father Bugnini's reflections, which as we have seen, make it evident that the changes brought to the 1955 reform are quite marginal, and are the fruit of a natural evolutionary process. Though certainly, as it was with the new *Ordo Sabbati Sancti,* the *Ordo Hebdomadae Sanctae* also experienced some practical difficulties in its applications. These were largely due to the transition from the old to the new discipline. For this reason, the decree contained some criteria designed to resolve such problems.

The following quote is a remark of Antonelli's which expresses the hope of every Catholic, and it is with this that we shall conclude:

> The reform of Holy Week, while from the point of view of the liturgy is an event of supreme importance, is from a pastoral perspective certainly a precious gift given to the Church by Pius XII in his capacity of Supreme Pastor. Its object was to facilitate the participation of all the faithful in the great mysteries of our redemption.[70]

* * *

Undoubtedly the liturgical reform required much study, debate, revision, updating, and modification. This was possible thanks to the intelligence, tenacity, and sense of responsibility of the members of the Commission. Father Antonelli explicitly acknowledged this: "This period was a kind of novitiate. It was spent in the midst of proposals, counter-proposals, retakes, and rewordings, projects of major importance, and fruitful discussion".[71] Many things had to be borne in mind and above all attention had to be given to the directives guiding the work of the Commission. Antonelli summarizes these as follows:

> There were three major elements: simplify things, revitalize the inherent qualities of the sacred ceremonies during these days, help the people to understand the rites, which in themselves are so eloquent and, once freed from later accretions, increase the vital force of the Church through Sacramental Communion.[72]

Antonelli, in a document addressed to the Holy Father, elucidates the difficulties encountered by the reform and emphasizes his certain conviction of the spiritual benefits deriving from the reform:

> The Commission is also of the view that, apart from the usual criteria of those, who either from indolence or lack of liturgical sensibility do not want anything to change, the bishops in general, like all of the liturgists and all others with a healthy understanding of the liturgy, are said to be highly positive in their praise of the reform (as they already are of the reform of Holy Saturday.) They are said to be profoundly grateful to the Holy Father.
>
> More important, however, is the conviction that this reform will bring the faithful more easily to an understanding of the mysteries of the passion, death, and resurrection of our Savior, and to a more intensive living-out of those same mysteries, thereby certainly bringing copious spiritual benefits.[73]

In one of his manuscripts Antonelli again expresses his confidence in the work of the Commission:

> This is something very important. Much is expected of it. We are aware of the sacramental efficacy of the liturgy, which is especially rich during these days. Ideally speaking, Lent and Holy Week should conclude with the renewal of baptismal promises. The days of Holy Week have a special meaning and character: Palm Sunday, the triumph of Jesus, the Messianic King; Holy Thursday, a day of gratitude for the gifts of the Eucharist, the priesthood, and charity; Good Friday, a day of sorrow; Holy Saturday, a day of mourning ending in the joy of Easter.[74]

The reform started out with a new concept of the nature and ends of the liturgy which Antonelli describes:

> The liturgy is not an archeological museum, it is the most vital expression of the Church; and life is not something static. The liturgy, apart from being worship of God, is also a school for the Christian life and in that school, the scholar must be able to understand and follow the lessons. The liturgy is also a religious pedagogy. The faithful, by means of gestures and formularies, must be brought to perceive and re-live the mysteries of the redemption.
>
> In short, for the liturgy to be what it should be, both worship of God and a

school of the Christian life, the faithful must be able to participate in it actively and consciously. In the liturgical action, the faithful are never merely spectators, rather they are actors.

Thus the reform of the liturgy must seek to bring the faithful to a conscious and active participation in the celebration of the Sacred Mysteries. In order to reach this goal, the faithful must be able to see, understand, and follow the liturgical action. They must therefore be interested in the liturgical action and they have to be encouraged to play their part in that action. This is precisely a return to the ancient. "This is a constant and evident preoccupation of the present reform of Holy Week".[75]

[1] F. ANTONELLI, *La Riforma liturgica della Settimana Santa*, in *ALV*, pp. 1-4.

[2] *Ibidem*, p. 1.

[3] *Ibidem*.

[4] *Ibidem*, p. 2.

[5] *Ibidem*, pp. 3-4.

[6] *Ibidem*, p. 4.

[7] *Ibidem*, pp. 4-5.

[8] *Ibidem*, p. 5.

[9] CPRL, *Intorno alla Settimana Santa*, May 30, 1954, in *SCCS*, p. 1.

[10] *Ibidem*, pp. 1-2.

[11] *Ibidem*, p. 2.

[12] *Ibidem*.

[13] F. ANTONELLI, *Sulla sistemazione del giovedì e venerdì Santo*, in *SCCS*, p. 2.

[14] *Ibidem*.

[15] *Ibidem*, p. 3.

[16] F. ANTONELLI, *Sulla riforma del giovedì e venerdì Santo*, in *SCCS*, p. 2.

[17] CPRL, *Verbali*, cit., p. 125.

[18] Cf. F. ANTONELLI, *L'anno liturgico. Lezioni di Liturgia, 1945-1967*, pp. 2-3.

[19] F. ANTONELLI, *La riforma liturgica della Settimana Santa*, in *VeP*, 39 (1956), pp. 151-152.

[20] *Ibidem*, p. 152.

[21] *Ibidem*.

[22] *Ibidem*.

[23] Cf. *ibidem*, p. 153.

[24] *Ibidem*.

[25] *Ibidem*, p. 153.

[26] F. ANTONELLI, *Sulla sistemazione*, cit., p. 4.

[27] *Ibidem*.

[28] *Ibidem*.

[29] F. ANTONELLI, *La riforma*, cit., p. 7.

[30] *Ibidem*, p. 8.

[31] *Ibidem*.

[32] F. ANTONELLI, *Sulla sistemazione*, cit., p. 4.

[33] *Ibidem*, p. 8.

[34] *Ibidem*, pp. 4-5.

[35] *Ibidem*, p. 5.

[36] *Ibidem*.

[37] *Ibidem*.

[38] *Ibidem*, p. 5.

[39] *Ibidem*.

[40] *Ibidem*.

[41] F. ANTONELLI, *L'anno liturgico*, cit., pp. 145-146.

[42] Cf. F. ANTONELLI, *La riforma*, cit., p. 155.

[43] F. ANTONELLI, *La Domenica della Palme*, manuscript dated July 8, 1954 containing the Schema for presentation to the Commission for the Liturgical Reform, in *SCCS*, pp. 3-4.

[44] F. ANTONELLI – J. Löw, *Annotazioni intorno alla riforma della liturgia della domenica delle Palme*, in *SCCS*, p. 1.

[45] *Ibidem*, p. 5.

[46] *Ibidem*.

[47] *Ibidem*, p. 3.

[48] Cf. P. MARAVAL, *Egérie, Journal de voyage*, SCH 296, Paris 1982, pp. 68-69.

[49] F. ANTONELLI – J. Löw, *Annotazioni*, cit., pp. 3-4.

[50] F. ANTONELLI, *Promemoria sulla Riforma Liturgica della Settimana Santa. Stato della questione*, manuscript marked "*per il S. Padre*", August 1954, in *SCCS*, pp. 6-7.

[51] F. ANTONELLI – J. Löw, *Annotazioni*, cit., p. 5.

[52] *Ibidem*, p. 6.

[53] Cf. *ibidem*.

[54] Cf. *AAS*, 47 (1955), pp. 383-847; *EL*, 70 (1956), pp. 5-14.

[55] F. ANTONELLI, *Importanza e carattere pastorale della Riforma Liturgica della Settimana Santa: L'Osservatore Romano*, November 27, 1955, p. 2.

[56] F. ANTONELLI, *La Riforma dell'Ordo Liturgico della Settimana Santa*, manuscript for a broadcast on RAI, in *ALV*, p. 4.

[57] *Ibidem*.

[58] F. ANTONELLI, *Importanza*, cit., p. 2.

[59] *Ibidem*, p. 6.

[60] F. ANTONELLI, *Importanza*, cit., p. 2.

[61] F. ANTONELLI, *Promemoria*, cit., p. 9.

[62] The text of Fr. Antonelli's lecture on the reform of Holy Week may be found in *L'Osservatore Romano*, March 22, 1956, p. 3.

[63] F. ANTONELLI, *La Riforma dell'Ordo*, cit., p. 5.

[64] F. ANTONELLI, *Importanza*, cit., p. 2.

[65] *Ibidem*.

[66] F. ANTONELLI, *La Riforma dell'Ordo*, cit., p. 6.

[67] F. ANTONELLI, *Importanza*, cit., p. 2.

[68] A. BUGNINI, *La Riforma liturgica*, cit. p. 124.

[69] Cf. *ibidem*, pp. 124-127.

[70] F. ANTONELLI, *Importanza*, cit., p. 2.

[71] F. ANTONELLI, *Per l'adunanza del 10 giugno 1952*, in *SCCS*, p. 2.

[72] F. ANTONELLI, *Sulla riforma*, cit., p. 5.

[73] F. ANTONELLI, *Promemoria*, cit., pp. 15-16; cf. F. ANTONELLI, *I motivi storici delle riforme nella liturgia della Settimana Santa: Giornale d'Italia*, March 30, 1956, p. 3.

[74] F. ANTONELLI, *La Riforma liturgica della Settimana Santa*, brown notebook entitled "*Liturgia*", in *ALV*, p. 14. Concerning the *Apostolic Exhortation* of Pius XII to the parish priests and lenten preachers of Rome, see *L'Osservatore Romano*, March 11, 1955, pp. 1-2.

[75] F. ANTONELLI, *La riforma liturgica della Settimana Santa. Importanza, attuazione, prospettive*, in *La Restaurazione liturgica nell'opera di Pio XII. Atti Primo Congresso Internazionale di Liturgia pastorale (Assisi 1956)*, Genoa 1957, pp. 179-197.

Chapter 7

The Preparation of *Sacrosanctum Concilium,* 1960-1963

History

Any understanding of Father Antonelli's work for the Second Vatican Council requires a knowledge of his activities during the period from 1959 to 1970. By mid-November of 1959, Antonelli was no longer the Rector of the *Antonianium* due to his nomination as an ecclesiastical Assistant to the *Missionarie della Regalità di Nostro Signore Gesù Cristo*, an appointment that was made by decree of the Congregation for Religious on August 8, 1959. Additionaly, he was no longer the *Relator-Generalis* of the Historical Section in the Sacred Congregation of Rites, but on November 21, 1959 he was appointed to the position of *Promotor Generalis Fidei*. "He was promoted to this office by the paternal trust of Pope John XXIII and signed by the late Cardinal Tardini which was published in the *Acta Ordinis*, 79 (1960), 102".[1]

During the preparatory years leading up to the enormous event of the Second Vatican Council, Father Antonelli experienced many joys and sorrows in addition to the vast amount of work that was handled by his office. We have not found a single text of Antonelli relating to the preparatory work of the Liturgical Commission for the Council, of which he was no longer a member, presumably because of the demands placed on him by his work in the Sacred Congregation of Rites. The silence in his documentation continues until February of 1962 when he comments on some new developments.

In the early 1960s Antonelli closely collaborated with the Prefect of the Sacred Congregation of Rites, Cardinal Amleto Cicognani, who died on February 5, 1962 and was succeeded by Cardinal Larraona[2] who knew Antonelli[3] very well. On March 14, 1962 after a long and cordial conversation with the new Prefect, Cardinal Larraona mentioned the idea of nominating him Pro-Secretary of the Sacred Congregation of Rites: "I said nothing. He replied that with my experience in the Congregation, I would be able to take the world wide liturgical movement in hand immediately, not to stop it, but to give it a uniform line and free it from extreme positions".[4]

Since Cardinal Larraona was required to nominate *periti* to the Council, he also consulted Father Antonelli:

> On Friday, March 17, 1962 Cardinal Larraona handed me a letter with a request for the Conciliar Commission on the Liturgy, and he asked for my proposals. Yesterday evening I responded with my proposals, giving him the following names:
>
> *Italy*
> Msgr. Mario Righetti (Genoa)
> Msgr. Pietro Borella (Milan)
> Dom Cipriano Vagaggini, OSB (Rome)
>
> *France*
> Msgr. Amato Giorgio Martimort (Toulouse)
> Père Roguet, OP (Paris)
> Dom Antoine Chevasse (Strasburg)
> Msgr. Marcelo Noirot (Lyon)
>
> *Germany*
> Joseph Jungmann, SJ (Innsbruck)
> Msgr. Johannes Wagner (Trier)
> Msgr. Theodore Schnitzler (Cologne)
>
> *Spain*
> Gregorio Martinez de Antoñana (Madrid)
> Dom Ignazio Oñatibia
> Dom Brasó (Monserrato) or Dom Adalberto Franquesa (Montserrat).
>
> I also added that it would be necessary to have an English speaking representative and gave the following three names:
>
> Dom Godfried Diekmann, OSB (Collegeville, Minnesota, U.S.A.)
> Msgr. Frederick McManus (Washington)
> Dom John-Baptist O'Connell (Builth Wells, England)
>
> I did not mention Fr. Joseph Löw's name because it was my understanding that, according to the Cardinal, the members of the Roman Congregations, such as Fr. Löw, would also be appointed to the Commission. He also told me that I too would be named a member.[5]

Unfortunately, Father Löw died suddenly of a heart attack on September 22, 1962. In his notes Antonelli wrote:

> With Father Löw's death, I lost a friend and a friendship which is not easy to describe. While we were never very close, we fully understood each other. I called him to Rome in November of 1935, with Pius XI's permission, in order to have him nominated as the *Vice Relator-Generalis* of the Historical Section. From that time on, up until my appointment as *Promotor Fidei* (November 21, 1959), he remained my closest and most valuable collaborator in the Historical Section while working on hagiographies and especially on the liturgy. It was a complete and harmonious collaboration always carried out with a mutual respect and trust. It was also a fruitful and honest collaboration, as Father Löw had

an extraordinary historical and liturgical knowledge, a most vivid imagination, and a notable capacity for work. He was, however, somewhat mechanical and not always very lucid. If am not mistaken, I always brought a note of clarity, simplification, and a freer style to the work.[6]

The result of this collaboration was that the work produced was always valuable and well acknowledged. Unexpectedly, on October 5, 1962 Father Antonelli received a communication from Cardinal Larraona who communicated the following message:

> October 4, 1962: Cardinal Arcadio Larraona respectfully and cordially salutes Father Antonelli, and has the pleasure to communicate to him today, on the feast of St. Francis while the Holy Father is in Assisi, his nomination as Secretary General of the Conciliar Commission on the Sacred Liturgy. Have no fears about the work, or about the Commissions. You will see that we will find a way to make everything compatible. Thus "*in passione socius*". We shall speak tomorrow. In the meantime I commend myself to your holy prayers and believe me to be devotedly obliged. *In Domino*, Arcadio M. Cardinal Larraona.[7]

Antonelli immediately understood the importance of this position and the grave responsibilities facing him. He noted: "I felt in my heart this was a great undertaking that had fallen on my shoulders. I thanked the Cardinal for his trust and told him that I would try to serve, as always, in the best possible manner".[8]

Father Antonelli's appointment was received with surprise and apprehension by the members of the Commission,[9] as Martimort recalled:

> His appointment gave rise to surprise and unease not because of his person but because Father Bugnini, former Secretary of the Preparatory Commission, had already been proposed for this position. The failure to confirm his nomination was considered an affront and attack by the Curia on the work of the Preparatory Commission and on its Secretary, who, subsequent to his appointment as *peritus* of the Commission, retreated to an absolute silence for the entire conciliar period. Father Antonelli's position was not easy but he discharged his duties with total loyalty, with a serenity that was often meritorious, and above all with an efficiency which was a model for other Conciliar Commissions.[10]

A note written by Antonelli contains an account of the first meeting of the Commission which took place a few days after his nomination as Secretary of the Conciliar Commission on the Sacred Liturgy.

In this chapter we shall refer to the minutes of the meetings of the Liturgical Commission, on the basis that it has been possible to reconstruct the course of this same Commission. The minutes were kept by Father Falsini and may be complemented by material extracted from Antonelli's papers and with extracts from his diaries.

Meeting I (October 21, 1962)

> Today, Sunday, at 10:30 a.m. the Conciliar Commission on the Sacred Liturgy met for the first time in the *Sala del Congresso* of the Sacred Congregation of Rites. Cardinal Larraona named two Vice Presidents, Cardinal Giobbe and Cardinal Jullien. This gave rise to a certain amount of surprise, especially since both were members of the Curia. Cardinal Lercaro, however, who was the sole Cardinal

directly elected by the General Congregation, and greatly esteemed as a liturgical expert, was overlooked. He then communicated the nomination of myself as Secretary and announced that he would convoke several *periti*, not only liturgists but also theologians and priests. I spent the afternoon preparing a commentary on the Schema for the following day.[11]

Shortly after, a decision was made to hold the meetings of the Commission on working days at 5 p.m., and a discussion of some judicial procedures then ensued. The new Secretary, Fr. Antonelli, was assisted by Carlo Braga and Rinaldo Falsini. On the following day, October 22, Antonelli gave a detailed description of the General Congregation of the Council held in St Peter's.

This morning shortly after 10 a.m. in the Council *Aula* [Hall], following the announcements made by the Secretary General concerning the constitution of the final three Commissions, the Council proceeded to examine the first Schema presented to the Council Fathers, namely, that on the Liturgy. Cardinal Larraona, the president of the Commission, was the first to speak. He announced that he had charged Father Antonelli with the preparation and general explanation of the Schema in accordance with article 31 of the *Ordo Celebrandi Concilium Oecumenicum Vaticanum II*.

Then I was conducted to the speakers' platform. The immensity of the Basilica has a curious echo caused by the loudspeakers. I adjusted to it quickly, and although I had a slight cold and found it troublesome to speak, I was able to arrive at my point without too much difficulty. I spoke for about 15 to 20 minutes.[12]

The following is an extract from the discourse prepared and read by Antonelli:

... *capitulum de Sacra Liturgia non tantum magni momenti ex natura sua sed et summae actualitatis in praesens censendum est duabus praesertim causis:*

Primo quia quam plurimi sacri Pastores et omnes in re viri periti unanimi sententia, gravibus quidem suffulta argumentis, tenet libros liturgicos, seu textus ac ritus in illis contenutos, genuina profecto servata liturgica traditione, opportuna indigere emendatione et ad nostrae aetatis ingenium ac necessitates accomodatione.

Accedit secundo ratio pastoralis gravissima. Inde siquidem a media aetate, multisque de causis quas hic recensere non possumus, christfideles in liturgicis actionibus adstantes, muti potius spectatores facti sunt quam actores prout res ipsa postulat... .[13]

Father Antonelli spoke and gave a short presentation of the Schema *De Sacra Liturgia*. In his introduction he suggested that a constitution on the liturgy should be an objective of the Council's work, and giving the following two reasons: the need to improve and adapt the liturgical books, texts, and rites; and on account of the pastoral demands of the times. Referring to this last point, Antonelli maintained that Christians were gradually being reduced to the role of silent spectators instead of active participants in the liturgy. However, the renewal and nourishment of the Christian life would be derived in great measure by a return to the sources of grace, that were clearly present in the liturgy, rooted in an active and personal participation in the liturgy itself. In such a point of view Antonelli referred himself to Pius X's hopes for the liturgical movement, to the contribution of Pius XII's establishing the Commission of 1946, to the results following that Commission, which have become concretized in the Council called by John XXIII, and to the Preparatory Commission on the Liturgy instituted in 1960.[14] Immediately after his presentation and illustration of the Schema on the Sacred Liturgy, *Sacrosanctum Concilium,* Antonelli noted the reactions he provoked:

> I returned to my seat and was congratulated by many. I was surprised by the cordial response of Msgr. Amleto Tondini, the Secretary of Briefs to Princes, regarding my Latin. Others gave similar praise. Msgr. Martimort was also happy with the content, as well as Msgr. Wagner and Fr. Jungmann, SJ. For this I give thanks to the Lord.[15]

Antonelli's constant efforts and his liturgical training were greatly appreciated by the *periti* of the Commission. It is also worth recalling the name of A.G. Martimort with whom Antonelli remained good friends until his death.[16] It is clear that he also desired to maintain cordial relations with Fr. Bugnini, as the following episode illustrates:

> This morning I saw Fr. Bugnini at the Congregation, and I asked him to come over because I wanted to talk to him. I mentioned that perhaps he was unhappy with what had happened to him, and I told him I could well understand. I then told him how things had happened, and he reacted violently. [...] He stressed that there must have been some malicious people who had portrayed him in a bad light to the Cardinal. He complained that the Cardinal had never called him (so he said). I remained silent, and only told him that I had been called and presented with the nomination already signed.[17]

When Bugnini encountered difficulties with the Institute for Pastoral Theology where he taught liturgy, Antonelli was very displeased and was ready to intervene in his favor.[10] Moreover, when he had to present the Commission with the names of experts for the reform of the liturgical books, he suggested Bugnini for several of the study groups.

After much work, Antonelli was able to present its fruits to the *Osservatore Romano* on December 4, 1963, the day on which the Constitution on the Liturgy *Sacrosanctum Concilium* was promulgated.[19] After Antonelli's presentation of the Schema *De Sacra Liturgia* at the fourth General Session of the Council, the first discussions on the Schema began. The task of the Commission was to revise the Schema of the Constitution on the basis of the emendations [*emendationes*] and modifications [*modi*] proposed by the Council Fathers. We will now follow with a description of all the sessions of the Commission and of the various changes made during the meetings. For convenience we will give an account of the minutes of the meeting in the body of the text and refer to the original Schema of *De Sacra Liturgia* in the notes. This will allow us to see clearly the progress of the Commission leading to the definitive text of *Sacrosanctum Concilium.* We will follow closely the various vicissitudes, the prudent study of the Conciliar Fathers, the difficulties in accepting the many modifications put forth by the various Sub-commissions, as well as the various dispositions and the sensitivity with approving such modifications due to a fear of damaging a healthy tradition. The following chapter will contain Antonelli's commentary and a presentation of *Sacrosanctum Concilium*.

Meeting II (October 22, 1962)

The meeting began at 5 p.m. and a detailed discussion ensued which moved point by point and took two meetings (October 22 & 23, 1963). "In the first two days there were some 29 interventions on the text as a whole".[20]

Meeting III (October 23, 1962)

At this meeting we discussed the introduction along with chapter 1 and its general principles. This discussion was extended to the 29th of October: 88 Fathers spoke.[21]

Meeting IV (October 26, 1962)

The Conciliar Commission on the Sacred Liturgy met in the Congregation of Rites at 5 p.m. under the presidency of Cardinal Larraona. All the Fathers and *periti* were present. After praying the *Adsumus* the President asked the *peritus* Msgr. Bonet to speak on the *Regolamento* [Code] of the Commission. The President then read the text and commented on the more important points of the *Regolamento*. Following the reading of the text, it was approved.

The President announced the nomination of a theological Sub-commission in order to examine some points in the Schema which the Conciliar Fathers had commented on and in this way it would not be necessary to constitute a mixed Conciliar Commission. The following were members of this Sub-commission: Father Gagnebet, OP, Professor of the *Angelicum*, President; Father D. van den Eynde, OFM, Rector of the *Antonianum*; Msgr. Masi, Professor of the Lateran University. Two *periti* who had been members of the Preparatory Commission were added: Father Vagaggini, OSB and Canon Martimort.

The meeting closed after the Secretary had made some announcements and said the prayer.[22]

Meeting V (November 5, 1962)

The entire Conciliar Commission on the Sacred Liturgy met in the *Aula* [Hall] of the Sacred Congregation of Rites at 5 p.m.. The President, Cardinal Larraona, announced the nomination of the various Sub-commissions which would examine the observations made by the Council Fathers on the Schema for the Sacred Liturgy.

The first Sub-commission will be a theological one, and the second commison will be juridical. These two technical Sub-commissions will avoid the need to create a mixed Conciliar commission, and will collaborate, each according to its expertise, with the other Sub-commissions. The President of the Commission (Cardinal Larraona) and the two Vice-Presidents (Cardinals Jullien and Giobbe) along with the Secretary (Fr. Antonelli) will not be members of the Sub-commissions.

The Secretary, Father Antonelli, announced the names of the Presidents and members of the various Sub-commissions which, including those for theological and juridical matters, numbered 13. Each Sub-commission will examine that part of the Schema assigned to it. Having consulted the theological and juridical Sub-commissions, which have to read over the whole of the Schema, the Sub-commissions will then present a detailed report in a plenary meeting of the Commission.

The reason for the absence of the Council Fathers from the theological and juridical Sub-commissions was discussed. The President explained that the Sub-commissions were empowered merely to express a technical judgement on the matters placed before them. Hence they played an auxiliary role. A discussion ensued on the procedure to be followed in the Sub-commissions and on the competence of the Commission itself.

The President invited the Commission to meet again on November 7, recited the prayer, and declared the meeting closed.[23]

Meeting VI (November 7, 1962)

The meeting took place in the *Aula* of the Sacred Congregation of Rites, and Cardinal Lercaro, President of the third Sub-commission, presented a report on the work of that Sub-commission.

With regard to the note prefacing the Schema, it was decided to omit it because it did not belong to the Schema. Concerning the *Declarationes*, whose distribution to the Council *Aula* had been called for by some Fathers, Cardinal Larraona observed that they did not form part of the Schema which had been approved by the Pope. However, he was not opposed to their distribution if it helped the Fathers' understanding of the Schema.

Cardinal Lercaro's report was then discussed. Some problems which had not yet been resolved were discussed: i.e. whether or not the term *ritus latinus* should be conserved or replaced by *ritus romanus*, whether the word *Missiones* ought to be retained or replaced by the expression *Ecclesiae nuper erectae*, and whether the citations from Pontifical documents should be excluded from the Schema, etc..

The meeting ended at 7 p.m..[24]

Meeting VII (November 9, 1962)

The Conciliar Commission on the Sacred Liturgy met at 5 p.m. in the *Aula* of the Sacred Congregation of Rites, and no absences were reported. The President, having said the prayer, read a letter signed by some members of the Commission proposing that a more expeditious method be adopted so as to advance the work of the Commission.

After some minutes Msgr. Malula spoke. He stood up and, turning to the President, he expressed his dissatisfaction with the mode of procedure employed by the Commission, which he said was slow and inconclusive. He implored him to change the process so as to avoid further wasting of time. The President, after a short firm response, continued with the discussion which had been interrupted.

Concerning the questions which had remained undecided since the last meeting, it was decided:

a. the phrase *ritus latinus* or *romanus* would be discussed when examining the preamble;

b. it was considered convenient to retain the expression *Missiones*;

c. ecclesiastical documents would not be reproduced in the text and Scripture would be quoted only if the exact phrase appeared in the text;

d. the question of the Episcopal Conferences would be discussed again at an opportune time, when the proper occasion arose in the text of the Schema.

The *Agimus* was prayed and the meeting was adjourned.[25]

Meeting VIII (November 12, 1962)

The entire Commission met in the *Aula* of the Sacred Congregation of Rites at 5 p.m.. After the prayer, the Secretary read a letter sent by the President of the Council in which the Commission was asked to print and distribute to the Fathers of the Council both the *declarationes* of the Schema on the liturgy and a list of other questions on the other Schemas. After having commented on the files and pages which had been distributed, he asked the Presidents of the Sub-commissions to submit their reports on time. The Fathers then approved Cardinal Lercaro's report with unanimous agreement.

It was proposed that Cardinal Lercaro would present the report of the third Sub-commission, already approved by the Commission, to the Council. Msgr. Bonet, a *peritus*, noted that it might be an opportune time to include the Preamble, so that the Council might be able to proceed to a vote. Once it had been read by Cardinal Lercaro, it was unanimously decided to propose a general vote on the Schema on the Sacred Liturgy to the Fathers of the Council. The Cardinal President decided that the text to be presented to the Council Fathers would be presented at the following meeting.

The President of the fourth Sub-commission, Msgr. Martin, read his report on the Preamble. The text of the Preamble, together with the modifications made by the Sub-commission, were then read. The modifications were examined one by one, and the most important modifications proposed by the theological Sub-commission that were approved by a majority vote were the following: the phrase "*quidquid ad unionem fratrum separatorum in Ecclesiae*", changed to, "*quidquid ad unionem omnium in Christum credentium*" (two Fathers disagreed); the phrase "*opus nostrae Redemptionis exercetur*" placed in inverted commas (all in agreement); the phrase "*Ecclesiae naturam ... visibilem et invisibilem*", changed to, "*visibilem invisibilibus praeditam*" (all in agreement).

After the prayer, the meeting was adjourned.[26]

Meeting IX (November 14, 1962)

The entire Conciliar Commission met in the *Aula* of the Sacred Congregation of Rites at 5 p.m.. The President said the prayer and asked the Secretary to read a reply to the Commission's recent letter which had been sent by the president of the Council, Msgr. Felici.

It was asked if it was necessary, or at least useful, to present Cardinal Lercaro's report on the general observations of the Schema to the Council Fathers. Psychological reasons would recommend it – and it was so decided. Cardinal Lercaro read his report and the Commission approved it unanimously.

Discussion on the Preamble was thus concluded, and attention was then centred on the report and the discussions of articles 1-9 of Chapter I. Three Fathers opposed adding the phrase "*Spiritu Sancto unctum*" to the phrase "*verbum carnem factum*" (line 5, page 159 of the Schema). All the other members were favorable.

It was unanimously agreed to change the word "*causa*" to "*instrumentum nostrae salutis*". Two other modifications of article 1 were also unanimously agreed. All accepted the substitution of the word "*exercent*" with the word "*efficerent*" in article 2.

Msgr. Martin then read the amended text of the Preamble, together with the stylistic changes which had been made by Abbot Egger (a *peritus*). The Commission gave its unanimous approval, and the meeting was adjourned.[27]

Meeting X (November 16, 1962)

The Conciliar Commission on the Sacred Liturgy met in the *Aula* of the Sacred Congregation of Rites at 5 p.m.. The President said the prayer. The Secretary then asked the various Sub-commissions to prepare complete drafts of the amended texts, together with their reports, before consulting the theological and juridical Sub-commissions, and to send them to the Secretariat in order to have them reproduced and distributed to the members of the Commission. This was intended to expedite the work done at the meetings of the Commission.

The President made some announcements and said that the Council Fathers would vote on the Preamble and on the Schema the following day. Msgr. Martin was asked to prepare a report to be read to the Council Fathers.

Msgr. Martin resumed reading the report prepared by the IV Sub-commission which led to a discussion. A vote was taken on the phrase in n. 2 of the Schema *"per sacrificium et sacramenta exercerent"*. A proposal made by some of the *periti* to include the word *"sacrificium"* was opposed by three Fathers [28] The final part of n. 2 of the Schema was the object of a rather lively debate, but modifications were not proposed. Instead, notable changes were made to the first paragraph of n. 3, and the Commission unanimously voted to accept the new text.[29] Of the other articles, only article 6 was particularly contested because of the phrase, which was part of § 5, *"Liturgia est culmen ad quod omnia tendere debent et simul fons a quo omnia procedunt"*.[30] In spite of a number of emendations made by the Sub-commission the text encountered difficulties, especially from Cardinal Jullien and Msgr. Enciso. A proposal was accepted not to use the expression *"culmen vitae Ecclesiae"* (title of n. 5), but *"culmen actionis Ecclesiae"*, since the Liturgy, as the principle means of sanctification, is the goal towards which all the Church's activity tends.

Slight changes were approved for articles 7, 8, and 9; and the meeting concluded after 7 p.m..[31]

Meeting XI (November 19, 1962)

The Conciliar Commission on the Sacred Liturgy met in the *Aula* of the Sacred Congregation of Rites at 5 p.m.. After the opening prayer, the President thanked Cardinal Lercaro and Msgr. Martin for the report which they delivered to the Council that morning.

Msgr. Enciso made some comments about his having distributed a text to the Council Fathers already containing the amendments that had to be voted on. According to the rules, these should only have been inserted after the vote was taken by the Council. The President replied that the rule was not absolute. The Secretary, reflecting the mind of the Secretary General of the Council, said the Fathers only voted on substantial amendments and that amendments of this kind were not to be found in the Preamble. Msgr. Martin then read the text of the first nine articles which were corrected by the Latinists and would be proposed to the Fathers.

Msgr. Martimort, a *peritus*, complained strongly about the numerous corrections made by the Latinists, and he proposed that words and expressions derived from the liturgical texts and from the Fathers should be conserved since they represented traditional use. The Commission accepted Msgr. Martimort's proposal.

The way in which the voting on each of the specific articles should occur was then discussed. The President proposed that votes be taken on each individual article.

The Secretary proposed moving the titles of articles 1-9 to the margins of the text and printing them in small characters. All agreed to the proposal.

The discussion raised by Msgr. Martimort was resumed and concentrated on the expression "*per sacrificium et sacramenta exercerent*" since the term "*sacramentum*" included the concept of "*sacrificium*".

Some changes were made to the texts of articles 7, 8, and 9 following the corrections made by the Latinists. The Secretary regarded the expressions "*sacra exercitia*" in article 9 as inopportune, since Ecclesiastical documents only distinguished between liturgical actions and pious exercises. Jungmann and Wagner, referring to the usage of the German dioceses supported using the phrase "*sacra exercitia*".[32] The text retained the phrase "*sacra exercitia*".

At the end of the meeting Msgr. Grimshaw proposed a new work method, and the meeting concluded with a prayer.[33]

Meeting XII (November 21, 1962)

The Conciliar Commission on Sacred Liturgy met in the *Aula* of the Sacred Congregation of Rites at 5 p.m.. Following the opening prayer and the announcement made by the Secretary, the President Cardinal Larraona invited Msgr. Grimshaw to speak. He was President of the V Sub-commission which was examining articles 10-15 and 32-36 of Chapter 1. Msgr. Grimshaw read a report prepared by the Sub-commission which was then discussed. Article 10, with the modifications proposed by the Sub-commission, was unanimously approved.[34] There ensued a wide and lively debate concerning the phrase in article 11 "*Scientia de Sacra Liturgia in seminariis et facultatibus theologicis inter disciplinas principales est habenda*". The President questioned each of the Fathers and subsequently each of the *periti* on the matter. The point of the discussion is evident from the addition of the adjective "*potiores*" or "*principales*" in the expression "*inter disciplinas necessarias et potiores*". Two Fathers regarded "*necessarias*" as sufficient but others supported the inclusion of "*potiores*" or "*principales*". While the majority of *periti* tended towards "*principales*", there was no unanimity among them. The Secretary observed that the new text spoke of seminaries and theological faculties: these should be distinguished. Consequently, the terminology of the Apostolic Constitution "*Deus scientiarum Dominus*" was adopted, and the new text amended to: "*In Seminariis ... inter disciplinas necessarias et potiores... in facultatibus Theologicis inter disciplinas principales*".

The President submitted both parts of the formula to a secret vote. The first part, concerning the teaching of the liturgy in seminaries received the following vote: 19 *placet*, 4 *non placet*. The second part: 22 *placet* and 1 *non placet*. The Sub-commission proposed the addition of the phrase "*et gentis suae indolem*" to the phrase "*et religiosae culturae gradum*" in article 14. The proposal was voted on by raising hands and defeated by 23 votes to 18.

Msgr. Grimshaw continued reading his report on articles 32 and 33. An addition to article 32 (referring to the churches of Religious) was rejected as it was regarded as out of place. The purpose of this article of the Schema was not to recall the idea of the parish, especially the territorial parish, as a visible expression of the Church and fount of worship of the Christian community.[35]

Meeting XIII (November 23, 1962)

The Conciliar Commission on the Sacred Liturgy met in the *Aula* of the Sacred Congregation of Rites at 5 p.m.. After the prayer, the Secretary made some announcements. Cardinal Lercaro asked the President to increase the number of Commission meetings and to request the President of the Council to dispense the Fathers who were members of the Commissions from attendance at the General Congregations of the Council so as to allow them to finish their work as soon as possible. The President promised to look into the matter but remarked that the sessions of the Commission could not be increased if the Sub-commissions had not finished their work. Moreover, it was difficult to imagine that the President of the Council would dispense all the members of the Commission from attendance at the General Congregations of the Council.

Other questions followed, one regarding the vote to be taken on the first nine articles of Chapter I, and another about the declarations. Concerning the declarations, the III Sub-commission was asked to indicate the most useful among them, and the Secretariat to see to having them printed.

The President then invited the Fathers to express their views with regard to a suitable date on which to suspend the Commission's work (he proposed December 8), and to suggest a date on which the Commission might resume working before the Second Session of the Council.

At the suggestion of Msgr. Jenny, it was proposed that the first chapter be presented to the Council Fathers for their vote and that it should be subsequently promulgated. The President replied that a general vote on the entire chapter could only take place after a vote had been taken on each amendment and on each article. Promulgation was unrealistic.

Msgr. Calewaert, Head of the VI Sub-commission which examined numbers 16-31 of Chapter I, read his report which was then discussed. All approved the new numeration proposed by the Sub-commission. The other amendments were unanimously accepted, with the exception of determining a date for the reform of the liturgical books,[36] which was to happen not only "*inter paucos*" but also "*quam citissime*", and the question of adding bishops to the members of the Commission for the Reform (n. 16). Msgr. Frutaz, *peritus*, strongly criticized a passage in the report which claimed that the recent reforms had been executed outside of the S.R.C.. He said that the Sacred Congregation of Rites, often through its Historical Section, was the Pope's expert means of carrying out a reform, even when extraneous *periti* were aggregated to it. The Secretary observed that the expression "*quam citissime*" was too strong and should be replaced by "*cito*". He also maintained that the inclusion of bishops in a future Commission would create serious difficulties. The new text which spoke of "*quam primum*" (and not "*citissime*") and of "*de consultis Episcopis*" was approved by a show of hands, with 21 Fathers in agreement and 2 against.

The proposal of a liturgical Code was unanimously rejected by the Commission since it would not be necessary once the new liturgical books had been published. The rubrics of the liturgical books would also contain the new legislation.

The meeting concluded with a prayer at 7 p.m..[37]

Meeting XIV (November 24, 1962)

The Conciliar Commission on the Sacred Liturgy met in the *Aula* of the Sacred Congregation of Rites at 5 p.m. with Cardinal Larraona presiding.

Following the prayer, the Secretary read the notices. With regard to voting on the amendments, he proposed distinguishing between formal or stylistic amendments and substantial ones. Only the latter, after approval by the Commission, would be submitted to the Council Fathers. The system was based on that used at the First Vatican Council as related by Msgr. Maccarone.

Msgr. Pichler asked if it would be possible to approve and promulgate Chapter I. The President thought that there might be some hope of having it approved but noted that its promulgation was a matter reserved to the Pope. The Secretary asked that the titles of the articles which were not part of the text be omitted. All agreed to suppress the titles.

Msgr. Calewaert, Head of the VI Sub-commission examining articles 16-31 of Chapter I, resumed reading his report starting with article 20. All approved the amendments proposed by the Sub-commission. To article 25 (27 in the amended text), the Sub-commission proposed adding a paragraph on the celebration of the Word of God, the so-called Biblical vigils.[38] First, Cardinal Jullien made an objection and then the Secretary to the addition of the word "*liturgica*". "*Liturgico*" properly speaking, only refers to the contents of the liturgical books. Everything else is to be regarded as "*pia exercitia*". The Commission agreed that "*liturgica*" should be suppressed and replaced it with the word "*sacra*".

The meeting closed with a prayer.[39]

Meeting XV (November 26, 1962)

The Conciliar Commission on the Sacred Liturgy met in the *Aula* of the Sacred Congregation of Rites at 5 p.m.. Following the prayer, and the announcements made by the Secretary, the President, Cardinal Larraona, invited the Head of the VI Sub-commission, Msgr. Calewaert, to continue reading his report, commencing with article 20 of the Schema.

Articles 20 and 21 provoked a long discussion which came to no practical conclusions. Approval of these two articles was postponed to the following meeting. The discussion was interrupted by the distribution of the drafts of a facsimile of the *Emendationes* to articles 1-9 which would be presented to the Council Fathers for their vote. The Secretary explained the criteria used in selecting the *Emendationes* which were of two kinds: important additions or substantial changes in the text. Msgr. Martin read both amendments and the complete text of both articles, as it stood after the insertion of the *Emendationes*. The Commission approved them unanimously.

The meeting closed with a prayer.[40]

Meeting XVI (November 27, 1962)

The Conciliar Commission on the Sacred Liturgy met in the *Aula* of the Sacred Congregation of Rites at 5 p.m.. The President said the prayer, and the Secretary made his announcements indicating the date for the distribution of all the fascicles together with the "*animadversiones*" of the Council Fathers. The President, Cardinal Larraona, indicated that he would decide on the work schedule of the Commission once the Fathers had expressed their intentions. Msgr. Calewaert, President of the VI Sub-commission examining articles 16-31 of Chapter I, resumed reading his report. Articles 20-22 of the Schema (40-48 of the amended text) were discussed and unanimously approved by the Commission. Article 21 (39) concerning the competence of Episcopal Conferences was the object of particular discussion.[41]

Since the Council had not yet approached the question of the Episcopal Conferences, and to avoid prejudice to any eventual decision, it was considered desirable that the text should be formulated such that it would easily adapt to any subsequent dispositions. Hence, the text speaks of: "*coetus episcopales territoriales competentes...*".

Article 24 concerning the liturgical language was then analyzed. Msgr. Calewaert continued reading his report which was then discussed.

A new draft of this article, prepared by the Sub-commission in four paragraphs, was generally approved by all except by Msgr. Dante who opposed section 2 concerning the introduction of the Mass in the vernacular.[42]

Meeting XVII (November 28, 1962)

The Conciliar Commission on the Sacred Liturgy met in the *Aula* of the Sacred Congregation of Rites at 5 p.m.. After the prayer, the Secretary made some announcements. The President invited Msgr. Calewaert, President of the VI Sub-commission, to read the new text consisting of four paragraphs of article 24 of the Schema on language.[43] Concerning paragraph 1, a discussion on the expression *ritu romano* or *latino* ensued and a decision to adopt the expression *ritibus latinis*, was approved by a show of hands. Slight changes were made to paragraph 2 which was equally approved by a show of hands.[44] On paragraph 3[45] much discussion centred on the expression "*actis ab apostolica sede recognitis*". The President, Cardinal Larraona, proposed the term "*probatis*". Several *periti* commented. In the end, a majority of the Fathers of the Commission favored Cardinal Larraona's proposal. Paragraph 4, as drawn up by the Sub-commission, was not accepted by the Commission. Some suggested its suppression. A new draft was prepared and accepted by all the Fathers.[46]

Finally the Commission unanimously approved the amendments to articles 10-15 which were chosen by the Secretariat of the Commission to be presented to the Council Fathers for their vote.

The meeting ended with a prayer.[47]

Meeting XVIII (November 30, 1962)

The Conciliar Commission on the Sacred Liturgy met in the *Aula* of the Sacred Congregation of Rites at 5 p.m.. Following the prayer and announcements made by the Secretary, the President, Cardinal Larraona, asked the Fathers whether they preferred to return to Rome to resume the work of the Commission before or after Easter. By a slight majority the post-Easter period was preferred.

Msgr. Spülbeck, *peritus*, intervened to note that the term "*probatis*" in paragraph 3 of article 24 of the Schema (concerning language) was not in exact accordance with usage of the CIC (Code of Canon Law). He suggested replacing it with the word "*confirmatis*". The President did not consider it opportune to revisit this subject. Msgr. Grimshaw, Head of the V Sub-commission, was asked to speak. He read a report on articles 34-35 which had been suspended while awaiting the conclusions of the VI Sub-commission on the powers of Episcopal Conferences and on the diocesan and *supra* diocesan liturgical Commissions connected with them. The articles in question, as amended by the Sub-Commission, were unanimously approved by the Commission.[48]

The Secretary presented the amendments to be made to articles 16-31. 11 substantial amendments would have to be voted on by the Council Fathers. The first five were approved by the Commission without reservation. The sixth amendment, on language, (paragraph 3 of article 24 of the Schema) which spoke of "*actis ab Apostolica Sede probatis*" opened a lively discussion. The meaning of "*probatis*" and of "*seu confirmatis*" was clarified, and it was decided to add the more precise term "*seu confirmatis*" to the text. The remaining five amendments were unanimously approved by a show of hands. Finally, the President proposed reading the report that Msgr. Calewaert would give to the Council before the vote on articles 16-31. Father Bugnini was asked to do this. The Commission expressed its complete agreement with the report.

At the end, Msgr. Rossi, *peritus*, asked the President to ascertain from the President and Secretariat of the Council the reason why the Mass in the Council *Aula* which had been sung in polyphony was now sung in Gregorian.

After the prayer the meeting was adjourned.[49]

Meeting XIX (December 3, 1962)

The Conciliar Commission on the Sacred Liturgy met in the *Aula* of the Sacred Congregation of Rites at 5 p.m.. After the prayer, the Secretary announced that a work-plan for the Sub-commission during the suspension of the Council had been prepared and distributed.

The amendments to articles 32-36 of the Schema were presented. These would be voted on by the Council. The Commission unanimously approved the choice of emendations. Msgr. Grimshaw, President of the I Sub-commission, read a report on articles 32-36 of the Schema, which would be read and distributed to the Conciliar Fathers. The Commission unreservedly approved the report.

The President proposed discussion of the order of business to be followed during the suspension of the Council. The Secretary read the *Regolamento* governing the work of the Sub-commission which was unanimously approved.

With regards to the date which the Commission would resume, Cardinal Larraona asked the opinion of the Fathers. The majority favored resuming after Easter. The period between April 22 and May 4, 1963 was chosen with the hope of having all business completed in two weeks. The Secretary asked the Sub-commission to accelerate their work and to forward their reports by the beginning of March so that they could be reproduced and circulated.

Finally, Cardinal Larraona invited Msgr. Enciso to speak. He acted as President of the VII Sub-commission which was examining Chapter II of the Schema dealing with the Eucharist. A discussion followed his reading of a report on the general observations made with regard to Chapter II. Some problems concerning the competence of the Commission were clarified.

The meeting ended with a prayer.[50]

Meeting XX (December 4, 1962)

The Conciliar Commission on the Sacred Liturgy met in the *Aula* of the Sacred Congregation of Rites at 5 p.m.. The absence of some of the Fathers and *periti* was noted.

After the prayer, the Secretary announced the distribution of a volume containing the comments of the Conciliar Fathers on Chapter IV (in total 205 pages). The fascicles on the other chapters together with an appendix containing comments which had arrived late to the Secretariat, would be ready for the meeting on January 7. A general index would be forwarded through the mail before Christmas.

Msgr. Dante asked to speak on a point raised in Msgr. Calewaert's report which was to be read to the Council on the following day. It concerned the explanation contained in the report of the words "*probatis seu confirmatis*" (article 36, paragraph 3 of the amended text). He preferred that the expression "*confirmatis*" be suppressed since it rendered redundant any act of superior authority. Cardinal Larraona accepted that the explanation given in the report was not completely accurate, but a change in the text at this point was impossible as the report had already been printed. He did not agree with Msgr. Dante about the word "*confirmatis*". He said that it was perfectly acceptable since it referred to an imperfect act posited by an inferior authority which had to be confirmed by a higher authority in order for it to be perfected. Several *periti* continued the discussion. It was decided to retain the text as printed. Msgr. Rau, *peritus*, speaking on behalf of a number of bishops, lamented the fact that other amendments, including grammatical ones, would not be placed before the Conciliar Fathers.

The President replied that a general vote could subsequently be taken on all the minor amendments. The Secretary intervened to say that it would have been impossible to submit all the amendments to the Conciliar Fathers' vote. The Commission had agreed unanimously to the criteria used in selecting the amendments. These had been perfectly acceptable to the Secretariat of the Council.

The President announced that he would assume the Presidency of the Sub-commission on the Divine Office, since Cardinal Albareda had asked to be relieved.

Msgr. Enciso, President of the III Sub-commission examining Chapter II, resumed reading his report on the general observations and on the Preamble to Chapter II. When he finished, the Commission briefly discussed its ability to treat of some of the amendments proposed by the Fathers. The text of the Preamble as amended by the Sub-commission was then examined. Generally, the amendments were unanimously accepted by the Commission.

The President, Cardinal Larraona, indicated his desire to offer a reception to the Fathers and *periti* of the Commission. He settled the invitation for the afternoon of December 6 and called a meeting for that date.[51]

Meeting XXI (April 23, 1963)

The Conciliar Commission on the Sacred Liturgy met in the *Aula* of the Sacred Congregation of Rites at 5 p.m.. The President said the *Adsumus* and greeted the Fathers and the *periti*. He referred to those absent: Cardinal Lercaro, Msgr. Malula, Msgr. Grimshaw, Msgr. van Bekum, Msgr. Ramos, and Fr. Schweiger. The Secretary, Father Antonelli, then spoke. He saluted the Fathers and the *periti* and wished them well in their work. He then presented a brief report on the work of the Secretariat and the actual state of the remaining chapters of the liturgical Schema.

On January 18, 1963 the Secretariat dispatched copies of the fascicle together with the final *animadversiones* on the Schema to all the Fathers and *periti* of the Commission. A souvenir photograph of the Commission had also been sent with the fascicle. On March 26 – 27, Presidents and Secretaries of all the Sub-commissions were reminded to send on their reports as quickly as possible. The report on Chapter III arrived on March 13; Chapter IV came on March 30; the reports on Chapters II and III, and the reports completed by the theological and juridical Commissions reached the Secretariat on April 8; the report on Chapter VI arrived on April 10, and Chapter VIII reached the Secretariat on April 16.

The report on Chapter V (*De anno Liturgico*) was still awaited but would be ready in a few days. Five fascicles were distributed to the members of the Commission containing respectively: an appendix to the *animadversiones* of the Fathers and the *placet iuxta modum* expressed in relation to Chapter I; the report and revised text of Chapter II (Sub-commission VII); report and revised text of Chapter III (Sub-commission VIII); report and revised text of Chapter IV (Sub-commission IX).

The Secretary announced that the next meetings of the Commission would take place in the *Aula* of the Hospice of Santa Marta in the Vatican at 9:30 in the morning. The President then set the next meeting for that time and at that place. The discussion on Chapter II, *De sanctissimo Eucharistiae mysterio*, would then resume.

The President then mentioned two of the problems: the possibility of reducing the liturgical Schema to four or five chapters so as to harmonize it with the other Schemata; and the treatment of questions which did not directly fall under the competence of the Commission but which could arise during the various discussions. In relation to the first question, a Sub-commission would eventually be nominated; in relation to the other an effort would be made to come to a working arrangement with the respective Commissions.

Following the announcement that a Sub-commission would be formed to examine the *placet iuxta modum* on Chapter I, a discussion opened. It was, however, still born. Msgr. Enciso briefly referred to the work of the Sub-commission on Chapter II. The Secretary proposed that the reports to be read in the Council *Aula* and the revised texts, together with any amendments to be voted on, should be ready before the end of the present session. In September it would then be possible to submit material for the Council's vote. It was therefore important that the reports should be very accurate so as to avoid as much as possible votes cast *placet iuxta modum*

The meeting concluded with a prayer.[52]

Meeting XXII (April 24, 1963)

The Commission met at 9:30 a.m. in the *Aula* of the Hospice of Santa Marta in the Vatican. The Fathers who had been absent the previous day were also not present at this meeting. After the prayer, the President asked Msgr. Enciso, President of the VII Sub-commission for the examination of Chapter II, to speak. He began by reading the reports (see p. 6) on the observations made in regard to article 37 of the Schema (article 50 according to the new numeration).

Discussion centred on acceptance of the suppression of the phrase "*sive in generali dispositione sive in singulis partibus*". While Msgr. Dante was against it, Father Jungmann was favorable. Others, such as Msgr. Wagner and Father Dirks, proposed making the text more clear. Msgr. Nabuco's proposal of speaking of various types of Masses was not accepted. The President sent the question back to the Sub-commission for further study. Msgr. Jenny spoke and referred the meeting back to the *Declarationes* on the Schema. The discussions resumed, and it was judged helpful not to get into too much detail, and to include matter needing clarification in the reports to be read in the Council *Aula*. The Secretary observed that it would be more expeditious were the text of the report to be read initially and the text of each of the amended articles subsequently.

The President proposed a discussion of the amended text of article 47 of the Preamble. After a short discussion, Msgr. Martimort lamented the suppression of the word "*fontem*". Msgr. Enciso explained that this was done because of the acceptance of a phrase of St. Augustine which did not contain that word. It was decided to postpone a definitive approval of the text prepared by the Sub-commission until the following day.

Article 48 of the Preamble was then examined. The insertion of the phrase "*muti spectatores*", as in the original Schema[53], was proposed. Cardinal Jullien asked that the word "*actuose*" be inserted after the adjectives "*conscie, pie*" Msgr. Fey commented on the complicated style of the phrase and suggested splitting it into two parts.

Three modifications were made to article 49 of the Preamble by the Sub-commission. The first two were accepted, and the third was suppressed. This had read: "*ceterarum Missae formarum curam remittentes ad generalem rubricarum recognitionem*".

Article 50 (previously 37) revised by the Commission was not acceptable to Cardinal Jullien. The President recommended that the Sub-commission prepare a new text taking into account the following points: maintain the substance, greater clarity in the rite, and omission of duplication or what appeared difficult.[54]

In article 51 (previously 38) Jungmann proposed substituting "*plurium annorum*" with "*aliquot annorum*". Father Dirks suggested suppressing the word "*ditior*"[55]. This implied the suppression of the phrase "*mensa eucharistica*", which was accepted, notwithstanding Msgr. Martimort's reservations.

Mention of the obligation to preach[56], as in article 52 (previously 39) seemed superfluous to Cardinal Jullien who noted that it was already in the Code. Hence, it sufficed to say "*ad normam*". Msgr. Bonet noted that the Code would have to be adapted to the Council and not vice-versa. The President proposed adding the expression *"sacrae vel doctrinae expositio"* to the homily so as to be able to give a complete course in Christian doctrine. This caused a heated debate. Fathers Enciso, Pichler, and Jenny, and the *periti* Gagnebet and Vagaggini intervened. The President insisted that the homily could not lack doctrine. The Secretary proposed the expression: *"Homilia in qua tota oeconomia salutis exponetur"*. The President asked the Sub-commission to prepare a new text.

Article 53 (previously 40) appeared superfluous to Cardinal Jullien who noted that diverse intentions were already included in the prayers of the Mass.[57] The Commission did not accept this observation. Msgr. Spülbeck proposed adding the intention *"pro salute mundi"*. The Commission agreed.

Article 54 (previously 41) on language was discussed.[58] Msgr. Enciso defended the addition: *"Provideatur tamen ut fideles... "*. Msgr. Martimort lamented that nothing about the use of the vernacular had been clarified. He suggested an insertion at article 36 of the Schema. The discussion was interrupted and postponed to the following day.[59]

Meeting XXIII (April 25, 1963)

The Conciliar Commission on the Sacred Liturgy met in the *Aula* of the Hospice of Santa Marta in the Vatican at 9:30 a.m.. The Fathers absent at the previous meeting did not attend. Following the prayer, the President asked the Secretary to speak. He recommended brevity in the discussions so as to ensure that the business of the Commission might be completed by May 10 as everybody desired.

Msgr. Enciso of the Sub-commission on Chapter II resumed reading his report. He explained the reason for the addition of article 54, previously 41, which recommends that the faithful learn to "say or sing" in Latin the easier parts of the Mass.

The President, Cardinal Larraona, asked about the distinction between a sung Mass and a said Mass. A discussion ensued during which Msgr. Wagner and Msgr. Martimort vigorously insisted that the vernacular not be excluded from use at sung Masses. They objected to the distinction between the Solemn Mass *"in cantu"* and the Solemn Mass merely sung by the clergy. Appeal was made to the concession made by the Holy Office on the proclamation of the readings in which a distinction is drawn between a *Missa Cantata* and a Solemn Mass. The *peritus* Msgr. Anglés said that no distinction could be made on the basis of Mass being sung.

The President asked the Sub-commission to prepare a new text. Msgr. Jenny preferred changing the article. Msgr. Fey asked that the door not be closed to further concessions and to bear in mind the difficulties experienced throughout Latin America. Msgr. Dante lamented the hostility to Latin and proposed that the precise use of the vernacular and Latin in the Mass be clarified. Msgr. Enciso said that he would be prepared to examine any written proposals, so the Sub-commission was asked to prepare a new text.

Msgr. Enciso read a report on Article 55 (previously 42) on Communion under both species.[60] The President asked if it might not be opportune to foresee the case of Matrimony. Msgr. Enciso replied affirmatively because there was no intention to exclude the laity. However, on the other hand, Msgr. Zauner maintained that it was most useful to specify the cases in which Communion might be received under both species because the Fathers did not believe it desirable to have a wide extension of Holy Communion under both species. Msgr. Martimort proposed suppressing the instance of marriage and to replace it with the Baptism of adults. Msgr. Dante asked for the suppression of the entire article for reasons of hygiene. Drinking from the same vessel offended common sense and other solutions were unsatisfactory.

Msgr. Pichler stated that Holy Communion under both species would not present difficulties once the laity had been educated in it. The use of the 'spatula' was easy and hygienic. In the article, however, it should be left to the Holy See to determine the instances on which Holy Communion under both species might be permitted. The application of the concession should be left to the judgment of the bishops. Otherwise, a two thirds majority would never be attained. The discussion continued without arriving at anything new. The President referred the matter to the Sub-commission which was asked to mention specific instances when presenting the revised text.

Two objections were made to article 56 (previously 43).[61] The President was not happy about the suppression of the adverb "..." [not in original text]. He therefore proposed that the text be revised. The Secretary was unhappy with the addition of "*Praesertim quando ex praecepto...*" which presupposed a dangerous distinction between the two types of Masses.

Msgr. Rossi replied to the Secretary, and Msgr. Enciso, who had added it, and emphasized that he wished it inserted for pastoral reasons. It was directed against those moralists who retained that the faithful were only obliged to attend the second part of Mass. Msgr. Wagner thought the phrase too benign and demanded a stronger formulation.

Msgr. Enciso resumed reading article 57 (previously 44) on concelebration.[62] During the discussion, Abbot Prou asked that the occasion of an Abbatial Blessing be included among the list of occasions upon which the concession might be made while Father Dirks asked that the unity of the priesthood be included among the reasons recommending concelebration. Msgr. Martimort read out a documented peroration in favor of the inclusion of the *Coena Domini* Mass among the occasions on which concelebration might be permitted. The proposal was greeted by applause. The Secretary, Father Antonelli, informed the Commission that the proposal to allow concelebration at *Coena Domini* Mass was rejected during the Reform of Holy Week, however, Msgr. Jenny proposed including also the Easter Vigil. Cardinal Jullien did not like the limitation *"eodem tempore in eodem ecclesia"* for the *"Missa privata"*. Msgr. Martimort stated that the purpose of the limitation was to avoid confusion in the same church.

The President, Cardinal Larraona, wished to extend concelebration to those participating at an ordination. Father Jungmann proposed prefacing the article with the phrase *"Episcopi indicio"*. The President maintained that it would create a problem. Msgr. Enciso was of the opinion that the bishop's judgment should also be sought in the case of churches of Religious so as to avoid losing the faithful from parish churches.

Msgr. Martimort said that concelebration happened frequently in the East without the presence of the bishop. Abbot Prou asked that the *"Ordinario loci"* be replaced by the term *"Ordinario"*. Msgr. Enciso had no difficulty in accepting the proposal with regard to monasteries but not for Religious because of eventual abuses. Abbot D'Amato responded that in the event of abuses the Ordinary would intervene. Father Dirks, a *peritus*, could not understand why abuses would arise in the churches of Religious. Msgr. Jenny made the observation that the faithful attended the churches of Religious in large numbers. Father Dirks objected: if the faithful can attend Solemn Mass in the churches of Religious, why can they not attend concelebrated Masses in the same churches? Article 58 (previously 46) on the rite of concelebration did not merit discussion.[63]

Various questions were then posed by the President: could the domenical precept be anticipated on Saturday? Could a priest binate after concelebration? Msgr. Martimort expressed his reservations on this final point.

The meeting closed at 12:30 p.m..[64]

Meeting XXIV (April 26, 1963)

The Conciliar Commission on the Sacred Liturgy met in the *Aula* of the Hospice of Santa Marta in the Vatican at 9:30 a.m. The Fathers who had not been present at the previous meetings were absent. Cardinal Larraona said the prayer, and the Secretary made some announcements.

Msgr. Paul Hallinan, President of the Sub-commission examining Chapter III, began his report. A discussion centred on its Preamble containing three paragraphs. In the first paragraph, Father Dirks asked for greater clarification of the idea of the unity of the Church, and proposed *"aedificationem corporis"*. Msgr. Wagner thought it would be better to place the sanctification of the Church first, and subsequently the sign of her unity.[65]

Discussion on paragraph two amounted merely to explanations and clarifications. Abbot D'Amato did not like paragraph three, and Msgr. Enciso shared his opinion. The phrase *"quibus eorum natura et finis minus eluceant"* was too severe a judgment on the present rite.[66]

A long discussion ensued on article 47 of the Schema concerning the vernacular. Msgr. Fey did not like the limitation "*praeterquam in forma sacramentorum*" as the principle did not apply to marriage and also because it was the form which made the sign intelligible. Thus, he asked that the door not be closed on further developments.

The President observed that it was necessary to ensure obtaining a two thirds majority. Msgr. Stickler observed that the vernacular could not be extended to the whole rite and said that a majority might be obtained by adding the clause "*salva auctoritate territoriali*".

Msgr. Martimort did not believe that it was right to distinguish between sacramental form and the rite in its entirety. On the other hand, the extent of the use of the vernacular would have to be clarified, since it is promised in article 36 of Chapter I. A text would have to be made which took into account the various celebrations since the sacramental form varies according to the different sacraments: Penance, for example, takes place in two moments; the same for the Anointing of the Sick, etc.. Msgr. Enciso proposed omitting reference to the form altogether by simply saying "*praesertim cum dialogo*".

Msgr. Wagner said that the distinction between *Pontificale* and *Rituale* had to be retained. In the *Pontificale* the limitation of Latin to the sacramental form could be conserved, but it would practically be reduced to ordination, while in the *Rituale* the vernacular could be proposed.

However, Msgr. Enciso was interested to see the use of the vernacular also for the Sacrament of Orders. Father Vagaggini also remarked that the consecration of a church was contained in the *Pontificale* and that it would not be advantageous to compile all of the *Pontificale* in Latin.

The Secretary, Father Antonelli, proposed to explicitly permit the use of the vernacular for all the Sacraments except Orders, if all were in agreement that the ordination be in Latin. Msgr. Wagner agreed with the proposal, provided that the distinction between the *Pontificale* and the *Rituale* be made in accordance with the formula proposed by Msgr. Martimort.

After a short break, the discussion was resumed, and the President of the Sub-commission, Msgr. Hallinan, requested that proposals be made in writing to the Sub-commission. The discussion moved to paragraph two on the new *Rituale*.[67] Msgr. Wagner said that it should be called "*Praeter nova*" instead of "*super nova*". Father Antonelli proposed: "*iuxta nova*". Father Vagaggini observed that the article only referred to a new *editio typica* of the *Rituale*. Jungmann proposed that the new Ritual should have two sections: one valid for all and the other for the particular churches. The President feared that such restrictions might impede future developments.

Article 48 met with several difficulties[68], as did article 49.[69] Msgr. Malula wanted to add the phrase "*de iudicio Ordinarii*" to the latter, but it was noted that this was a matter for the Commission on adaptations for Missionary countries, as indicated in Chapter I of the Schema.

Abbot D'Amato, referring to article 50[70], did not easily envisage Mass for Baptism. The Missal has its proper Mass with Baptism which is that of Easter, while on the other hand it was already referred to in Mass at the *Hanc igitur.*

Article 51 was easily approved.[71] Msgr. Fey thought the phrase "*infantis rationis nondum compatis aptetur*" seemed ridiculous. The Secretary proposed: "*Ratione habita infantis rationis nondum compatis*".

Article 52 was approved without comment.[72]

The second half of article 53 attracted the attention of the *periti* and of the Fathers.[73] Father Dirks proposed specifying the significance of the new rite for converts by adding the phrase "*in Ecclesiam recipiendi*". The President proposed "*in communione cum Ecclesia*". Abbot D'Amato disliked speaking of a new rite, but Father Dirks said that a new rite was desired in America. Father Gagnebet called attention to the theological difficulties. Father Vagaggini presented a new formulation: "*ritus ex novo... qui possit significare, ecc.*". The Commission accepted the proposal.

Article 54 was devoted to the blessing of baptismal water during the rite itself and outside of Easter time.[74] In a response to a desire of the President to have a blessing before Baptism, Msgr. Martimort said that the object of the article was not to abbreviate or hasten the rite but to allow for the possibility of an authentic catechesis on Baptism. Msgr. Wagner expressed his reservations about the word "*praesertim*" which had been inserted by the Sub-commission. He was not inclined to permit the blessing during Easter time for other times, because then no one would use the water blessed during the Vigil. Msgr. Martimort agreed with Wagner's proposal, and in replying to an objection of Msgr. Bonet, who saw a risk with regards to the baptismal fonts, he suggested that the inconvenience could be overcome by blessing the water in the font.

The President recommended that different circumstances would have to be taken into account, especially in Latin America. Itinerant priests could not be expected to carry water blessed at the Easter Vigil with them all the time.

The meeting ended at 12:30 p.m..[75]

Meeting XXV (April 27, 1963)

The Conciliar Commission on the Sacred Liturgy met in the *Aula* of the Hospice of Santa Marta in the Vatican at 9:30 a.m.. The absence of the Fathers who had not attended the previous meetings was noted.

After the prayer, discussion on article 54, and specifically on the word "*praesertim*", resumed. Msgr. Jenny wished to have it suppressed so as better to underline the relationship between Baptism and the Easter Vigil. The Commission agreed to the proposal.

Article 55 spoke of confirmation.[76] Msgr. Dante opposed the administration of Confirmation during Mass and challenged the reasons given for it in the Sub-commissions report. From the ensuing discussion two points emerged: There were no historical reasons for administering Confirmation *infra Missam*. However, pastoral reasons and a certain liturgical tendency to bring all the sacraments and sacramentals *infra Missam* recommended the proposal. Father Dirks remarked on the somewhat ambiguous formulation of the text, and Fathers Jenny and D'Amato also agreed. Fathers Rau, Malula, and the President returned to the question of Confirmation during Mass and raised several difficulties. It was decided that the text should be more clear and that the details of the rite be remitted to the Post Conciliar Commission.

Article 56 on Penance was approved without discussion.[77]

Article 57 on Extreme Unction was rather different.[78] Gagnebet raised a strong theological objection: here it gave the impression of wanting to change the common teaching. It was proposed that the word "*saltem*" be omitted and "*certe administrari potest in periculo mortis*" be added. It was considered good to specify that the anointing was to be administered to those who were gravely ill. Msgr. Jenny observed that all the prayers of the rite spoke of the healing of the sick person. Father Vagaggini explained that the idea of the Sub-commission had not been to resolve the disputed question, rather, it had been an attempt to avoid confirming the current opinion which reserved the sacrament to the dying. Msgr. Gagnebet replied that the connection between the sacrament and death could not be overlooked. Father Jungmann explained the history of the name "Extreme Unction". Msgr. McManus, a *peritus*, observed that the reasons for changing the name of the sacrament were valid in all countries. Msgr. Martimort took it that the article had been accepted by the Fathers, as only one had spoken against it. The President replied that such was a dangerous form of reasoning. Two-thousand Fathers had not yet spoken. At the end, the President asked the Sub-commission to examine the individual proposals.

Article 58 spoke of the time for the administration of the Anointing of the Sick[79], i.e. after Penance and before *Viaticum*. Msgr. Martimort explained that the object of the article was that of conveying the idea that the anointing was complementary to Penance. This usage was very ancient and it had been revived in various rituals.

The President mentioned that many died without *Viaticum* because they were opposed to Extreme Unction. Father Jungmann replied that the change of name had been suggested to counter this objection. Msgr. Wagner recognised that the difficulty raised by the President was real, and thus account would have to be taken of the possibility in some cases of administering the Anointing after *Viaticum* – as was the case in Germany. In placing it immediately before the *Viaticum*, as experience demonstrated, it was to be hoped that the change would be well received. Father Prou wished to have "*Eucharistiae*" substituted for "*Viatici*". The

President assigned the Sub-commission the task of revising the text.

Article 59 on the rite of Anointing remained unchanged[80] and was approved without difficulty. Article 60, on the recommendation of the Sub-commission, was omitted by general agreement of the Commission. The article had raised the possibility of allowing a priest to bless the oil, at least in certain circumstances. The President observed that it was a matter to be referred to the competence of the Post-Conciliar Commission. Msgr. Wagner proposed that it should be mentioned in the report to be presented to the Council.

On article 61, concerning Orders[81], Msgr. Jenny proposed that Ordinaries should be granted the faculty to give the allocutions in the vernacular. Msgr. Stickler regarded as suspect the addition approved by the Sub-commission, which spoke of the imposition of hands by all bishops present at an episcopal ordination. Msgr. Martimort defended this addition which reflected the history of the rite and was paralleled in priestly ordination. The President regarded the phrase as too strong and proposed attenuating the obligation.

Msgr. Wagner feared the reaction of the Council and suggested that the question should be mentioned only in the report and remitted to the Post-Conciliar Commission. The President did not foresee any need for anxiety, provided the Commission was unanimous.

Msgr. Bonet noted that the expression "*lingua fidelibus nota*" departed from the terminology of the Schema which said "*lingua vernacula*". If this were intended to mean the vernacular, as understood by the Commission, then it would be better to add the phrase "*the language in which the homily is given*".

Article 62 dealt with Matrimony.[82] The President proposed the use of the phrase "*funditus recognoscatur*". The question of mixed marriages seemed very delicate. Msgr. Bonet exhorted all to recall the text already prepared by the Commission on the Discipline of the Sacraments, while Cardinal Giobbe proposed suppressing the addition. Msgr. Martimort accepted Cardinal Giobbe's proposal.

Article 63 concerned the celebration of marriage.[83] Father Jungmann was not favorable to the phrase which proposed changing the text for the blessing of the spouses. It was important to explain the meaning and value of this prayer which should be conserved in its entirety. Abbot D'Amato agreed with Father Jungmann. Father Vagaggini, while against changing the formula, wondered if the spirit of the formula had not changed today, and in this case if it should insist only on the woman's fidelity. Cardinal Giobbe wished to know at what point during the Mass would Matrimony be administered and proposed "*after the Gospel*".

After the prayer, the meeting ended at 12.30 p.m..[84]

Meeting XXVI (April 29, 1963)

The Conciliar Commission on the Sacred Liturgy met in the *Aula* of the Hospice of Santa Marta in the Vatican at 9:30 a.m. with Cardinal Larraona presiding. The

Fathers already mentioned were absent. A new *peritus*, Msgr. Borella, was present. The prayer was said, and the Secretary made his announcements.

Msgr. Hallinan, President of the Sub-commission examining Chapter III, resumed reading his report. The discussion recommenced on article 64, concerning the revision of the sacramentals.[85] Msgr. Grimshaw requested dropping the word "*funditus*", and the President agreed.

With regard to an additional paragraph on the sacramentals which can be administered by the laity, Msgr. Enciso asked which sacramentals these might be. Father Vagaggini replied: for example, funerals. Msgr. Jenny suggested hearing the theologians on the question, and Msgr. Gagnebet replied that the matter did not fall within the power of orders. The President proposed that the text should speak of "*laicis qualificatis*", and the proposal was accepted. A discussion followed on the need for further clarification, e.g. the blessing of children by parents, and the blessing of superioresses for their subjects. It was decided to remit questions of detail to the post-Conciliar Commission.

Cardinal Jullien observed that the Code only mentions "*clerics*". Extending power to the laity would involve a change in the meaning of a sacramental. Msgr. Enciso replied that administration is something external which does not affect nature; Msgr. Martimort explained that the Code depended on medieval usage; Father Jungmann pointed out that in antiquity catechists could lay on hands, etc.. The President requested the Sub-commission to revise the text.

With regard to article 65, on religious professions,[86] the President observed that the present context referred to religious profession as a liturgical act, properly speaking. There were, of course, other uses worthy of respect. He proposed attenuating the obligations of making religious profession during Mass. Msgr. Martimort suggested that an amendment proposed by a Father in the *Aula* be accepted which urged that "*infra*" be changed to "*inter*". With regard to profession he had noted that many of the Fathers had requested a common rite. After a brief discussion, the President asked the Sub-commission to prepare a new text.

With regard to article 66, a very short discussion centred on the liturgical color.[87] While the President recognized that many had sought a change in the liturgical color, he retained that this was a matter for the Episcopal Conferences. Msgr. Martimort said that the question of the liturgical color did not fall into the general principles with which the Council was concerned, and with the approval of this article, the discussion on Chapter III closed.

The Commission moved to consider Chapter IV on the Divine Office. The President of Sub-commission VIII, Msgr. Martin, read the report on the Preamble and the discussion opened.[88]

Father Vagaggini deplored the suppression of the text of *Mediator Dei* which provided the theological basis for the entire Divine Office. The amended text was inadequate, and thus he suggested reviving the suppressed text. Msgr. Gagnebet, in the name of the theological Sub-commission, agreed with Father Vagaggini's proposal. The President also agreed that the suppressed text should be revived. All were in agreement that the text from St. Paul should be suppressed as well as the proposal for extension of prayer in the name of the Church (n. 2 Preamble).[89] Father Vagaggini underlined the importance of the deputation of the prayer of the Church which should not be understood in a merely juridic sense. This would be true also of the Oriental priests who, while not obliged, pray the Office with the faithful.

Msgr. Wagner emphasized the importance of the local Church assembled for prayer which in itself does not need deputation. Father Vagaggini noted the danger of considering pious exercises as official prayers.

In article 3 of the Preamble[90], Abbot Salmon objected to the phrase "*obligationem expleret*" because of its juridical overtone, and it merely referred to the external element of prayer (obligation) rather than to its nature.

Article 4 of the Preamble encountered difficulty.[91] On article 5 there was no agreement on the meaning and extent of the expression "*Officio romano*".[92] Msgr. Borella indicated that it could also include the Ambrosian rite, and Abbot Prou observed that it could not validly apply to the Benedictines. Msgr. Bonet held that it was necessary to retain the phrase in a general sense, otherwise all those who did not follow the Roman calendar would be excluded; in the individual articles changes to the Monastic Office should be avoided. Father Vagaggini had no difficulty with the text, and when the Roman Office would be approved, the Monastic Offices could be adjusted accordingly. The President proposed the title "*Breviario Romano*" and proposed inserting a clause in his report to the Council to the effect that not all of the proposed reforms to the Roman Breviary would be suitable for the Monastic Breviary. The Commission accepted the proposal.

The Commission then heard a report on article 68 (88 in the amended text) on the course of the hours[93], following which the discussion opened. Abbot Salmon read a long intervention on the hours for the Office. He spoke of three grades of Office: the Monastic, which was the ideal; the choral Office of the religious; and that recited privately. In the last case, he who prays the Office in private, in some sense participates in a common recital of the Office, since his prayer is a participation in the prayer of the Church. Substantially, he accepted the text of article 68.

Father Dirks proposed an alteration to the phrase: "*Horis veritas reddatur*" to read "*ut in horis persolvendis... veritas servari possit*", since the truth of the hours already exists. He also proposed dropping the word "*naturalis*". All were in agreement.

Msgr. Jenny recommended that the unity of the hours should be maintained and not broken when considering the reduction of the Office for those in pastoral activity. Msgr. Martimort was not of the same opinion. He believed that it was absolutely necessary to have two Breviaries. For him it was not a question of simply abbreviating the Breviary but rather of a true reform. Abbot D'Amato did not wish to have alterations to the Office and proposed referring the question to the Sacred Congregation of Rites.

Msgr. Wagner expressed desire that any reduction of the Breviary should not impede its being sung by those with choir obligations. Cardinal Jullien asked that chapters also be taken into consideration. The President agreed and added that account should be made of religious with or without ministry, and he recommended these various distinctions in order not to impose the same thing on all.

Father Vagaggini distinguished between the structure of the Office and the distribution of the Psalms; he recommended preserving its structure. Msgr. Bonet recommended the idea of the unity of the Church's prayer. The President also agreed with the proposal of having a single Office, albeit with some necessary adaptations. Msgr. Enciso insisted that the needs of those engaged in the pastoral ministry could not be accepted as normative.

On the other hand, Msgr. Rau asked if structure meant the actual distribution of the Psalms, readings, hymns, prayers, etc.. In this case, he regarded it as necessary to provide a different structure for those with the care of souls because some do not have sufficient time to say all of the Office. After a short discussion on the meaning of the term "*structure*", Msgr. Martimort proposed its suppression. The discussion closed because of the late hour, and after the prayer the meeting was adjourned. The President reminded the Commission that two meetings (morning and evening) would be held on the following day since May 1 was a holiday.[94]

Meeting XXVII (April 30, 1963)

The Commission met in the *Aula* of the Hospice of Santa Marta in the Vatican at 9:30 a.m.. Cardinal Larraona presided and read the prayer. The Secretary made some announcements, and he said that the *schede* [ballots] (*placet, non placet, placet iuxta modum*) for the vote on Chapter II would be distributed.

Msgr. Martin, President of the Sub-commission on the Divine Office, resumed reading his report which was followed by a discussion.

Article 8 of the report (68a of the Schema) concerning Lauds and Vespers was examined.[95] Msgr. Jenny wanted to underline the relationship between the Mass and the Office. Msgr. Martimort indicated that it had already been done in the Preamble. Msgr. Jenny was insistent, and the President recommended that the discussion avoid entering into details. Father Stickler asked the *periti* if there really was a connection between the Mass and Lauds. Father Jungmann replied saying the connection depended on the celebration of the one Christological mystery. On a historical level there was no connection, since Lauds were independent of the Mass. Father Vagaggini noted that in ancient times the connection was only made on the great feasts but not on the other days. Msgr. Martimort insisted on the relationship. As far as the texts were concerned it was doctrinal in character, and recently confusion had been created. Msgr. Jenny said that he did not intend a canonico-liturgical connection. All he intended was that the spiritual connection between the Mass and the Office be emphasized.

In his analysis of the text, Father Dirks proposed ending it with the word "*servandae*", thereby dropping "*utique celebrandae*". Msgr. Bonet regarded the term "*servandae*" as ambiguous and that it should be removed. The Secretary remarked that the purpose of the article was to highlight the two canonical hours. Msgr. Martimort proposed "*omnino servandae*". Msgr. Wagner proposed suppressing "*ubique*" and substituting "*praecipue*". The President intervened and summed up the two points which had emerged: i.e. to "*conserve*" and to "*celebrate*" Lauds and Vespers. The Sub-commission was asked to make the text more clear.

Consideration of the same article in the middle resumed. Compline encountered no difficulties.[96] With regard to Matins, Msgr. Salmon signalled that tradition gave more importance to the readings than to the Psalms, and Father Jungmann added that before the 11th century the readings had a spiritual character.

Cardinal Jullien saw a contradiction between this article and article 4. The latter says to pray without ceasing while in this case we are reducing the prayers (the readings are not prayers).[97] Father Vagaggini was asked to improve the initial phrase of the article. Msgr. Martimort proposed correcting the term "*Matins*". Msgr. Martin, President of the Sub-commission, replied that this question would be referred to the post-Conciliar Commission for clarification.

Abbot D'Amato was unhappy with the proposed suppression of Prime. Msgr. Martimort replied that from its inception, Prime had been a duplication of Lauds and that it was difficult to find a distinct hour for its recital. The President desired that at least some vestige of this canonical hour be retained.

With regard to the minor hours (68d of the Schema, amended to 88e)[98], the Sub-commission proposed the recital from memory of the same Psalm and their concentration into one hour when opportune. Abbot Salmon opposed this solution which ran contrary to the tradition and was an inadequate solution to practical difficulties. He preferred retaining all three hours, obliging the priest to one of them when he was busy. The choice could be made in accordance with the circumstances of the moment. The President pointed out that the Commission was not asked to suppress or impose anything as a general norm, and an apt formulation had to be chosen. Msgr. Enciso was not pleased with the text proposed by the Sub-commission: those who were busy could be dispensed, and for the others, the full obligation should remain and the same Psalm should not always be read. The President repeated the principle that a reduction should not be imposed on anyone who did not want it. Msgr. Martimort, replying to Msgr. Enciso, noted that the monks always recite the same Psalms and the rest was as it had been prior to St. Pius X.

The discussion continued between the Fathers and the *periti*, and the articles of the text proposed by the Sub-commission were approved as they went along. Finally, the Secretary proposed retaining the hours as they were but making only one of them mandatory for those not obliged to choir. In this way, it would be easy to attain the approval of the Council. Msgr. Bonet did not wish to introduce the idea of obligation in this context. The President asked the Sub-commission to propose a new text.[99]

Abbot Salmon spoke at length on Article 69 of the Schema (91 of the amended text) concerning the Psalms.[100] He defended the use of the entire Psalter, including the imprecatory Psalms, and he opposed the criteria proposed for the revision of the text because they would lend themselves to the choice of a monoretic text. Msgr. Enciso hoped that the original text of the Psalter might be emphasized. Father Jungmann held the view that historically, while the entire text of the Psalter was used, criteria had been employed to select texts. Msgr. Martimort indicated that the criteria for the selection of texts had not intended the exclusion of any texts. Msgr. Anglés suggested that Gregorian chant be taken as one of the criteria for the revision. At this point, there ensued a long discussion against the new version of the Psalter published by the Biblical Institute.

Article 71 was approved without much discussion.[101] Msgr. Bonet expressed his perplexity regarding the suppressions and feared that the Fathers would vote against it in the Council *Aula*. Msgr. Martin assured him that the report would deal with this problem. Father Jungmann suggested that the Spiritual Fathers should also be taken into consideration in the lessons of the Office.

All agreed to the suppression of article 72.[102]

The meeting ended at 12:30 p.m., and the Commission would meet again at 5 p.m..[103]

Meeting XXVIII (April 30, 1963)

The Conciliar Commission on the Sacred Liturgy met at 5 p.m. in the same *Aula* as in the morning. Those absent in the morning did not attend. The President said the prayer, and the Secretary made a brief announcement. The President of the Sub-commission on the Divine Office resumed reading his report. A discussion ensued and articles 73, 74, and 75 of the Schema (articles 95, 96, 97, 98, and 100 of the revised text) were examined.[104]

Regarding the faculty conceded to bishops to dispense from the Office, Msgr. Bonet requested that the question be referred to the competent Conciliar Commission. Abbot Prou observed that the faculty conceded to bishops had been dealt with, and that the text now spoke of faculties conceded to religious Ordinaries. Msgr. Martimort favored retaining the paragraph.

Abbot Salmon requested that article 16 of the text be changed because it was not accurate; one cannot speak of part of the Office being in competition with a liturgical act. Msgr. Wagner explained that the paragraph wanted to show that those who were impeded from reciting the canonical Office, because they performed a liturgical action, etc., could set aside some time equal to that of the monks who recite the Office, albeit in a different way.

The President intervened to defend the little hours against any impositions. The President preferred to say that they should be fulfilled "*ad modum Officii divini*". Msgr. Pichler and Fr. Jungmann favored the proposal to a certain extent. Msgr. Gagnebet noted that in order to have an exact notion of the Church's prayer it was necessary that the delegation and the form of the prayer be approved by the Church. The President asked the Sub-commission to produce a better formulated text.

Article 77 of the Schema (101 of the amended text)[105] on the language was discussed. Msgr. Martin, President of the Sub-commission, said that between the proposals of remitting the faculty to use the vernacular to the Episcopal Conferences or on to individual bishops, the Sub-commission had chosen the latter. Msgr. Jenny asked that both proposals be submitted to the Council. He was told that such a thing would be technically impossible and that the Commission had to come to a decision on the matter. Father Egger suggested that the term "*Ordinary*" be used instead of "*bishop*" so as to include religious.

The discussion became confused as several interventions in favor of Latin were made (*periti* Monsignors Anglés and Vagaggini) while others were against it. The President asked the Sub-commission to examine the written proposal which would be sent.

The revised text of article 9, which had been kept separate, was then examined. It was concerned with the relationship between the Office and private piety and mentioned the Commission for the Reform.

Msgr. Bonet did not think that the formulation was correct. Up to now the document had mentioned a special Commission but in article 25 of Chapter I a specific Commission was now being mentioned. Msgr. Martimort proposed that reference be made to the post-Conciliar Commission. The President observed that this was a delicate matter as they could not foresee a permanent Commission being established, and neither could anything more specific be envisaged. The primacy of the Pope had to be borne in mind. The Council would not be prolonged indefinitely.

Msgr. Jenny saw an agreement between private and public piety in article 9 as it was formulated. Msgr. McManus judged this article far too clerical. He proposed the expression "*qui recitant*" instead of speaking only of those obliged ("*qui adstricti*"). The article was acceptable to Abbot D'Amato; he thought it "*extra locum*" (he would put it in the Preamble to the Chapter), and he would have liked a clearer redaction of the article which said that private devotion had to be modeled on public devotion.

The prayer was said and the meeting concluded.[106]

Meeting XXIX (May 2, 1963)

The Conciliar Commission on the Sacred Liturgy met in the *Aula* of the Hospice of Santa Marta in the Vatican at 9:30 a.m. with Cardinal Larraona presiding. Cardinal Jullien and the other Fathers mentioned in the previous meeting were absent.

The prayer was said, and the Secretary made some announcements. A brief discussion on the vote on Chapter II ensued. The scheda, to be returned within a few days, were distributed to the Fathers. The President announced that the Sub-commission had completed its work. At this point, the text would be examined by a Sub-commission consisting of the Presidents of all the Sub-commissions. He then asked Abbot D'Amato, President of Sub-commission "*de Musica Sacra*" to speak. He then read his report.

Father Vagaggini, during the discussion on the Preamble[107], asked for greater precision with the phrase "*indolem ministerialem dominici servitii*". Msgr. Martimort proposed "*cuius indolem*", however, Abbot D'Amato proposed "*indolem ministerialem in dominico servitio*", which was acceptable to all.

The Commission unanimously approved the suppression of article 90, proposed by the Sub-commission.[108]

In paragraph 2 of article 91 (amended text)[109] Msgr. Martimort proposed substituting "*nonnulli*" with "*quinam cantus*". Wagner agreed but the President noted that everything depended on article 54 (the language to be used at Mass) on which they would have to vote. Cardinal Lercaro observed that the addition of "*quinam*" would introduce something new. The discussion continued but all agreed that this article would have to be drafted in the light of the articles referring to the Mass, the Sacraments, and the Office. Article 92 spoke of *scholae cantorum* which would be a help to the people.[110] Abbot D'Amato said that they were mentioned elsewhere. Msgr. Jenny insisted that at no point should it be stated as a principle that the *schola's* role was to assist the people. Msgr. Martin observed that the object of the article was *actuosa participatio* and not the *scholae cantorum*. Msgr. Fey Schneider made some comments on style. Abbot D'Amato made some changes to the text and read it. It was approved by all.

Article 93 dealt with the teaching of music.[111] Msgr. Anglés explained its significance and defended an amendment proposed by the Sub-commission concerning the teaching of music in the universities and theological faculties. Msgr. Stickler did not see how that would be possible; specialist Institutes already existed. *Peritus*, Father De Clercq, countered Msgr. Anglés saying that the criteria of the civil universities could not be applied to the theological faculties because arts faculties existed in the former but not in the latter. Father Vagaggini proposed retaining the text by making music an optional rather than an obligatory subject. The President suggested calling it "special material". Cardinal Lercaro believed that the text could be retained. The President concluded the discussion and asked the Sub-commission for further precision.

Article 94 dealt with Gregorian chant and polyphony.[112] Msgr. Stickler was surprised that the Sub-commission had added the expression "*qui semper lingua latina cani debet*" when speaking of Gregorian chant. In Croatia, everything was sung in the vernacular since 1925 when the *Rituale* was translated, and then there is the Mass which is sung in old-Slavonic. The Sub-commission should not preclude the possibility of Gregorian chant being sung in other languages, and he proposed the suppression of this addition. Msgr. Zauner thought that the addition might be retained by adding the word "*generatim*". He mentioned that in Austria, Gregorian chant was also sung in the vernacular: this does not constitute an obstacle but rather is a help to the singing of Gregorian chant in Latin. Msgr. Rau noted that not all languages were opposed to Gregorian. Msgr. Overath intervened and supported the proposal of Gregorian in Latin; he said, if new translations had to be made then a new music adapted to the genius of the vernacular should be found. Msgr. McManus countered that Protestants used Gregorian in the vernacular.

Msgr. Stickler maintained that Gregorian chant could be used in other languages; you would have to know the other languages to deny that. Msgr. Jenny proposed softening the expression "*cani debet*" because it sounded too legalistic. Msgr. Martin immediately proposed softening the phrase by presenting it merely as a simple explicative proposition.

Msgr. Anglés distinguished between the ancient central core of Gregorian and more recent melodies. Abbot Prou recommended preserving the treasure of authentic Gregorian chant; its conservation was necessarily bound to Latin. Msgr. Wagner made a long contribution objecting to the addition made by the Sub-commission, and gave examples of translations and music approved in German.

After a short pause, the discussion resumed. Msgr. Malula spoke against the addition referring to usage in the Congo. Msgr. Richler intervened, and in the end, Abbot D'Amato said that he was prepared to amend the text, and the President referred the matter to the Sub-commission.

Discussion moved to paragraph 2 of the relevant article. Msgr. Bonet raised the issue of the suppression of the phrase "*actuosa participatione*". Msgr. Frutaz and Abbot D'Amato replied that they favored the participation of the laity but the Sub-commission did not retain the phrase so as to avoid using it too frequently or embarrassing the polyphonic schools. Bonet, Martimort, and Rau favored restoring the phrase. The President referred it to the Sub-commission.

Articles 95, 96, 96b, and 97 were approved without discussion. On article 98, Msgr. McManus deplored the suppression of the phrase "*actuosa participatione*".[113] Msgr. Martimort proposed an emendation to article 99: it ought to read that hymns should not only conform to Scripture but their texts should be Biblical where possible.

The meeting ended at 12:30 p.m..[114]

Meeting XXX (May 3, 1963)

The Conciliar Commission on the Sacred Liturgy met in the *Aula* of the Hospice of Santa Marta in the Vatican at 9:30 a.m. with Cardinal Larraona presiding. The prayer was said, and the Secretary made some announcements and read a letter from the President announcing the establishment of a Sub-commission comprised of the heads of all the Sub-commissions for the scrutiny of the votes. The *periti* would be excluded. Msgr. Enciso made some clarifications to the text of Chapter II and explained the amendments proposed by the Sub-commission.

Msgr. Rossi, President of the Sub-commission on Sacred Art, read his report which was then discussed. Father Jungmann observed a lack of clarity in the first paragraph and proposed changing "*plurimum*" to "*quamplurimum*".

With regard to article 99 of the Schema[115], Msgr. Enciso proposed adding the phrase "*ut fini suo respondeant*" so as to make clear to artists that a work of art is directly destined for cult and must serve devotional needs. Cardinal Lercaro preferred to leave free reign to new styles while insisting on liturgical functionality. Msgr. Fey Schneider proposed adding another functionality to the use of art: the education of the people. The President asked the Sub-commission to examine the various proposals.

Msgr. Dirks made a stylistic observation about article 100.[116] Cardinal Lercaro did not approve the dropping of the phrase "*artis opera*". Msgr. Wagner suggested changing it to "*opificium opera*". Cardinal Lercaro observed that the final phrase in the article should be changed from "*eorundem sanctorum*" to "*Eiusdem Sancti*". Msgr. Gagnebet noted that the abuse of statues of Saints also touched on other parts. Msgr. Enciso proposed avoiding two extremes: excessive zeal and opposition to the cult of images and statues.

With regard to article 101, the President observed that the Commission should confine itself only to the conservation of sacred art. The other prescriptions did not fall within the competence of the Commission.[117] Msgr. Rossi believed that everything in the article, in some way or other, fell within the competence of the Commission. Msgr. Bonet proposed dropping the last phrase since provision had been made elsewhere.

Article 102 was not amended.[118] Msgr. Wagner proposed a slight change to article 103 by adding "*quadam*" to "*imitatione*".[119]

With regard to article 104, both the President and Msgr. Dante did not think it was the place to speak of relics, but reliquaries, however, could be mentioned.[120] Cardinal Giobbe proposed inserting the word "*criteriis*" to article 105. Education should not be limited merely to history but should also teach principles.[121]

After a brief pause, the Commission began its examination of Chapter V: the liturgical year. The Head of the relative Sub-commission read his report and the discussion opened.

Father Jungmann proposed substituting the phrase "*primo hebdomadae dies*" with the term "*prima dies*" in article 1 of the Preamble;[122] saying it is not true that Sunday is the first day of the week (Jewish tradition) and neither is it the conclusion of the week. It is the perfection of the week (Christian blessing). After a brief discussion of the point, Father Jungmann's proposal was accepted.

Father Dirks, referring to article 2 of the Preamble, suggested that it be rewritten in the third person as the Schema was. Msgr. Enciso did not agree with the application of the term: "*spem salutis*" to Our Lady, but Father Gagnebet defended the proposed text. Article 3 of the text passed without observations. Cardinal Giobbe proposed that "*instructione*" should precede "*operibus caritatis*" in article 4.[123]

Article 80 of the Schema treats Sunday.[124] An initial discussion arose where the text said that Sunday was a "*dies laetitiae*". Father Vagaggini did not like this formulation so he proposed "*etiam dies laetitiae*". Father De Clercq was not happy with the formulation and feared that the joy referred to would be connected with resting. The President suggested that the word "*culto*" should be added, and Msgr. Wagner proposed suppressing "*spiritualis*" and simply leave "*dies laetitiae*".

Msgr. Jenny broached the problem of first Vespers and the Sunday precept. He proposed that the celebration of Mass on Saturday evening should be considered a Sunday Mass, following the example of the Easter Vigil. Msgr. Martimort replied that he was scandalized and said that this way of celebrating Sunday, after the fashion of the Easter Vigil, led to the suspicion that the Easter Vigil was celebrated on Saturday evening. Father Calewaert opposed the proposal because it would gravely damage Sunday. The President thought that any danger might be avoided by conceding a faculty to local Ordinaries: it would not be the first time and it would help meet pastoral needs. Msgr. Jenny proposed renewing the Friday penance, and Msgr. Grimshaw replied saying that the actual practice was sufficient. Father Jungmann observed that penance could be recommended "*una cum Passione Domini*". The President asked the Sub-commission to provide for this.

Article 79, which had been moved by the Sub-commission, was examined and approved. [125]

After the usual prayer, the meeting ended at 12:30 p.m..[126]

Meeting XXXI (May 4, 1963)

The Conciliar Commission on the Sacred Liturgy met in the *Aula* of the Hospice of Santa Marta in the Vatican at 9:30 a.m. with Cardinal Larraona presiding. Those whose absence previously had been noted did not attend, except Msgr. Jop who had arrived the previous day from Poland. The prayer was said, and the Secretary made his announcements.

Msgr. Jenny explained the reasons for his intervention on the previous day with regard to anticipating Mass on Saturday evening. He said that Sunday is intimately related to Easter and that Holy Week is the type for every other week. As the celebration of Easter begins after Sunset, so too the Sunday Mass could be celebrated after sunset. With regard to Sunday, it should be noted that the festive day extends from Saturday evening to Sunday evening. Thus, the Mass expresses the meaning of Sunday, and then there were pastoral reasons to be borne in mind.

Msgr. Zauner resumed reading the report on the liturgical year. Some comments were made in relation to article 81.[127] Various observations were made in relation to article 82 on Lent.[128] Msgr. Rau declared that he had not well understood the phrase "*indoles peccatorum personalis et socialis*". He remarked that both adjectives referred to "*indoles*". The President proposed "*peccati*" instead of "*peccatorum*". Msgr. Gagnebet proposed the expression "*indole propria*" instead of "*indoles personalis*".

Abbot Salmon observed that the old name had been "*domenicale*" and not "*de tempore*". Agreeing, Wagner intervened proposing the conservation of the actual term as it would be easier for the Fathers to understand.

Msgr. Jenny desired to have the missionary character of Lent emphasized. Msgr. Zauner replied that the whole year had a missionary character, but Msgr. Jenny said that it was particularly strong during Lent. Msgr. Zauner retorted that it was stronger after Pentecost. Wagner said that Sunday had an internal and external missionary character, however, any clarification of that character had to do with the instruction of the faithful. The President intervened and reminded the Commission that small details should not be put into the Schema but left for the post-Conciliar Commission. Msgr. Fey Schneider proposed revising the style of the article, however, Abbot Egger who had proposed the emendation, did not agree.

Msgr. Nabuco, *peritus,* commented on article 83 which spoke of the penitential practices observed during Lent.[129] He proposed that the Lenten fast should end at mid-day on Holy Saturday. The President replied that the Commission was not competent to examine the subject. The formulation of the text was not acceptable to Father Vagaggini, who asked for it to be reworked.

Father Jungmann asked that the expression "*Sacrosancta Synodo*" be dropped. Msgr. Borella proposed a revision of the time of Lent. Reading from a script, he suggested suppressing the pre-Lenten period. Wagner asked him to forward his text to the post-Conciliar Commission, and to drop what had been said in the report about Ash Wednesday. Abbot D'Amato opposed Msgr. Borella's proposal.

Father Jungmann lamented the fact that nothing had been said about revising the Octave of Christmas and the time of Epiphany. The Secretary said that the historical questions were not all together clear but that these points would have to be looked at in the future. In the end, agreement was made that the reference to Ash Wednesday should be suppressed.

Msgr. Nabuco said, in relation to article 84, that it was not convenient to refer to sacred images in the text of the article since the subject had been dealt with in the chapter on sacred art.[130] Msgr. Wagner replied that this was the place to speak of images. The President thought that the expression "*veneratio sanctorum ne...*" was too weak.

In the view of the Sub-commission, articles 85 and 86 on the revision of the calendar were outside of the Schema to be approved by a declaration of the Council.[131] Wagner proposed taking them out of the chapter and placing them at the end since he did not agree that they should be omitted from the Schema. Father Jungmann regarded the expression "*non obstat*" as inappropriate for a Council. Msgr. Zauner replied that if the Catholic Church were not opposed, the others could do what they liked. Msgr. Jenny feared losing the rhythm of the weeks as he recalled that in the *Aula* a mixed Commission of Catholics and separated brethren was proposed to deal with civil governments. Msgr. Zauner observed that the establishment of the calendar is dependent on the fixing of the date of Easter.

Martimort thought that there were two questions to be addressed, and two methods had to be employed in responding to them. The first referred to the date of Easter. He said that this concerned only Christians. Hence it was preferable to use "*non obstat*" so as to avoid the impression that Catholics had set the initiative in motion, which would not be acceptable to the separated brethren. The second question was of concern to Jews and Muslims: were an initiative to be made by civil governments, then the Church could insist on conditions. The Secretary, Father Antonelli, mentioned some negotiations that had taken place some years previously between the United Nations and the Holy See. The question then arose of the wisdom of raising the matter in a Conciliar document.

The President said that while it was a delicate matter, the text could be presented in the Council *Aula*. Msgr. McManus announced that he had visited the United Nations in the name of the Preparatory Commission and said that a Conciliar declaration would be desirable.

After a brief pause, Msgr. Hallinan, President of the Sub-commission on Sacraments and Sacramentals, read a brief report explaining the new amended text prepared by the Sub-commission after the preceding discussion. Msgr. Grimshaw, President of the Sub-commission on Sacred Furnishings, read his report which was followed by a further discussion.

Msgr. Bonet did not agree with the suppression of a paragraph in the Preamble because it threatened to block the reform, and Msgr. Grimshaw responded that nobody wished to condemn progress.

Msgr. Bonet insisted that at least something should be said about poverty. The President, Cardinal Larraona, said that it could be mentioned without imposing anything. Not everybody thinks like St. Francis. Msgr. Enciso intervened saying that an addition should be made to the effect that furnishings should be accommodated to the spirit of the Church. The President approved.

Msgr. Wagner suggested fusing the two chapters on sacred art and sacred furnishings. Msgr. Grimshaw replied that the proposal should be examined directly by the respective Sub-commissions. The President agreed and asked him to report back to the Commission.

In article 87 Msgr. Wagner believed the first and second parts to be discordant. He proposed a revision of the entire arrangement of the chapter, allowing the territorial authorities greater possibility to intervene. Msgr. Jenny observed that the general laws had to be at the basis of this. Msgr. Bonet proposed an amendment to the text, which was accepted, to the effect: "*Servatis legis generalibus, erit competentis...*".

With regard to article 89, Msgr. Bonet observed that the juridical Sub-commission had proposed an amendment which had not been taken into account.

The meeting ended at 12:30 p.m. with the usual prayer.[132]

Meeting XXXII (May 6, 1963)

The Conciliar Commission on the Sacred Liturgy met in the *Aula* of the Hospice of Santa Marta in the Vatican at 9:30 a.m. Cardinal Larraona presided. In addition to those absent on previous occasions, two others were not present: Msgr. Malula who had left for the Congo and Cardinal Jullien who was ill.

The Secretary made several announcements, and among other things, he announced the nomination of a Sub-commission of Presidents, which would meet at the Sacred Congregation of Rites at 5 p.m.. He also announced the establishment of two further Sub-commissions: one for Latin, the other for citations.

The voting scheda on Chapter II were collected from the Fathers and *periti.*

Msgr. Martin read a brief report from the Sub-commission on the Divine Office explaining the amended text drawn up by the Sub-commission following the discussions of the previous days. Abbot D'Amato read another report on sacred music, Msgr. Zauner on the liturgical year, and Msgr. Rossi on sacred art. The Commission unanimously charged the two Sub-commissions on sacred art and sacred furnishings to fuse both chapters into one.

Finally, the Sub-commission for citations was asked to improve the structure of Chapter I, if it was opportune.

After the usual prayer, the meeting ended at 10:30 a.m..[133]

Meeting XXXIII (September 27, 1963)

The Conciliar Commission on the Sacred Liturgy met in the *Aula* of the Hospice of Santa Marta in the Vatican at 9:30 a.m. with Cardinal Larraona presiding. All the Fathers were present except Cardinal Lercaro, Msgrs. Van Bekkum, Fey Schneider, and Malula, and the *periti.*

The final drafts of the fascicles containing Chapters II and III and the amendments to be voted on were distributed to the Fathers and the *periti* along with the reports, the original texts, and the amended texts.

The President said the prayer and welcomed all present. The Secretary reported on the work which had been done since the previous meetings (April 23-May 10). The text had been revised for style and the quotations carefully checked. A small Commission had examined the reports and amendments on Chapters II-VIII.

Msgr. Enciso proposed that the amendments to Chapter II could be voted on by the Council. Msgr Wagner called attention to the lack of clarity in the division of article 57 (previously 44). Cardinal Albareda proposed adding the clause "*de praecepto*" to article 56 (previously 43). This proposal was accepted.

The report was not read since the Secretary announced that only two slight changes had been made by the Commission. Concerning the first change, relating to concelebration and the presence of the bishop, Msgr. Enciso said that he was happy, but given that it was a new insertion, he asked that the Conciliar Fathers be alerted to it. Msgr. Martimort proposed including it in the report, and it was decided to add the word "*etiam*" to the phrase "*Agimus etiam de Concelebratione absque praesenti Episcopi*". Father Dirks asked to have the *declarationes* added to the report. The President was not against the proposal but made no decision about it.

The entire text of Chapter II, as revised by the Latinists, was then read. An animated debate on article 57 followed. It was claimed that the structure of the article was confused. The President postponed a decision about it until the following day and asked the Sub-commission to formulate a new text.

Msgr. Hallinan read the amendments to Chapter III. These were then discussed. A long debate ensued concerning the expression "*actis ab Apostolica Sede confirmatis vel probatis*" in article 63 (previously 47). It was attacked by Msgr. Spülbeck and Msgr. Wagner who insisted on the use of the phrase "*probatis seu confirmatis*"; the President Cardinal Larraona defended the clause. He said that the difference between Chapter I, which had "*probatis seu confirmatis*", and the present text posed no difficulties. Chapter I was concerned with matters at a general level, while here particular matters were considered.

The Secretary announced that some paragraphs in the report had been eliminated, among them was the paragraph on the time for the Anointing of the Sick and the frequency with which this sacrament could be repeated. Approval of these changes was postponed until the following day. A debate ensued on the word "*praepositae*" which had been chosen by the Latinists, and on the word "*praeponendae*" in article 63b.

The revised text was read. Father Dirks proposed a stylistic change to article 79 which was accepted. After the usual prayer, the meeting closed at 12:15 p.m..[134]

Meeting *XXXIV* (*September 28, 1963*)

The Conciliar Commission on the Sacred Liturgy met in the *Aula* of the Hospice of Santa Marta in the Vatican at 9:30 a.m.. Cardinal Larraona presided. Two Fathers who had been absent the previous day were present: Msgrs. Van

Bekkum and Fey Schneider. The prayer was said. The President proposed that a message of condolence be sent to Cardinal Lercaro whose brother had died.

Msgr. Hallinan, President of the Sub-commission on the Sacraments and Sacramentals (Chapter III), asked to speak. He read a typewritten script and made various proposals including submitting three further changes in the text for the approval of the Commission. The Cardinal announced that an approved text cannot be revised. The most that might be considered would be some stylistic changes in the approved text.

Discussion resumed and centred on the phrase *"probatis vel confirmatis"*. Msgr. Hallinan proposed that the Commission express its opinion by means of a vote. Following a contribution from Msgr. Wagner, the President postponed further discussion of the matter until the following day so as to allow time to have Msgr. Hallinan's and Msgr. Wagner's contributions printed and distributed to all.

The Secretary asked the Commission to move to the approval of Chapter II on the Eucharist. Msgr. Enciso presented the proposals of the Sub-commission on article 57. It suggested dividing the article into paragraphs. The phrase *"in Cena Domini"* was added to paragraph two which began *"Salva tamen"*. The proposal was accepted by a majority with three against it. The President accepted the inclusion of the *declarationes*, as recommended by Msgr. Jenny and all approved the report.

Msgr. Martin, President of the Sub-commission on the Divine Office (Chapter IV), read the amendments to be placed before the Council. The Fathers accepted the choice of amendments, and the Secretary announced the suppression of some parts of the report on the Office which had been suggested by a small Commission that met in Rome from July 18-19, 1963. The Commission approved unanimously.

The Presidency of the Commission was assumed by Cardinal Giobbe, the Vice-President, because Cardinal Larraona had to attend an audience with the Pope. Msgr. Martin asked the reason for the suppression of another part of his report on the Office. Msgr. Bonet replied that it was because the paragraph did not indicate changes that had to be voted on. Msgr. Martin accepted the suppression of the paragraph but asked that it be reinserted in the final text of the report of the restricted Commission that met from July 18-19. The Commission had omitted it because it was considered too severe in some expressions and rulings. The proposal was put to vote and accepted unanimously. The final text was duly changed, and it was newly reinserted. Msgr. Martin read the amended text which was approved by all.

Msgr. Zauner, Head of the Sub-commission on Chapter V, read his report and the amendments to it, and everything was approved.

In relation to article 106 of the amended text (previously article 80), some clarifications were asked for with regard to the origins of Sunday. The words *"coepit in originem ducit"* were changed so as to affirm that the tradition, and not the Sunday, derives its origin from the resurrection of Christ. The amendment was unanimously accepted.[135]

Meeting XXXV (September 30, 1963)

The Conciliar Commission on the Sacred Liturgy met in the *Aula* of the Hospice of Santa Marta in the Vatican at 9:30 a.m. with Cardinal Larraona presiding. Cardinal Lercaro and a new *peritus*, Father Diekmann, were present. The prayer was said, and the Secretary read the announcements. Abbot D'Amato, the President of the Sub-commission for Chapter VI on Music, spoke.

The amendments to Chapter VI were approved without difficulty. The report was also approved with the *proviso* that all references to the Fathers who had spoken in the Council *Aula* be removed. Some minor changes were made to the text. Thus in article 112 the phrase *"prae ceteris artibus excellentem"* of the original text was replaced with *"maxime excellens inter ceteras artis expressiones"*. This was done on the recommendations of Cardinal Lercaro following a proposal made by Msgr. Martin. The addition *"commendatur quoque scholae cantorum"* in article 115 requested by Msgr. Enciso was suppressed because it was considered repetitive, but the addition of *"praesertim apud ecclesias cathedrales"* was added to article 114. On Msgr. Pichler's advice, the phrase *"organum... quod Ecclesiae caeremoniis mirum addit"* in article 120 was changed to *"... cuius sonus mirum addere valet splendorem"*.

Msgr. Rossi, the President of the Sub-commission on Chapter VI on Sacred Art and Sacred Furnishings, read both the amendments and his report: neither encountered any difficulties. The only change made to the amended text was the insertion of the word *"Episcopi"* in paragraph 2 of Article 124 since the matter pertained to their competence. A proposal made by Msgr. Enciso, to the effect that provision should be made for private devotions in the building of new churches, was not accepted. The Commission unanimously approved the amendments, the report, and the amended text.

The Commission then considered the proposals which had been distributed and had been made in writing by Msgr. Hallinan, the President of the Sub-commission on Chapter III on the Sacraments and Sacramentals. The first proposal asked that the phrase *"actis ab Apostolica Sede probatis vel confirmatis"* be changed to the formulation contained in Chapter I. After a heated debate, it was unanimously decided to revert to the original text *"actis ab Apostolica Sede Recognitis"*.

The second proposal concerned the name of Extreme Unction and recommended returning to the original text of article 73 (previously 57) *"deinceps Unctio Infirmorum vocabitur"*. The theological Sub-commission under the presidency of the *peritus* Fr. Gagnebet proposed *"quae etiam et melius Unctio Infirmorum vocabitur"*. All approved.

The third proposal relating to article 80 (previously 65) requested that the original text of the article, which provided for religious professions during the Mass, be revived. The Commission unanimously accepted Martimort's proposal so that the text might read: "*Professio religiosa laudabiliter intra Missam fiet*".

A fourth proposal relating to the time of administration of Extreme Unction was not accepted because of the opposition of the theological Sub-commission (cf. typed script).

The meeting closed with the usual prayer.[136]

Meeting XXXVI (October 7, 1963)

The Conciliar Commission on the Sacred Liturgy met in the *Sala del Congresso* of the Sacred Congregation of Rites at 6 p.m. with Cardinal Larraona presiding. The prayer was said, the Secretary made some announcements, and Cardinal Lercaro read a report on the work of the Commission which was to be distributed and read in the Council *Aula*. The report was approved without discussion.

The insertion of a text to be put into the report on Chapter III on the Sacraments and Sacramentals was discussed and approved. It explained the formula "*actis ab Apostolica Sede recognitis*". The text was approved without difficulty.

The Commission also approved a proposal made by Msgr. Jenny changing the amended text of the chapter on the liturgical year. In the final sentence of the decree on the revision of the calendar after the words "*hebdomadarum successio intacta*" the phrase "*nisi accedant gravissimae rationes de quibus Apostolica Sedes iudicium ferat*" was added. A reference in the notes to the International Association on the Calendar was eliminated.

After the usual prayer, this brief meeting was concluded.[137]

Meeting XXXVII (October 17, 1963)

The Conciliar Commission on the [Sacred] Liturgy met in the *Sala del Congresso* of the Sacred Congregation of Rites at 6 p.m.. The President, Cardinal Larraona, said the opening prayer and the Secretary made some announcements. He announced the establishment of four study groups to study the *placet iuxta modum* votes on Chapter II which had been cast on October 11.

The President announced that matters relating to the criteria to be applied in the examination of the *modi* [modifications], their value, context, etc., would be amended by the juridical Sub-commission which had been asked to prepare a report for the Commission as soon as possible. Msgr. Dante requested that a decision of an administrative tribunal be awaited because he, along with others, had made recourse to the tribunal because they regarded the vote on Chapter II as invalid on the basis of the *Ordo* of the Council. First the President responded, and then Bonet, that such a recourse could not impede the Commission from carrying on with its work.

A short discussion ensued on the criteria to be applied in examining the *modi*. Msgr. Jenny proposed taking into account only the more important *modi* while Martimort thought that it was necessary to reply to all the *modi* so as to persuade all the Fathers who had proposed them.

Awaiting the reply of the juridical Sub-commission, the Commission would be summoned in writing.

The meeting concluded with the usual prayer.[138]

Meeting XXXVIII (October 23, 1963)

The Conciliar Commission on the Sacred Liturgy met in the *Sala del Congresso* of the Sacred Congregation of Rites at 5 p.m. with Cardinal Larraona presiding. After the Secretary made some announcements, the President of the juridical Sub-commission, Msgr. Bonet, read and commented on a report of the Sub-commission on the juridical quality of the *placet iuxta modum*.

The President clarified some points, namely the following: the *placet iuxta modum* were positive votes; *modi* contrary to the text could not be accepted; and, provided that it agrees with the text, a non-contrary formula could instead be proposed.

Msgr. Enciso reported on the *modi* to Chapter II. The letter of the report was postponed to the next meeting.

The report on the *modi* to Chapter III were accepted, and there was a brief discussion on the application of the Constitution. Msgr. Rossi proposed a disposition, on the basis of which, examination of the articles of Chapter I began. Seeing the difficulties however, he requested the formation of a Sub-commission so as to make a more thorough examination. The President accepted this proposal and asked the Secretary to alert all concerned.

After the usual prayer, the meeting ended at 6:40 p.m..[139]

Meeting XXXIX (October 25, 1963)

The Conciliar Commission on the Sacred Liturgy met in the *Sala del Congresso* of the Sacred Congregation of Rites at 5 p.m. with Cardinal Larraona presiding. The prayer was said, and the Secretary made some announcements.

Msgr. Enciso began his report on the *modi* to Chapter II. A long discussion ensued on the number of votes and the order to be followed. As regards the number of votes, a clear distinction was proposed between *modi* (which were few in number because the same concerns had been mentioned several times) and votes. On the order to be followed and the criteria to be used in examining the *modi*, a difference of opinion was noted between Msgr. Bonet and the President. Finally, the President decided to have the juridical Sub-commission prepare a text on the criteria which would be discussed in the Commission. The text, if the case warranted it, could also be read in the Council *Aula*.

Msgr. Enciso continued reading his report. At the request of the Fathers and the *periti* several amendments were made to the text.

After the usual prayer the meeting was adjourned.[140]

Meeting XL (October 29, 1963)

The Conciliar Commission on the Sacred Liturgy met in the *Sala del Congresso* of the Sacred Congregation of Rites at 5 p.m. with Cardinal Larraona presiding. Various absences were noted among whom: Cardinals Lercaro, Giobbe, and Jullien, and Monsignors Zauner, Hallinan, Malula and Schweiger.

After the Secretary made some announcements, Msgr. Enciso resumed reading his report on the examination of the *modi* to Chapter II. Msgr. Calewaert opposed the view of the Sub-commission to propose an extension of the vernacular to the priestly prayers (article 54) for the vote of the Council Fathers. This would render the previous paragraph void. It was decided to propose nothing for the vote of the Fathers. Instead, a convenient explanation would be provided.

On the question of administering Holy Communion under both species, the Commission agreed that the case of spouses should not be submitted for a vote of the Council, but it was not satisfied with the reasons given for this decision by the Sub-commission. Mention should not be made of a lack of piety on the part of spouses, nor of other pastoral reasons. Extension of Holy Communion under both species would be determined by further indults of the Holy See.

Numerous *placet iuxta modum* were registered with regard to concelebration. Many of them called for the addition of the word "*loci*" to "*Ordinario*". The Sub-commission prepared a new formulation to be presented to the Fathers for their vote. The Commission decided to suppress the addition "*in singulis casibus*" which had been accepted by the Sub-commission (article 57, n. 2), and a reference to article 22, paragraph 1, in the new paragraph, saying that the bishop was responsible for regulating the discipline of concelebration in his diocese.

Abbot Prou called for greater precision with regard to the meaning of the formula "*disciplinam concelebrationis moderari*". Msgr. Enciso replied that this referred to the establishment of conditions with regard to time, simultaneous celebrations, frequency, etc.. In general terms, the report was approved.

Msgr. Dante reproposed his objection against the criteria used to determine the voting in the Council. He called for a vote on each article rather than on whole chapters. Msgr. Bonet replied that the *Ordo* of the Council spoke only of "*partes*," and the moderators had interpreted this to mean the individual chapters. The President intervened saying that the issue did not fall within the competence of the Commission.

Msgr. Rossi proposed a different ordering of the report than that proposed by Msgr. Enciso and the proposal was accepted. The Head of the juridical Sub-commission, Msgr. Bonet, read out a new version of the text concerning the examination of the *modi*. He believed it would be useful to read this report in the Council *Aula* before taking a vote on Chapter II. The reading was interrupted by the late hour so, after the usual prayer, the meeting was adjourned.[141]

Meeting XLI (October 30, 1963)

The Conciliar Commission on the Sacred Liturgy met in the *Aula* of the Sacred Congregation of Rites at 5 p.m. with Cardinal Larraona presiding. The following were absent: Cardinals Lercaro, Giobbe, and Jullien, and Monsignors Malula, Zauner, and Bekkers. After the prayer, the Secretary read the notices.

Msgr. Bonet, President of the juridical Sub-commission, resumed reading his report on the criteria to be used for the examination of the *modi*. A long discussion began on the way of voting on the *modi* in the Council *Aula*. Msgr. Bonet took it that it would be sufficient to take a cumulative vote on the *modi*. The President tended to the idea that a vote had to be taken on each *modus*. While he accepted Bonet's idea, the President believed that it would be opportune to ask the Council or indeed the President of the Council to approve the procedure proposed by the Commission. He then asked the Commission if it agreed with the idea of proposing to the Council only those *modi* which presented special difficulties and to reject the others. The Commission agreed.

Msgr. Bonet resumed the discussion by presenting three proposals: a) voting "*de modo accepto*"; b) voting "*de modo accepto*" and "*de relatione*"; c) voting "*de modo accepto*", "*de modis non acceptis*" (intending here *modi* presented by several Fathers) and "*globatim*" for all other *modi*.

When put to a vote, the first proposal (a) was rejected; the second (b) was favored by all the Commission; the third (c) received conditional acceptance: it might be used in exceptional circumstances.

The President asked the Commission if the report of the juridical Sub-commission should be printed and circulated in the Council *Aula*. Msgr. Bonet desired that the report should remain internal to the Commission. The matter was decided in his favor. Msgr. Wagner proposed that an explanation of the method followed by the Commission when examining the *modi* should be included in the reports made to the Council.

Msgr. Martin, President of the Sub-commission on the Divine Office, read a resumé of all the *modi* proposed for each article of Chapter IV. A reply would be prepared to each *modus* as soon as possible.

The only intervention made was by Father Jungmann who defended the meditative character of Matins using historical arguments.

After the usual prayer, the meeting concluded at about 7 p.m..[142]

Meeting XLII (November 6, 1963)

The Conciliar Commission on the Sacred Liturgy met in the *Sala del Congresso* of the Sacred Congregation of Rites at 5:30 p.m. with Cardinal Larraona presiding. Several Fathers were absent: 4 Cardinals and 5 Bishops.

The prayer was said and the Secretary read the notices. In the absence of Msgr. Hallinan, Msgr. Spülbeck read the report on the *modi* to Chapter III, *De ceteris Sacramentis et Sacramentalibus*.

The Sub-commission had accepted the *modus* of Msgr. Van Bekkum and other Fathers, concerning the consecration of the world by new sacramentals. It was to have been inserted in the Preamble, but the Commission rejected the *modus* as provision had already been made for the subject in articles 27-41 of Chapter I and in article 67 of Chapter III (new sacramentals).

Concerning the language used (article 63), Msgr. Rossi proposed a new formula to be submitted to the Council. Martimort believed it to be more opportune to propose the formula to the Council without taking a position on it. Then, *peritus* Msgr. Wagner proposed a new formula distinguishing between "*Pontificale*" and "*Rituale*". Msgr. McManus contradicted him, observing that the text had already been voted on. The President closed the discussion proposing that Msgr. Rossi's formula be submitted to the Council without any recommendation, and the Commission agreed.

The reply of the Sub-commission on the *modi* to article 79 (sacramentals) was deemed insufficient, especially in relation to the application of the term "*Ordinariorum*" to reserved blessings, and with regard to the addition of the word "*loci*" to "*Ordinario*" when referring to sacramentals administered by the laity. Msgr. Wagner proposed, in relation to the former, that it had not been the Commission's intention to reserve special faculties not enjoyed by bishops to Religious superiors. To the latter, he proposed dropping the word "*loci*" since the laity had only one superior: the bishop. Then, concerning the vote to be taken in the Council *Aula*, it was proposed to ask simply "*an placet responsio Commissionis*" or "*expensio modorum circa art. 79*". The Commission's report was approved and the President closed the meeting with the usual prayer.[143]

Meeting XLIII (November 7, 1963)

The Conciliar Commission on the Sacred Liturgy met at 5 p.m. in the *Sala del Congresso* of the Sacred Congregation of Rites and Cardinal Larraona presided. The other four Cardinals were absent as were Monsignors Dante, Stickler, Hallinan, and Malula.

Following the prayer, the Secretary made his announcements, and Msgr. Martin, who had been asked by the President to examine the *modi* to Chapter I, read his report. Father Vagaggini commented on article 10, which speaks of the liturgy being the summit and the source of the Church's activity. He observed that the original text had been clearer in its formulation than the present, from which the phrase "*in suo centro Eucharistiae*" had been excised. Msgr. Jenny proposed restoring the phrase. The President objected since it was sufficient to make a declaration about it in the report. Some further small corrections and emendations were then made to the text which was approved by the Commission.

Msgr. Zauner, President of the Sub-commission on Chapter V (the liturgical year), read his report on the examination of *modi* to Chapter V. Two brief discussions ensued, one on Sunday as "*dies prima*", the other on the ecclesiastical law requiring abstinence from work on Sunday. The report was eventually approved unanimously by the Commission.

Msgr. Jenny proposed concluding the Apostolic Constitution with a Biblical text and with a liturgical text. As it stood, the Constitution concluded with a chapter on pontificals [*pontificalia*]. The President said the prayer and closed the meeting.[144]

Meeting XLIV *(November 8, 1963)*

The Conciliar Commission on the Sacred Liturgy met in the *Sala del Congresso* of the Sacred Congregation of Rites at 5 p.m. with Cardinal Larraona presiding. Cardinals Lercaro, Giobbe, and Jullien were absent as were Monsignors Hallinan and Jenny.

The Secretary read out various communications. The President announced that the Constitution on the Liturgy would in all probability be published during the current session of the Council. He asked if anyone had proposals to make.

Father Vagaggini proposed changing the opening of the Constitution. He then made a disquisition on the opening formulae used at various Councils. The Secretary replied that the Secretariat General of the Council was studying this question. The Commission, however, was not competent to decide the matter. Msgr. Frutaz, who had been asked to investigate a concluding formula for the Constitution, replied that from his analysis of the various Councils no particular formula had been settled upon.

Msgr. Martin, Head of the Sub-commission on Chapter IV (Divine Office), read a report on the examination of *modi*. Father Jungmann commented on the question of Matins. He asked that the *modus* proposing the substitution of Biblical readings for Matins be referred to the post-Conciliar Commission. Msgr. Martimort replied that the question was a matter for the Conciliar Commission. The President did not think it convenient to refer the matter to the Council, and Msgr. Martin agreed with the President. Father Jungmann then asked that the Commission's reply be at least softened, and the proposal was accepted.

It was decided that Msgr. Martin would insert into the report what he had written and spoken in the Council *Aula* on the proposal to substitute Matins with Biblical readings.

Msgr. Dirks intervened with regard to the minor hours and those obliged to the choir but could not participate for pastoral reasons. He asked that these be regarded as equiparate to the secular clergy as far as having the liberty to choose one of the three minor hours. The President replied that the Commission did not intend to say anything further on this question. Given the diversity shown on the subject in the *relationes,* the matter would have to be regulated by particular law.

With regard to article 99 on the common recital of the Breviary, the *modus* of several Fathers, proposing that "*curandam*" be changed to "*optandum*" was partly accepted by the Commission. For stylistic reasons, the Commission preferred to use the verb "*suadetur*".

A long discussion ensued with regard to two *modi* recommending the suppression of the clause "*singulis casibus*" in article 101, and on the substitution of "*grave*" with "*verum impedimentum*" in the same article. The Commission accepted the latter *modus* but rejected the former. The Commission decided to give a better explanation for its decision with regard to the rejection of the former proposal. Eventually, it was also decided to reject the second proposal and to insert explanations for both decisions into the report to the Council in the hope of satisfying the Fathers. The text of the article, therefore, remained unchanged. The meeting then concluded with the usual prayer.[145]

Meeting XLV (November 11, 1963)

The Conciliar Commission on the Sacred Liturgy met at 5 p.m. in the *Aula* of the Sacred Congregation of Rites. Cardinal Larraona presided and Cardinals Lercaro, Giobbe, and Jullien were absent, as were Monsignors Dante, Jop, Schweiger, and Martin.

The prayer was recited and the Secretary read out his announcements. Abbot D'Amato, President of the Sub-commission on Chapter VI (Sacred Music) read his report on the *modi.* There was a brief discussion on the pipe organ and other instruments. Having clarified replies to two questions, the report was approved.

Msgr. Rossi, President of the Sub-commission for Chapter VII (Sacred Art and Furnishings), read his report on the *modi* to Chapter VII. There was a long discussion on a *modus* requesting the addition of the phrase "*aut in benedictione abbatiali*" after the words "*in consecratione episcopali*" in the final article of the Constitution. The *modus* had been proposed by the Abbots, and the Sub-commission had accepted it. While the Commission was sympathetic to the reasons advanced by the Abbots for this modification, it disagreed with the view of the Sub-commission. It did not regard it as opportune to refer the question to the Council *Aula* for a vote. A satisfactory reply would therefore be made to the Abbots in the report to the effect that for Abbots who exercised the office, the article would present no difficulties, while for titular Abbots there was no intention of departing from current usage. This suggestion, proposed by Msgr.

Wagner, was accepted by all. The report was subsequently approved unanimously, and the meeting ended after the usual prayer.[146]

Meeting XLVI (November 13, 1963)

The Conciliar Commission on the Sacred Liturgy met in the *Aula* of the Sacred Congregation of Rites at 5 p.m. with Cardinal Larraona presiding. Cardinal Lercaro was absent as were other Fathers.

Following the prayer, Cardinal Giobbe immediately spoke and presented greetings to the Cardinal President for his name day [*onomastico*]. The Secretary then made the announcements and, in the absence of Msgr. Martin, he presented the draft copy of the fascicle of the report on Chapter I, which also contained the printed text of the Schema. He drew the attention of the Commission to some corrections which had been made to the original text and read the text of a number of articles. The Commission suggested some minor emendations and then definitively approved the report on the *modi* to Chapter I.

The President then raised the matter of the application of the Constitution on the Liturgy. He proposed both that a formula be prepared and discussed in the Commission, and that the faculties granted to Episcopal Conferences contained in the Constitution also be granted to those regions where such Conferences had not yet been established. Then, after the usual prayer, the meeting ended at 6:15 p.m..[147]

Meeting XLVII (November 14, 1963)

The Conciliar Commission on the Sacred Liturgy met at 5:30 p.m. in the *Aula* of the Sacred Congregation of Rites. Cardinal Larraona presided and Cardinals Jullien and Lercaro were absent as were Monsignors Dante, Pichler, Martin, and Enciso, Abbot Prou, and Father Schweiger.

The President said the prayer, after which the Secretary made his announcements. In the absence of Msgr. Enciso, the Secretary read the report on the examination of the *modi* to Chapter II (the Mass). He emphasized the salient points and indicated the corrections that had been made to the text. It was decided to avoid the term "*emendatio*" which would have required a further vote on the *modi*. Instead, the term "*mutatio*" (sic) would be used.

Article 54 provided a long and animated discussion on the use of the vernacular in the Mass. Msgr. Grimshaw observed that the Constitution only provided for the retention of Latin in the Collect in the first part of the Mass. This island of Latin would be incomprehensible to many of the Fathers unless an adequate explanation were given in the report. The Secretary replied that the removal of this island would not be acceptable to many of the Fathers. Msgr. Hallinan contested the explanation provided for article 54 and suggested the suppression of paragraph 3 of the reply. Father Diekmann opposed the retention of Latin in the

Collects. Martimort replied that this represented the *via media* proposed by the Commission. The President then intervened and asked the Commission to bear in mind that only 108 of the Council Fathers had approved the use of the vernacular in the Collects. He called on the Commission to respect the wishes of the Council as expressed in the *Aula*.

Msgr. McManus appealed to article 36 of Chapter I which spoke of "*nonnullis orationibus*" and Martimort replied that the phrase refers to the liturgy in general. On the other hand, it states that the faithful must be able to sing and say in Latin at least the easier responses. Father Jungmann proposed referring the question to the post-Conciliar Commission and Martimort opposed this saying that the question of language was not the competence of the post-Conciliar Commission but of the territorial authorities. The President wondered if the question should be referred to the Council. With some preoccupation, Msgr. Jenny observed that the Constitution risked shipwreck over a comma. Father Calewaert observed that the principle should be applied which required the faithful to know the Latin responses to the Mass, and the proposal was accepted.

Msgr. Zauner observed that the principle was always valid for the *Missa Cantata*. Msgr. Wagner added that the use of the word had not been explicitly mentioned so as not to exclude the vernacular in the liturgy of the Eucharist. At this point it was decided to rework the reply of the Commission. The new text, which began "*Omnibus perpensis quae Patribus...* ", was approved by all.

With regard to article 57, on concelebration, Msgr. Fohl observed that the reference to canon 609 in the reply of the Commission did not correspond to the text of the Code. On the suggestion of Msgr. Bonet, the President decided to quote nothing, and the Commission unanimously approved the text of the report.

At this point, the President called for a discussion of a note which he had prepared on the application of the Constitution. He then distributed two typed pages together with a list. Martimort suggested distributing the articles into the following categories: a) immediate application; b) application by the territorial authorities; c) non applicable. During the discussion another category was suggested: articles on doctrinal principles. Then, after the usual prayer, the meeting concluded.[148]

Meeting XLVIII (November 18, 1963)

The Conciliar Commission on the Sacred Liturgy met in the *Aula* of the Sacred Congregation of Rites at 5 p.m., with Cardinal Larraona presiding. Cardinals Jullien, Lercaro, and Giobbe were absent as were Monsignor Enciso, Abbot Prou, Abbot D'Amato, and Father Schweiger.

The Secretary read out various announcements, and Msgr. Rossi reported on the work of the Sub-commission on the application of the Constitution. He observed that the work of the Commission was somewhat laborious and hence still required some time. Martimort read out his proposal for those articles of the Constitution which required the intervention of the territorial authorities, Episcopal Conferences, Plenary Councils, etc.. At the request of the President, the text would be distributed to the members of the Commission.

The Commission then examined the drafts of the report on the *modi* to Chapter IV. Msgr. Martin read the more controversial points. Some corrections were proposed, which had already been decided upon but by an oversight they had not been integrated with the text that had been sent to the printers. The report was again approved by all present.

Msgr. Rossi presented the proposals of the Sub-commission on the application of Chapter I of the Constitution to the Commission. Each article was reviewed with relative ease, and the meeting ended at 6:30 p.m. with the usual prayer.[149]

Meeting XLIX (November 19, 1963)

The Conciliar Commission on the Sacred Liturgy met in the *Aula* of the Sacred Congregation of Rites at 5 p.m. and Cardinal Larraona presided. Cardinals Jullien, Lercaro, and Giobbe were absent, as were Monsignors Dante, Masnou, Pichler, and Hallinan, and Father Schweiger.

The Secretary read the announcements, and the Commission then moved to the examination and definitive approval of the reports of the *modi* to Chapters V, VI, and VII. While the first two reports were approved without difficulty, the third report once again encountered difficulties concerning the "*pontificalia*" [pontificals].

Msgr. Nabuco objected to a faculty being granted to priests to bless or consecrate altars. He explained his objection by reference to the Church's great reverence for Chrism whose use is reserved, ordinarily, to the bishop. Martimort then contradicted him, referring to the faculty given to priests to administer Confirmation, and that the usefulness of a concession allowing priests to consecrate fixed altars was therefore also something that depended on pastoral needs. The Secretary, replying to Msgr. Nabuco, pointed to the use of Chrism in the rite of Baptism. During the discussion, the President was obliged to leave the *Aula* to attend to other business. The report was then approved and the meeting ended at 6 p.m. with the usual prayer.[150]

Meeting L (November 21, 1963)

The Conciliar Commission on the Sacred Liturgy met in the *Sala del Congresso* of the Sacred Congregation of Rites at 5 p.m. with Cardinal Larraona presiding. Cardinals Jullien, Lercaro, and Giobbe were absent, as were Bishops Pichler and Enciso, and Father Schweiger.

At the outset of the meeting, immediately after the prayer, Msgr. Nabuco asked the President to obtain an audience with the Pope for the Commission. The

President assured him that he was interested in the matter.

The Secretary read the announcements, and the President asked the Commission for its opinion with regard to certain faculties in liturgical matters that the Pope intended to concede to bishops. The Commission was favorable to the proposals with the exception of permitting the faithful to receive Holy Communion outside of the liturgy on Good Friday.

While awaiting the drafts of the Constitution, a document prepared by Martimort on episcopal assemblies, of which there had been much mention in the Constitution, was examined by the Commission. The President said that it was necessary to take the minimum as a point of departure (Provincial Councils, Provincial Conferences, Regional Councils, etc.). Msgr. Jenny raised the question of the participation of auxiliary bishops. Msgr. Rossi believed that all Bishops should attend episcopal assemblies.

Having distributed the drafts of the Constitution, the Secretary asked whether the notes were to be placed at the foot of every page or at the end of the document. While Msgr. Rossi favored the former solution, the Commission voted for the latter.

Martimort suggested a number of stylistic changes which were accepted. They were: using "*paenitentia*" in place of "*poenitentia*"; the elimination of "*quidem*" in article 9 and of "*sub*" in article 20; and the following substitutions: replacing "*persolvendi*" with "*persolvere*" (article 96); using "*vero*" instead of "*tantum*" (article 7); and "*autem*" in place of "*vero*" (article 107).

A report on the application of the Constitution prepared by Msgr. Rossi was then examined. Msgr. Martimort presented two questions: 1) He asked whether the text represented the private *votum* of the Commission or was it a *votum* that would be presented to the Pope; 2) He asked that in the list of articles which had been drawn up, that a clear distinction be made between those matters for which the post-Conciliar Commission would have responsibility, and those matters which would be required of the episcopal assemblies, or of the Holy See. The President replied that, with regard to the first point, the Commission could only make proposals on this matter, while in relation to the second matter, everything had already been considered.

Msgr. Rossi began reading the text, and Martimort asked that a further distinction be made between what the Pope could concede and what the Secretary could.

The Secretary, in the name of the Secretariat of the Council, asked that account be taken of three distinctions: those articles to be applied immediately; the *vacatio legis*; and those articles which would require further provisions to be made.

The President suspended further discussion, and he invited the members of the Commission to revise the text and to make possible proposals.

The meeting concluded at about 7 p.m. with the usual prayer.[151]

Meeting LI (November 28, 1963)

The Conciliar Commission on the Sacred Liturgy met in the *Aula* of the Sacred Congregation of Rites at 5 p.m. with Cardinal Larraona presiding. Cardinals Jullien, Lercaro, and Giobbe were absent, as were Bishops Hallinan and Martin. After the prayer, the Secretary made some announcements.

Msgr. Bonet, *peritus*, began reading a text regarding the "*vacatio et exsecutio Constitutionis*" which had been drawn up by a group of experts with Cardinal Larraona. Msgr. Nabuco asked that the *declaratio* annexed to the chapter on sacred art be published, and the President replied that such a thing was beyond the competence of the Commission. Some stylistic changes were made to the text, and the discussion, properly speaking, began with the examination of appendix C concerning episcopal assemblies.

Msgr. Zauner observed that Episcopal Conferences had no competence in liturgical matters. Msgr. Bonet replied that there was no desire to create a new body but simply to confirm these powers *ad interim* on bodies already existing while awaiting clarification of the nature of Episcopal Conferences.

Msgr. Pichler regarded it as dangerous to invite auxiliary bishops to such assemblies. The President believed that all residential bishops ought to be called to these assemblies. Msgr. Wagner, summing up the discussion, observed that the problems were with regard to the competence of the Conferences and the membership of the Conferences. Thus he asked that provision be made for all eventualities while remaining within the general law, but auxiliary and titular bishops should be excluded.

The President replied that account would have to be taken of those who had the right to attend Conferences already in existence. Msgr. Pichler desired that the participation of auxiliary bishops be limited to particular cases. It was finally decided that all auxiliary bishops could be invited to participate in the episcopal assemblies, but they would only have a consultative vote.

Msgr. Diekmann, supported by Msgr. McManus, opposed appendix D which proposed, by Papal concession, the application of article 89. They regarded it as too clerical and proposed the application of article 28 of the Constitution. It was observed that article 28 referred to a future reform.

The Commission was reticent about an immediate suppression of Prime, and the President interrupted the discussion since the subject was not pertinent to the Commission.

Following the Secretary's concluding remarks, the meeting ended at 6:30 p.m. with the usual prayer.[152]

[1] F. ANTONELLI, *Diario n. 16*, cit., p. 3.

[2] Cf. B. FRISÓN, *Cardenal Larraona*, Madrid 1979.

[3] F. ANTONELLI, *Diario n. 16*, cit., p. 33.

[4] *Ibidem*, p. 54.

[5] *Ibidem*, pp. 55-57.

[6] *Ibidem*, pp. 66-70.

[7] *Ibidem*, pp. 80-83. For further details see B. FRISÓN, *Cardenal Larraona*, cit., pp. 458-460.

[8] *Ibidem*, p. 83.

[9] Father Bugnini writes: "Of all the secretaries of the preparatory commissions for the Council, only Fr. Bugnini was not confirmed as secretary of the Liturgical Commission. This was the first sign that the new president of the liturgical commission, Cardinal Arcadio Larraona, was going to follow a line other than that laid down by the Constitution which was following its *iter* to be presented in the Council. Cardinal Larraona pursued his objective by dismissing the secretary and much of the preparatory work. This was Fr. Bugnini's first exile... and it was a direct repressive act of Cardinal Larraona, assisted by some who wished better to serve the Church and the liturgy". For further information on these events, cf. A. BUGNINI, *La riforma liturgica*, cit., p. 41. Also cf. J. WAGNER, *Mein Weg zur Liturgiereform (1936-1988)*, Erinnerungen, Freiburg-Basel 1993, p. 61 where it affirms that Antonelli was a good choice for secretary.

[10] A.G. MARTIMORT, *In memoriam*, cit., p. 426; cf. IDEM, *La Constitution sur la liturgie de Vatican II. Esquisse historique*, in *Bullettin de littérature ecclésiastique*, 85 (1984), pp. 60-74. R. FALSINI also deals with the subject in *Il mistero cristiano e la sua celebrazione*, Milano 1994, p. 182 as does A. VERHEUL, *De leden van de conciliaire commissie voor de liturgie*, in *Tijdschrift voor liturgie* 47 (1963), pp. 88-90, p. 89.

[11] F. ANTONELLI, *Diario n. 16*, cit., p. 122.

[12] *Ibidem*, pp. 123-125.

[13] *Acta Synodalia Sacrosancti Concilii Oecumenici Vaticani II*, vol. I, p. 305.

[14] G. ALBERIGO, *Storia del Concilio Vaticano II*, vol. II, Bologna 1996, p. 131.

[15] F. ANTONELLI, *Diario n. 16*, cit., pp. 125-126.

[16] Cf. *ALV*, folder *Corrispondenze*.

[17] F. ANTONELLI, *Diario n. 16*, cit., p. 84.

[18] Cf. *ibidem*, pp. 95-96.

[19] Cf. F. ANTONELLI, *Antecedenti, importanza e prospettive della Costituzione Liturgica*: L'Osservatore Romano, December 8, 1963, p. 6.

[20] G. ALBERIGO, *Storia del Concilio Vaticano II*, vol. II, Bologna 1996, p. 133.

[21] *Ibidem*, p. 133.

[22] *Verbali delle riunioni della Commissione Conciliare di Sacra Liturgia*, in *SCCS*, Archivio fondo Antonelli, p. 1.

[23] *Ibidem*, p. 2.

[24] *Ibidem*, p. 3.

[25] *Ibidem*, p. 4.

[26] *Ibidem*, p. 5. In order to obtain a complete reading and to have in hand the necessary elements to be able to confront the original text of the Schema that was changed through various modifications by the Conciliar Commission on the Liturgy, we will present each time the original text *Schema Constitutionis de Sacra Liturgia. SACROSANCTUM OECUMENICUM CONCILIUM VATICANUM SECUNDUM, Commissio Conciliaris de Sacra Liturgia, Schema Constitutionis de Sacra Liturgia, Emendationes*, I, Proemium, Typis Polyglottis Vaticanis, 1962. Line n. 5 p. 1: *quidquid ad unionem fratrum separatorum in Ecclesia quoquo modo conferre potest, fovere;et quidquid ad omnes in sinum Ecclesiae vocandos concurrit, roborare; suum esse ducit peculiari ratione etiam de instauranda atque fovenda Liturgia curare.* Line n. 11 p. 1: *Liturgia enim, per quam, maxime in suo centro, divinae scilicet Eucharistiae Sacrificio, opus Redemptionis exercetur, summe confert ut fideles vivant et aliis manifestent*

mysterium Christi et genuinam verae Ecclesiae naturam: cuius proprium est esse simul humanam et divinam, visibilem et invisibilem, Ecclesiam actionis et contemplationis, in mundo praesentem et tamen peregrinam.

[27] Cf. *Verbali delle riunioni della Commissione Conciliare di Sacra Liturgia*, in *SCCS*, Archivio fondo Antonelli, p. 6. *SACROSANCTUM OECUMENICUM CONCILIUM VATICANUM SECUNDUM, Commissio*, cit. *Textus Schematis*, Caput I, nn. 1-9, Line n. 5 p. 5: *Deus, qui "omnes homines vult salvos fieri et ad agnitionem veritatis venire"* (1 Tm 2:4), *"multifariam multisque modis olim loquens patribus in prophetis"* (Heb 1:1), *ubi venit plenitudo temporis, misit Filium suum Verbum carnem factum ad evangelizandum pauperibus, ad sanandos contritos corde, "medicum carnalem et spiritualem", Mediatorem Dei et hominum. Ipsius namque humanitas, in unitate personae Verbi, fuit causa nostrae salutis.*

[28] Line n. 2 p. 6: *Nam, sicut Christus missus est a Patre, ita et ipse, "totius Ecclesiae mirabile sacramentum" instituens, Apostolos eorumque successores misit, non solum ut, praedicantes evangelium omni creaturae, annuntiarent Filium Dei morte sua nos a potestate satanae et a morte liberasse, ac resurrectione sua in regnum Patris transtulisse, sed etiam ut opus salutis, quod annuntiabant, per Sacramenta efficerent.*

[29] N. 3 line n. 41 p. 6: [... *ob praesentiam ipsius christi in Liturgia*, ...]. Ad tantum vero opus perficiendum, Christus Ecclesiae suae semper adest, praesertim in actionibus liturgicis, ipse qui promisit: "ubi sunt duo vel tres congregati in nomine meo, ibi sum in medio eorum" (Mt. 18,20). *Ipse est qui loquitur dum verba sacrae Scripturae in Ecclesia leguntur et explicantur; qui opus salutis quod degens in terra patraverat, in Sacramentis pergit; ipse denique nunc in Sacrificio Missae se offert "sacerdotum ministerio, qui seipsum tunc in Cruce obtulit".*

[30] N. 5 line n. 6 p. 8: [Liturgia in se non amplectitur totum ambitum actionis Ecclesiae]. Licet sacra Liturgia non amplectatur totum ambitum actionis Ecclesiae, *est tamen in suo centro, quod est divinum Eucharistiae Sacrificium, culmen ad quod omnia tendere debent, et simul fons a quo omnia procedunt.* N. 6, line n. 33, pag. 8: [*Eucharistiae Sacrificium fons vitae Ecclesiae*]. *Labores autem apostolici ad id tendunt, ut qui receperunt fidem et paenitentiam egerunt filii Dei fiant per Baptismum, in unum conveniant, in medio Ecclesiae Deum laudent et cenam dominicam manducent.*

[31] *Verbali delle riunioni della Commissione Conciliare di Sacra Liturgia*, in *SCCS*, Archivio fondo Antonelli, p. 7.

[32] N. 9 line n. 37 p. 9: [*Pia exercitia approbata et commendata*]. Pia populi christiani exercitia, si legibus Ecclesiae conformia sint, valde commendantur, praesertim cum de mandato Sancta Sedis fiunt.

[33] *Verbali delle riunioni della Commissione Conciliare di Sacra Liturgia*, in *SCCS*, Archivio fondo Antonelli, p. 9.

[34] N. 10 line n. 3 p. 6: [*Magistri in Sacra Liturgia formandi*]. Magistri, qui sacrae Liturgiae scientiae in seminariis et facultatibus theologicis docendae praeficientur, ad munus suum in istitutis ad hoc speciali cura destinatis probe instituendi sunt. The modifications of the Sub-commission were: Magistri, qui sacrae Liturgiae *disciplinae* in seminariis, *studiorum domibus religiosis* et facultatibus theologicis docendae praeficintur, ad munus suum in istitutis ad hoc speciali cura destinatis probe instituendi sunt.

[35] *Verbali delle riunioni della Commissione Conciliare di Sacra Liturgia*, in *SCCS*, Archivio fondo Antonelli, p. 11.

[36] N. 16 line n. 5 p. 21: [*Libri liturgici recognoscendi*]. Libri liturgici recognoscantur, *peritis* ex universo orbe adhibitis; et intra paucos annos adantur.

[37] *Verbali delle riunioni della Commissione Conciliare di Sacra Liturgia*, in *SCCS*, Archivio fondo Antonelli, p. 13.

[38] N. 25 line n. 19 p. 23: [*Lectio sacrae Scripturae, praedicatio et catechesis liturgica*]. Ut clare appareat in Liturgia ritum et verbum intime coniungi: ...

[39] *Verbali delle riunioni della Commissione Conciliare di Sacra Liturgia*, in *SCCS*, Archivio fondo Antonelli, p. 14.

[40] *Verbali della riunioni delle Commissione Conciliare di Sacra Liturgia*, in *SCCS*, Archivio fondo

Antonelli, p. 15.

[41] N. 21 line n. 15 p. 25: [*Limites aptationis*]. Limites servandi in hac aptatione facienda ita a legislatione ecclesiastica statuantur ut, intacta vi editionis typicae librorum liturgicorum a Sancta Sede editorum aut edendorum, Ordinariis singularum provinciarum vel regionum, vel etiam Conferentiae Episcopali nationali, maior concedatur facultas divinum cultum ordinandi, imprimis autem quoad administrationem Sacramentorum et Sacramentalium, processiones, linguam liturgicam, musicam sacram et artes, actis a Sancta Sede recognitis (cf. can. 291). The corrections of the Sub-commission were: Intra limites in editionibus typicis librorum litugicorum statutos, erit competentis auctoritatis ecclesiasticae territorialis, de qua in art. 22 § 2, aptationes definire, *praesertim* quoad administrationem Sacramentorum, *quoad* Sacramentalia, processiones, linguam liturgicam, musicam sacram et artes, iuxta tamen normas fundamentales quae hac in constitutione, habentur.

[42] *Verbali delle riunioni della Commissione Conciliare di Sacra Liturgia*, in SCCS, *Archivio fondo Antonelli*, p. 16.

[43] N. 24 line n. 9 p. 24: [*Lingua liturgica*]. Latinae linguae usus in Liturgia occidentali servetur. The changes of the Sub-commission were: § 1 Linguae latinae usus, salvo particulari iure, in *Ritibus latinis* servetur.

[44] N. 24 line n. 11 p. 24: Cum tamen "in non paucis ritibus vulgati sermonis usurpatio valde utilis apud populum existere" possit, amplior locus ipsi in Liturgia tribuatur, imprimis autem in lectionibus et admonitionibus, in nonnullis orationibus et cantibus. The changes of the VI Sub-commission were: § 2: Cum tamen, sive in Missa, sive in Sacramentorum administratione, sive in aliis liturgiae partibus, *haud raro linguae vernaculae* usurpatio valde utilis apud populum existere possit, amplior locus ipsi *tribui valeat*, imprimis autem in lectionibus et admonitionibus, in nonnullis orationibus et cantibus, iuxta normas quae de hac re in sequentibus capitibus singillatim statuuntur.

[45] N. 24 line n. 20 p. 24: Sit vero Conferentiae Episcopalis in singulis regionibus, etiam, si casus ferat, consilio habito cum Episcopis finitimarum regionum eiusdem linguae, limites et modum linguae vernaculae in Liturgiam admittendae Sanctae Sedi proponere. The changes were: § 3: *Huiusmodi normis servatis, est competentis auctoritatis ecclesiasticae territorialis, de qua in art.* 22 § 2, etiam, si casus ferat, consilio habito cum Episcopis finitimarum regionum eiusdem linguae, *de usu et modo* linguae vernaculae statuere, actis ab Apostolica Sede probatis seu confirmatis.

[46] The new draft proposed by the Sub-commission read as follows: §4 Conversio textus Latini in linguam vernaculam in Liturgia adhibendam, a competenti auctoritate ecclesiastica territoriali, de qua supra, approbari debet.

[47] *Verbali delle riunioni della Commissione Conciliare di Sacra Liturgia*, in SCCS, *Archivio fondo Antonelli*, p. 17.

[48] N. 23 line n. 14 p. 23: [*Structura rituum*]. Ritus modo simplici et claro extruantur, sint brevitate perspicui et repetitiones inutiles evitent, sint fidelium captui accomodati, neque generatim indigeant multis commentariis ut intellegantur. The modifications made by the V Sub-commission were: n. 34: Ritus *nobili simplicitate fulgeant,* sint brevitate perspicui et repetitiones inutiles evitent, sint fidelium captui accomodati, neque generatim multis indigeant *explanationibus.* The text proposed for n. 25 line n. 19 of the Schema was: [*Lectio sacrae Scripturae, praedicatio et catechesis liturgica*]. Ut clare appareat in Liturgia ritum et verbum intime coniungi ….The modifications made were: N. 35: Ut clare appareat in Liturgia ritum et verbum intime coniungi…

[49] *Verbali delle riunioni della Commissione Conciliare di Sacra Liturgia*, in SCCS, *Archivio fondo Antonelli*, p. 18.

[50] *Ibidem*, p. 19.

[51] *Verbali delle riunioni della Commissione Conciliare di Sacra Liturgia*, in SCCS, *Archivio fondo Antonelli*, p. 20-21.

[52] *Verbali delle riunioni della Commissione Conciliare di Sacra Liturgia*, in SCCS, *Archivio fondo Antonelli*, p. 22-23.

[53] N. 48 line n. 13 p. 25: Itaque curat Ecclesia ut christifideles huic mysterio fidei non velut inertes

et mutui spectatores intersint, sed ut ritus et preces bene intellegentes, ea actuose, conscie et pie participent, mensa cum verbi tum corporis Domini reficiantur, gratias Deo agant, immaculatam hostiam una sacerdote offerendo seipsos offerre discant, et de die in diem ad perfectiorem unitatem transferantur ut sit Deus omnia in omnibus. The Sub-commission proposed the following corrections: N. 48: Itaque Ecclesia *sollicitas curas eo intendit ne* christifideles huic mysterio *tamquam extranei vel muti spectatores* intersint, sed *per* ritus et preces *id* bene intellegentes, *sacram actionem* conscie, pie et actuose participent, *verbo Dei instituantur*, mensa Corporis Domini reficiantur, gratias Deo agant, immaculantam hostiam, *non tantum per sacerdotis manus, sed etiam una cum ipso offerentes*, seipsos offerre discant, et de die in diem *consummentur, Christo Mediatore, in unitatem cum Deo et inter se*, ut sit *tandem* Deus omnia in omnibus.

[54] N. 37 line n. 13 p. 26 of the original Schema read: [*Ordo Missae instaurandus*]. Ordo Missae ita recognoscatur, sive in generali dispositione sive in singulis partibus, ut clarius percipiatur et actuosam fidelium participationem faciliorem reddat. The modifications of the Sub-commission were: n. 50: Ordo Missae ita recognoscantur, *ut singularum partium propria ratio necnon mutua connexio clarius pateant, atque pia et actuosa fidelium participatio facilior raddatur. Quamobrem ritus, probe servata eorum substantia, simpliciores fiant; ea omittantur quae temporum decursu duplicata fuerunt vel minus utiliter addita; restituantur vero ad pristinam sanctorum Patrum normam nonnulla quae temporum iniuria deciderunt, prout opportuna vel necessaria videantur.*

[55] N. 38 line n. 26: [*Lectiones in Missa*]. Ut fidelibus cum mensa eucharistica etiam ditior mensa verbi Dei paretur, thesauri biblici largius aperiantur, ita ut, decursu plurium annorum, praestantior pars Scripturarum sanctarum populo praelegatur.

[56] N. 39 line n. 32: [*Homilia*]. Homilia, tamquam pars ipsius Liturgiae, valde commendatur, praesertim diebus dominicis et festis de praecepto. The Sub-commission modified this to read: n. 52: Homilia, qua per anni liturgici cursum ex textu sacro fidei mysteria et normae vitae christianae exponuntur, *ut* pars ipsius liturgiae, valde commendatur; quinimmo in Missis quae diebus dominicis et festis de praecepto concorrente populo celebrantur, ne omittatur, nisi grave de causa.

[57] The original text of the Schema proposed the following for n. 40 line n. 3 p. 27: [*Oratio communis*]. Oratio communis, seu fidelium, post Evangelium et homiliam, saltem diebus dominicis et festis de praecepto, redintegretur, ita ut, populo participante, obsecrationes fiant pro sancta Ecclesia, "pro omnibus hominibus, pro regibus et omnibus qui in sublimitate sunt". The modifications of the Sub-commission were: n. 53: "Oratio communis" seu "fidelium", post Evangelium et homiliam, *praesertim* diebus dominicis et festis de praecepto, *restituatur*, ut populo *eam* participante, obsecrationes fiant pro sancta Ecclesia, *pro iis qui nos in potestate regunt, pro iis qui variis premuntur necessitatibus, ac* pro omnibus hominibus *totiusque mundi salute.*

[58] N. 41 line n. 11 p. 27: [*Lingua*]. Linguae vernaculae in Missis cum populo congruus locus tribuatur, imprimis autem in lectionibus, oratione communi et nonnulis cantibus, ad normam articuli 24 huius Constitutionis. The Sub-commission proposed the following changes: Linguae vernaculae in Missis cum populo *celebratis* congruus locus tribui possit, *praesertim* in lectionibus *et* "oratione communi", ac, pro condicione locorum, etiam in partibus quae ad populum spectant, ad normam *art.* 36 huius Constitutionis.

[59] *Verbali delle riunioni della Commissione Conciliare di Sacra Liturgia*, in *SCCS, Archivio fondo Antonelli*, p. 24-25.

[60] N. 42 line n. 29 of the original Schema proposed: [*Communio sub utraque specie*]. Communio sub utraque specie, sublato fidei periculo, pro certis casibus a Sancta Sede bene determinatis, uti, v.g., in Missa sacrae Ordinationis, iudicio Episcoporum, tum clericis et religiosis, iudicio Episcoporum, tum clericis et religiosis, tum laicis concedi potest. The modifications of the Sub-commission were: n. 55: Valde commendatur illa perfectior Missae participatio qua fideles post communionem sacerdotis ex eodem sacrificio corpus dominicum sumunt. Communio sub utraque specie, firmis principiis dogmaticis a Concilio Tridentino Statutis, *in casibus ab Apostolica Sede definiendis,* tum clericis et religiosis, tum laicis concedi potest, de iudicio Episcoporum, *veluti ordinatis in Missa sacrae suae ordinationis, professis in Missa religiosae suae professionis, neophitis in Missa quae Baptismum subsequitur.*

The Preparation of *Sacrosanctum Concilium*, 1960-1963

[61] N. 43 line n. 37 p. 27: [*Praeceptum Missae festivae*]. Liturgia Missae duabus partibus quodammodo constat, liturgia nempe verbi et eucharistica. Hae duae partes tamen ita intrinsece coniunguntur, ut unicum actum cultus efformant. Proinde animarum pastores, in catechesi tradenda, fideles sedulo instruant, ut integrae Missae celebrationi intersint. The modifications of the Sub-commission were: *Due partes e quibus Missa* quodammodo constat, liturgia nempe verbi et eucharistica, *tam arcte inter se* coniunguntur, ut *unum* actum cultus *efficiant. Sacra proinde Synodus vehementer hortatur* animarum pastores *ut,* in catechesi tradenda, fideles sedulo *doceant de integra Missa participanda,* praesertim diebus dominicis et festis de praecepto.

[62] N. 44 line n. 8 p. 28: [*Usus amplificetur*]. Concelebratio tam in Ecclesia Orientali quam in Occidentali in usu hucusque remansit. Concilio facultatem concelebrandi ad sequentes casus extendere placet: *a)* ad Missam chrismatis, feria V in Cena Domini; *b)* ad conventus sacerdotum, si ad singulares celebrationes aliter provideri non possit et de iudicio Ordinarii. The modifications of the Sub-commission were: n. 57: § 1. Concelebratio, qua unitas sacerdotii opportune manifestatur, in Ecclesia tam Orientali quam Occidentali *usque adhuc* in usu remansit. *Quare* facultatem concelebrandi ad sequentes casus Concilio extendere *placet:* 1°*a)* Feria V in Cena Domini, tum ad Missam Chrismatis, tum ad Missam Vespertinam; *b)* ad Missas in Conciliis, conventibus Episcopalibus et Synodis; *c)* ad Missam in Benedictione Abbatis; 2° Praeterea, accedente licentia Ordinarii, cuius est de opportunitate concelebrationis iudicare eiusque disciplinam moderari: *a)* ad Missam conventualem et ad Missam principalem in Ecclesiis, cum utilitas christifidelium singularem celebrationem omnium sacerdotum praesentium non postulet; *b)* ad Missas in conventibus cuiusvis generis sacerdotum tum saecularium tum religiosorum.

[63] N. 46 line 36 p. 28: [*Ritus concelebrationis*]. Quoad ritum, servari possunt rubricae Pontificalis romani. Attamen quaedam aptationes fiant, scilicet: *a)* ut concelebrantes, oblatione peracta, stent circa altare, vestibus sacerdotalibus, aut saltem alba et stola, induti; *b)* ut minuatur numerus precum a concelebrantibus simul dicendarum; *c)* ut communicare possint sub utraque specie; *d)* ut solus celebrans principalis gestus faciat et benedicat. The modifications of the Sub-commission were: n. 58: *Novus ritus concelebrationis conficiatur, Pontificali et Missali Romano inserendus.*

[64] *Verbali delle riunioni della Commissione Conciliare di Sacra Liturgia,* in *SCCS, Archivio fondo Antonelli,* pp. 26-28.

[65] Preamble cap. III *De Sacramentis et Sacramentalibus,* p. 19: Sacramenta et Sacramentalia ordinantur ad cultum debite Deo reddendum et ad hominem sanctificandum, utpote vero signa "ad instructionem pertinent". Unde fidem non solum supponunt, sed "verbis ac rebus" alunt; et ita eorum celebratio liturgica fideles ad cultum Deo debite reddendum et ad gratiam fructuose recipiendam etiam proxime disponit. Ideo "sacramenta fidei" dicuntur. The modifications the Sub-commission made were: n. 59 line n.1: Sacramenta ordinantur *ad santificationem hominum, ad aedificationem Corporis Christi,* ad cultum *denique* Deo reddendum; *ut* signa vero *etiam* alunt, *roborant, exprimunt; quare* fidei sacramenta dicuntur. *Gratiam quidem conferunt, sed* eorum celebratio fideles *optime* etiam disponit ad *eandem* gratiam fructuose recipiendam, *ad Deum rite colendum et ad caritatem exercendam.* Preamble line n. 12 p. 19: Maxime proinde interest ut qui ad fidem vocantur, Baptismum verum signum fidei inveniant, et fideles, ad propriam vitam christianam alendam, Sacramenta impensissime frequentent. The modifications were: Maxime proinde interest ut *fideles signa Sacramentorum facile intellegant et ea* Sacramenta impensissime frequentent, *quae ad vitam christianam alendam sunt instituta.*

[66] Preamble of the Original Schemata line 20 p. 20 reads: Cum autem, decursu temporum, non sine fidelium detrimento, quaedam in ea irrepserint quae praedictae eorum naturae minus bene respondeant, Sacrosanctum Concilium ea quae sequuntur decernit. The modifications of the Sub-commission were: n. 62: cum autem, *successu* temporum, quaedam in *Sacramentorum et Sacramentalium ritus* irrepserint, *quibus eorum natura et finis nostris temporibus minus eluceant, atque adeo opus sit quaedam in eis ad nostrae aetatis necessitates accommodare,* Sacrosanctum Concilium ea quae sequuntur *de eorum recognitione* decernit.

[67] N. 47 line n. 1 p. 21: [*Ritualia particularia*]. In nova editione "typica" Ritualis romani paranda, clare indicentur partes, quae, in Ritualis particularibus, lingua vulgari dici possunt. Super huiusmodi autem

131

Ritualis romani editione, Ritualia particularia, singularum regionum necessitatibus aptata (cf. art. 21 huius Constitutionis), a Conferentiis Episcopalibus quam primum parentur, et, actis a Sancta Sede recognitis (cf. can. 291), in respectivis regionibus adhibeantur. In his autem Ritualibus vel peculiaribus Collectionibus rituum conficiendis, ne omittantur instructiones pastorales et rubricales, quae in Rituali romano singulis ritibus praemittuntur. The Sub-commission made the following modifications: *b) Iuxta novam Ritualis romani editionem,* Ritualia particularia, singularum regionum necessitatibus, *etiam quoad linguam, accomodata, a competenti ecclesiastica actuoritate territoriali de qua in art.* 22 § *2 huius Constitutionis* quam primum parentur, et, actis *ab Apostolica* Sede recognitis, in regionibus *ad quas pertinet* adhibeantur. In iis autem Ritualibus vel peculiaribus Collectionibus rituum conficiendis, ne omittantur instructiones, in Rituali romano singulis ritibus *praepositae, sive* pastorales et rubricales, *sive quae peculiare momentum sociale habent.*

[68] The original Schema read as follows· [*Restauratio cathecumenatus*]. Instauretur chatecumenatus adultorum pluribus gradibus distinctus, ita ut tempus cathecumenatus, instructioni destinatum, de iudicio Ordinarii loci, sacris quoque ritibus successivis temporibus celebrandis, santificari possit.

[69] N. 49 line n. 17 p.21: [*Elementa initiationis a traditione populorum derivata*]. In terris Missionum, praeter ea quae in traditione christiana habentur, illa etiam elementa initiationis admittantur, quae apud unumquemque populum in usu reperiuntur, quatenus ritui christiano aptari possunt.

[70] N. 50 line n. 29: [*Ordo Baptismi adultorum*]. Ritus ad baptizandos adultos recognoscatur, ratione habita catechumenatus instaurati; et Missali romano Missa propria in collatione Baptismi inseratur.

[71] N. 51 line n. 34: [*Ordo Baptismi parvulorum*]. Ritus ad baptizandos parvulos condicioni reali infantis rationis nondum compotis aptetur; partes etiam parentum et patrinorum in ipso ritu melius in luce ponantur.

[72] N. 52 line n. 4 p. 22: [*Ordo brevior Baptismi*]. Conficiatur Ordo brevior Baptismi, qui, in terris Missionum, a catechistis, et generatim, in periculo mortis, a fidelibus, absente sacerdote vel diacono, adhiberi possit.

[73] The second part of N. 69 of the modifications of the Sub-commission read: Item *novus ritus* conficiatur pro valide iam baptizatis, *ad sacra catholica conversis, quo significetur eos in Ecclesiae communionem admitti.*

[74] N. 54 line n. 20 [*Benedictio aquae baptismalis*]. Aqua baptismalis, extra tempus paschale, in ipso ritu Baptismi, ex iusta et rationabili causa, formula breviore et apta, benedici potest.

[75] *Verbali delle riunioni della Commissione Conciliare di Sacra Liturgia,* in *SCCS, Archivio fondo Antonelli,* pp. 29-31.

[76] The original Schema of N. 55 p. 22 reads: [*Ritus Confirmationis*]. Ritus Confirmationis ita recognoscatur, ut clarius eluceat huius Sacramenti intrinseca connexio cum tota initiatione christiana; et ideo, pro opportunitate, Confirmatio etiam intra Missam conferri possit; eamque praecedat renovatio promissionum Baptismi. Ipsa administratio Sacramenti aptioribus liturgicis formulis introducatur. The modifications of the Sub-commission were: n. 71: Ritus Confirmationis recognoscatur *etiam* ut huius Sacramenti *intima* connexio cum tota initiatione christiana clarius eluceat; *quapropter* renovatio promissionum Baptismi *convenienter ipsam Sacramenti susceptionem praecedet.* Confirmatio, pro opportunitate, intra Missam conferri *potest; ad ritum autem extra Missam quod attinet, paretur formula ad modum introductionis adhibenda.*

[77] N. 56 of the original Schema: [*Ordo Poenitentiae*]. Ritus et formulae Poenitentiae ita recognoscantur, ut effectum Sacramenti clarius exprimant. The modifications of the Sub-commission were: n. 72 Ritus...., ut *naturam et* effectum...

[78] N. 57 of the original Schema, line n. 1 p. 23: [*Nomen et natura Sacramenti*]. Sacramentum, quod communiter "Extrema Unctio" nuncupatur, deinceps "Unctio infirmorum" vocabitur; nam non est per se Sacramentum morientium, sed graviter aegrotantium, ac proinde tempus opportunum illud recipiendi est statim ac fidelis in gravem morbum inciderit. The modifications of the Sub-commission were: n. 73: "Extrema Unctio", quae etiam et melius "Unctio infirmorum" vocari potest, non est Sacramentum eorum tantum qui in extremo vitae discrimine versantur. Proinde tempus opportunum id recipiendi iam certe habetur cum fidelis incipit esse in periculo mortis propter infirmitatem vel senium.

The Preparation of *Sacrosanctum Concilium*, 1960-1963

[79] N. 58: [*Collatio Sacramenti*]. Unctio infirmi regulariter locum habeat post Confessionem et ante receptionem Eucharistiae. The modifications of the Sub-commission were: n. 74: *Praeter ritus seiunctos Unctionis infirmorum et Viatici, conficiatur Ordo continuus secundum quem Unctio aegroto conferatur* post confessionem et ante receptionem *Viatici*.

[80] N. 59: [*Ritus Sacramenti*]. Unctionum numerus pro opportunitate aptetur (cf. art. 21 huius Constitutionis), et orationes quae ritum Unctionis infirmorum comitantur, ita recognoscantur, ut respondeant diversis condicionibus infirmorum, qui Sacramentum recipiunt. The modifications of the Sub-commission were: Unctionum numerus pro opportunitate *accommodetur*, et orationes *ad* ritum unctionis infirmorum *pertinentes* ita recognoscantur, ut respondeant *variis* condicionibus infirmorum, qui Sacramentum *suscipiunt*.

[81] N. 61: [*Ritus Ordinationum recognoscendi*]. Ritus Ordinationum a peritis, sive quoad caerimonias sive quoad textus, recognoscantur. Allocutiones Episcopi, initio cuisque Ordinis, fiant lingua fidelibus nota. The modifications of the Sub-commission were: n. 76: Ritus Ordinationum sive quoad caerimonias sive quoad textus, recognoscantur. Allocutiones episcopi, initio cuiusque *Ordinationis aut Consecrationis, fieri possunt lingua vernacula*. In Consecratione Episcopali impositionem manuum fieri licet ab omnibus episcopis praesentibus.

[82] N. 62: [*Ritus Matrimonii*]. Ritus celebrandi Matrimonium, qui exstat in Rituali romano, funditus recognoscatur et ditior fiat, ita ut gratia Sacramenti clarius significetur. The modifications of the Sub-commission were N. 77: Ritus celebrandi Matrimonium, qui exstat in Rituali romano, funditus recognoscatur et ditior fiat, *quo* clarius gratia Sacramenti significetur *et munera coniugum inculcentur.*

[83] N. 63: [*Celebratio Matrimonii*]. Matrimonium ordinarie infra Missam celebretur, post lectionem Evangelii et homiliam, ante orationem fidelium. Oratio super sponsam, ita opportune emendata ut supra utrumque coniugem recitari valeat, dicatur lingua vernacula. Si vero Sacramentum Matrimonii extra Missam, sed in ecclesia, celebratur, lectiones de Epistola et Evangelio Missae pro Sponsis legantur in initio ritus. The modifications of the Sub-commission were: n. 78: Matrimonium *ex more intra* Missam celebretur, post lectionem Evangelii et homiliam, ante "orationem fidelium". Oratio super sponsam, ita opportune emendata ut *aequalia officia mutuae fidelitatis utriusque sponsi inculcet, dici potest* lingua vernacula. Si vero Sacramentum Matrimonii *sine Missa* celebratur, Epistola et Evangelium Missae pro sponsis legantur in initio ritus et benedictio sponsis semper impertiatur.

[84] *Verbali delle riunioni della Commissione Conciliare di Sacra Liturgia*, in *SCCS, Archivio fondo Antonelli*, pp. 32-34.

[85] N. 64. [*Recognitio Sacramentalium*]. Sacramentalia funditus recognoscantur, prae oculis habito principio de conscia, actuosa et facili participatione fidelium, et attentis hodiernis necessitatibus. In Ritualibus recognoscendis, etiam nova Sacramentalia, prout necessitas expostulat, addi possunt. Benedictiones reservatae perpaucae, et in favorem tantum Episcoporum, habeantur. The modifications of the Sub-commission were: N. 79: Sacramentalia recognoscantur, *ratione habita nermae primariae* de conscia, actuosa et facili participatione fidelium, et attentis *nostrorum temporum* necessitatibus. In Ritualibus recognoscendis, *ad normam art. 63*, etiam nova Sacramentalia, prout necessitas expostulat, addi possunt. Benedictiones reservatae perpaucae *sint*, et in favorem tantum Episcoporum *vel Ordinariorum*. Provideatur ut quaedam Sacramentalia, saltem in specialibus rerum adiunctis et de iudicio Ordinarii, a laicis congruis qualitatibus praeditis, administrari possint.

[86] N. 65 line n. 4 p. 25: [*Ritus vestitionis et professionis religiosae*]. Conficiatur ritus vestitionis et professionis religiosae et renovationis votorum, qui valde optatam unitatem, sobrietatem et dignitatem inducat, ita tamen ut quidam ritus particulares non excludantur. Professio religiosa infra Missam fieri potest. The modifications of the Sub-commission were: n. 80: *Ritus Consecrationis Virginum, qui in Pontificali romano habetur, recognitioni subiciatur.* Conficiatur *praeterea ritus professionis religiosae et renovationis votorum*, qui *ad maiorem* unitatem, sobrietatem et dignitatem *conferat, ab iis qui professionem vel votorum renovationem intra Missam peragunt, salvo iure particulari, assumendus.* Professio religiosa *laudabiliter intra* Missam *fiet.*

[87] N. 66: [*Ordo exsequiarum*]. Ritus exsequiarum sensum paschalem mortis christianae clarius exprimat, et condicionibus ac traditionibus singularum regionum melius aptetur. The modifications

of the Sub commission were: Ritus exsequiarum paschalem mortis christianae *indolem manifestius,* exprimat, *atque* condicionibus *et* traditionibus singularum regionum, *etiam quoad colorem liturgicum,* melius *respondeat.*

[88] Preamble *De Offico Divino* caput IV line n.1 p.31: Summus Novi atque aeterni Testamenti Sacerdos, Christus Iesu, "humanam naturam assumens, terrestri huic exilio hymnum illum invexit, qui in supernis sedibus per omne aevum canitur. Universam hominum communitatem ipse sibi coagmentat, eandemque in divino hoc concinendo laudis carmine secum consociat".

[89] N. 2 of the Preamble: Ecclesia autem, sacerdotio mirabili in suo Capite insignita, et divinam ipsius missionem in terris pergens, "pro hominibus constituitur in iis quae sunt ad Deum", ut Deum sine intermissione laudet et pro singulis interpellet. Quod munus absolvit non solum per celebrationem Eucharistiae, sed etiam per mirabile illud laudis canticum, in Officio divino exstans, quod christianorum omnium nomine eorumque in beneficium adhibetur Deo, cum a sacerdotibus aliisque fiat, in hanc rem ipsius Ecclesiae instituto delegatis. The modifications of the Sub-commission were: Illud enim sacerdotale munus per ipsam suam Ecclesiam pergit, *quae non tantum Eucharistia celebranda,* sed etiam aliis modis, praesertim *Officio divino persolvendo, Dominum* sine intermissione laudat et pro *totius mundi salute interpellat.* Moreover, line n. 84 adds: *Divinum Officium ex antiqua traditione christiana ita est constitutum ut totus cursus diei ac noctis per laudem Dei consecretur.* Cum vero mirabile illud laudis canticum rite peragunt sacerdotes aliique ad hanc rem Ecclesiae instituto deputati vel chrisitifideles una cum sacerdote forma probata orantes, tunc vere vox est ipsius Sponsae, quae Sponsum alloquitur, immo etiam oratio Christi cum ipsius corpore ad Patrem.

[90] N. 3 of the Preamble line n. 6 p. 32: Omnes proinde qui hoc munere funguntur tum gravem Ecclesiae obligationem, tum summum Sponsae Christi honorem participant, quia unusquisque in Officio divino orando ante thronum Dei stat nomine Matris Ecclesiae. The modifications of the Sub-commission were: line n. 85: Omnes proinde qui *haec praestant, tum Ecclesiae officium explent,* tum summum Sponsae Christi honorem participant, *quia laudes Deo persolventes stant* ante thronum Dei nomine Matris Ecclesiae.

[91] N. 4 of the Preamble: Huiusmodi Ecclesiae precatio ex antiqua traditione ita est constituta, ut totus cursus diei ac noctis per sacrificium laudis, a labiis confitentium Deo oblatum, consecretur.

[92] N. 5 of the Preamble: Quo vero divinum Officum a sacerdotibus aliisque Ecclesiae membris, in fragilitate humana atque difficillimis temporum adiunctis constitutis, "tamquam sanctificatio diversarum horarum diei" facilius et perfectius peragatur, Sacrosancto Concilio quae sequuntur placuit decernere. The modifications of the Sub-commission were: n. 88: ut *autem* divinum Officium, sive a sacerdotibus *sive ab aliis* Ecclesiae membris *melius et* perfectius *in rerum adiunctis* peragatur, Sacrosancto Concilio, *instaurationem ab Apostolica Sede feliciter inceptam persequenti, de Officio iuxta ritum romanum ea* quae sequuntur placuit decernere.

[93] N. 68 of the original Schema line n. 35 p. 32: [*Cursus Horarum*]. Cum santificatio diei naturalis sit finis Officii divini, cursus Horarum ita instauretur ut "Horis" veritas, in quantum fieri potest, reddatur ratione tamen habita diversarum condicionum vitae hodiernae in determinatione iuridica temporis ad satisfaciendum obligationi Officii divini recitandi. The modifications of the Sub-commission were: n. 88: Cum santificatio diei sit finis Officii, cursus Horarum *traditus* ita instauretur ut Horis veritas *temporis,* quantum fieri potest, reddatur, *simulque ratio habeatur* vitae hodiernae condicionum *in quibus versantur praesertim ii qui operibus apostolicis incumbunt.*

[94] *Verbali delle riunioni della Commissione Conciliare di Sacra Liturgia,* in *SCCS, Archivio fondo Antonelli,* pp. 35-38.

[95] N. 68a of the Schema reads: ut autem cursus traditionalis Officii divini servetur ac simul hodiernae vitae necessitatibus cleri congruentur aptetur, hae normae prae oculis habeantur: *a) Laudes ac Vesperae,* ex venerabili traditione Ecclesiae universalis duplex cardo Officii divini cotidiani, ubique tamquam Horae praecipue celebrandae sunt. The modifications of the Sub-commission were: *a)* Laudes, *ut preces matutinae,* et Vesperae, *ut preces vespertinae,* ex venerabili *universae* Ecclesiae *traditione* duplex cardo Officii cotidiani, Horae praecipue *habendae sunt et ita* celebrandae.

[96] N. 68b: *Completorum* ita instruatur, ut aperte appareat ipsius natura ultimae precationis in fine diei.

The Preparation of *Sacrosanctum Concilium*, 1960-1963

The modifications were: *b)* Completorium ita instruatur, *ut fini diei apte conveniat.*

[97] N. 68c: Hora quae *Matutinum* vocatur, quamvis indolem nocturnae laudis retinens, ita aptetur ut qualibet diei hora recitari valeat. The modifications were: *c)* Hora Matutinum vocatur, quamvis *in choro* indolem nocturnae laudis *retineat*, ita *accomodetur* ut qualibet diei hora recitari *possit, et e Psalmis paucioribus lectionibusque longioribus constet.*

[98] N. 68d: *Horae minores* ita instruantur ut tempore competenti recitari possint, ad sanctificandum laborem cotidianum. The modifications were: *d) Hora Prima supprimatur; e) in choro, Horae Minores Tertia, Sexta, Nona serventur. Extra chorum e tribus unam seligere licet, diei tempori magis congruentem.*

[99] N. 90 of the Sub-commission: *Cum praeterea Officium Divinum, utpote oratio publica Ecclesiae, sit fons pietatis et orationis personalis nutrimentum, obsecrantur in Domino sacerdotes aliique omnes divinum Officium participantes, ut in eo persolvendo mens concordet voci, ad quod melius assequendum, liturgicam et biblicam, praecipue psalmorum, institutionem sibi uberiorem comparent. In instauratione vero peragenda, venerabilis ille Romani Officii secularis thesaurus ita aptetur,ut latius et facilius eo frui possint omnes quibus traditur.*

[100] N. 69 of the original Schema line n. 1 p. 34: [*Psalmi*]. Ut cursus Horarum, in articulo praecedenti propositus, reapse observari possit, psalmi non amplius per unam hebdomadam, sed per longius temporis spatium distribuantur. Opus revisionis psalterii, feliciter inchoatum, perducatur ad finem, respectu habito latinitatis et usus liturgici. The modifications of the Sub-commission were: n. 91: Ut cursus Horarum, in art. 89 propositus, reapse observari possit, psalmi non amplius per unam hebdomadam, sed per longius temporis spatium distribuantur. Opus *recognitionis* Psalterii, feliciter inchoatum, *quamprimum* perducatur ad finem, respectu habito latinitatis *christianae*, usus *liturgici etiam in cantu necnon totius traditionis latinae Ecclesiae.*

[101] N. 71 of the Schema: [*Lectiones*]. In revisendis lectionibus, haec serventur: *a)* Lectiones *Sacrae Scripturae* ita distribuantur, ut thesauri Verbi divini in pleniore amplitudine expedite adiri possint. *b)* Doctrina Patrum debitum suum locum et modum, iuxta Ecclesiae traditionem, obtineat; proinde *lectio ex Patribus* et sublimioribus theologiae spiritualis Magistris, dummodo agatur de textibus a structura et mente Liturgiae non discrepantibus, mensura largiore instauranda est et simul revisenda. *c)* Passiones seu *vitae Sanctorum* ad fidem historica reddantur. The modifications made were: n. 92: *Ad Lectiones quod attinet,* haec serventur: *a) lectio sacrae Scripturae ita ordinetur,* ut thesauri verbi divini in pleniore amplitudine expedite adiri possint; *b) lectiones de operibus Patrum, Doctorum et Scriptorum ecclesiasticorum depromandae melius seligantur; c)* Passiones seu vitae Sanctorum fidei historicae reddantur.

[102] N. 72: [*Orationes*]. *a) In Laudibus ac Vesperis feriarum per annum dicantur "Orationes matutinales ac vespertinales", quae praesto sunt in Sacramentariis; b) Vesperis cotidie "Preces" inserantur pro variis necessitatibus mundi et Ecclesia; c) In fine Horarum minorm, loco orationis diei, dicatur oratio dominica seu "Pater noster".*

[103] *Verbali delle riunioni della Commissione Conciliare di Sacra Liturgia,* in *SCCS, Archivio fondo Antonelli,* pp. 39-41.

[104] N. 73: [*Obligatio*]. Cum infirmitas humanae naturae postulet ut quid minimum orationis praescribatur, et aliunde totum pensum divini Officii servandum sit, hae normae erunt observandae: *a) Communitates choro obligatae* tenentur Officium divinum cotidie in choro celebrare, et quidem: - *totum Officium,* Ordines Canonicorum, Monachorum et Monialium; - saltem *Laudes aut Vesperas,* Capitula residentialia; - *totum Officium aut partem illius,* ceteri Ordines et Congregationes religiosae, secundum proprias Constitutiones. Omnes autem illarum Communitatum clerici, si sunt in Ordinibus maioribus, et omnes sollemniter professi, exceptis conversis, tenentur ad recitationem totius Officii, etiam a solo factam, si totum aut partem in choro non absolvunt. *b) Clerici choro non obligati,* si sunt in Ordinibus maioribus, cotidie, sive in communi, sive a solo, tenentur totum Officium persolvere. *c) Fratres, Sorores, ac laici cuiusvis Instituti status perfectionis observent Constitutiones proprias. Ipsis autem enixe commendatur ut, in quantum fieri potest, Laudes ac Vesperas celebrent sicut in Breviario.* N. 95 of the Sub-commission: Communitates choro obligatae, *praeter Missam conventualem,* tenentur Officium divinum cotidie in choro celebrare, et quidem: *a)* totum Officium, Ordines Canonicorum,

135

Monachorum et Monialium, *aliorumque Regularium ex iure vel constitutionibus choro adstrictorum;* *b)* Capitula *cathedralia vel collegialia, eas partes Officii, quae sibi a iure communi vel particulari imponuntur; c)* Omnes autem illarum Communitatum *sodales, qui* sunt aut in Ordinibus maioribus constituti aut solemniter professi, conversis exceptis, *debent eas Horas canonicas soli recitare, quas in choro non persolvunt.* N. 96 of the Sub-commission: Clerici choro non obligati, si sunt in Ordinibus maioribus *consituti,* cotidie, sive in communi, sive *soli, obligatione* tenentur totum Officium persolvere, *ad noemam art. 89.*

N. 74 of the original Schema: [*Sodales religiosi*]. Sodales cuiusvis Instituti status perfectionis, qui, vi Constitutionum, partes aliquas divini Officii absolvunt, orationem publicam Ecclesiae agunt. Item, publicam Ecclesiae orationem agunt, si quod parvum Officium, vi Constitutionum, recitant, dummodo in modum Officii divini confectum ac rite approbatum sit. The Sub-commission did not make any modifications.

N. 75 of the original Schema: [*Fidelium participatio in Officio divino*]. Curent animarum pastores ut Horae praecipue, vel ad minus Vesperae, potissimum diebus dominicis et festis sollemnioribus in ecclesiis et oratoriis celebrentur communes. Commendatur ut et ipsi laici celebrent Officium divinum, vel cum sacerdotibus, vel inter se congregati, vel immo unusquisque solus. The modifications of the Sub-commission were: n. 100: Curent animarum pastores ut Horae praecipue, *praesertim* Vesperae, diebus dominicis et festis sollemnioribus in ecclesia *communiter* celebrentur. Commendatur ut et ipsi laici *recitent* Officium divinum, vel cum sacerdotibus, vel inter se congregati, *quin* immo unusquisque solus.

[105] N. 77 of the original Schema: [*Lingua adhibenda in recitatione Officii divini*]. *a)* Iuxta saecularem traditionem Occidentalis Ecclesiae, in Officio divino lingua latina clericis servanda est. *b)* Monialibus, necnon sodalibus, sive viris non clericis sive mulieribus, Institutorum statuum perfectionis, in Officio divino, tam in choro aut in communi quam a solo celebrando, a proprio Ordinario, annuente Sancta Sede, concedi potest ut lingua vulgari utantur. *c)* Quivis Officio divino adstrictus, si Officium divinum una cum fidelibus laicis, vel cum iis qui sub *a)* et *b)* nominantur, lingua vernacula celebrat, suae obligationi satisfacit, dummodo textus versionis sit legitime approbatus. The modifications of the Sub-commission were: n. 101: § 1 Iuxta saecularem traditionem *ritus atini,* in Officio divino lingua atina clericis servanda est, *facta tamen Ordinario potestate usum versionis vernaculae ad mormam art. 36 confectae concedendi, singulis pro casibus, iis clericis, quibus usus linguae latinae grave impedimentum est quominus Officium debite persolvant.* § 2 Monialibus, necnon sodalibus, sive viris non clericis sive mulieribus, Institutorum statuum perfectionis, in Officio divino, *etiam* in choro celebrando, concedi potest *a Superiore competente* ut lingua vernacula utantur, *dummodo versio approbata sit.* § 3 Quivis clericus Officio divino adstrictus, si Officium divinum una cum *coetu fidelium vel cum iis qui sub* § 2 *recensentur,* lingua vernacula celebrat, suae obligationi satisfacit, dummodo textus versionis sit approbatus.

[106] *Verbali delle riunioni della Commissione Conciliare di Sacra Liturgia,* in *SCCS, Archivio fondo Antonelli,* pp. 42-43.

[107] Preamble Chapter VII *de Musica Sacra*: Musica traditio sanctae Ecclesiae thesaurum constituit inaestimabile, maxime excellens inter ceteras artis expressiones, cum Musica sacra efformet necessariam Liturgiae sollemnis partem et directe sacram Actionem comitetur. Efficaciam spiritualem sacri concentus in cultu divino laudibus, extulerunt sancti Patres atque Romani Pontifices, qui hac nostra praesertim aetate, praeeunte sancto Pio X, Musicam sacram "ad fontes" revocantes, ipsius characterem ministerialem dominici servitii pressius ostenderunt. *Etsi relationes statuantur, limites tamen in generibus musicis haud ponuntur,* cum Ecclesia omnes verae artis expressiones, debitis praeditas dotibus, amplectatur et in cultum admittat. Normas ac praecepta ecclesiasticae traditionis et disciplinae secutum, prae oculis habens finem ultimum Musicae sacrae, qui "gloria Dei est, santificatio exemplumque fidelium", Sacrosanctum Concilium ea quae sequuntur statuit.

[108] N. 90, suppressed by the Sub-commission, read: [*Natura Musicae sacrae*]. Musica sacra tam nobilem in Liturgia locum ex Patrum traditione habet, ut ei velut ancilla seu administra famuletur, modo orationem suavius exprimens vel unanimitatem fovens, modo ritus sacros maiores sollemnitate comitans. Tanto ergo pulchrior et sanctior erit, quanto actioni liturgicae arctius connectetur.

[109] N. 91 of the original Schema: *Liturgia sollemnis principem locum tenet*]. Forma nobilior celebrationis

136

liturgicae est Liturgia sollemnis, lingua latina celebrata, cum participatione populi. *Ut autem fideles et scholae cantorum ad Liturgiam sollemniter celebrandam progressive ducantur, gradus ipsorum captui et condicioni accomodati statuantur. Proinde sit Conferentiae Episcopalis in singulis regionibus proponere ut nonnulli cantus lingua vernacula peragi possint, ad normam articuli 24 huius Constitutionis.*
[110] N. 92 of the original Schema line n. 21 p. 16: [*Participatio fidelium numquam excludenda*]. Quamvis thesaurus artisticus Musicae sacrae summa cura servandus et fovendus sit, et scholae cantorum assidue provehendae, Episcopi ceterique animarum pastores sedulo provideant ut in qualibet sacra actione, vel sollemnissima, universus fidelium coetus actuosam participationem sibi propriam in cantu praestare possit. The modifications made were: n. 114: Thesaurus Musicae sacrae summa cura *servetur et foveatur.*Scholae cantorum assidue *provehantur, praesertim apud ecclesias cathedrales;* Episcopi *vero* ceterique animarum pastores sedulo *curent* ut in qualibet actione sacra *in cantu peragenda* universus fidelium coetus actuosam participationem sibi propriam praestare *valeat, ad normam art. 28 et 30.*
[111] N. 93 of the original Schema: [*Institutio musica*]. Magni habeatur institutio et praxis musica in Seminariis, in Religiosorum utriusque sexus novitiatibus et studiorum domibus, necnon in ceteris institutis et scholis catholicis; ad quam institutionem obtinendam, magistri, qui Musicae sacrae docendae praeficiuntur, sedulo praeparentur. Cantores vero et musicae artifices, praeter musicam, solida formatione liturgica donentur, iuxta Ecclesiae traditionem et pastoralem populi utilitatem, quibus eorum servitium spiritu ac mente perficiatur. *Fideles quoque, iuxta ipsorum condicionem, sicut in Sacra Liturgia ita in cantu sacro opportune edoceantur, "ut vocem suam sacerdotis vel scholae vocibus, ad praescriptas normas, alternent".*
[112] N. 94 of the original Schema [*Cantus gregorianus et polyphonicus fovendus*]: Ecclesia Romana cantum gregorianum agnoscit tamquam suae Liturgiae proprium: ideo in actionibus liturgicis, ceteris paribus, principem locum obtineat. Alia tamen genera Musicae sacrae, praesertim vero polyphonia, in celebrandis divinis Officiis minime excluduntur, dummodo fidelium actuosam participationem ne impediant, neque dignitati, gravitati et sanctitati Liturgiae repugnent.
[113] N. 98 of the original Schema: [*Organum et instrumenta musica*]. Organum est instrumentum musicum traditionale Ecclesiae occidentalis, ad sacros ritus maiore sollemnitate donandos. Cetera vero musica instrumenta, de iudicio et consensu loci Ordinarii in cultum divinum admitti possunt, quaetenus usui sacro aptari possunt, templi dignitati congruunt, atque communi fidelium actuosae participationi favent. *Nova technicae artis inventa ad sonos producendos vel transmittendos, in sacris celebrationibus Ecclesia haud respuit, dummodo sonitum omnino decorum gratumque edant et talia instrumenta, non modo mere mechanico seu automatico, sed directa et personali artificis actione tractentur.*
[114] *Verbali delle riunioni della Commissione Conciliare di Sacra Liturgia,* in *SCCS, Archivio fondo Antonelli,* pp. 44-46.
[115] N. 99 of the original Schema:[*Omnem stilum artis Ecclesia admittit*]. Ecclesia nullum artis stilum veluti proprium habuit, sed omnium temporum modos semper admisit. Nostrorum etiam temporum atque omnium gentium et regionum ars liberum in Ecclesia campum habet, quae sacris aedibus sacrisque ritibus debita reverentia debitoque honore inserviat; ita quidem ut eadem ad mirabilem illum gloriae concentum quem summi viri per revoluta iam saecula catholicae fidei cecinere, suam queat adiungere vocem. The modifications were: Ecclesia nullum artis stilum veluti proprium habuit, sed *secundum gentium indoles ac condiciones atque variorum Rituum necessitates modos cuiusvis aetatis admisit, efficiens per decursum saeculorum artis thesaurum omni cura servandum.* Nostrorum etiam temporum atque omnium gentium et regionum ars liberum in Ecclesia *exercitium habeat, dummodo* sacris aedibus sacrisque ritibus debita reverentia debitoque honore inserviat; ita quidem ut eadem ad mirabilem illum gloriae concentum quem summi viri per *praeterita* saecula catholicae fidei cecinere, suam queat adiungere vocem.
[116] N. 100 of the original Schema: [*Opera artis fidei et pietati contraria arceantur*]. Curent locorum Ordinarii ut artis opera quaecumque, quae fidei et moribus ac christianae pietati aperte repugnant sensumque vere religiosum, vel ob insanam formarum depravationem, vel ob artis insufficientiam, mediocritatem ac simulationem, offendunt, ab aedibus sacris arceantur ac prorsus expellantur.
[117] N. 101 of the original Schema: [*In diiudicandis artis operibus, periti adhibeantur*]. In diiudicandis

artis operibus, Ordinari curent audire Commissionem dioecesanam de Arte sacra et, si casus ferat, alios viros valde peritos. In causis autem quae, undique spectatae, difficliores evenerit, adeant consilia ceterorum provinciae vel regionis Episcoporum eorumque peritorum. Si etiam horum consultu iudicium tutum non invenitur, rem Sanctae Sedi proponant. The modifications were n. 126: In diiudicandis artis operibus, Ordinari *locorum audiant* Commissionem dioecesanam de Arte sacra et, si casus ferat, alios viros valde peritos, *necnon Commissiones de quibus in articulis 44, 45, 46. Sedulo advigilent Ordinarii ne sacra supellex vel opera pretiosa, utpote ornamenta domus Dei, alienentur vel disperdantur.*

[118] N. 102: [*Commissiones de Arte sacra*]. *Commissiones de Arte sacra tum dioecesanae, tum provinciales vel regionales vel nationales vel etiam internationales, congregentur, in quantum possibile, ex utroque clero et laicis peritis.*

[119] N. 103: [*Artificum institutio*]. Episcopi, vel per se ipsos vel per sacerdotes qui peculiari facultate et amore praediti sunt, artificum curam habeant, ut eos spiritu Artis sacrae et sacrae Liturgiae imbuant. Artifices autem omnes, qui, ingenio suo vocati, gloriae Dei in Ecclesia sancta servire intendunt, semper prae oculis habeant agi de sacra quadam Dei Creatoris imitatione et de operibus cultui catholico, Ecclesiae aedificationi necnon fidelium religiosae instructioni destinatis.

[120] N. 104: [*Disciplina ecclesiastica de Arte sacra opportune revisenda*]. Canones et statuta ecclesiastica, quae rerum externarum ad sacrum cultum pertinentium apparatum spectant, praesertim quoad aedium sacrarum, dignam et utilem constructionem, altarium formam et aedificationem, tabernaculi eucharistici nobilitatem et securitatem, baptisterii aptitudinem et honorem, necnon sacrarum imaginum, decorationis et ornatus convenientiam, moderationem et ordinem, recognoscantur: quae Liturgiae instauratae minus congruere videntur, emendentur aut aboleantur; quae vero ipsi favent, nova et vetera, retineantur vel introducantur.

[121] N. 105: [*Cleri institutio in Arte sacra*]. Clerici, dum sacrae Liturgiae studio incumbunt, instruantur etiam de mutuis relationibus inter Artis sacrae historiam et christianae fidei ac disciplinae evolutionem, quatenus Ecclesiae venerabilia quaecumque monumenta aestiment et servent, necnon artificibus, in novis Artis sacrae operibus efficiendis, illuminata consilia praebere queant. Ad hoc obtinendum, in Universitatibus omnibus catholicis, sacrae Theologiae scholis necnon Facultatibus, principia et historia Artis sacrae doceantur.

[122] Preamble of cap. V *De anno liturgico*: Sponsi divini opera salutifera, statutis diebus in anni decursu pia Mater Ecclesia sacra semper recordatione celebrare contendit. Primo hebdomadae die, quem "dominicum" vocavit, memoriam habuit Resurrectionis Domini, quam etiam semel in anno, solemnitate magna Paschatis, una cum beata ipsius Passione, frequentavit. Totum vero Christi mysterium per anni circulum explicavit, ab Incarnatione et Nativitate usque ad Ascensionem, ad diem Pentecostes et ad exspectationem beatae spei et adventus Domini. Recolendo taliter mysteria Redemptionis, aperuit fidelibus divitias virtutum atque meritorum Domini sui, ita ut omni tempore quodammodo praesentia fiant, et ipsi illa attingant et gratia salutis repleantur. Quin immo, per omnia mysterio Christi unitum, Sancta Ecclesia, in annuo festorum circulo, etiam mysterium beatissimae Dei Genetricis Mariae cum amore frequentat, in quo et praecellentem Redemptionis fructum merito exaltat, et veluti in purissima imagine, id quod ipsa tota esse cupit et sperat cum gaudio contemplatur. The modifications of the Sub-commission were: Pia Mater Ecclesia *suum esse ducit* Sponsi *sui* divini *opus salutiferum, statis diebus per anni decursum* sacra recordatione celebrare. *In unamque hebdomada, die quam Dominicam vocavit,* memoriam *habet* Resurrectionis Domini, quam semel etiam in anno, solemnitate *maxima* Paschatis, una cum beata ipsius Passione, *frequentat.* Totum vero Christi mysterium per anni circulum *explicat,* ab Incarnatione et Nativitate usque ad Ascensionem, ad diem Pentecostes et ad exspectationem beatae spei et adventus Domini. Mysteria Redemptionis, *ita recolens,* divitias virtutum atque meritorum Domini sui, *adeo* ut omni tempore quodammodo praesentia *reddantur,* fidelibus aperit, *qui ea* attingant et gratia salutis repleantur. N. 103: In hoc annuo mysteriorum Christi circulo celebrando, sancta Ecclesia beatam Mariam Dei Genetricem cum peculiari amore veneratur, quae indissolubili nexu cum Filii sui opere salutari coniungitur; in qua praecellentem Redemptionis fructum miratur et exaltat, *ac* veluti in purissima imagine, id quod ipsa tota esse cupit et sperat cum gaudio contemplatur.

[123] N. 4 of the Preamble: In exercitationibus denique, diversis anni temporibus, iuxta traditas disciplinas aggrediendis, fidelium formationem perficit, per illas animi et corporis actuositates, quae in predicatione, in ieunio et instructione vim suam attingunt.

[124] N. 80 of the original Schema, *de anno liturgico instaurando:* Peculiaris natura diei dominici pietati fidelium quam maxime proponatur et inculcetur, quatenus est "dies Domini" et hebdomadalis commemoratio mysterii paschalis et christianae fidelium regenerationis. Aliae proinde celebrationes, nisi revera sint magni momenti; ipsi ne praeponantur. The modifications of the Sub-commission were: n. 106: Mysterium Paschale Ecclesia, ex traditione apostolica quae originem ducit ab ipsa die resurrectionis Christi, octava quaque die celebrat, quae dies Domini seu dies dominica merito nuncupatur. Hac enim die christifidelibus in unum convenire debent ut, verbum Dei audientes et Eucharistiam participantes, memores sint Passionis, Resurrectionis et gloriae Domini Iesu, et gratias agant Deo qui eos "regeneravit in spem vivam per resurrectionem Iesu Christi ex mortuis" (1 Pt. 1:3). Itaque dies Dominica est primordialis dies festus, qui pietati fidelium proponatur et inculcetur, ita ut etiam fiat dies laetitiae et vacationis ab opere. Aliae celebrationes, nisi revera sint maximi momenti, ipsi ne praeponantur, quippe quae sit fundamentum et nucleus totius anni liturgici.

[125] N. 79 of the original Schema: [*Annus liturgicus in genere*]. Annus liturgicus ita recognoscatur ut, servatis aut restitutis sacrorum temporum traditis consuetudinibus et disciplinis iuxta nostrae aetatis condiciones, ipsorum indoles nativa retineatur, ad fidelium pietatem debite alendam in celebrandis mysteriis Redemptionis christianae, maxime vero mysterio paschali, quod est totius anni liturgici veluti centrum et culmen.

[126] *Verbali delle riunioni della Commissione Conciliare di Sacra Liturgia*, in *SCCS, Archivio fondo Antonelli*, pp. 47-49.

[127] N. 81 of the original Schema: [*Proprium de Tempore*]. Fidelium animi dirigantur imprimis ad dies festos Domini, qui mysteria salutis in anno celebrant. Proinde "Proprium de Tempore" aptum suum locum obtineat super festa Sanctorum, ut integer mysteriorum salutis cyclus debito modo recolatur.

[128] N. 82: [*Tempus quadragesimale*]. Duplex character temporis quadragesimalis, praeparatio nempe vel saltem memoria Baptismi et actio poenitentialis, tam in Liturgia quam in catechesi liturgica plenius in luce ponatur. Proinde: *a) ad profundiorem fidelium eruditionem, eorumque ad celebrandum mysterium paschale praeparationem*, elementa baptismalia liturgiae quadragesimalis propria abundantius adhibeantur; quaedam vero ex anteriore traditione, pro opportunitate, restituantur; *b)* idem autem fiat de elementis poenitentialibus. Quoad catechesim autem imprimis inculcentur animis fidelium socialis peccati indoles perniciosa, et partes Ecclesiae in actione poenitentiali; atque oratio pro peccatoribus urgeantur. The modifications made by the Sub-commission were: n. 109: Duplex indoles temporis quadragesimalis, quod praesertim per memoriam vel praeparationem Baptismi et per poenitentiam fideles, instantius verbum Dei audientes et orationi vacantes, componit ad celebrandum Paschale Mysterium, tam in Liturgia quam in catechesi liturgica *pleniore* in luce ponatur. Proinde: *a)* elementa baptismalia liturgiae quadragesimalis propria abundantius adhibeantur; quaedam vero ex anteriore traditione, pro opportunitate, restituantur; *b)* idem *dicatur* de elementis poenitentialibus. Quoad catechesim autem animis fidelium inculcetur, una cum consectariis socialibus peccati, illa propria poenitentiae natura quae peccatum, prout est offensa Dei, detestatur; *nec praetermittantur* partes Ecclesiae in actione poenitentiali; atque oratio pro peccatoribus urgeantur.

[129] N. 83: [*Praxis poenitentialis Quadragesimae opportune restituenda*]. Indoles poenitentialis temporis quadragesimalis non tantum spiritualiter et individualiter colatur, sed in vita quoque practica fidelium suam partem externam et socialem habeat. Instauretur, proinde, iuxta nostrae aetatis et diversarum regionum possibilitates necnon fidelium condiciones, opportuna praxis poenitentialis. The modifications made by the Sub-commission were: n.110: *Poenitentia* temporis quadragesimalis non tantum *sit interna et individualis*, sed quoque *externa et socialis*. Praxis vero poenitentialis, iuxta nostrae aetatis et diversarum regionum possibilitates necnon fidelium condiciones, *foveatur, et ab auctoritatibus, de quibus in art. 22, commendetur.*

[130] N. 84 of the original Schema: [*Festa Sanctorum festis mysteria salutis recolentibus ne praevaleant*]. Festa Sanctorum mirabilia quidem Christi in servis eius praedicant, et fidelibus opportuna praebent

virtutum exempla imitanda: attamen festis ipsa mysteria salutis recolentibus ne praevaleant. Immo plura ex his particulari cuique Ecclesiae vel Nationi vel Religiosae Familiae relinquantur celebranda, iis tantum ad Ecclesiam universam extensis, quae Sanctos memorant momentum universale revera prae se ferentes. The modifications made were n. 111: *Sancti iuxta traditionem in Ecclesia coluntur, eorumque reliquiae authenticae atque imagines in veneratione habentur.* Festa Sanctorum mirabilia quidem Christi in servis eius praedicant, et fidelibus opportuna praebent, exempla imitanda. *Ne festa Sanctorum* festis ipsa mysteria salutis recolentibus, plura ex his particulari cuique Ecclesiae vel Nationi vel Religiosae Familiae relinquantur celebranda, iis tantum ad Ecclesiam universam extensis, quae Sanctos memorant momentum universale revera prae se ferentes.

[131] N. 85 of the original Schema: II *De Calendario Recognoscendo* [*Festum Paschatis certae dominicae assignandum*]. Ut festum Paschatis certae dominicae in calendario gregoriano assignetur, assentientibus iis quorum intersit, praesertim fratribus separatis, Sacrosanctum Concilium commendat. Variorum autem systematum, quae ad calendarium perpetuum stabiliendum excogitata sunt, illis tantum non obstat, quae hebdomadam septem dierum servant et tutantur. The modifications made were: Appendix [Ad Schema Constitutionis de Sacra Liturgia] Concilii Vaticani secundi de Calendario Recognoscendo Declaratio – Sacrosanctum Concilium Oecumenicum Vaticanum secundum, haud parvi momenti aestimans multorum desideria de festo Paschatis certae Dominicae assignando et de Calendario stabiliendo, omnibus sedulo perpensis, quae ex inductione novi calendarii manare possint, haec quae sequuntur declarat: 1. Sacrosanctum Concilium *non obnititur quin* festum Paschatis certae dominicae in Calendario Gregoriano assignetur, assentientibus iis quorum intersit, praesertim fratribus *ab Apostolicae Sedi communione seiunctis.* N. 86 of the original Schema: [*Calendarium fixum inducendum*]. Sacrosanctum Concilium declarat se non obstare mediis et iceptis, quibus tenditur ad calendarium perpetuum in societatem civilem inducendum. The modifications were: 2. *Item* Sacrosanctum Concilium declarat se non *obsistere* iceptis, *quae conferant* ad calendarium perpetuum in societatem civilem inducendum. Variorum autem systematum, quae ad calendarium perpetuum stabiliendum *et in societatem civilem inducendum excogitantur,* iis tantum *Ecclesia non obsistit,* quae hebdomadam septem dierum *cum dominica* servant et tutantur, *nullis diebus extra hebdomadam interictis, ita ut hebdomadarum successio intacta, nisi accedant gravissimae rationes de quibus Apostolica Sedes iudicium ferat, relinquatur.*

[132] *Verbali delle riunioni della Commissione Conciliare di Sacra Liturgia,* in *SCCS, Archivio fondo Antonelli,* pp. 50-53.

[133] *Ibidem,* p. 54.

[134] *Verbali delle riunioni della Commissione Conciliare di Sacra Liturgia,* in *SCCS, Archivio fondo Antonelli,* pp. 55-56.

[135] *Ibidem,* pp. 57-58.

[136] *Verbali delle riunioni della Commissione Conciliare di Sacra Liturgia,* in *SCCS, Archivio fondo Antonelli,* pp. 59-60.

[137] *Ibidem,* p. 61.

[138] *Ibidem,* p. 62.

[139] *Verbali delle riunioni della Commissione Conciliare di Sacra Liturgia,* in *SCCS, Archivio fondo Antonelli,* pp. 63-64.

[140] *Ibidem,* p. 65.

[141] *Verbali delle riunioni della Commissione Conciliare di Sacra Liturgia,* in *SCCS, Archivio fondo Antonelli,* pp. 66-67.

[142] *Ibidem,* p. 68.

[143] *Verbali delle riunioni della Commissione Conciliare di Sacra Liturgia,* in *SCCS, Archivio fondo Antonelli,* p. 69.

[144] *Ibidem,* p. 70.

[145] *Verbali delle riunioni della Commissione Conciliare di Sacra Liturgia,* in *SCCS, Archivio fondo Antonelli,* pp. 71-72.

[146] *Verbali delle riunioni della Commissione Conciliare di Sacra Liturgia,* in *SCCS, Archivio fondo*

Antonelli, p. 73.

[147] *Verbali delle riunioni della Commissione Conciliare di Sacra Liturgia*, in *SCCS, Archivio fondo Antonelli*, p. 74.

[148] *Verbali delle riunioni della Commissione Conciliare di Sacra Liturgia*, in *SCCS, Archivio fondo Antonelli*, pp. 75-76.

[149] *Ibidem*, p. 77.

[150] *Ibidem*, p. 78.

[151] *Verbali delle riunioni della Commissione Conciliare di Sacra Liturgia*, in *SCCS, Archivio fondo Antonelli*, pp. 79-80.

[152] *Ibidem*, pp. 81-82.

Chapter 8

Historical and Pastoral Reasons
for the Liturgical Renewal

In the previous chapter we presented the minutes of the meetings of the Conciliar Commission on the [Sacred] Liturgy and described those meetings as they were recorded by Father Rinaldo Falsini. Fr. Falsini had been chosen by Antonelli to keep the minutes of the Commission's meetings. Publishing these minutes will be useful for those wishing to study the manner in which the Commission set about its work and the topics it discussed at the various meetings. They will also permit a closer study of the various Fathers and *periti* who comprised the Commission and offer an insight into their preoccupations as well as the difficulties which they encountered while presenting the various themes discussed at the meetings of the Commission. The minutes will illustrate the seriousness with which the Commission set about its work and dispel certain impressions which were widespread at the time of the Council, as well as today, that the Commission on the Liturgy was slow in its work. It is also interesting to observe those points which most preoccupied the Council Fathers and confront these with subsequent ideas concerning the Council's work.

This chapter will present the history of the liturgical reform as recorded in Antonelli's writings. It will also allow us to see Antonelli's perception of the reform, to present his thoughts on the Constitution *Sacrosanctum Concilium*, and to study the work of various study groups set up to examine the liturgical books, to which Antonelli made a significant contribution.

From the Council of Trent to "Sacrosanctum Concilium"

The Conciliar Constitution on the Liturgy "has closed an epoch in the history of the liturgy and opened another. It has closed the Tridentine era and opened what one might call the era of Vatican II".[1]

The Tridentine form of the liturgy lasted exactly four hundred years, the Council of Trent having been closed on December 4, 1563 in the wake of the reform of the liturgical books. *Sacrosanctum Concilium* was promulgated on December 4, 1963.

The Development of the Liturgical Reform

The liturgical outlook of the Tridentine Fathers certainly had many positive elements, but it had been undoubtedly superseded. Yet it is still useful to know "so as to understand the spirit, principles, and objective of the Conciliar Constitution. The antecedents must always be known, primarily the merits and lacunae of the Tridentine era".[2]

The Merits

Antonelli recognized that one of the great merits of the Council of Trent was to have carried out an accurate revision of the liturgical books:

> In the short span of seven years, the two fundamental books, the Breviary and the Missal, were revised and published:
>
> 1568: The Roman Breviary
> 1570: The Roman Missal
>
> The Revised edition of the other books followed:
>
> 1584: The Roman Martyrology
> 1596: The Roman Pontifical
> 1600: The Ceremonial of Bishops
> 1614: The Roman Ritual.[3]

Despite the value of the new editions and the increased ability to diffuse them due to the advent of printing, "there was great confusion. Every diocese had its own books into which many obsolete and improper elements had been introduced".[4]

The Council's invitation to uniformity was not, in fact, accepted by all. In some Churches dispensations from the use of the new books became necessary:

> Exceptions were made for Churches which could show that they possessed their own liturgical books and wished to conserve them. Thus, different liturgical books continued for:
>
> The Ambrosian liturgy;
> The Dominicans;
> The Carmelites;
> The Carthusians;
> The (Bracarense) liturgy;
> The Mozarabic liturgy in Toledo.
>
> The stability brought to the liturgical books due to the foundation in 1588 of the Congregation of Rites, must not be overlooked. This Congregation was given the competence to oversee the various editions of the liturgical books and the observance of the Rubrics.[5]

Lacunae

Notwithstanding the good will and competence of those who had collaborated in the liturgical Reform of the Council of Trent, lacunae soon emerged in the Breviary, Missal, and other books.

This was easily understandable: "Excellent men, such as Cardinal Sirleto (†1585) had worked on the reform, but they were obliged to use the means then at their disposal. There were no critical editions and there was no history of the liturgy".[6]

A further shortcoming was the importance given to externals to the detriment of the true nature of the liturgy:

> In accordance with the spirit of the times, the ceremonial part of the liturgy was emphasized to the detriment of its soul. The very name of the Congregation of Rites, underlines the secondary aspect of the rite. Throughout the seventeenth century ritual and ceremony were further encouraged in the atmosphere of the Baroque.[7]

Another error comprehensible in the light of the pre-Tridentine confusion, was the highly rigid outlook of the Congregation of Rites, which excluded all innovation, even in peripheral matters:

> No changes: A ritual and rubrical crystallization set in which discouraged the participation of the faithful in the liturgy and which ran contrary to its very nature. While the liturgy has immutable elements, it continually adapts to the changed circumstances of the times.[8]

As Paul VI remarked to the *Concilium*, the liturgy "is like a vigorous tree which is rooted in the ground, and whose trunk is covered with new branches and leaves".[9]

A further serious lacuna in the Tridentine Reform was the fact that it did not promote active participation on the part of the faithful. By the time of the Council of Trent this aspect of the liturgy had already been lost for several centuries.

> The great defect of the Tridentine epoch was not to have rediscovered [active participation by the faithful.] Neither did it make any effort to rediscover it. The rubrics of the old liturgical books speak of celebrant, ministry, clerics, and the *schola*, but never of the people. The mention of people appeared in the rubric for the Easter Vigil of 1951.[10]

The faithful became passive spectators at the liturgy for several reasons:

1. From the 7th – 8th centuries the vernacular language was no longer understood;
2. The *schola cantorum* silenced the people;
3. The multiplication of read Masses;
4. The ceasing of the Offertory;
5. The silence during the Canon;
6. Individualistic tendencies created and promoted by the *devotio moderna*.[11]

All of these tendencies led to the clericalization of the liturgy. "The faithful were simply spectators who were obligated to attend without understanding or participating in what was happening".[12]

Preparatory factors for a Renaissance in modern times

Several factors contributed to the development of a more adequate understanding of the liturgy, which culminated in *Sacrosanctum Concilium*. Firstly, the publication of various critical editions of the liturgical books and published works which:

> Highlighted the lacunae and rediscovered the real meaning of the liturgy. Among these are the works of Mabillon (†1707), Muratori (†1750), Martène (†1739). Don Guéranger was one of the first to promote a revival of Sacred Music and of a liturgical sense".[13]

The liturgical movement also made great contributions to the development of the liturgy. Above all, it promoted an awareness of the liturgy "initiallly among the clergy and subsequently among the faithful, from 1909 until its last gathering: the International Congress of Assisi in 1956".[14]

Mention must also be made of the support given to the embryonic liturgical movement by St. Pius X. The *motu proprio Tra le Sollecitudini* published on November 22, 1903 states that "The faithful draw the Christian life from its primary and indispensable font, which is active participation in the most holy mysteries and from the public and solemn prayer of the Church".[15]

Other documents and partial reforms had a positive effect. Father Antonelli signals the following:

November 20, 1947:	*Mediator Dei*;
December 30, 1948:	*Memoria della Riforma*;
February 26, 1951:	Easter Vigil;
March 23, 1955:	*Simplificatio Rubricorum*;
November 16, 1955:	Reform of Holy Week;
September 3, 1958:	*Instructio de Musica Sacra et Sacra Liturgia*;
July 26, 1960:	*Codex Rubricarum*.[16]

Two other factors contributed to the rediscovery of the true nature of the liturgy: the present historical moment which is masked by profound and rapid change; and the eminently pastoral nature of the Second Vatican Council. Had the First Vatican Council produced a liturgical Constitution, it would probably have been doctrinally solid but would have been likely to have been deficient in other respects. The Second Vatican Council gave maximum consideration to the role of the faithful. It was the first Ecumenical Council to treat the liturgy in all of its aspects.[17]

We can gain further information about the elaboration of the liturgical Constitution from an article published by Father Antonelli in the *Osservatore Romano* on December 8, 1963:

> The original schema was drawn up by the Pontifical Preparatory Commission on the Sacred Liturgy, constituted by John XXIII on June 15, 1960. The Commission, which was headed by the late Cardinal Gaetano Cicognani, consisted of 25 members, and 35 consultors, drawn from among the most eminent figures in the science of pastoral liturgy. The secretary was the Very Reverend Fr. Annibale Bugnini. The Commission met in plenary session some 36 times and worked intensely for more than a year.

This schema, once revised and amended by the Central Commission was the first to be placed before the Fathers in October 1962. The Council devoted 15 General Congregations to the schema from the 5th session (October 22) to the 19th session (November 13).

On October 22, 1962 the Council Fathers had elected a Conciliar Commission for the Sacred Liturgy, composed of 26 members, which was representative of the entire Catholic world. Cardinal Larraona, President of the Commission, chose 28 *periti* to assist the Commission. These ensured that the Commission had access to experienced theologians, proven Canonists, and particularly to experts in liturgy and pastoral theology.[18]

Antonelli then outlines the complex work conducted by the Conciliar Commission. Here we shall only cite the more significant data:

The Fathers made 662 interventions during the examination of the schema: 328 were read in the Council *Aula*, and the remainder were in writing. The Secretariat of the Commission rapidly reproduced all of these interventions in 12 fascicles comprising, in all, more than 1,200 pages, subsequently 13 Sub-commissions were created. A theological Sub-commission and a juridical Sub-commission examined the entire schema. The other Commissions were asked to examine the observations of the Fathers with regard to specific parts of the schema.

The reports compiled by the Sub-commissions were then examined by the plenary sessions of the Commission, of which there were 54 in all. This led to the printing of 11 fascicles of *Emendations*, which were distributed gradually to the Fathers of the Council.

Every fascicle contained a *Relazione* on the analysis of the observations made by the Fathers, together with the text of the schema in double columns, one containing the original text the other, an amended text. Some 85 votes were taken on the more important amendments. Most were favorable. There was no shortage of votes cast *juxta modum*, which gave conditional approval to certain chapters which were regarded as acceptable once certain changes had been made. Each of these proposals was examined by the Commission. The conclusions were again voted on by the Council Fathers. A report on each *modus* was printed and, all in all, some 5 fascicsles were distributed on the *modi*.

The concluding vote on this work was taken on December 4. The Fathers approved the Constitution almost unanimously (2,147 votes in favor and 4 against). This event, while a source of great satisfaction for all who had collaborated in drafting the Constitution and for all who foster the sacred liturgy, was a clear and authoritative proof that the reform which it provided for, was a real response to the pastoral needs of our time.[19]

Here we must underline the precision with which these events are recorded, for Antonelli day by day, kept careful minutes of the Conciliar sessions.

The Constitution on the Sacred Liturgy entered into force on February 16, 1964, the first Sunday of Lent. Antonelli records that

in the meantime a document was published, clearly indicating those dispositions of the Constitution which had immediate effect, and those which could not be implemented until after the revision of the liturgical books, or following particular dispositions enacted by ecclesiastical authority.[20]

The Development of the Liturgical Reform

Antonelli's comments on the Constitution allow us to discover those matters of particular concern to himself as well as to profit from his wise counsels:

> The inattentive reader might easily have the impression that, basically, it contained nothing new. In reality, many things would remain the same until the liturgical books would have been revised. However, it contained one great novelty, namely, the spirit by which the Constitution was animated.

> Everything converged on a single objective: to allow the faithful easily to understand the rites, follow them and turn to them, as they should, as actors and not as mere spectators at the liturgical ceremonies. This was an essential point which, unfortunately, had been lost for centuries. This aspect of the liturgy would be slowly regained in the following decades, and the Constitution would bring it to full vigor. This is something which cannot be achieved in a few months or years. When the masses have to be reeducated, one has to think in terms of generations. Prospects, however, are promising. We have started out well. The Constitution will become a kind of *magna carta* for the pastoral liturgy of the clergy, and for the liturgical life of the faithful.[21]

Antonelli then turns to the importance of assuring that the clergy are adequately formed in the liturgy. He regards this as an indispensable prerequisite for the education of the laity:

> When the people return to active participation in all of liturgical life, the hope of an authentic rebirth of Christian life will be consolingly archived. It was this hope that induced Pope John to call the Second Vatican Council and which moved the Fathers to approve the Constitution.[22]

Antonelli's article concludes quoting Paul VI in his promulgation of the Constitution:

> We recognize here a scale of values and duties. In the first place God; prayer is our first obligation, the liturgy is head spring of the divine life communicated to us, the first school of the spiritual life, the first gift that we can give to the Christian people. In our faith and prayer, it is our first invitation to the world so that the mute tongue might be unfettered in true and blessed prayer, and hear the desirable regenerating power of singing with us the divine praises and the hopes of mankind through Christ our Lord, in the Holy Spirit.[23]

Fr. Antonelli adds a reflection on the past and on the future:

> When St. Peter's Basilica resounded with these great words, the bones of St. Pius X exulted. The Constitution on the Liturgy is nothing but the precious fruit of a small seed sown by him. It is also the beginning of a new era in the liturgical life of the Church.[24]

Pastoral Expectation of "Sacrosanctum Concilium"

Here we wish to analyze the content of the Constitution on the Liturgy. What objectives did it have? Antonelli writes: "The objective of the liturgical renewal is essentially to bring the faithful to an active and conscious participation in the liturgical life (of the Church) and especially in the Mass which is the center of the liturgy".[25]

We see the points on which the Council Fathers based themselves when drawing up the Constitution on the Liturgy. Antonelli lists them as follows: "The entire Constitution tends towards an enrichment of the Biblical readings, the revaluation of the sermon as a catechesis on the word of God, the revival of the *Oratio fidelium*, and the revision of the *Ordo Missae*".[26]

The question of language was much discussed but Antonelli comments that "the most striking innovation is the wide concession for the use of the vernacular in all the liturgy, including the Mass".[27]

In his manuscript notes, Antonelli underlined in red the problem presented by the vernacular, as if to signify the importance of the conflict which it evoked. He writes:

> It is a question of two conflicting values. Undoubtedly, Latin has been the language of the Latin liturgy for 1,600 years. It is a sign and source of unity as well as a defense of doctrine, not because of the language so much, but because it is a language no longer subject to changes. There are so many beautiful texts which can never have the same effectiveness in translation. Lastly, Latin is bound to an extremely precious heritage of melody, Gregorian chant and polyphony. On the other hand, it is beyond doubt that if we wish to bring the faithful, all the faithful, to a direct conscious and active participation in the liturgy, then we must speak to them in the language which they speak. The Constitution chose the only solution possible in this case: that of a compromise. Certain parts of the Mass, such as the Canon, remain in Latin, while others, especially those directed to the people, such as the readings and the restored *Oratio fidelium,* can take place in the vernacular.[28]

To understand why Latin remained obligatory for many centuries and to understand why Antonelli believes that the time was ripe for the introduction of the vernacular, a historical fact, dating from the Council of Trent, must be borne in mind:

> One thing must be clear. The Council of Trent did not directly prohibit the use of the vernacular. In the face of the protestant denial of the sacrificial character of the Mass and their assertion that the Mass was nothing other than a memorial, and that it was essential to understand this memorial (thereby implying that the Mass had to be celebrated in the vernacular), the Council of Trent, in correcting this doctrinal error, affirmed the validity of the Mass even when celebrated in a language unknown to the faithful. The use of the vernacular, therefore, *patribus visum est non expedire.* This implies that were the circumstances to change, the *non expedire* might also change. The Second Vatican Council clearly retained that the circumstances had changed and, consequently, it changed the *non expedire* of the Council of Trent.[29]

Antonelli was not unaware of the difficulties connected with the new norms:

> A community celebration involving all in a collective action and excluding solitary subjectivism, is not easily realized, especially when it implies a move from Latin to the vernacular and the introduction of new ritual forms to replace cherished habits and usage.[30]

In this regard, Antonelli proposes several recommendations and helpful suggestions:

> The application of the instruction of September 26, which comes into force on

March 7, is a major advance. But, it is not going to be easy. The bishops, in the first instance, and all concerned with the care of souls are committed to its implementation. But all have to cooperate. The spirit and the letter of the provisions of the Constitution and the appended instruction must be understood. The letter is necessary but more so the spirit.[31]

It is of interest to note Antonelli's suggestion regarding the method to be adopted in applying the reform in such a way as to avoid negative reactions:

It is a question of changing mentality. When the people come together they constitute a sacred assembly, the assembly of the people of God. The faithful have to be brought to a realization that the liturgical action is a community action in which no one is a spectator. All must become actors. When it is a question of changing mentality, or of bringing the masses with you, the time span has to be reckoned in generations rather than in months or years. Patience, therefore, is necessary. Success will be assured by patience and perseverance.[32]

Looking at the future, the manuscript ends quoting Paul VI's discourse to the monks of Montecassino on October 24, 1964: "The liturgy must return to being a school for the Christian life, a school conducted in the light of a new religious pedagogy which the Constitution on the Liturgy intends to restore to the Christian people".[33]

General View of the Composition of the Constitution

Antonelli offers a general view of the Constitution on the Liturgy in the manuscript draft of a lecture given on September 8, 1964, which analyzes the spirit and the letter of *Sacrosanctum Concilium*. Having noted that the Constitution consists of a preamble, seven chapters, and an appendix, he notes that:

The preamble is solemn, as it should be in such a document.

The first chapter, treating of the value and importance of the liturgy, is the most developed chapter and also the most important one.

a) Nature of the liturgy and its importance for the Church (articles 5-13): These articles require meditation. They embrace the entire economy of salvation that is accomplished in Christ (*sacramentum primordiale et fontale*) that is given to men by the Church (*sacramentum generale*) through the sacraments, which are the channels of grace. The whole application of salvation is achieved in the liturgy, which is the "summit towards which all her power flows" (article 10);

b) The liturgical formation of the clergy and faithful;

c) The liturgical reform and the establishment of the criteria for that reform.[34]

Antonelli then poses the question of whether the times are favorable for the introduction of liturgical changes and replies: "I do not know. We are in a period of change. The Constitution is accelerating that change but it also confirms it. Some things, perhaps, need further maturing, for example, concelebration".[35]

Having commented on articles 47-58, concerning the Eucharist, "focal point of liturgical life",[36] Antonelli poses some further questions and suggests some answers:

> Many will ask what the innovations in the Mass are. A brief reply may be made. A revision of the *Ordo Missae* is foreseen. It will have to be carried through with optimum care and attention. The biblical readings will be enriched. The ancient *Oratio fidelium* will be restored. This will take the form of the prayers which are already well known from Good Friday ceremonies. It will be shorter, however. The introduction of concelebration is also foreseen. This takes the form of Mass celebrated by more than one priest in certain well-defined cases.

> All these things will be introduced with the reform of the liturgical books. For the moment, nothing will change. A certain use of the vernacular in the Mass is also envisioned; particularly for the biblical readings, and in certain other parts which will be determined by the ecclesiastical authority in the various countries, and approved by the Holy See.[37]

With regard to the other sacraments and sacramentals, Antonelli recognizes the importance given to them by the Constitution, but adds that the chapter needs to be reformed in some important respects. He affirms that sacramentals can be administered by trained lay people,[38] he hopes for "a wider use of the vernacular in the sacraments and sacramentals. This is a logical and opportune development, given that the sacraments are more directly addressed to the individual".[39]

Speaking of the chapter on the Breviary, Antonelli reveals the importance of the recent reform of the Breviary which clarified many of the objectives of the Commission on the Liturgy:

> There are dispositions which were introduced some years ago which could have given the impression of a tendency to reduce the official prayer of the Church. This would be erroneous. The Constitution is preoccupied with ensuring that priests can better and more fruitfully recite the great public prayer of the Church Two things must be observed: a desire to have the laity participate to the greatest extent in this prayer, especially on Sundays and holy days; and, the fact that all who belong to a state of perfection, including members of secular institutes, share in the public prayer of the Church even when they recite some little office, duly approved and permitted by their proper Constitutions.[40]

Commenting on the liturgical year, Antonelli briefly outlines the objectives to be pursued:

> By means of a healthy and intense pastoral presentation of the liturgy, it tries to bring Christian people to live, consciously, joyfully, fruitfully, every year the mysteries of the Redemption accomplished by Christ, which has blossomed in the saints and above all in Our Lady. Hence the great cycles of Christmas and Easter, the cycle of Marian feasts, and the celebration of the martyrs and saints.[41]

In chapter 6 on sacred music he only mentions that these are "many prescriptions enjoining and promoting the proper function of music, which is not something merely decorative, but the highest and most perfect expression of prayer".[42]

Referring to the chapter on sacred art and furnishings, effectively Antonelli says that the Constitution "does not exclude any expression of genuine art, it seeks to distance from the sanctuary anything repugnant to Christian piety or offensive to religious sensibilities".[43]

The Development of the Liturgical Reform

Some General Principles of the Constitution

Antonelli constantly distinguished the liturgy from ceremonialism and rubricism. He always regarded the liturgy as an integral part of the Church's life. Referring to Article 7 of the Constitution he says:

> "The Church's purpose is to continue the work of Redemption in the world. That essential mission is effected in the liturgy. The nobility of liturgical actions derives from this as well as the precedence which must be given to them "because they are works of Christ, the Priest, and of his Body which is the Church" (art. 7).[44]

The centrality of Easter is a further point underlined in the Constitution:

> The Paschal mystery, the hinge of the history of salvation (article 5), the central point and corner of worship (article 10) is perfectly expressed in the Eucharistic sacrifice (article 47). From it derives the effectiveness of the sacraments (article 61). It is prolonged in the liturgical year with Sunday, the weekly Easter.[45]

The rediscovery of the Word of God is one of the most important points of the Constitution. Antonelli explains the historical reasons for a certain diffidence with regard to the Bible and draws some practical conclusions from the Liturgical Constitution.

> The undervaluing of Sacred Scripture in the liturgical life is a post-Tridentine reaction to Protestantism. The point had been reached at which translations of the Missal were prohibited. The first translations only date from the last century. The liturgy is woven from Sacred Scripture. The Constitution desires to:
>
> 1. See that ample scriptural pericopes are introduced into the Mass (article 51) and the Divine Office (article 90a), and indeed into all liturgical celebrations (article 35, 1);
>
> 2. Make the homily obligatory, as a part of the liturgical actions (article 52);
>
> 3. Have celebrations of the Word of God (articles 35, 4). These are useful and should be done. They can end with benediction of the Blessed Sacrament;
>
> 4. Introduce adaptations to the culture and temperament of the various nations (article 37), especially in the sacraments (article 63), while conserving the unity of the Roman Rite (article 38);
>
> 5. Favor decentralization. The local ecclesiastical authorities can intervene and propose adaptations.[46]

Promemoria on the Revision of the Liturgical Books

Father Antonelli was still Secretary of the Conciliar Commission on the liturgy at the time of the promulgation of *Sacrosanctum Concilium*. He was asked to devise a schedule of work for the revision of the liturgical books, which had been enjoined by *Sacrosanctum Concilium*.[47] To this end, he drew up a *Promemoria*, which clearly illustrates his liturgical and historical culture. He writes:

> The Constitution of the Sacred Liturgy in article 25 prescribes a revision of the liturgical books. Articles 26-40 provide the general principles for that revision.

Historical and Pastoral Reasons for the Liturgical Renewal

By way of preface, I wish to point out that after the Council of Trent, the Reformed Breviary by St. Pius V in 1568 took five years to produce, while the Missal, published in 1570, took seven years to prepare. Taking into the account the fact that such a work is more complex today, given the numerous available fonts and the copious bibliographies, a well-organized work schedule must be prepared if this work is to be brought to completion within a relatively short period of time. The preparatory work will have to be subdivided among various groups of people, each assigned to a specific area. This work has to begin immediately.

Having said that, I would suggest the following study groups, among which the preparatory work might be divided.[48]

Following an expert presentation of the task, Antonelli devotes a detailed study to the working groups that would have to be established. He divides them according to what the Constitution says with regard to the liturgical books, citing the relevant article and explaining his thoughts about it.

The study groups should be established immediately and should be kept small: three to five particularly well-trained persons and a head. The following study groups could be established:

Group One: Definitive Revision of the Psalter

Article 91, paragraph 2 of *Sacrosanctum Concilium* says, "*Opus recognitionis Psalterii, feliciter inchoatum, quamprimum perducatur ad finem, respectu habito latinitatis christianae, usus liturgici etiam in cantu, necnon totius traditionis latinae Ecclesiae*".

This is one of the more urgent tasks to be done, since the Psalter is an essential element of all the liturgical books.[49]

Having introduced this study group and explained the importance of the Psalter for the Church, Antonelli traces the history of the reform of the Psalter:

Some years ago, Father Weber, a Benedictine who has worked on the Vulgate at San Girolamo (St. Jerome) for many years, published a new version of the Psalter which tried to preserve as much as possible of the traditional text of the Vulgate, while taking advantage of the version published by the *Biblicum*. With these two versions, that of Father Weber and that of the *Biblicum*, it should not be too demanding to furnish a text which respects the demands of the original while taking into account the tradition of Latin Christianity and the norms for the *cursus* which govern the singing and recital of the Psalms.[50]

Group Two: The Revision of the Universal Calendar of the Church.

Article 111 of *Sacrosanctum Concilium* provides the criteria on which many of the feasts of local saints are to be remitted to the local diocesan calendars or to those of the religious orders. The general calendar will contain "*quae Sanctos memorat momentum universale revera prae se ferentes*". This revision should be carried out immediately. The revision of the historical and patristic readings cannot be effected for as long as we do not know which saints are to remain in the Breviary. This is a very complex and delicate work but much material has already been prepared by the Pontifical Commission for the Reform of the Liturgy created by Pius XII in 1948.[51]

Group Three: Distribution of the Psalter into two weeks

Instead of reciting the entire Breviary in one week, article 91 of the Constitution provides for its distribution *per longius temporis spatium*. Naturally, one thinks of a bi-weekly distribution as is found in the Ambrosian liturgy.[52]

Group Four: Revision of the Biblical Readings in the Breviary

Article 92a prescribes: *Lectio sacrae Scripturae ita ordinetur, ut thesauri verbi divini in pleniore amplitudine expedite adiri possint.*

This implies a revision of the actual order of the Biblical readings in the Breviary. It is desired by all. Indeed, there are several parts that could be omitted without any harm, while there are others, the Sapiential books for example, that could be beneficially introduced into the Breviary.[53]

Group Five: Revision of the Patristic Readings in the Breviary

Article 92b prescribes the following in relation to these readings: *Lectiones de operibus Patrum, Doctorum et Scriptorum ecclesiasticorum depromendae melius seligantur.*

As with the Biblical texts, this revision calls for men particularly competent in Patrology.

Group Six: Revision of the Historical Readings

Article 92b states: *Passiones seu vitae sanctorum fidei historicae reddantur.* All are agreed of the need for such a revision. The Historical Section with a group of their consultors, together with some members drawn from among the Bollandists, would be able to do this work.

Group Seven: Revision of the Hymns of the Breviary

Article 93 provides for a revision of the Breviary's hymnological patrimony and lays down the criteria for it. A small expert group could easily complete the task.

Group Eight: Revision of the *Ordo Missae* with the addition of the Prefaces and the *Oratio communis*

Article 50 provides for a revision of the *Ordo Missae*, while article 53 calls for the revival of the *oratio fidelium*. It is commonly desired that various Prefaces be added and that certain votive and ferial Mass formulas be revised. This is a delicate task and will have to be assigned to a group of chosen specialists.

Group Nine: The distribution of the Pericopes from the Epistles and Gospels used in the Mass into a threefold series

Article 51 states: *Quo ditior mensa verbi Dei paretur fidelibus, thesauri largius aperiantur, ita ut, intra praestitutum annorum spatium, praestantior pars Scripturarum Sanctarum populo legatur.*

This calls for a group of specialists in Sacred Scripture and in liturgy.

Group Ten: New Rite of Concelebration and Rubrics for the distribution of Holy Communion under both species

Articles 55, 57, and 58 of the Constitution provide for these matters. Two competent people could easily carry out this work.[54]

With regard to the remaining groups, Antonelli proposed the following to the Conciliar Commission:

Group Eleven: Revision of the Roman Pontifical

The Pontifical Commission for the General Reform of the Liturgy, instituted by Pius XII in 1948, has already conducted a reform of the second part of the *Pontificale*, which has already been published. The revision of the first and third parts remains to be done.

The Constitution expressly provides for a revision of ordinations (article 76) and for the consecration of virgins (article 80). This is a demanding task. It requires a group of experts who are prepared to undertake some serious work. I believe, however, that it is possible and that it should be able to be effected within a reasonable period of time.

Group Twelve: Revision of the Roman Ritual

This is provided for in article 63b and is something necessary. It will require a protracted amount of work, which will not always be very easy. It requires a group of competent experts who are prepared to undertake some serious work.

Group Thirteen: A Complement to the *Editio Typica* of the Books of Gregorian Chant

Article 117 of the Constitution provides for this. The monks of Solesmes, naturally, are best prepared for a work of this kind.

Group Fourteen: Revision of the Roman Martyrology

The Constitution makes no explicit mention of a revision of the martyrology but such falls within the general prescription of article 25, which speaks of revising the liturgical books. This is a most complex work. However, it is aided by two commentaries published by the Bollandists, one on the Hieronomian Martyrology (1931) and another on the Roman Martyrology (1940).

While the revision of the martyrology is necessary, it is less urgent than the reform of the Breviary and Missal. All of the saints who will remain in the general calendar are historical figures, and will most certainly be retained in the martyrology.[55]

Division of Labor and of the Study Groups

Following his detailed exposition of the various study groups for the revision of liturgical books, Antonelli considered some different suggestions for both the organization of the work and the membership of these groups.

The establishment of the various study groups and the specifications of their competence is relatively easy. More challenging, however, are the tasks of organizing the work and choosing the persons to whom it will be entrusted.

As for the organization of the work, it would seem absolutely necessary to constitute some body over and above the various groups. It would decide competence, establish criteria, and resolve questions that might arise. In the context of the Council, it would not seem opportune to assign this task to the Sacred Congregation of Rites as such. That, however, would not preclude the use of some elements from the said Congregation, chosen for their knowledge and experience. This cannot be overlooked.

Neither would it appear advisable to commit the direction of this work to the Conciliar Commission on Sacred Liturgy. With all respect, it must be said that several of its members do not have the specific qualification to carry forward this work. Given the large number of members and their geographical distribution, it would be difficult to convoke them. In practical terms, the Commission would not be able to function.

On the other hand, the members and *periti* of this commission, having followed the various discussions, know better than anyone else the problems, difficulties, limits and objectives of the reform of the liturgical books.[56]

From the foregoing, Antonelli's vision, his wisdom, and the equilibrium with which he approached the problem emerge, as well as his respect for the experts in the liturgical field. This is proved by acceptance of his suggestion and the constitution of the Commission for the reform of the liturgical books.[57] Antonelli also outlined the basis on which its members should be selected:

In choosing the members of this commission, account should be taken of their competence, balanced judgment, capacity for and possibility of work, and of choosing them so as to represent the various languages and countries.[58]

By way of suggestion, the following names might be mentioned:

1. Cardinal Larraona, as President of the Conciliar Commission, has followed and directed all of the work;

2. Cardinal Lercaro followed the work of the Commission with interest and competence;

3. Monsignor Grimshaw, Archbishop of Birmingham, a very balanced person: he could represent the English language;

4. Monsignor Martin, Bishop of Nicolet in Canada, made a notable contribution to the Commission;

5. Monsignor Zauner, Bishop of Linz, could represent the German language in the Commission. He appeared open and balanced.

A number of experts would have to assist the cardinals and bishops. They could be chosen from those who have given proof of competence and capacity for work, and it should be easy to convoke them. Among them, mention could be made of:

1. Msgr. Martimort, Toulouse;

2. Msgr. Martin, Trier;

3. Msgr. Bonella, as a representative of the Ambrosian liturgy;

4. Msgr. Fautaz, Historical Section of the Sacred Congregation of Rites;

5. Father Bugnini, Editor of *Ephemerides Liturgici*;

6. Father Vagaggini, OSB, liturgist and theologian;

7. Father Dirks, OP, Director of the Institute of Friars Preachers at Santa Sabina;

8. Father Ferdinando Antonelli, Secretary of the Conciliar Commission on the Sacred Liturgy.

A commission such as this could be an effective and balanced force to direct the preparatory work at a general level, which, even if pushed to the limit, will necessarily require some years to discharge its work.

The Secretariat of the Conciliar Commission on Sacred Liturgy has all the relevant material in hand and could easily act as a Secretariat for this Commission.[59]

Following this long list of liturgical experts, all of whom had been known to Antonelli both before and during the Council, he proceeds to outline the immediate and future work which awaits the Commission.

Competence of the Commission

This commission should meet as soon as possible, in January or February, to settle the general criteria for the work and to distribute it to the various study groups. It should be able to meet from time to time to decide important questions that might arise. It could also reply to queries concerning the interpretation of the constitution. Evidently, all of this will have to be submitted for the decision of the Holy Father.[60]

He subjoins a list of the study groups together with a reference to one or two specialists.

The Composition of the Study Groups

Antonelli lists the various groups and suggests the names of several experts, but always invites the Commission to provide alternatives. It is interesting to note how the division of competence led him to see how some parts of the revision would be more difficult than the others:

One of the first duties of the Commission would be to distribute the work to the various study groups. These can be made up of just a few specialists. For more complex work it would seem better to entrust it to a religious institute with particular competence in a specific field, rather than to individuals or groups of persons.

By way of suggestion, the names of some persons and Institutes with special competence can be indicated. However, the Commission may find other solutions.[61]

Group One: Definitive Revision of the Psalter

This task should be given to the monastery of San Girolamo which is always working on the Vulgate. Some representatives from the Pontifical Biblical Institute would need to be added to the group. In this respect, one might think of Msgr. Garofalo, who is a biblicist, and of some other expert on the *cursus*.[62]

Group Two: Revision of the Universal Calendar of the Church

This is a very delicate question. Some material has already been prepared by the Historical Section for the Commission for the General Reform of the Liturgy. The present *Relator-Generalis*, Msgr. Frutaz, could be asked to work on the project together with some others, such as Msgr. Martimort, Msgr. Wagner, a Bollandist (for example Father De Gaiffin). Father Antonelli, who worked with the Commission, may also be able to give helpful advice.[63]

Group Three: Distribution of the Psalter into two weeks

Perhaps the same persons charged with the reform of the Psalter, the Monastery of San Girolamo, together with some other specialists could undertake this work. Here mention could be made of: Msgr. Balthasar Fischer of Trier, together with a specialist in the Ambrosian liturgy, which already has a bi-weekly Psalter, such as Msgr. Cattaneo or Msgr. Borella.[64]

Group Four: Revision of the Biblical Readings of the Psalter

This is a very demanding task. Perhaps the Abbey of Mont César in Louvain, and Dom Botte, who is very expert in the matter, could be asked to undertake this work. The Abbot, Father Van Doren, is competent and has sound judgment. Were Mont César to decline, then the Abbey of Clerveaux might be approached.[65]

Group Five: Revision of the Patristic Readings of the Breviary

This is also a very demanding task and the Abbey of St. Calcat in France might be approached to undertake it. Otherwise, the Benedictines at Steenbrugge in Belgium, who publish *Corpus Christianorum,* might be considered.[66]

Group Six: Revision of the Historical Readings of the Breviary

From the point of view of competence and experience, the best qualified body to conduct this work would appear to be the Historical Section of the Congregation of Rites. There are several experts in hagiography among its Consultors as well as a Bollandist.[67]

Group Seven: Revision of the Hymns of the Breviary

This work does not cause particular preoccupations. It should be given to two or three experts. In this regard, Msgr. Del Ton may be helpful.[68]

Group Eight: Revision of the *Ordo Missae*

This is an extremely delicate question. We need qualified men, but of highly balanced judgment. I would not recommend a religious institute to undertake this work. A group of very balanced persons should be created directly. Among these, the following might be included:

Cardinal Lercaro;

Father Jungmann;

Msgr. Martimort;

Dom Botte, OSB;

Msgr. Wagner;

Father Antonelli;

Father Bugnini;

Msgr. Cattaneo.[69]

Group Nine: Distribution of the Pericopes of the Epistles and Gospels in the Missal into several series

Given the correspondence between the reading in the Mass and the Breviary, this task could be assigned to those working on the Breviary. They might be assisted with a number of specialists on the Missal. In this respect, the name of Dr. Kahlefeld of Munich immediately comes to mind, as well as that of Dom Jounel of Paris, and others.[70]

Group Ten: New Rite of Concelebration and the Rubrics for Distribution of Holy Communion under both species

This is a relatively easy task that can be done quickly. Martimort would appear particularly suitable to address the questions of concelebration.[71]

Group Eleven: Revision of the Roman Pontifical

This task is mainly concerned with the first and third parts of the *Pontificale* since part two has already been revised. The first part is more urgent. From this question, Father Bugnini and his collaborators at the *Ephemerides Liturgicae* might be approached.[72]

Group Twelve: Revision of the Roman Ritual

This is a great amount of work and needs to be done urgently. Father Gy, OP, of the Dominican House of Studies at Soulchoir, Professor at the Catholic Institute in Paris, might be approached. He could be assisted by other people, such as Msgr. Wagner of Trier, Msgr. McManus of Boston, Father Vagaggini could represent Italy, along with others.[73]

Group Thirteen: Completion of the *Editio Typica* of the books of Gregorian Chant

The matter could be given to the monks at Solesmes, without, however, excluding the Pontifical Institute for Sacred Music.[74]

Group Fourteen: Revision of the Martyrology

This involves an enormous amount of work. It could be given to an institute, such as the Bollandists, under the direction of the Historical Section of the Congregation of Rites, which has already acquired a wide experience of the eulogies of the martyrology. This work, if it is to be seriously undertaken, requires a great amount of work. In terms of the reforms enjoined by Constitution, it is not urgent.[75]

It is interesting to note how Antonelli qualifies his suggestions for the reform of the liturgical books. His comments are marked by prudence and experience. He frequently uses the conditional, invites the members to observe confidentiality, this amounts to something more than a mere counsel. He displays the same courtesy in his dealings with the Commission, to which the possibility of finding more qualified people is always left open.

One observation. Great discretion must be required of the persons and institutes to which this work is entrusted. It must be firmly laid down that nothing may be published in relation to their work, so as to avoid harmful and useless polemics.

Finally, I wish to reiterate that the suggestions I have made with regard to the persons and institutes that might be approached with regard to the reform of the liturgical books are merely illustrative. Further investigation may well suggest other persons or institutes better qualified for this task.[76]

Among Antonelli's papers concerning the liturgical reform subsequent to the publication of *Sacrosanctum Concilium*, there is copious documentation relating to the creation of a new organism called the "*Consilium ad exsequendam Constitutionem de Sacra Liturgia*" of 1964, about which more will be said in the next chapter.

The Development of the Liturgical Reform

[1] F. ANTONELLI, *Antecedenti, principi e scopo della Costituzione Conciliare sulla Sacra Liturgia*. Lectures on Liturgy, January 12, 1965, in *ALV*, p. 1. Cf. F. ANTONELLI, *La Costituzione della Sacra Liturgia*, a note given to the Press Agency ANSA, November 30, 1963, in *ALV*, pp. 1-3.

[2] F. ANTONELLI, *Antecedenti, principi*, cit., p. 1.

[3] *Ibidem*, p. 2.

[4] *Ibidem*.

[5] *Ibidem*, p. 3.

[6] *Ibidem*, p. 5.

[7] *Ibidem*.

[8] *Ibidem*.

[9] *Ibidem*; cf. PAUL VI, *Discourse at the first Audience granted to the Concilium*, October 29, 1964, in *Insegnamenti di Paolo VI*, vol. II, Vatican City 1964, p. 619.

[10] F. ANTONELLI, *La Costituzione Conciliare sulla Sacra Liturgia. Antecedenti e grandi principi*, lecture, December 26, 1964, in *ALV*, p. 4.

[11] *Ibidem*, p. 5.

[12] F. ANTONELLI, *Antecedenti, principi*, cit., p. 6b.

[13] *Ibidem*, p. 7.

[14] F. ANTONELLI, *La Costituzione Conciliare*, cit., p. 7.

[15] PIUS X, *Tra le Sollecitudini*, in A. BUGNINI, *Documenta*, cit., pp 12-13.

[16] F. ANTONELLI, *La Costituzione Conciliare*, cit., p. 7.

[17] *Ibidem*, p. 8.

[18] F. ANTONELLI, *Antecedenti, importanza*, cit., p. 6.

[19] *Ibidem*.

[20] *Ibidem*.

[21] *Ibidem*.

[22] *Ibidem*.

[23] *Discourse of Paul VI at the close of the second phase of the Council*, 3rd Session: December 4, 1963, in *EV*, 1/212.

[24] F. ANTONELLI, *Antecedenti, importanza*, cit., p. 6.

[25] F. ANTONELLI, *La Costituzione Conciliare*, cit., p. 9.

[26] *Ibidem*.

[27] *Ibidem*, pp. 8-9.

[28] *Ibidem*, pp. 10-12.

[29] *Ibidem*, pp. 12-13.

[30] *Ibidem*, pp. 13-14.

[31] *Ibidem*, pp. 14-15.

[32] *Ibidem*, pp. 15-16.

[33] *Ibidem*, p. 18.

[34] F. ANTONELLI, *La Costituzione liturgica nella lettera e nello spirito*. Lectures on Liturgy, September 8, 1964, in *ALV*, pp. 4-5.

[35] *Ibidem*, p. 5.

[36] *Ibidem*, p. 5b.

[37] F. ANTONELLI, *Antecedenti, importanza*, cit., p. 6.

[38] Cf. F. ANTONELLI, *La Costituzione liturgica nella lettera*, cit., p. 5b.

[39] F. ANTONELLI, *Antecedenti, importanza*, cit., p. 6.

[40] *Ibidem*, p. 6.

[41] *Ibidem*.

[42] *Ibidem*.

[43] *Ibidem*.

[44] F. ANTONELLI, *La Costituzione liturgica nella lettera*, cit., p. 6.

[45] *Ibidem*, pp. 6-7.

[46] *Ibidem*, pp. 7-8.

[47] A. BUGNINI also speaks of this *Promemoria* on the revision of the liturgical books in his book (p. 71): "The work of the Conciliar liturgical secretariat was, more or less, to organize the Preparatory Commission. It allowed for 14 study groups dependent on a Commission which represented neither the Sacred Congregation for Rites nor the Conciliar Commission. It was, however, supposed to be a small Commission. On this subject, Fr. Antonelli drew a proposal concerning its composition – 5 bishops and 8 experts. Secretarial services for the Commission, it was clarified, could be provided by the Conciliar Commission. Finally, the most qualified persons for every group were indicated".

[48] F. ANTONELLI, *Promemoria sulla revisione dei libri liturgici in esecuzione della Costituzione Conciliare della Sacra Liturgia*, December 19, 1963, in *SCCS*, pp. 1-2.

[49] *Ibidem*, p. 2, Antonelli briefly outlines the problem of the Psalter: "We must resolve the anomolous situation in which we have the Vulgate Psalter which is still officially in use, and the version of the Psalter produced by the Pontifical Biblical Institute in 1945 which has been permitted, but not required, for liturgical use. No one can deny the worth and advantage of this version but it has also been criticized and an echo of that criticism is to be found in article 91 of the Constitution".

[50] F. ANTONELLI, *Promemoria sulla revisione dei libri liturgici*, cit., p. 3.

[51] *Ibidem*, pp. 3-4.

[52] *Ibidem*, p. 4.

[53] *Ibidem*, pp. 4-5.

[54] *Ibidem*, pp. 5-7.

[55] F. ANTONELLI, *Promemoria sulla revisione dei libri liturgici*, cit., pp. 7-8.

[56] *Ibidem*, second part, pp. 1-2. Antonelli continues: "On the basis of these considerations, it appears that responsibility for the work of reforming the liturgical books should be entrusted to a small Commission comprised of persons who have already been members of or expert advisors to the Conciliar Commission. Such people know the problems [that have arisen] not only in the abstract but also in the concrete situation of the conciliar discussions. These people can afford adequate counsels.

[57] A. BUGNINI, *La riforma liturgica*, cit., p. 71; new edition, p.74..

[58] F. ANTONELLI, *Promemoria sulla revisione dei libri liturgici*, cit., p. 2.

[59] *Ibidem*, pp. 2-3.

[60] *Ibidem*, p. 4.

[61] *Ibidem*.

[62] *Ibidem*, p. 5.

[63] *Ibidem*.

[64] *Ibidem*.

[65] *Ibidem*, p. 6.

[66] *Ibidem*. Antonelli advised: "For an opinion as to whether some significant excerpts of Syriac, Coptic, or Armenian patristic writings could be introduced into the Breviary, the University of Louvain could also be approached. It is the only Catholic institute equipped for [the study of] Oriental patristic literature.

[67] F. ANTONELLI, *Promemoria sulla revisione dei libri liturgici*, cit., p. 6.

[68] *Ibidem*, p. 7.

[69] *Ibidem*.

[70] *Ibidem*, pp. 7-8.

[71] *Ibidem*, p. 8.

[72] *Ibidem*.

[73] *Ibidem*.

[74] *Ibidem*, pp. 8-9.

[75] *Ibidem*, p. 9.

[76] *Ibidem*.

Chapter 9

From the *Consilium ad exsequendam Constitutionem de Sacra Liturgia* to the Congregation for Divine Worship

History

In the preceding chapter we followed the preparation of *Sacrosanctum Concilium*, seeing the difficulties that arose, its objectives, the reactions to it, and the efforts made to have it implemented. As with all reforms effected by decree, the Constitution on the Liturgy was followed by an instruction, *Inter Oecumenici*, setting out the practical norms for its application.

Pope John XXIII died on June 3, 1963 and he was succeeded on June 21 by Giovanni Battista Montini who took the name of Paul VI. From his previous experience, he well understood the difficulties that had been experienced in the various Commissions, especially in the one on the liturgy, of which he had been a member. His election seemed like an act of God. On August 21, 1963 he nominated four new members to the Commission coordinating the Council's work. These were Cardinals Agagianian, Lercaro, Döpfner, and Suenens. On September 14, 1963 the four moderators who would oversee the conciliar debates were officially announced. Msgr. Martimort writes:

> On September 27 my German colleague, Msgr. Wagner, and I went to visit Cardinal Lercaro at the Catacombs of St. Priscilla. We wanted to alert him to some irregularities that had happened during the summer. Efforts to change Chapter III of the schema of modifications had been made without the knowledge of the competent Sub-commission or of the plenary Commission. The opening of the new session of the Council and the orientation determined by the new Pope had silenced opposition for the moment.[1]

On October 8 Cardinal Lercaro proposed drawing up a *Relatio generalis* setting out the actual state of the Commission's work. On October 10, 1963 Paul VI received the four Cardinal moderators of the Council. During this audience he made clear his desire to distribute a document at the close of the second session of the Council which would indicate clearly those articles of the Constitution that could be activated.[2] This document was to be consigned to the Fathers of the

Council before they left Rome. Cardinal Lercaro asked Father Bugnini, Secretary, to present him with a list of names as quickly as possible.

On October 12 Father Bugnini presented his list. That afternoon, nine experts met with Cardinal Lercaro at the monastery of Benedictine nuns of St. Priscilla on the Via Salaria. The work was thus distributed: Msgr. Martimort was asked to research what could be useful in Chapter I of the Constitution; Father Jungmann was assigned to Chapter II (Mass); C. Vagaggini and Professor McManus to Chapter III (Sacraments); H. Schmidt to Chapter IV (Divine Office); Msgr. Wagner to Chapters VII and VIII (Art and Sacred Music); Msgr. E. Bonet was asked to take charge of the juridical part; and Fr. Bugnini was asked to be Secretary of the group.[3]

The *periti* met again at San Gregorio al Celio on October 19 and 20. Cardinal Lercaro asked them to prepare a report to be presented in the Council *Aula* early in November. Martimort presented an interesting problem:

> In November, given that the *modi* had to be presented in the *aula*, Msgr. Bonet, Msgr. Wagner, and I feared that some of the bishops were disoriented by the new procedures. We suggested a second meeting with Cardinal Lercaro, which was arranged for Sunday evening, November 17 during a working supper to which Cardinal Larraona, Father Antonelli, and we three would be invited.[4]

Martimort himself writes, "This was read the following morning, November 18, so that voting on the *modi* could begin as soon as possible".[5] Then, we read that, "On November 22, Lercaro seemed pleased with the outcome of the Council session at which he presided. The schema on the Sacred Liturgy had been approved by 2,158 votes to 19. On December 4, 1963 the Constitution was solemnly promulgated".[6] About two months later on January 25, 1964 Paul VI, commemorating the fifth anniversary of the Council's indiction, published the *motu proprio, Sacram Liturgiam*, in which he instituted a Commission whose principal competence was to activate the prescriptions of *Sacrosanctum Concilium* in the best possible way.[7]

The new organism, called the *Consilium ad exsequendam Constitutionem de Sacra Liturgia*, was comprised of Cardinals Giacomo Lercaro, Paolo Giobbe, and Arcadio Larraona. The Secretary was Father Annibale Bugnini.[8] Shortly after the constitution of this new organism, several meetings were held to choose persons with expertise in the liturgy, who would form its main body. Antonelli's diary speaks of these initial meetings and it may be assumed that he was involved in the project at both its inception and at its decisive stage. He records his conversation with Cardinal Larraona on February 17, 1964 concerning the second meeting of the *Consilium*:

> They proposed an enormous Commission: about 50 members drawn from the Council Fathers; different consultors, among them myself. We shall see. A small meeting: Dante, myself, Frutaz, Bugnini on concelebration at the Holy Thursday Chrism Mass, which is desired by the Pope.[9]

The frenetic work continued so as to decide on the persons to be nominated to the *Consilium*.

From the *Consilium ad exsequendam Constitutionem de Sacra Liturgia* to the Congregation for Divine Worship

Today, at noon, there was a meeting in the Congregation of the Section on the Conciliar Liturgy. It was decided to nominate a certain number of members. I drew up the letter and gave it to Msgr. Dante. A first meeting will be held on Wednesday. I proposed the preparation of an *Instructio* on the parts of the Constitution that were already in force, in the wake of the *motu proprio* of January 24. All agreed.[10]

The instruction was prepared on the basis of a project drawn up by Antonelli.

I went to the Cardinal and showed him a draft for the *Instructio* on the execution of the *motu proprio, Sacram Liturgiam* of January 25, 1964. We shall examine it on Wednesday morning.

[On Wednesday morning:]

At 11 a.m. we held a meeting of the *Commissari* in the Congregation to examine some questions relating to the interpretation of the *motu proprio, Sacram Liturgiam* of January 25, 1964. We learned that yesterday a second edition had been published, in a separate fascicle which would be sent to all the bishops and published in the *Acta Apostolicae Sedis*. That disturbed the meeting. I then examined the text. I do not believe it was free from error and uncertainty. The very fact of publishing a second edition of a *motu proprio*, varying in many instances from the original text, sometimes substantially, is a negative development. If the discussions continue, as they will, it will be detrimental to the Constitution.[11]

Father Antonelli's name appears in his manuscripts where he contributed to the history of the Council.

At 12:45 p.m. Father Braga brought me two documents: a letter from the Cardinal Secretary of State, N. 13419 of February 27, communicating that the Holy Father had nominated me a member of the Commission for the implementation of the Constitution on the Liturgy; and a letter from Cardinal Lercaro, President of the *Concilium ad exsequendam Constitutionem de Sacra Liturgia* dated March 2, 1964, n. 198/64, inviting me to a meeting to be held at Santa Marta on March 11, 1964 at 9:30 a.m..[12]

Meeting I (March 11, 1964)

The meeting was held in the Apostolic Palace of Santa Marta at 9:30. Cardinal Lercaro presided. The following were present: Cardinals Agagianian, Giobbe, Confalonieri, Larraona together with many members. Cardinal Lercaro, after a brief comment on the competence of the *Consilium*, announced the appointment of a vice-president. Cardinal Confalonieri's name was mentioned. Cardinal Cicognani had written to the effect that the nomination would have to be presented to the *Consilium* of the Council. Cardinal Confalonieri was of course named. Father Bugnini then spoke of the *Ratio laboris*:

1. A plan of work had been prepared;

2. Each working group will be composed of seven Consultors;

3. Each group will prepare a schema. It will be sent to 20-30 *periti*. A new draft will be made and sent again to the *periti*;

4. The Consultors. They will not be few in number. The Counselors who

will examine the schemata will be even greater in number. The names of the Consultors will not be published;

5. There will be a study group for doctrinal, theological, Biblical, scriptural, chant, art style, and pastoral considerations, etc.. These will conduct the revisions;

6. The task of the *Consilium*. When the schemata produced by the various groups (Breviary, Missal, etc.) are ready, all the *periti* who participated in their preparation will examine them. Only at that point will the schemata be submitted to the *Consilium* of the Council. Parts of the schemata, however, may be presented to the *Consilium* (e.g., the Psalter);

7. The *Coetus* for the revision of the Psalter had been constituted on February 17.

A Commission was set up to prepare the *Instructio* on the Constitution and on the *motu proprio, Sacram Liturgiam*. The draft will be sent to many Consultors. The observations of the *periti* will be collected after Easter and the schema will subsequently be submitted to the *Consilium*.[13]

Antonelli concludes his description of the first meeting of the *Consilium* on a personal note: "Things are still nebulous. These are grandiose projects, but it will not be easy to realize them".[14] In the meantime, a certain friction emerged between the *Consilium* and the Sacred Congregation of Rites. The Congregation accused the *Consilium* of acting as an improvised organ of government when in fact it was merely a consultative organ erected for study purposes.[15]

The second meeting of the *periti* of the *Consilium* took place on March 17, 1964 at 9:30 a.m. in Santa Marta. The following were present: Father Bugnini, Father Braga, Father Antonelli, Msgr. Bonet, Father Dirks, OP, Father Schmidt, SJ, Father Neunheuser, OSB, and Father Vagaggini.

1. The object of the meeting was to examine the material to be examined by the *Consilium* on the following Friday, March 20;

2. The instruction will not be ready before May and the *Consilium* will meet on April 17;

3. Seven or eight points will be included in the *Instructio*. These could be sent to the Nuncios immediately and passed on to the Presidents of the Episcopal Conferences;

4. The *Consilium* has some twenty Consultors. Some will be nominated. The Consultors will also attend the meetings of the *Consilium* with a consultative vote.[16]

Antonelli's impressions at the end of the meeting are interesting:

I am not enthusiastic about this work. I am unhappy at how much the Commission has changed. It is merely an assembly of people, many of them incompetent, and others well advanced on the road to novelty. The discussions are extremely hurried. Discussions are based on impressions and the voting is chaotic. What is most displeasing is that the expositive Promemorias and the relative questions are drawn up in advanced terms and often in a very suggestive form. The direction is weak. It is unpleasant that the question of article 36 has again been re-opened. Msgr. Wagner was unhappy. It is unpleasant to find that questions which, in themselves are not very important but which have serious consequences, should be discussed and decided by an organ which functions such as this. The Commission or *Consilium* is composed of 42 members: yesterday evening we were 13, not even a third of the members.[17]

Meeting II (April 17-20, 1964)

Article 51 of Chapter II of the Constitution, *De sacrosancto Eucharistiae mysterio,* was discussed. Having noted the various interventions of the Fathers, Antonelli concludes with his general impressions:

1. The *Instructio* is still poor both in form and content;

2. Father Braga read most of the articles, instead of Father Bugnini who is unwell. He read them too quickly. His explanations were delivered in a dry and unfriendly manner;

3. Everything is approved because that is the atmosphere of the *Consilium*;

4. There is always great haste and no time is taken for reflection;

5. Finally, it must be borne in mind that a text is distributed and its examination is begun, without having had any time to reflect on it;

6. Again, I wonder if the modifications made to Article 51, on the *Ordo Missae*, at least in some of them, are opportune, especially when it will have to be revisited when the *Ordo Missae* is revised. Important questions. But these minds are agitated and they are determined to move ahead.[18]

It is interesting to note Antonelli's experiences of the *Consilium* and the atmosphere which pervaded its work. These he recorded in his diary. It emerges that the *Consilium* not only discussed specific problems. Liturgical experiments were also made. On June 19, 1964 at 8:30 a.m. Antonelli wrote:

The *Consilium* was invited to the abbatial church of Sant'Anselmo on the Aventine Hill to assist at a concelebrated Mass which had been organized for experimental purposes. The Abbot Primate celebrated, and there were twenty concelebrants. The entire sung Pontifical Mass was finished in an hour and a quarter.[19]

Antonelli's impression of this rite is recorded as follows:

The rite is positive on the whole. Naturally, the church favored the rite: the position of the altar, the quality of the concelebrants, the commitment, the trials done in advance. I repeat on the whole it was positive.[20]

Despite a substantially positive impression, Antonelli did harbor reservations.

Communion should take place at the altar, one after the other. Communion from the chalice, the same chalice, as it was done was not too bad, everything considered. I wonder if the placing of the concelebrants in the sanctuary, away from the altar, was good. I wonder if the extension of the right hand during the consecration is to be recommended. Father Vagaggini says that it is a sign to indicate the coming of the Holy Spirit: a kind of epiclesis. This does not reassure me very much.[21]

Meeting III *(June 18-24, 1964)*

The *Consilium* met for the last time before the autumn of June 20, 1964. On one page of his diary, Antonelli notes:

> Looking back over the past three days, it must be recognized that much work was done and much has been accomplished. On the other hand:
>
> 1. the atmosphere which is too innovating is unfortunate;
> 2. the tone of the discussions is hasty and at times tumultuous which is unfortunate;
> 3. it is unfortunate that the President did not intervene and ask an opinion from every member.
>
> In conclusion, the things to be completed are momentous. I am not sure if the time is opportune.[22]

During the summer recess, Antonelli seems to have had time to reflect. He made efforts to prevent re-opening the problems connected with the various questions raised at the meetings of the *Consilium*. He reflected and, as can be seen from his diary entry for July 27, 1964, he wrote:

> I am going to see Msgr. dell'Acqua and present to him:
>
> 1. Cardinal Larraona's letter of July 23, 1964;
> 2. The observations on the *Instructio*. These two items, as I have said, I wrote myself following the discussions and recorded their results;
> 3. The observations on concelebration, or better, on the Rite of Concelebration;
> 4. Observations on Holy Communion under both species. Numbers 3 and 4 were written by Msgr. Dante, in agreement with and incorporating the observations of the Congregation.[23]

Meeting IV *(September 28 – October 1, 1964)*

The subjects presented to the Council Fathers were almost exclusively concerned with the Mass and Divine Office. During a discussion on one point, Antonelli made the following intervention:

> I said that the invocation of the divine assistance on the work and the offering of that work was something very useful. If it has to be added to any of the hours, then it should be added to Lauds, since it is not discordant with its character of praise. The *Consilium* proposed the *Oratio communis*. The martyrology cannot be retained but the embolism from the martyrology could be retained: *sancta Maria.* Then, after the final prayer, the following would come: *Adiutorium nostrum in nomine Domini: Oremus: Omnipotens sempiterne Deus...Per Christum Dominum Nostrum, Sancta Maria et omnes sancti etc....*[24]

Concerning the Patristic readings (question 9), or the readings from the Fathers as the *Consilium* called them, to be included in the Office of Readings, Antonelli notes what Msgr. Pellegrino read from his report, which he concluded with the question:

> *Utrum lectiones in Breviario proponi liceat, ex scriptis aliquorum scriptorum*

ecclesiasticorum antiquorum iuxta criteria exposita deprompta qui vel nota sanctitatis authentice recognitae carent, vel qui in aliis suis scriptis forsitan sententias orthodoxas fidei non omnino conformes docuerunt.[25]

While Msgr. Pelegrino mentioned no names in his questions, he cites the names of Tertullian, Origin, Eusebius of Caeseria, Theodore of Mopsuestia, and others in his report. Antonelli intervened with the following contributions:

> Gratulor inprimis eruditissimo et carissimo domino Pellegrino de optima sua Relatione. Propositum vero quaesitum, suadentem quidem ponit questionem, quae tamen attentam postulat considerationem. Etenim: Lectiones in Breviarium recepta, praeterquam ex Sacra Scriptura, desumebantur hucusque vel ex Patribus, vel a Doctoribus, vel ex scriptoribus ecclesiasticis inter sanctos relatis. Hi autem omnes, Patres, Doctores, Scriptores, cultu sanctorum in Ecclesia fruuntur (Utique allatae sunt etiam Encyclicae RR Pontificum, sed exempla sunt recentiora.)

> Nunc vero proponitur, ut lectiones desumi possint etiam ex Scriptoribus qui cultu Sanctorum in Ecclesia non gaudent.

> Non nego emolumenta quaedam inde trahi posse. Id autem quod ad propositionem admittendam me retinet, est praesertim consideratio haec: contra antiquissimam et nunquam intermissam traditionem nos hoc modo, in Ecclesia et in actu pubblici cultus, post Sacram Scripturam, idest verba Dei, audiemus verba virorum qui nullo cultu gaudent; imo, quod peius est, verba quandoque audiemus et honorem hoc modo daremus viris, qui, etsi multa bona nobis reliquerint, nihilominus, vel vere haeretici fuerunt, uti Tertullianus, vel materialiter saltem haeretici ut Origenes et Eusebius Caesareensis.

> Porro si principium admittimus quod lectiones desumi possint ex scriptoribus non sanctis, infinitus erit numerus eorum qui petunt ut admittantur.

> Solutio quaedam per compromissum dari forsitan potest, ut scilicet aliqua excerpta ex scriptoribus communi opinione probatis, vel etiam ex scriptoribus antiquis non semper et in omnibus probatis, uti Tertulliano, Origene, Eusebio Caesareensi et aliis, inseri possint in Lectionarium illud patristicum, ad libitum adhibendum, de quo supra sermo factus est.[26]

Antonelli's perspicacity and equilibrium should be noted. He is not against the proposal but he does point to some of the negative effects and proposes a compromise.

Meeting V (April 26-30, 1965)

A second notebook, entitled *Consilium 2*, contains a long contribution made by Antonelli during the course of the fifth meeting of the *Consilium* on the historical and practical aspects of the *Confiteor* in the Mass:

> I asked for and was given permission to speak. In substance, I said the following: I could well understand the difficulty encountered by Msgr. Wagner and his collaborators. The earliest historical sources, Justin and Hippolytus, make no mention of any penitential act during the Mass. Neither do the early *Ordinis Romani*. On the other hand, St. Paul envisages such an act: *Probet autem seipsum homo, et sic de pane illo edat et de calice bibat*, etc.. There is also an important reference in chapter 14 of the *Didachè*: *Die autem Dominica congregati frangite*

> *panem et gratias agite, postquam confessi eritis peccata vestra, ut mundum sit sacrificium vestrum.*
>
> It is to be remembered that anyone who wishes to revive institutions which have ceased to exist and are no longer effective simply because they existed in the past smacks of archeologism, as indeed do those who refuse to accept useful elements simply because they did not exist in antiquity. The *Confiteor* is medieval; it entered the Mass in the 10th century and has had its present form since the time of Pope Pius V (1570). Today its theological and pastoral utility is obvious. I cannot imagine how it can be overlooked. I would prefer to see it at the beginning of Mass, after the priest has kissed the altar and greeted the assembly. The form could be reduced. For example: *Fratres carissimi, confiteamur peccata nostra Deo et veniam impetremur. Omnes: Confiteor Deo quod peccavi nimis cogitatione, verbo et opere. Domine miserere.*
>
> I would suggest adding the absolution which is a sacramental whose usefulness and effectiveness for the purification of the soul at this time we have already mentioned. It would be sufficient to have a formula such as: *Indulgentiam peccatorum nostrorum tribuat nobis omnipotens et misericors Deus.*[27]

Father Antonelli had to leave the meeting immediately after his intervention because he had an audience with the Pope.[28] He points out, however, that his comments did not go unnoticed. "I am told that after my support for the penitential act, a favorable vote took place recommending that there should be a penitential act in the Mass and, I believe, at the beginning".[29] In his absence there was a discussion about the *Kyrie* and *Gloria*, the Liturgy of the Word, and about the Offertory. We know Father Ferdinando's thoughts on these questions from the following note:

> I do not know the decisions reached in relation to the *Kyrie, Gloria*, the Liturgy of the Word and the Offertory. With regard to the Offertory, I am told that the passage from Proverbs 9: 1-2 (*Sapientia aedicavit sibi domum... immolavit victimas suas, miscuit vinum et proposuit mensam suam. Gloria tibi Deus in saecula*) was regarded as artificial. Had I been there, I would have pointed out that this practice was deplored by Durandus of Mende who rejected the selection of Scripture passages simply because they contained a ritual word. In terms of Wisdom, the bread and wine are its counsels and the doctrine deriving from Wisdom. What has this to do with the Eucharist?
>
> In any event, I shall ask somebody what decisions were reached.[30]

At the close of the fifth meeting, Antonelli expressed a somewhat worried conclusion.

> Today at 12:30 p.m. the meeting of the *Consilium ad exsequendam Constitutionem* concluded. It was a constructive meeting. However, I do not like the atmosphere. There is a spirit of criticism and intolerance of the Holy See that cannot lead to good ends. Then there is the rationalist study of the liturgy and no concern for true piety. I am afraid that one day we will have to say of this reform that which was applied to Urban VIII's reform of the hymns: *accepit latinitas, recessit pietas.* In this case, it will be: *accepit liturgia, recessit devotio.* I would love to be able to deceive myself.[31]

From the *Consilium ad exsequendam Constitutionem de Sacra Liturgia* to the Congregation for Divine Worship

Meeting VI (October – December 1965)

Eight schemata were examined during this period: *Ordo Missae*, Baptism of adults, burial, revision of the Psalter, ordination of bishops, priests and deacons, ceremonial of bishops, Divine Office, and an introduction on sacred music. Question five, concerning the recital of the formula of ordination by consecrating bishop alone or by all concelebrating bishops, caused prolonged discussion in the *Aula*. Antonelli certainly made an important contribution to the discussion of this topic:

> The relator, Dom Botte, citing the Constitution *Sacrosanctum Ordinis* published by Pius XII in 1940, observed that it obliged the two co-consecrators to recite the preface and the prayers *submissa voce*. He proposed returning to the former use whereby the co-consecrator imposed hands but said nothing, leaving it to the principal consecrator to recite the preface and the other prayers. In support of his proposal, he categorically stated that until the 12th century and later, the general tradition in all of the churches, including the Roman Church, required the consecrating bishop alone to pronounce the formula, while the other bishops imposed hands in silence, thereby consecrating *sacramentaliter et non tantum caeremonialiter*.[32]

> The text reads: *Certe enim dum coniugia in mundo celebrantur, coniugati quique convocantur, ut in via quam coniugii praecesserunt in subsequentis quoque copulae gaudio misceantur; cum non ergo et in hac spiritali ordinatione, qua per sacrum mysterium homo Deo coniungitur, tales conveniant, qui vel pro eius custodia omnipotenti Domino preces pariter fundant?* (St. Gregory, *Registrum epistolarum*, Ed. Hartmann II, p. 336.)

> Also Gregory II writing to St. Boniface in the 8th century said: *Ut quoties episcopum consecraveris, duo vel tres conveniat tecum episcopi, ut Deo sit gratum quod geritur et eis convenientibus ipsisque praesentibus consacres.*

> According to both of these Popes, the assisting bishops do not perform a true consecration, their presence being more *ad honorem et decus*. He must conclude that Dom Botte's affirmation of a universal practice in all of the Churches up to the 12th century of bishops preserving a silent consecration, while the principal consecrator recited the prayer, is not correct.

> Having briefly pointed out this lack of unanimity on tradition, mentioned by the relator, Dom Botte, to the effect that consecrating bishops who only impose hands without pronouncing a formula, do not perform a valid ordination, or at the very least would be regarded as having conducted a dubious ordination according to the actual state of sacramental theology. I conclude therefore that the consecrators must pronounce the words of consecration as laid down by Pius XII.[33]

Following Antonelli's report, the question was put to a vote. Of 27 votes, 15 registered a *non placet* while 12 registered a *placet*. Antonelli noted:

> According to the 12 Fathers who gave their *placet*, the two consecrating bishops perform a true consecration (for nobody wishes to accept a merely ceremonial consecration), by placing the matter (*impositio manuum*) but not the form (words of the formula). For them, the principle of a true consecration is thus saved by uniting their intention with that of the consecrator. That is what Rahner proposed for the Eucharist. The priests present at the Mass consecrate with the

celebrant even if they do not say the words of consecration. One would have to ask those who vote *placet*: what do those priests do who impose hands on a newly ordained priest without saying anything?

Do they perform an ordination like the two assistant bishops at an Episcopal ordination? To my mind, this is a grave matter and Dom Botte's proposal cannot be admitted.[34]

Meeting VII (October 6-15, 1966)

For the first time, observers from the protestant churches[35] attended the meeting. Eleven questions were examined: calendar, sacred orders, the whole problem of minor orders, the readings of the Mass, baptism of children, matrimony, Divine Office, ceremonial of bishops, prefaces and prayers, consecration of oils, instruction on the Eucharistic mystery. On behalf of his office, Antonelli clarified an important point concerning priestly ordination.

Number 44 on page 19 was reviewed. In his allocution to the *ordinandi,* which is new, in the second paragraph, when the bishop speaks to those present he explains what the priesthood is, saying: *Sacerdotio Episcoporum coniungendi, Christo configurandi, summo et aeterno sacerdoti, in veros Novi Testamenti sacerdotes sunt consecrandi ad evangelium praedicandum, populum Dei pascendum cultumque divinum celebrandum.*[36]

It was with some surprise that Antonelli noted the absence of any mention of the priests' principal task, namely to offer the *sacrificium eucharisticum.*

This caused me to observe that the bishop speaks of sacrifice when he immediately turns to the ordinands and instructs them on what they must do. On p. 20, in fact, when the bishop addresses the *ordinandi* he says: *Munere item sanctificandi in Christo fungemini. Ministerio enim vestro sacrificium spirituale fidelium perficitur, Christi sacrificio coniunctum, quod per manus vestras super altare incruenter in mysterio offertur.*[37]

Father Antonelli regarded this text as too vague and believed that it was not acceptable.

At least on one of these occasions, when the bishop describes the *munera presbyteri* to the faithful, or to the *ordinandi*, it should be clearly stated that the priest has the *praecipuum munus offerendi sacrificium eucharisticum.*[38]

Many of the Fathers accepted Antonelli's proposal. Following further reflection on the question, he noted:

I am not doubting that the *periti* have conducted an exhaustive study of tradition and of the texts for the Ordination of Deacons, Priests, and Bishops. They are guided by Dom Botte, OSB, who has an excellent knowledge of all the relative material. I have the impression, however, that the body which decided in the matter, in this case 35 members of the *Consilium,* were not competent enough to deal with the question. There is also a negative factor: the haste to drive on simply because *tempus urget.* I can understand such haste in one who has set himself a vast program of work. He has to blaze the trail in order to complete it. In such important things, however, haste is a bad counselor.[39]

Meeting VIII (April 10-19, 1967)

At this meeting Antonelli was very struck by the discourse delivered during the audience with Paul VI on April 19. He reflects and writes:

> It is clear that Paul VI closely followed the work of this *Consilium*. I well remember that Paul VI personally intervened at one of the meetings of this *Consilium* (that of April 19, 1967). The fact struck me that Paul VI, speaking of the course taken by the implementation of the liturgical reform, declared that he had been hurt by certain arbitrary liturgical experiments and pained by a certain tendency to de-sacralize the liturgy. He re-confirmed his confidence in the *Consilium*, however. The Pope did not seem to realize that all the difficulties had been created by the manner in which the reform was interpreted by the *Consilium*.[40]

In order to understand the real situation of the *Consilium*, we transcribe Antonelli's comments of April 23, 1967, which reveal enormous shortcomings at an organizational and procedural level:

1. There is no denying that colossal work has been done.

2. There is a lack, however, of that kind of organization which favors mature judgment. Move on, move on, get it out. Schemata are multiplied without ever arriving at a considered form.

3. The system of discussion is bad:

    a. There are 50 Fathers: sometimes they do not all come, but there are always at least 30. Few have any specific competence. In itself, it would be difficult to conduct a discussion involving so many people;

    b. Often the schemata arrive just before the discussions. Sometimes, and in important matters, such as the new anaphoras, the schema was distributed the evening before the discussion was to take place;

    c. Cardinal Lercaro is not the man to direct a discussion. Father Bugnini has only one interest: press ahead and finish.

4. The voting system is worse. It is ordinarily done by a show of hands, but nobody counts who has raised a hand and who has not. Nobody says 'so many approved' and 'so many said no'. It is disgraceful. Although the question has been asked several times, nobody has succeeded in ascertaining whether the necessary majority must be absolute or two thirds of the votes. Voting by scheda only takes place at the request of the Fathers. The scheda are subsequently examined by those from the Secretariat.

5. A further grave lacuna is the absence of any minutes of the meetings. There certainly has been no reference to them and they certainly have never been read.[41]

The situation could not have continued and it became necessary to lay down certain essential norms for the *Consilium*.

> In its first three years, the *Consilium* operated on the basis of a few norms laid down initially by the Cardinal President. The manner in which the work progressed, and certain difficulties concerning the competence of the President and the Secretariat which emerged subsequent to the publication of certain

documents by other Dicasteries, mentioning that they had been approved by the *Consilium* without their having been so approved by the *plenum* of the *Consilium*, clearly demonstrated the need to revise certain aspects of the structure and order of the *Consilium*.

Cardinal Lercaro explained the matter to the Holy Father at an audience granted on September 22, 1966. Following the Pope's general consent, the members of the *Consilium,* meeting the following October, examined the organizational problem of the *Consilium*, and established the following:

1. … the functions and responsibilities of the relators, the consultors, etc., are to be revised and more clearly defined in an internal *regolamento* to regulate those functions and responsibilities;

2. it also appeared opportune to establish greater certainty with regard to the statutes so that they can better govern the organization of the *Consilium* (President, Presidential Council, Secretariat, General Meetings, and Special meetings) and regulate the proceedings of its meetings.[42]

The Holy Father was informed of their decision by Cardinal Lercaro in an audience of November 10, 1966. He consigned the statutes to the Pope requesting that they be approved for three years, *ad experimentum*, as had happened with the statutes of other similar organizations.[43] Under strictly reserved cover, Paul VI gave the proposed *Statutum Consilii* to Msgr. Antonelli[44] who immediately began an examination. After two months, he returned the papers to the Pope.

On May 9, 1967 I received all the documentation together with the statutes of the *Consilium*, and the two schemata *De Sacris Ordinibus* and *De Calendario*.

Yesterday morning, before going to the audience, I read these observations to Cardinal Larraona, having spoken to him on several occasions about them. The Cardinal approved the observations. During the audience, I returned all the documentation to the Holy Father with these notes and observations on July 15, 1967.[45]

Since it is important to know Antonelli's reaction to the proposed statutes of the *Consilium*, we now transcribe the observations which he made to the Pope.

General Observations:

Firstly, it must be said that for several reasons, the liturgical reform must be accelerated as much as possible. In the first place, there is widespread and notable disquiet amongst both clergy and laity because of the continuous changes that are being made; secondly, this instability and uncertainly about the future promotes the arbitrary and continues to lower all respect for the liturgical laws; thirdly, if the reform is not carried out quickly, then when we arrive at the end, that which has been decided on principle will no longer be valid (we are already experimenting); finally, for as long as the Holy See will dispose of two entities to deal with liturgical matters, the Sacred Congregation for Rites and the *Consilium*, albeit with each having theoretically well-defined areas and competence, in practice, it will be difficult to avoid the inconvenience of a certain diarchy.

In view of these opening remarks, the question could be posed if it might not be opportune to set aside the proposed Statutes, which by their very name and contents give the impression of a permanent institution, or at least to postpone any decision in their regard for the time being, while collating the necessary practical disposition in a *regula* or internal *regolamento*, mentioned in articles 9 and 14, but which have yet to be drawn up as article 15 states.

Particular Observations:

Page 4: *Praeterea ipsius Consilii est experimenta moderari ac disciplinam liturgicam tueri usquedum novae liturgiae formae et instituta certa definiantur.*

It would appear necessary to draw attention to the fact of the experiments. Experiments are necessary to verify the functionality of new rites. These, however, should be few in number, limited in time, and restricted to a few expert locations. Only responsible people should be involved in these. The fact that experiments have been carried out on a vast scale, and the scope permitted to them, has resulted in many priests, practically everywhere, regarding themselves as authorized to attempt the most outrageous things under the pretext that they are being done *ad experimentum*. In conclusion: experiments yes, but few in number, limited in time, and permitted to a small number of qualified persons.

Page 4, paragraph 4: *Proinde, Patribus ipsi Consilio efformando deputatis approbantibus, praesens Statutum seu lex peculiaris paratum est.*

It is something novel for an organ of the Holy See to prepare and approve its own statutes (*Patribus approbantibus*), and have them merely confirmed by the Holy Father. Everybody knows that a revision of the Roman Curia is in course. However, no Dicastery has ever presumed to revise its own competence.

Page 4, n. 4: The promulgation of the definitive text prepared by the *Consilium* is reserved to the Sacred Congregation of Rites. Nothing, however, is mentioned of its part in preparing these texts. It is evident that the Congregation cannot blindly sign such a document.

Page 5a, n. 5B 3: According to this paragraph, it pertains to the *Consilium corripere devios conatus, qui hic illic forte deprehendi possunt, pravos usus prohibere ac cohibere eos, qui proprio marte agunt.* It must be noted that in n. 4, it is said that the Sacred Congregation of Rites inherently has the competence to *tueri tum novas formas liturgicas definitas et instituta certa et obligantia, tum eas quae iam vigent.*

How can interference be avoided?

Page 6 n. 8: "*Membra (Consilii) non excedunt quinquaginta?*"

Are we sure that such a high number can function practically? It began with 40, and now 50 are proposed. What requires closer and more careful attention is what is proposed regarding the nomination of the members of the *Consilium*, its consultors, and other organs.

The nomination of the members of the *Consilium*, including Cardinals, and the selection of four-fifths of those participating in it are entrusted to the Presidential Council. The Pope is asked merely to confirm. (Evidently, the Pope need not confirm should he so desire, but in fact his choice is already determined.) The Pope may then directly select one-fifth of the *Consilium*, including, I repeat, the Cardinals.

This is an absolutely novel system amounting to nothing other than a continuation of the Council. There are no historical precedents for it. Once Trent and Vatican I had been closed, the Holy See reverted to having full autonomy. The Presidential

Council, which is composed of seven members of the *Consilium*, is elected by the plenary *Consilium*. The Vice-President is even elected by the *Consilium*. The Pope, again, merely confirms.

Think of the contrast between these and the canonical nominations. All members of every Dicastery of the Holy See, from the Cardinals to the Consultors, are chosen and nominated directly by the Pope. After these observations on the text, I hope that I may be permitted to stress the absolute necessity of imposing some discipline on the voting system of the *Consilium*. With such a large number of participants, often of very different views, it is vital to be able to decide the various questions by vote. But what criteria are to apply?

Is an absolute majority required or merely a two-thirds majority?

One of the most important things that must be decided is the system by which votes are cast: by scheda ballot or by show of hands. Up to now, the latter system has been widely used, but in a somewhat empirical manner. It was sufficient merely for a certain number to raise their hands to forge ahead, without anybody counting how many had approved or not. Then in the subsequent debates, appeal is often made to positive votes, without anybody being able to prove that a given vote had actually been positive.

Cardinal Felici might be asked for his opinion with regard to the voting in the *Consilium*. During its sessions, he has raised the question several times. The draft schemata: *De Sacris Ordinis* and *De Calendario*, are acceptable in general terms, prescinding from particular observations of secondary importance.[46]

It would seem that the statutes were cancelled in light of Antonelli's observations. Because of this, Antonelli had a rather surprising and painful altercation with Bugnini.

He told me openly that the proposed statutes had been wrecked because Msgr. Anonelli had expressed a negative view about them. When I told him that I had only made some serene and honest observations about them, he replied that he had not seen my text. Clearly, he has been told that I made observations. When I told him then that I had merely expressed some modest, firm observations, Father Bugnini asked why I had not expressed them during the meeting of the *Consilium*. I replied that the text of the statutes had only been circulated the night before the meeting. Moreover, the atmosphere of the *Consilium* was such that the Secretary of the Congregation of Rites could not have made observations on the subject without danger of being misunderstood. At that point, I had the opportunity to point out that the proposed statutes had returned to the Sacred Congregation of Rites, and that it would have been opportune had the Congregation been consulted. Father Bugnini replied that such had not been necessary since it involved a matter internal to the *Consilium*.[47]

In a note relating to all the events of 1967, Antonelli noted his impressions of the internal and external situation of the *Consilium*:

1. Confusion. No one has a sense any longer of the sacred and binding character of the liturgical laws. The changes continue. Sometimes, they are not clear, while at other times they lack logic. In my opinion, this is because of the deplorable system of experiments. It has breached the dykes. Everyone acts more or less arbitrarily.

2. There is weariness. All have grown tired of the continual reforms and all want to arrive at something stable.

3. The conservatives gain strength. The Synod of Bishops was not a success for the *Consilium*.

4. The work of de-sacralization continues on a vast scale. Now they call it secularization.

5. From this it is evident that the liturgical question, while having a large influence on the rapid development of a certain mentality, has, in its turn, been absorbed into a wider problem, which is fundamentally doctrinal.

6. The great crisis then is the crisis of traditional doctrine and the Magisterium.[48]

Antonelli's papers from 1968 no longer contain a detailed account of the meeting of the *Consilium*. He merely records the discourses given by the Fathers and the votes taken. An entry for October 12, 1968 is significant:

> The morning was spent at the *Consilium* where they discussed a reform of the Breviary, or more accurately, a great *Instructio de Breviario*. When this document is completed, it will have an important consequence for the public prayer of the Church. It is a pity both that it has not yet been finished to perfection and that the examination that was done of the document was very superficial. Chapter one should be a resumé of the doctrine on public prayer. It was drawn up by Prof. Lengeling. It is not bad but it must be perfected. I made some observations:
>
> 1. that the public prayer of the Church continues that of the synagogue;
> 2. it is an essential duty for the Church;
> 3. the question of the persons deputed to carry out the public prayer of the Church must be examined. The Constitution on the Liturgy mentions it.
>
> Now the progressives say that all are deputed to say the public prayer of Church: I well know that; but if nobody prays, what will happen? There have to be people who are obliged to say the public prayer of the Church. Deputed, here means, obliged.[49]

During 1969, Antonelli resumed the practice of accurately recording the meetings of the *Consilium*. On January 20 he noted a meeting of the *Consilium* with representatives of the Congregations to examine proposed norms for the Mass with several groups. He reflected:

> This is a growing phenomenon and a dangerous one. The following were present: Cardinal Gut, myself, Father Bugnini, Father Braga for the *Consilium*, Msgr. Casoria, and Msgr. Rossetti and Msgr. Barone for the Sacred Congregation of the Clergy.[50]

Regular meetings were held, and in his diary entry for February 10 he notes:

> The revision of the rite of matrimony continues, followed by the rite for the baptism of children. Some parts are well prepared, others less so. At the end of the doctrinal chapter, I ask: why is it that the entire chapter speaks of baptism for the remission of sins but never mentions original sin? It was only at that point that Father Braga said that the Holy Office had introduced a modification in this sense.[51]

It is worth transcribing Antonelli's observations on the meeting of February 20:

> This morning we finished the revision of the schema for the rite of baptism of children, which had been prepared by a group of liturgists from the *Consilium*. It is fine. There are some good things in it, but it is gigantic. Again this morning, I had to observe that where one would expect to highlight original sin, for instance when there is the little homily of catechatical character, it would appear that all trace of it had vanished. I dislike this new, vapid, theological mentality.[52]

The *Consilium* meetings for 1970 are recorded by Antonelli in a notebook marked "*April 9-10, 1970. Last meeting of the Consilium. Inauguration of the Sacred Congregation for Divine Worship*". Among other things we read:

> The meeting took place in the *Sala delle Congregazioni* in the Vatican at 9 a.m.. Many were present. Cardinal Gut opened the meeting. There was a brief history of the *Consilium* and of its work. It had tried to follow tradition and adjust the liturgy to the needs of today. The Congregation for Divine Worship is a continuation of the *Consilium*. Today we celebrate its final meeting. Gut read his text in Latin. Clearly, it had been prepared by others. *Ne verbum quidem* of the Sacred Congregation of Rites, of which he himself was the last Prefect.[53]

Father Bugnini's report followed Cardinal Gut's discourse. He introduced the agenda to be discussed during the meeting.[54] Antonelli comments:

> The text was distributed as Father Bugnini read it out. Many observations could be made about it, but one has to be mentioned: all the texts prepared by the *Consilium* were subsequently discussed by the Sacred Congregation of Rites which published them.
>
> Often the texts, at least in part, were circulated to the other Dicasteries, and especially to the Holy Office, before receiving approval. Father Bugnini felt obliged publicly to thank Msgr. Agustoni for his services at the Holy Office; but *ne verbum quidem* of the Sacred Congregation of Rites of which he was Under-secretary. *Res commentario non indigent.*[55]

A discussion on the martyrology followed Father Bugnini's report. Bugnini observed that the *Coetus* for this work had not yet been formed. Antonelli noted an omission in Bugnini's discourse, since he "did not mention that since 1964, in the printed list of the *Coetus*, the Bollandists and the Historical Section of the Congregation of Rites, logically, had been proposed to carry out this work".[56] A report followed by Father Jacques Dubois, OSB, Director *d'Études à L'Ecole Pratique des Hautes Études*, and a specialist on the history of martyrologies. The discussion began. Father Bugnini asked Msgr. Antonelli to speak. He gave the following contribution:

> I am very pleased with the report. I would ask one question: is it a certainty that there are some saints, authentic saints, who, through some error, have not been included in the martyrology, as it is certain that some saints have been inserted into the martyrology although they are not authentic? In these cases, the former should be introduced and the latter removed. But what is to be done in cases where doubts exist? These are much more numerous. Once upon a time it used to be said that *melior est conditio possidentis*. Is this criterion to be retained, or is it taken that it would be better to eliminate them?
>
> Father DuBois says that they are thinking of recovering them. I suggested

drawing up a *Commentarius Brevissimus*, similar to the one for the *Calendarium Romanum*, giving the reasons for the omissions, additions, and the exclusions made in doubtful cases. Cardinal Felici believed that these studies should be undertaken before proceeding with a revision of the martyrology. I said that we could take it that the studies had already been done. The two great volumes of the Bollandists, together with Father Delehaye's *Commentarius Perpetuus* and his *Martyrologium Hieronymianum* and his *Commentarius* on the Roman Martyrology, published with his collaborators, allows us to say with certainty if a saint is authentic or dubious.

On the other hand, an updated version of the martyrology is necessary for the important reason that on the many days on which the Mass of a saint can be said, it can be said of the saint found in the martyrology. For this same reason, Father Bugnini insisted on the need for an immediate revision of the martyrology.[57]

In the notebook containing the various sessions of the *Consilium*, Antonelli recorded the discussions of the Fathers, the votes, and the corrections. With regard to the final meetings of the *Consilium*, he gives the impression of many things being done in great haste:

> I ask myself: how can one give an opinion on these questions, some of them grave, when the text is changed at the last minute and presented as the meeting ends. This cannot be taken seriously (this happened in relation to the *Praenotanda* for the rite of confirmation).[58]

Again he writes:

> Personally, I ask myself, what authority or competence do we have to discuss these most intricate theological questions?[59] (about the difference between Baptism and Confirmation, between character and effects)

At the end of the first session of the final meeting of the *Consilium*, Antonelli went to the offices of Divine Worship on April 9, 1970. Here the work of the *Consilium* was formally closed and that of the Congregation for Divine Worship inaugurated. Antonelli writes:

> At 5 p.m. I went to the fourth floor of the *Palazzo delle Congregazioni* in Piazza Pio XII, 10. There was great excitement. Some chairs had been brought to the entrance. Against the wall, a bust of Paul VI, in bronze, had been placed on a table. Overhead, an inscription had been put up in marble. The Latin had been composed by Father Lentini, OSB.

> Cardinals Gut, Giobbe, Lercaro, Confalonieri, Tarancon, were present as were Bishops Boudon, Spülbeck, and others, many of the *periti*, but I did not see Msgr. Wagner. Cardinal Gut spoke, or rather, read out an address in Latin. Msgr. Boudon then spoke, at length in the name of the bishops as did Professor Pascher of Munich on behalf of the *periti*. Nothing of importance. Pascher used some baroque images. He said that visitors to Rome can admire the fountains with which the Popes had opened *fontes sitibundis*. Here Paul VI had opened the fount of the liturgy to a *populo sitienti*. We are back to 1600!

> It was interesting to observe that neither the discourse read by Cardinal Gut nor those of Boudon and Pascher mentioned *ne verbum quidem* of the Sacred Congregation of Rites. And, imagine, all of the work for the liturgical reform began here in the Historical Section.[60]

The *Consilium* met for the last time on the following day and went to an audience of the Holy Father. The Pope was very cordial. He spoke, but said with clarity from the outset, that the *Consilium*, *"post conditam Sacram Congregationem pro Culto Divino iam dimittitur"*.[61]

* * * *

The present chapter, having examined his papers, illustrates the figure of Antonelli as a liturgist and demonstrates how highly his opinions were valued during the life of the *Consilium*. It was unfortunate that he was not so much involved in the work of the liturgical reform, especially after the suppression of the Congregation of Rites. He felt this very much. Perhaps such is the destiny of pioneers: they open up the way, while others enter and forge ahead leaving the pioneers behind. Reading Antonelli's account of the meetings of the *Consilium*, his disappointment with the various decisions made with regard to the liturgical reform clearly emerges. He reacted in this manner because he regarded the liturgy as the base of all Christian formation. He expected that the liturgical reform would be seriously applied in an atmosphere of calm and considered judgment. His reaction to the reform of the rites contained in the *Rituale Romanum* is stimulating. Antonelli considered it highly important and requiring careful attention since the sacraments had been instituted by Christ for his people. Indeed, Antonelli remained so firmly convinced of his one great preoccupation, that of bringing the faithful to a living and active participation in the liturgy, that it permeated his entire liturgical sensibility. In the next chapter, we shall proceed to examine some further liturgical writings, particularly important for Msgr. Antonelli.

[1] A.G. MARTIMORT, *Mirabile laudis canticum*, Ed. Liturgiche, Roma 1991, pp. 380-381.

[2] A. BUGNINI, *La riforma*, cit., p. 65.

[3] *Ibidem*.

[4] F. ANTONELLI, *Diario n. 17*, p. 225: "Cardinal Larraona's car came to pick me up yesterday evening at the *Antonianum* and brought me to St. Priscilla. Those present were: Cardinal Larraona, President of the Liturgical Commission, Fr. Antonnelli, the Secretary, and three members: Msgr. Martimort (the *liturgical bomb* as Cardinal Lercaro usually called him), Msgr. Bonet, and Msgr. Wagner. We met to decide on a number of questions concerning the procedure for the last and definitive phase for the approval of the Schema. We concluded with a beautiful and fraternal supper. We left St. Priscilla at 10:30 p.m.".

[5] A.G. MARTIMORT, *Mirabile*, cit., p. 381.

[6] G. LERCARO, *Lettere dal Concilio*, Bologna 1980, p. 231.

[7] Cf. *EV*, 2/136. The Pope also announced that specific "opportune and authoritive instructions" would be given for the application of the Constitution on the Liturgy before the end of the *vacatio legis* which had been fixed for February 16, 1964, and that "appropriate post-conciliar structures" would be put in place to prepare the reforms: cf. PAUL VI, *Allocuzione ai Padri conciliare*, December 4, 1964, in *AAS*, 56 (1964), p. 34. Both the Secretariat of State and the Congregation of Rites began work in this regard in early January. The *Diario* for 1964 makes several references to this – including an Audience of the Pope granted on February 13: "He spoke to me about the *motu proprio, Sacram Liturgiam*, and of the reactions raised by article IX. He showed me a promemoria prepared by Father Bugnini. I approved in substance a number of changes. It seems they want to make many small changes. He showed me a long paper prepared by Msgr. Carli, Bishop of Segni. He seemed rather preoccupied. If the Council does not go well then it would be a set back for Rome and for the Church".

[8] Cf. A. BUGNINI, *La riforma*, cit., p. 60.

[9] F. ANTONELLI, *Diario*, cit., February 16, 1964.

[10] *Ibidem*, February 21, 1964.

[11] *Ibidem*, February 26, 1964.

[12] *Ibidem*, March 3, 1964. In the *Diario*, he speaks of a conversation with Cardinal Larraona who showed him a letter from the Cardinal Secretary of State in which the application of the Constitution on the Liturgy is deputed to the *Consilium ad exsequendam Constitutionem*. However, until contrary proofs are shown, the Congregation is the organ of government: if another governative organ is established confusion will ensue. Tomorrow, we shall have to see about this development".

[13] In a green coloured *Buffetti* notebook entitled *Consilium I*, in the *Fondo Antonelli* of the Congregation for the Causes of Saints, we find a complete chronological account of the meetings of the *Consilium*. F. ANTONELLI, *Note sulle Adunanze del Consilium I*, in *SCCS*, pp. 3-5.

[14] F. ANTONELLI, *Diario*, cit., March 11, 1964.

[15] F. ANTONELLI, *Diario*, cit., March 16, 1964. Antonelli notes: "This morning I had a long conversation with Cardinal Larraona. We were very saddened by the fact that the *Consilium* had arrogated to itself functions which logically inhered in the Congregation of Rites. The *Consilium* is a study organism: the Congregation is an organ of government".

[16] F. ANTONELLI, *Note sulle Adunanze*, cit., p. 6.

[17] *Ibidem*, p. 23.

[18] *Ibidem*, pp. 76-77.

[19] *Ibidem*, p. 79.

[20] *Ibidem*.

[21] *Ibidem*, pp. 79-80.

[22] F. ANTONELLI, *Diario*, cit., June 20, 1964.

[23] F. ANTONELLI, *Note sulle Adunanze*, cit., p. 83.

[24] *Ibidem*, p. 101.

[25] *Ibidem*, p. 119.

[26] F. ANTONELLI, *Note sulle Adunanze*, cit., pp. 120-121.

[27] F. ANTONELLI, *Note sulle Adunanze of the Consilium 2*, in *SCCS*, pp. 81-82.

[28] Cf. *ibidem*, p. 82.

[29] *Ibidem*, p. 83.

[30] *Ibidem*.

[31] F. ANTONELLI, *Diario*, cit., April 30, 1965.

[32] F. ANTONELLI, *Note sulle Adunanze*, cit., pp. 131-134. Here we transcribe Antonelli's discourse: "Now, we have to say that this tradition was never so constant. Msgr. Nabuco, for example, has reminded us that when the Pope consecrated he was not assisted by two co-consecrators. Moreover, ANDRIEU, in *Les Ordines Romani*, III, p. 586, cites a passage from a letter of St. Gregory the Great to St. Augustine of Canterbury which reads: *Et quidem, in Anglorum ecclesia, in qua adhuc solus tu episcopus inveniris, ordinare episcopum non aliter nisi sine episcopis potes. Cum igitur auctore Deo ita fuerint episcopi in propinquis sibi locis ordinate, per omnia episcoporum ordinatio sine adgregatis tribus vel quattuor episcopis fieri non debet.* However, St. Gregory continues to say that if others are invited to a wedding, why not invite other bishops to the ordination or consecration of a bishop?

[33] *Ibidem*, pp. 133-134.

[34] *Ibidem*, pp. 135-136.

[35] F. ANTONELLI, *Note sulle Adunanze of the Consilium 3*, in *SCCS*, p. 5.

[36] *Ibidem*, pp. 12-13.

[37] *Ibidem*, p. 13.

[38] *Ibidem*.

[39] *Ibidem*, p. 24.

[40] F. ANTONELLI, *Diario*, cit., April 19, 1967.

[41] F. ANTONELLI, Manuscript added to the *Diario 1967*.

[42] *Consilium [ad exsequendam Constitutionem de Sacra Liturgia]*, Statuto del *"Consilium"*, Prot. n. 594/67, Città del Vaticano, April 18, 1967, p. 1.

[43] Cf. *ibidem*, p. 2.

[44] Cf. Manuscript of Paul VI, in folder *"Intorno allo Statuto del Consilium"*, in *ALV*.

[45] F. ANTONELLI, *Manoscritto informale dell'Udienza avuta con Paolo VI il 15 luglio 1967*, in folder *"Intorno allo Statuto del Consilium"*, in *ALV*.

[46] F. ANTONELLI, *"Intorno allo Statuto del Consilium". Osservazioni generali*, in folder *"Intorno allo Statuto del Consilium"*, in *ALV*, pp. 1-5.

[47] F. ANTONELLI, *Diario*, cit., August 21, 1967 – August 28, 1967.

[48] *Ibidem*, November 1, 1967.

[49] *Ibidem*, October 12, 1968.

[50] *Ibidem*, January 20, 1969.

[51] *Ibidem*, February 10, 1969.

[52] *Ibidem*, February 20, 1969.

[53] F. ANTONELLI, *April 9-10, 1970. Ultima Sessione "Consilium", Inaugurazione S.C. Culto Divino*, in *SCCS*, pp. 3-4.

[54] Cf. *ibidem*, pp. 5-6.

[55] *Ibidem*, pp. 6-7.

[56] *Ibidem*, p. 8.

[57] *Ibidem*, pp. 8-11.

[58] *Ibidem*, p. 13.

[59] *Ibidem*, p. 16.

[60] *Ibidem*, pp. 23-25.

[61] *Ibidem*, p. 43.

Chapter 10

The Instruction *Inter Oecumenici*
(1964)

Foreword

> A fascicle entitled *Instructio ad exsecutionem Constitutionis de Sacra Liturgia recte ordinandam* was distributed to the Conciliar Fathers on October 16, 1964. It had been prepared by the *Consilium*, and various drafts had been drawn up and revised by the Congregation of Rites. It was agreed upon at a high-level meeting of the *Consilium* and the Sacred Congregation of Rites held on the September 21, 1964, and it was promulgated with the explicit approval of the Holy Father on September 26, 1964.[1]

After our long account of the person of Ferdinando Antonelli and of his valuable contribution to the work of liturgical reform of the Second Vatican Council while Secretary of the Conciliar Commission on the Sacred Liturgy and as a member of the *Consilium*, we now begin an analysis of a document containing his reflections on the Instruction of September 26, 1964. First, however, we intend to reproduce Antonelli's thoughts on the general liturgical situation a year after the liturgical reform. Speaking to the parish priests of the diocese of Rome on March 10, 1966, he stated that:

> A new era had begun in the history of the Church. For the liturgy, it began on December 4, 1963 with the approval of the Constitution on the Sacred Liturgy. The Tridentine era had great strengths but also great weaknesses. The Constitution was partially implemented on March 7, 1964, when the *Instruction* of September 26, 1964 came into force. In order to measure how far we have come, and how far we have yet to go, we need to know our final destination. Article 10 of the Constitution, a fundamental article, describes that objective. It provides a new vision of the Christian life and the pastoral apostolate.
>
> It is a matter of creating an awareness among the people of God of their participation in the Paschal mystery, which is a participation in the family of the Risen.[2]

The manuscript that we will now examine is dated December 27, 1964 and contains various reflections of Father Antonelli,[3] which are always clear and precise, and from them it is possible to deduce his total involvement in the new springtime of the Church initiated by the Second Vatican Council. Thus, we will be able to reflect on the importance of the liturgical reform and on Antonelli's concern, as well as those of the Council Fathers, for its implementation. In his introduction to the

The Development of the Liturgical Reform

Instructio, Father Antonelli stresses the importance of the revision of this document by the Sacred Congregation of Rites, of which he was Promotor of the Faith.

Value of the Instruction

Antonelli presents the nature of the *Instruction* as follows:

> This is a legal text which is not autonomous. It depends on another text, whose application, in concrete terms, it determines. Thus, the *Decretum Generale* of November 1955 on Holy Week, was also followed by an *Instructio*.

> The famous document, *Deus Scientiarum Dominus*, was followed by an analogous document, *Ordinationes Sacrae Congregationis de Studiis*.

> The Instruction is signed by Cardinal Larraona, Prefect of the Sacred Congregation of Rites, and by Cardinal Lercaro, President of the *Consilium*.

> A *vacatio legis* was determined to run until the first Sunday of Lent 1965, which fell on March 17. Of its nature, the *Instructio* must neither go against the Constituion nor exceed it.[4]

Contents

The content of the document under consideration is divided into the following chapters:

> The *Instructio* follows the order of the Constitution. Thus, it is comprised of a preamble and five chapters:

> Chapter 1: General Norms, the most developed chapter;

> Chapter 2: The Eucharistic Mystery;

> Chapter 3: The Sacraments and Sacramentals; ·

> Chapter 4: The Divine Office;

> Chapter 5: Disposition on the construction of churches and altars.

> It did not touch upon the material in Chapter V of the Constitution on the liturgical year or Chapter VI on Sacred Music. In all, there are five chapters.[5]

Object

Antonelli describes the object of the Instruction mainly by reference to Article 3:

1. Clarify the competence of the various Episcopal assemblies in liturgical matters;

2. Clarify some principles contained in the *motu proprio, Sacram Liturgiam,* of January 25, 1964;

3. Its principal objective is to outline those points of the Constitution which are already in force and which do not have to await the publication of the liturgical books.[6]

The Principles

The principles on which the *Instructio* is based are essentially: the spirit animating the constitution; a gradual application of the Constitution; the change in mentality it tries to effect; and the centrality of the Paschal mystery. Antonelli underlines the importance of entering into the spirit of the Constitution, which is extremely important. The *Instructio* also has to be given due consideration so as to ensure that what has been carefully constructed after years of study will not be swept away by any hastiness. Changes must come about gradually because what counts the most is not the external change, but the formation of a new mentality.

    a) Spirit of the Constitution

> Everything prescribed by the *Instructio* must be understood in reference to the spirit of the Constitution, which is that of promoting the participation of the laity in the liturgy.[7]

    b) Progressive application

> The reform will be more easily translated into practice if applied gradually. The principle is good, but it must be used sparingly. Indeed, no new dispositions are foreseen until the publication of the liturgical books.[8]

    c) Change of mentality

> It is not a question of revising this rite or that text, but rather, by means of enlightened pastoral activity, the Christian life should rediscover its true source in the liturgy.[9]

    d) The object of the reform, the Paschal mystery lived

> The liturgy inaugurates this plan and provides the means to accomplish it through the Sacraments which confer operative life.[10]

Antonelli concludes with the hope that the liturgy will once again become a school for the Christian life, and quotes a passage from Paul VI's discourse of October 29, 1964 to the *Consilium* in which he says that the liturgy should form piety, truth, and charity.[11] "All these principles, and the entire liturgical Constitution, if fully implemented should lead to a situation in which the liturgy will return to what it was for more than a millennium, a school of Christian life".[12]

Means of achieving a true liturgical reform

Referring to articles 14-20 of the Constitution, Antonelli outlines the fundamental condition for a true liturgical reform, namely, the liturgical formation of the clergy and the faithful. The *Instruction* dwells on the subject, and it proposes a detailed means and a series of practical measures to create a liturgical awareness among the faithful:

1. Liturgical formation of clerics (articles 11-13) in the seminary and in liturgical piety.

2. Spiritual formation of clerics (articles 14-17):

    a) Ascetical books, pious exercises in harmony with liturgical piety;

    b) The Mass, center of the spiritual life, sung on feasts and holy days, concelebrated at least on solemnities, and attending Mass in the cathedral;[13]

    c)   Divine Office, even if not *in sacris*, especially Lauds and Vespers, and Vespers in the cathedral.

3.   Liturgical formation of religious (article 18) and of the faithful (article 19).

Prescriptions Concerning the Mass

Antonelli then dwells on the rite of the Mass, bearing in mind the contents of the Constitution and the *Instructio*:

Sacrosanctum Concilium

1.   Article 50 of the Constitution contains 3 words which are explosive when compared to the actual state of things: *Ordo Missae recognoscatur.*

Therefore, the fixed parts of the Mass must be revised. In reality, they are not very ancient and they assumed their present form only in the Tridentine reform. The Canon, however, has remained unchanged since the time of Gregory the Great, simply because he believed it to be Apostolic in origin.

2.   The Constitution also gives the criteria for recognition:

    a)   *Singularum partium propria ratio necnon mutua connexio clarius pateant*, for example, distinguishing the place of the liturgy of the word and that of the Eucharist;

    b)   *Pia et actuosa fidelium participatio facilior reddatur*, simplifying some things, Psalm 42, for example;

    c)   *ritus simpliciores fiant*, for example some genuflections and many signs of the cross;

    d)   *ea omittantur quae duplicatur fuerunt*, for example, that the the celebrant should have to say alone the parts sung by the deacon or subdeacon;

    e)   *restituantur nonnulla quae deciderunt*, for example, the *oratio fidelium*.[14]

In Article 50 of the Constitution, which is very dense, lays down two indispensable conditions:

1.   *Ut substantia rituum servetur*, in such a way that were St. Pius V or St. Gregory the Great to come back, they would be able to say that the Mass had substantially remained the same.

2.   *Ad pristinam sanctorum Patrum normam*. This expression is taken from the Bull of St. Pius V of 1570 on the Missal. It means that the entire revision must be carried out in accordance with the tradition of the Church.[15]

Having considered the prescriptions of the Constitution with regard to the Mass, Antonelli continues with those contained in the *Instruction*.

The Instruction

I have dwelled on Article 50 of the Constitution so that nobody may be surprised by the innovation introduced by the Constitution. It must be said at the outset, that the prescriptions of Article 48 of the *Instructio* itself are valid up to the reform of the Mass, *donec integer Ordo Missae instauratus fuerit*. We can be sure that certain things which are now anticipated will be retained, and other things, about which some doubt exists, will remain unchanged.

The general principle contained in articles 32-33, especially 32, should be noted: *Partes quae ad scholam et ad populum spectant, si ab ipsis canuntur aut recitantur, a celebrante privatim non dicuntur.* Article 33: *Item a celebrante privatim non dicuntur lectiones quae a competenti ministro vel a ministrante leguntur aut canuntur.*

Having said that, we now turn to the prescriptions of Article 48.

It must be said at the outset that a *Ritus servandus* and the melodies for the chants, such as the *Pater noster* will soon be published:[16]

a) *Partes Proprii quae a schola vel a populo canuntur aut recitantur, a celebrante privatim non dicuntur.*[17] This is a sensible prescription. If the *schola* sings the *graduale*, it does so for the entire assembly, and its head, the priest, should not say it privately;[18]

b) *Partes Ordinarii celebrans potest una cum populo vel schola cantare vel recitare,* that is, the *Kyrie, Gloria, Credo, Sanctus,* and *Agnus Dei;*[19]

c) *Psalmus 42 in precibus ad gradus altaris omittitur. Omnes hae praeces omittuntur quoties actio liturgica praecessit.*[20] Those who know the history of these prayers will not be surprised. However, we always need to have a penitential act, and the definitive revision makes a provision for it. It already existed in the *Doctrina duodecim apostolorum* or the *Didachè;*[21]

d) *In Missa sollemni, patena a subdiacono non tenetur, sed super altare relinquitur;*

e) *Oratio secreta vel cantetur, vel in missa lecta elata voce dicatur;*

f) *Doxologia finalis "Per ipsum" cantetur aut elata voce dicatur, omissis signis crucis et genuflectitur solum post Amen.*[22]

It was permitted for the people and the celebrant to say the *Pater noster* in the vernacular at read Masses. In sung Masses, it could be sung by the people in Latin, unless the local authorities had obtained permission from the Holy See for chant in the vernacular set to melodies approved by the territorial authorities.[23]

The remaining details of the Instruction are transcribed by Antonelli without comment, and it is unnecessary to reproduce them here. Rather, we would like to dwell on point 4 of Article 56 of the Instruction which mentions *De oratione communi seu fidelium.*[24] Here we have an account of the historical development of the prayers of the faithful and of its pastoral importance during the celebration of the Mass.

Importance of the 'Oratio fidelium'

1. Already mentioned by St. Justin by the year 150.
2. Found in all liturgies after the readings and the dismissal of the catechumens (hence, *oratio fidelium*) with general intentions (hence, *oratio communis*).
3. A classical form, that of Good Friday, was used in Rome:

>   *a)*   for penitential days – these were said kneeling;
>
>   *b)*   the intentions were those of Good Friday.

4.   A litany form exists among the Orientals. The Deacon announces the intention and the people reply *Kyrie eleison*. It spread from the East to Gaul and Northern Italy (Milan).

5.   In Rome: the classical form is last mentioned during the reign of Felix III (483-492 cf. Epistula VII, P.L. 58.925). Pope Gelasius (492-496) transformed the Roman *Oratio fidelium* into a litany form (*Deprecatio Gelasii*). Shortly afterwards, it was moved from the beginning of the Liturgy of the Eucharist to the beginning of the Liturgy of the Word, since there were no longer any catechumens. However, the *Oremus* remained after the offertory. Then, later, St. Gregory the Great suppressed the *Deprecatio Gelasii*, retaining 9 of the 15 *Kyrie eleison*-s, and with the passage of time, to avoid repetition, the *Christe eleison* was introduced which already existed in Gaul by the 8th century. Amalarius of Metz († 850) retained a Christological sense of all 9 elements, but in theory he speaks of a Trinitarian sense.

6.   The restoration of the *Oratio fidelium* is important from the pastoral point of view and for the active communitarian participation of the faithful.[25]

At the end of this manuscript, in which Antonelli outlines elements which were of interest to him, it only remains to quote the conclusion which repeats some central points.

1.   The liturgical reform is a religious event of great importance for positive reflections on the Christian life;

2.   The texts must be known in spirit and in letter;

3.   Discipline must be maintained. The Bishop is moderator of the liturgy. Here we must repeat the dictum: *Nihil sine Episcopo*;

4.   A liturgical catechesis must be developed. Patience is required. The masses are educated over several generations. Small groups of leaders must be formed, and good readers and cantors must be found;

5.   Above all, a genuine religious sense is required. Perfect liturgical actions without a religious sense are merely aesthetics.[26]

[1] F. ANTONELLI, *Diario*, October 16, 1964, cit.

[2] F. ANTONELLI, *Bilancio sommario del 1° anno della Riforma liturgica*, a lecture delivered February 10, 1966, in *ALV*, pp. 1-2.

[3] F. ANTONELLI, *La "Instructio" del 26 settembre 1964: indole, scopo, principi e prescrizione concernente la Messa*, liturgical lectures, December 27, 1964, in *ALV*, pp. 1-20.

[4] *Ibidem*, p. 2.

[5] *Ibidem*, p. 3.

[6] *Ibidem*, p. 4.

[7] *Ibidem*, p. 5.

[8] *Ibidem*.

[9] *Ibidem*.

[10] *Ibidem*, p. 6.

[11] Cf. *Insegnamenti di Paolo VI*, vol. II, Città del Vaticano 1964, p. 619.

[12] Cf. *Allocuzione del Santo Padre ai conciliari*, December 4, 1964 in *AAS*, 56 (1964), p. 34.

[13] F. ANTONELLI, *La "Instructio"*, cit., p. 8.

[14] *Ibidem*, pp. 9-10. Cf. *EV*, 2/87, p. 90.

[15] *Ibidem*, p. 10.

[16] *Ibidem*, pp. 11-12.

[17] *EV*, 2/258.

[18] F. ANTONELLI, *La "Instructio"*, cit., p. 12.

[19] *Ibidem*.

[20] *EV*, 2/258.

[21] F. ANTONELLI, *La "Instructio"*, cit., p. 12.

[22] *EV*, 2/258.

[23] Cf. *ibidem*.

[24] *EV*, 2/266.

[25] F. ANTONELLI, *La "Instructio"*, cit., pp. 17-18.

[26] *Ibidem*, p. 20.

Chapter 11

Antonelli's Personal Notes
on the Development of the Reform
(1968-1971)

In a notebook entitled *Note sulla Riforma Liturgica*, covering the period from 1968 to 1971, we find Antonelli's comments on the final stages of the liturgical reform which had been approved by the Sacred Congregation for Divine Worship. Fr. Antonelli's great preoccupation with this phase of the reform is immediately evident. Clearly, he had come to doubt the utility of the reform itself. In the Preface to the notebook, he noted:

The day before yesterday, July 23, 1968, while speaking with Msgr. Giovanni Benelli, *Sostituto* of the Secretariat of State, I explained my concern for the liturgical reform, which is becoming more chaotic and deviant. I particularly noted:

1. Up to the Council, liturgical law was regarded as something sacred, for many it no longer exists. Everyone now takes it that they are authorized to do what they like, and many of the young do just that;

2. The Mass is an especially painful case. Masses in homes are becoming increasingly frequent, as are group Masses, often connected with common meals, for example, supper;

3. Concerning the Sacrament of Penance, a work of disintegration has begun;

4. I noted that part of the cause for the state of things must be related to the system of experiments. The Pope granted a faculty permitting experiments to the *Consilium*, and this faculty was used extensively by the *Consilium*. An experiment carried out in one or two confined circumstances (a monastery, or a working parish) and for a very limited period is acceptable and can be useful. However, when carried out on a widespread basis and without any strict time limitation, such experiments open the way to anarchy;

5. In the *Consilium*, there are few Bishops with a specifically liturgical expertise, and very few are really theologians. The most acute deficiency in the *Consilium* is the lack of theologians. In fact, it could be said that they had been excluded altogether, which is something dangerous. In the liturgy, every word and every gesture expresses an idea which is always a theological idea. Given that all theology is currently questioned, the various theories current among the progressive theologians influence

the formulae and the rites, and this has very serious consequences. While theological discourse remains at the high level of the educated, through the formulae and rites it begins to be spread among the people. I could illustrate this point with various elements from the *Instructio de cultu eucharistico*, published last year.[1]

From the foregoing, it can be deduced that in the post-Conciliar Commission for the reform of the liturgy, experiments had been conducted and continued over a period of time, and some priests had come to regard them as a right. In his Apostolic Letter, *Vicesimus Quintus Annus*, Pope John Paul II echoes this when he speaks openly of "erroneous applications" of the liturgical Constitution of the Council which still persisted.[2]

Given Antonelli's formation and character, it is easy to intuit that his convictions led him to oppose certain liturgical experiments and some of the directions taken by the liturgical reform which he regarded as dangerous. His evaluations of them display a certain pain and concern:

That which is sad [...] however, is a fundamental datum, a mutual attitude, a pre-established position, namely, many of those who have influenced the reform, [...], and others, have no love, and no veneration of that which has been handed down to us. They begin by despising everything that is actually there. This negative mentality is unjust and pernicious, and unfortunately, Paul VI tends a little to this side. They have all the best intentions, but with this mentality they have only been able to demolish and not to restore.[3]

The following judgment, expressed at the end of 1969, displays lucidity of analysis, sharpness, and objectivity:

My impressions of the liturgical reform are substantially good. The new *Ordo Missae*, which came into force on November 30, 1969, has many positive elements. Like all things, it might have been more perfect. Substantially, however, it is good. The *Institutio generalis Missalis Romani* is more imperfect. The substance is good. With time, it will be possible to counter-balance some of the positions contained in it.[4]

The publication of the *Ordo Missae* had a rather curious history:

The question of the *Ordo Missae* is interesting. The facts are thus: some days ago, Father Stickler, a Salesian, told me that Cardinal Ottaviani had prepared a doctrinal critique of the *Ordo Missae* and of the annexed *Instructio*. This news then appeared in the papers. Msgr. Laboa told me that the Pope had written a two page letter to Cardinal Seper asking him to examine the question. Cardinal Seper spoke of it, with alarm, to Cardinal Gut. Cardinal Gut, who was much taken, then spoke to Father Bugnini.[6]

It was decided to publish the *Instructio* immediately to avoid, perhaps, further criticism and the predictable manipulation by the media.

Yesterday morning, Msgr. Laboa told me more. He said that Cardinal Villot had written to Father Bugnini a few days previously asking him to suspend everything to do with the *Ordo Missae*. Then, I mentioned the unexpected publication of the *Instructio*. Msgr. Laboa told me that yesterday Msgr. Benelli had told Father Bugnini to publish the *Instructio* immediately since it had been ready for some time, and its publication would cut off the nascent press campaign. Then, this evening on October 31, the press-release from the Italian Episcopal Conference announced that an Italian version would be ready by November 30 and will go into force in Italy, although, they had already stated that this would not be possible.[7]

Disconsolate, Antonelli concludes: "We are in the kingdom of confusion. This pains me because it will have sad consequences".[8] He takes up this theme again on October 31:

> I am disturbed by the affairs surrounding the *Ordo Missae*. I cannot imagine why Cardinal Ottaviani's critique should have raised such anxiety and why, in reaction to noise stirred up in the press, the Congregation for Divine Worship should have published the *Instructio* in such haste, or why the communiqué published by the Italian Episcopal Conference should announce that everything would take effect on November 30 when we still do not have the text of the *Ordo Missae*. How can this be ready by November 15? How can a change of this magnitude be effected in the space of ten days?[9]

Questions must be asked about what happened. Even more so, questions must be asked about those who arranged all of this. Antonelli made the following suggestion:

> I am afraid that the reaction is due to the irascible insistence of the progressives on the one hand, and the blind conservatives on the other. Both of these are the deadly enemies of the authentic liturgical reform. Neither can it be denied that the dispositions of the *Instructio* are confused and that its very formulation is everything but clear and lucid.[10]

The matter did not end there. Msgr. Benelli telephoned Antonelli and asked him to prepare a note on the *Instructio* and on the *Ordo Missae*.[11] In a three page reply, Antonelli began by pointing out that the *Instructio* and the *Ordo Missae*, insofar as they had been approved by the Pope and published by the competent dicastery, had not yet appeared in the *Acta Apostolicae Sedis*.[12] He then proceeded to highlight the problems to which we have referred. Here will shall only mention his remarks with regard to the doctrinal aspects of the *Instructio*:

> In the meantime, very many criticisms have been made, some of a ritual nature, others doctrinal in character. We shall set aside the criticisms made of the rubrics, which are of secondary importance, and concentrate on the doctrinal criticisms. According to some critics the new *Ordo Missae,* and especially the annexed *Institutio generalis,* even contain heresies. We must say immediately that there are no doctrinal errors in the *Institutio generalis* and even less so in the *Ordo Missae*. The *Ordo Missae* is a very exhaustive text and is unassailable from a doctrinal point of view. The *Institutio generalis*, however, from a redactional perspective, might have been clearer, more coordinated in its contents and more accurate in its terminology. To take some particular examples, insistence on the idea of *cena* (meal) appears to be detrimental to that of sacrifice. Article 2, for example, speaks of the fruits of the Mass, *ad quos obtinendos Christus Dominus sacrificium Eucharisticum sui Corporis et sui Sanguinis instituit.* This, however, is an oblique reference. The idea of *cena* occurs frequently and in direct speech (cf. nn. 2, 48, 55d, 56, etc..)[13]

Antonelli's observations were well founded. Indeed, following them some were unhappy and highly surprised to find certain passages in the *Instructio*.

> Certain omissions have not served clarity. When speaking of the Mass, it would have been opportune to include, at the beginning of the *Instructio*, if not a definition, at least a description of the Eucharistic mystery, emphasizing all of its essential aspects. The absence of such a definition is all the more striking, when, at the beginning of Chapter II, which speaks of the structure of the Mass, the imprudent formulation of Article 7 seems to convey a definition of the Mass (the text reads: *Cena dominica sive Missae est sacra synaxis*, etc..) The text, in fact, does not intend to give a definition of the Mass, but merely to affirm the community character of the Eucharistic celebration. Taking Article 7 as a definition of the Mass, the critics have cried out, is scandalous.[14]

In the wake of the foregoing considerations, Antonelli proposed the following:

> Things being thus, I believe that it would be possible to close off all criticism of the *Instructio* by introducing into it the definition of the Mass given in Article 47 of the Conciliar Constitution on the Liturgy. This description could be inserted at the beginning of the *Instructio*, where it speaks of the dignity and importance of the Mass. Precisely in Article 2, using the same words as the Conciliar Constitution, it could be stated what the Mass is, thereby explaining why it is the center of all Christian life. The context of the present Article 2, could then follow stating *maxime interest* that all participate (in the Mass.)[15]

Having read Antonelli's personal notes on the liturgical reform, we now wish to turn to a number of other items that emerged at the final meeting of the *Consilium* in 1969:

> At 11:40, after the vote had been taken on the selection of 7 Bishops to be included as Members of the Congregation for Divine Worship, and in the presence of all the Fathers and some of the periti, who had been chosen on an *ad hoc* basis, Father Bugnini informed the assembly of certain incidents relating to the new *Ordo Missae* that had taken place during the month of October.[16]

Antonelli then lists the facts. From his conclusion, it is evident that the judgment expressed by him at that time was correct.

1. At the beginning of October the Holy Father asked for an Instruction on the application of the *Ordo Missae*;

2. The Instruction was promulgated on October 20 and sent to the Episcopal Conferences;

3. Two days later, on October 22, Cardinal Ottaviani wrote a letter to the Holy Father, which was also signed by Cardinal Bacci. It was an alarmist letter about the errors of the new *Ordo Missae*. Attached to it was a reproving exposition (of the errors);

4. The same day, the Holy Father remitted the entire question to the Sacred Congregation for the Doctrine of the Faith;

5. The Prefect of the Doctrine of the Faith ordered the suspension of everything to do with the *Ordo Missae*;

6. The Congregation for the Doctrine of the Faith had the question examined by three theologians. All three arrived at the same conclusion: there are no errors in the *Ordo Missae*. Cardinal Seper said that the *Ordo Missae* was fine but, in some small points, it could be improved.[17]

Antonelli's Personal Notes on the Development of the Reform (1968-1971)

The manuscript mentions the names of only two theologians. A blank space was left for the name of the third theologian. We are inclined to believe that the third theologian consulted on this question was Antonelli himself, given that Msgr. Benelli had already asked him to compile a report on the same problem. On article 7 of the *Institutio*, Antonelli comments as follows:

> Commenting on article 7 of the *Institutio*, Cardinal Seper warned that if it was intended as a definition of the Mass it was not exact and would have to be amended. Yesterday, November 13, Msgr. Benelli called Fr. Bugnini and told him to place the matter before the members of the *Consilium* and to draw up a revision of article 7 of the *Institutio*. The Pope also wants an article published in the *Osservatore Romano* reporting on this meeting of the *Consilium*. The same article was to touch on the subject of article 7 and on its revision.[18]

In the *Consilium*, the text of article 7 of the *Institutio* was immediately distributed together with a revised text. This text survives [in Antonelli's papers] and contains several corrections made by Antonelli. Antonelli recounts the following:

> Father Braga showed us the folio and read it. There was a discussion, but it was of the kind that happens among people who are not prepared. Cardinal Willebrands made a good observation: rather than saying *in qua sacrificium Crucis repraesentatur* the text should read *quo sacrificium Crucis repraesentatur*.

> Msgr. Hervas made a correct observation on the question of the [real] presence: he criticized the use of the term *maxime* for it would give rise to the impression that it was merely a question of degree. I would hold that there is a substantial difference between the presence of Christ in the Scriptures which are read; and his presence in the assembly which prays – a real but moral presence; and his presence in the sacraments – a virtual presence; and his presence in the Eucharist which is a real and substantial [presence], because there is present [on the altar] the body and blood and the person of Christ.[19]

Antonelli's intervention was taken with great seriousness but, to his great displeasure, a vote was taken immediately.

> It went as follows. Father Bugnini asked if the text was approved. There was no written vote. There was not even a show of hands. Someone said *placet*. Msgr. Hervas said – and I distinctly heard him say – *non placet ultima pars*. Msgr. Jenny also expressed his difficulties about the real presence in the sense as it was outlined here. It was after midday. Cardinal Gut thanked all the members and wished them well until the next meeting which would take place in April, and that was the end of the matter.[20]

Returning to the *Note sulla Riforma Liturgica*, Antonelli recorded all the changes that were made during the year, which he did not always agree with. He adds:

> Many things have happened between now and when I wrote last September. The Pope, relying on a remark made to him by Cardinal Larraona at the beginning of last summer, has reopened the question of dividing the Sacred Congregation for Rites.

> The Pope spoke to me about this in an audience at the end of 1968.[21] I would think that the matter has been sufficiently considered and, taking everything into account, the division should go ahead. I told the Pope that, and he was pleased. I was asked and charged with the task of making preparations for the

> division: I made the preparations. However, I delayed because, in the meantime, it was desired – and I desired as well – to prepare the *motu proprio* on the reform of the Instruction of Processes which was finally concluded with the publication of the *motu proprio* on March 19, 1968. Then, I began to draft the Apostolic Constitution for the division of the Congregation of Rites and, with the permission of the Pope, I consulted a canonist whom I trusted. The result was the Apostolic Constitution *Sacra Rituum Congregatio* on May 8, 1969.[22]

At this point, Antonelli's work with the Historical Section came to an end. Indeed, "after the division, I was named Secretary of the Congregation for the Causes of Saints while Fr. Bugnini, naturally, was nominated Secretary of the new Congregation for Divine Worship".[23] In his diary, however, Antonelli records the following memories:

> Thus, my immediate work and responsibility for the liturgy practically came to an end. My conscience is clear and has led me to act honestly, keeping me always within a line of healthy progress while observing a great veneration for the tradition, and at the same time, being careful to avoid modifications in the formulas and in the rites which rely on so many new theological ideas that are anything but tested and proven.[24]

Reviewing the work accomplished by the Congregation over many years, Antonelli felt pleased because he had always acted in a prudent and balanced manner, thoroughly examining the problems that had arisen and setting them within an interdisciplinary framework (historical, theological, magisterial, liturgical, etc.). Not everyone thought he had acted in this manner. His judgment on his successor, as with other judgments made by Antonelli, may appear too explicit and sharp at times, but it should not be forgotten that we are dealing with a man privately reflecting within himself:

> Father Annibale Bugnini, CM, has been appointed Secretary of the new Congregation for Divine Worship. I could say many things about this man. I have to add that he always had the backing of Paul VI. While I would like to be mistaken, I can say that his greatest lacuna was his lack of any theological training or sensibility. This was a grave defect and lacuna because in the liturgy, every word and every gesture expresses a theological idea. I have the impression that much has been conceded to the Protestant mentality, especially in matters regarding the sacraments. It is not that Fr. Bugnini created these ideas – no, that is not the case. He used the services of many people and, I do not know why, he admitted into this work so many able people of a liberal theological outlook. He either did not notice, or else he just did not oppose certain tendencies as he ought to have.[25]

He well recalls his contribution to the reform carried out by the Second Vatican Council; his interventions at the *Consilium* as well as his careful and precise work at the Sacred Congregation of Rites. The following extract clearly demonstrates the bitterness provoked by his detachment from the Congregation where he spent almost forty years. Here we can grasp some idea of his great intellectual and moral honesty, as well as his interior detachment from the ideas which he advanced, and of his just pride in the work he had done:

Antonelli's Personal Notes on the Development of the Reform (1968-1971)

> I made various interventions at the *Consilium*. I made even more interventions at the Sacred Congregation of Rites when the texts had to be revised by us: I succeeded in eliminating expressions and ideas that I did not believe were correct on various points. Notwithstanding all that, the pain remains. Time will tell whether all this was for better or for worse, or merely indifferent altogether.[26]

At the close of this historical excursus, which goes from 1963 to 1970, I wish to underline Antonelli's great intelligence, his extensive culture, his balance, his respect and cordiality in human relations, and his unreserved committment to service of the Church at a very difficult moment in her history.

Let us quote from his letter to Fr. Rinaldo Falsini which we regard as particularly interesting in so far as it witnesses to and sums up Antonelli's contribution to the liturgical reform from the time of the first Pontifical Commission, erected by Pius XII, from which flow the subsequent developments in the theory and practice of the liturgy:

> Dear Falsini […], with regard to Fr. Annibale Bugnini's book, *La Riforma Liturgica (1948-1975)*, I have leafed through it, and I too am not so enthusiastic about it. I shall make only one observation about the book. The title promises to treat the history of the liturgical reform from 1948-1975, and of those 27 years, 12 were occupied by the reform begun by the Commission established by Pius XII (1948-1960). It is true that the Commission, following the custom of the time, worked with a certain slowness. However, that which it accomplished has its importance for the history of the reform of the liturgy. In order to appreciate the reform initiated by Pius XII's Commission, albeit slowly, it suffices to mention the *Memoria sulla Riforma Liturgica* (1948), which you are aware of, as well as other successive and connected works, such as the reform of the Easter Vigil (1951), and the following reform of the *Triduum Sacrum* (1955) which went into force in 1956. It should be recalled that this Commission between 1948 and 1960 met 82 times. I chaired those meetings of the Historical Section of the Sacred Congregation of Rites as *Relator-Generalis*. Bugnini was the secretary and kept the minutes. However, with that being said, Fr. Bugnini covers the work of the Commission of Pius XII in 8 pages of his book (pp. 8-25).[27]

The principle characteristics of Cardinal Antonelli that emerge from his papers are: humility and Franciscan gentleness; objectivity and clarity in his judgments; a capacity for minute analysis and for great synthesis; an openness to new ideas tempered by a capacity to see their consequences as well as to integrate them into the healthy tradition of the Church without causing detriment to her; and above all a great love of God which brought him to become a religious and allowed him to dedicate himself totally to the renewal of the liturgy. He was convinced that the liturgy was a formidable instrument in promoting the faith in the hearts of man. For us, the diaries were a lesson in life, and I must ask him to excuse me for having entered into his interior world without having asked for his permission – but I could not do otherwise.

The Development of the Liturgical Reform

[1] F. ANTONELLI, *Note sulla Riforma Liturgica* (1968-1971), in *SCCS*, pp. 1-3.

[2] IOANNES PAULUS II, Litterae apostolicae *Vicesimus quintus annus,* quinto iam lustro expleto conciliari ab promulgata de sacra liturgia constitutione *Sacrosanctum Concilium*, December 4, 1988, n. 13, in *EV*, 11/999.

[3] F. ANTONELLI, *Note sulla Riforma Liturgica,* cit., pp. 4-5.

[4] F. ANTONELLI, *Diario,* cit., January 2, 1970.

[5] [Editors note: Here and in the following instances in Chapter XI, *Instructio* and *Institutio* both refer to the *Institutio generalis Missalis Romani*. It would have been known to Antonelli under both of these titles.]

[6] F. ANTONELLI, *Diario,* cit., October 31, 1969.

[7] *Ibidem.*

[8] *Ibidem.*

[9] *Ibidem,* notes.

[10] F. ANTONELLI, *Diario,* cit., notes.

[11] Cf. *Ibidem,* November 9, 1969.

[12] Cf. *Breve appunto compilato su richiesto di S. Ecc. Mons. G. Benelli sostituto della Segreteria di Stato intorno all'Ordo Missae e alla annessa IGRM,* in *SCCS*, p. 1.

[13] *Ibidem,* pp. 1-2.

[14] *Ibidem,* p. 2.

[15] *Ibidem.* In a separate folio, the relevant citations from *Sacrosanctum Concilium* are listed, nn. 14, 19, 26, 28, 30, and 47: cf. *Allegato IGMR*, p. 2.

[16] F. ANTONELLI, *Manoscritto* dated November 14, 1969, in *SCCS*, p. 1.

[17] *Ibidem,* pp. 1-2.

[18] *Ibidem,* pp. 2-3.

[19] *Ibidem,* pp. 3-4.

[20] *Ibidem,* p. 4.

[21] Cf. F. ANTONELLI, *Diario,* December 21, 1968.

[22] F. ANTONELLI, *Note sulla Riforma,* cit., pp. 17-19.

[23] *Ibidem,* p. 19.

[24] *Ibidem,* p. 20.

[25] *Ibidem,* pp. 19-21.

[26] *Ibidem,* pp. 21.

[27] F. ANTONELLI, *Lettera a P. Falsino,* November 21, 1983, in *ALV*, pp. 1-2.

General Conclusion

At the end of our discourse a few concluding notes seem opportune.

1. I have tried to research a little known period of the Church's history, the liturgical reform, which I take to have begun in 1948 with the institution of the Commission by Pope Pius XII. I have continued to follow the progress of the reform through the Council and the post-Conciliar period up to 1970 when Antonelli left active service in the liturgical field. In this context, I have attempted to do justice to the important role played by Cardinal Antonelli in the liturgical reform. In many ways he is the missing link between two distinct periods in that reform.

2. Antonelli was remarkable for his expertise in the field of theoretical and pastoral liturgy and for his balanced judgment and ecclesial sense. He worked diligently for the Pontifical Liturgical Commission instituted by Pius XII during the first phase of the liturgical reform, and Father Antonelli's principal commitment was to the reform of Holy Week and the Easter Vigil. These first fruits of the Liturgical Commission demanded great exertions, but they were also destined to be taken up by the reform of the Second Vatican Council. In this regard, Father Bugnini's remarks on the occasion of Msgr. Antonelli's episcopal consecration (1966) are significant:

> The preparatory work took four years. Finally, in 1951, the first reformed rite was announced: the Easter Vigil. It came like a sweet scented spring in full blossom. It began with Easter, the very heart of the liturgy, so that its precocious light might spread rapidly, bringing a breath of new life to the whole Church. It is not necessary to outline all the stages of his reform, which found full expression in the Conciliar Constitution on the liturgy, to which Father Antonelli dedicated himself so much, just as he continues to do in his valued and distinguished contribution to our *Consilium*.[1]

Father Falsini concurs with this testimony concerning the reform of Holy Week when he said that Antonelli, "had a sure influence at the Council, at which the then Father Antonelli appeared, and indeed excelled, as a *Relator*, a pioneer, [and an] organizer."[2]

3. In following the various stages of the liturgical reform, I have drawn attention to Antonelli's personal contribution at each phase of that reform. I have also sought to draw attention to his personal reflections as well as to his judgments about the reform and his assessment of it. Rather than repeating the data and

events, which are already well known through other studies, I have tried to see them from Antonelli's perspective, highlighting his particular contribution and his own specific point of view. All of his writings have been carefully examined, and I have found many things that were unknown until now in his personal notes, lectures, conventions, and both published and unpublished writings.

Particular importance must be given to Antonelli's conviction that the liturgical reform's object was to remedy some of the lacunae of the Tridentine period. This is especially true of one area, which was completely overlooked by the reform of the Council of Trent, namely, the participation of the faithful in the liturgical life of the Church. Antonelli noted, "In order to find a reference to the participation of the faithful in a liturgical text, you have to turn to the restored *Ordo* for the Easter Vigil of 1951. In short, the liturgy, even after the Council of Trent, remained a clerical liturgy. The faithful were merely spectators."[3] This was the reason motivating the request made to the Holy Father to authorize a reform of the Easter Vigil and of Holy Week – the progress and various stages of which we have seen earlier. The pastoral desire to promote the participation of the faithful in the liturgy was the sole reason for the reform of the Easter Vigil and Holy Week. This concern would later become the vital force for the Conciliar Constitution on the Sacred Liturgy and the subsequent post-Conciliar reform. Father Bugnini comments that so many

> millions and millions of souls can praise and pray to the Lord today, with a renewed sense of the sacred and of the mystery, in their own tongues, with intelligence, understanding, with greater conviction and love, it is because of the humble, constant, hidden work of those laborers whom the Lord has chosen and who are at the source of this great wave of grace. May I say that among these our beloved Msgr. Antonelli is to be found in the front line, occupying a place of honor.[4]

4. Antonelli dedicated an impressive amount of work to the liturgical cause, in return for which he experienced both joy and sorrow. In reviewing the history of the liturgical reform initiated by Pius XII and carried out by the Council, we have encountered a man who lovingly and serenely devoted himself to the various offices to which he was appointed. It suffices to recall just two of the difficulties which he experienced during his ecclesial service: his nomination as Secretary of the Conciliar Commission of the Sacred Liturgy, which was not welcomed by all, and the division of the Sacred Congregation of Rites which we spoke of earlier.

5. We have also remarked that, with the passage of time, especially following the erection of the *Consilium*, Father Antonelli became increasingly concerned with the manner in which the liturgical reform developed and with its implementation. He grew increasingly and openly critical of certain persons whom he was rather severe with in his judgments.

He refused, in fact, to concede that any governing function had ever been attributed to the *Consilium*. Furthermore, though he was substantially positive in his appraisal of the liturgical reform in general and of many particular elements of it, he never approved of the methods adopted by the *Consilium*. He did, however, recognize the tremendous amount of work accomplished by the *Consilium*.

Antonelli was especially opposed to the haste with which decisions and votes were taken. He reacted to the excessive disparaging of the past and to a certain mentality towards the Holy See, which at times bordered on intolerance. He deplored the lack of a spirit of piety in the system of liturgical experiments and in the manner in which these experiments were carried out. As the reform progressed he also encountered a situation, which was not sufficiently clear or defined.

We can suppose that the concerns which are to be found in his notes may well derive from the excess of the times, which were in part caused by a contest of opposing mentalities, often lamented by Antonelli himself. These concerns may also derive from Antonelli's experience of the method of work employed by the Sacred Congregation of Rites, which differed notably from that of the *Consilium*. Only with the passage of time will it be possible to arrive at a balanced and conclusive historical appraisal of his life and contribution to the liturgical reform. This is true too of other persons of differing outlooks employed in the service of the Church.

6. Many facets of this book tend to suggest a certain rivalry between two relatively contemporary ecclesiastics: Father Ferdinando Antonelli (1898-1993) and Father Annibale Bugnini (1912-1982.) Both had a liturgical foundation, which began with the study of Christian archaeology and which was subsequently enriched through personal research, publications, teaching, and by various contacts with Italian and non-Italian liturgists.

Father Bugnini had a very distinguished liturgical background From the outset of his career he had specialized in liturgy which allowed him to concentrate his energies in that field. Father Antonelli, on the other hand, had to divide his interests between both liturgical and other studies, while at the same time occupying various ecclesiastical offices.

Both worked together on the Commission established by Pius XII (1948-1960): Bugnini acted as Secretary, and Antonelli undertook the necessary research and directed the work of the Commission, especially during its reform of Holy Week.

With regard to the liturgical reform of the Second Vatican Council, Bugnini had been Secretary to the Preparatory Commission, while Antonelli was appointed Secretary of the Conciliar Commission in 1962 amid circumstances that gave rise to apprehension and criticism. Such, however, were not directed against his person.

With the institution of the *Consilium* (January 3, 1963), the difficulties between Bugnini and Antonelli were accentuated since they both had different views regarding the competence and function of the *Consilium*. Throughout the Second Vatican Council, Antonelli made a first class contribution to the Council's work of reform in the preparation and drafting of various documents, in addition to his responsibilities at the Congregation of Rites. Father Bugnini was secretary of the *Consilium* and spent much of his efforts organizing and activating the work of the *Consilium*, and he was less sensitive to traditional standards and methods.

Having been involved in all phases of the liturgical reform, both Antonelli and Bugnini ended their ecclesiastical careers in other areas. Father Antonelli's work received official recognition to the extent that he was created a Cardinal. In our judgment, however, his contribution to the liturgical reform has not been sufficiently appreciated by those who have studied the reform. Father Bugnini, on the other hand, who had been the target of much criticism at various levels, has not been officially rehabilitated. Many who have studied the reform, nonetheless, continue to regard him as the architect of the Conciliar liturgical reform.

7. We conclude this study with a double quotation in the hope of clarifying the life and work of Cardinal Antonelli. First, we will return to a text which we have already seen, and in the second we will read from a note written by Father Falsini who had always been close to Antonelli. In his diary, Antonelli noted:

> I made various interventions at the *Consilium*. I made even more interventions at the Sacred Congregation of Rites when the texts had to be revised by us: I succeeded in eliminating expressions and ideas that I did not believe were correct on various points. Notwithstanding all that, the pain remains. Time will tell whether all this was for better or for worse, or merely indifferent altogether.[5]

In commemoration of Cardinal Antonelli at the 1994 Pastoral-liturgical Convention, Father Falsini wrote:

> The pages of history, when the veil is lifted, demonstrate that the great deeds and achievements of the Church, such as those accomplished in the liturgical reform, do not happen by accident. They must always be sown and matured. They demand time, effort, and patience so as to be accepted and implemented. Following the season for sowing silently and laboriously, there came the spring and the flowering during the Council. Thirty years separate us from the Sacred Congregation and these are still too few to enable us to grasp its fruits.

> We are at the outset of a new journey. We have the right, indeed the duty, to make that journey and to hope with confidence and with serenity. Such is the witness and testimony of Cardinal Antonelli.[6]

[1] A. BUGNINI, *Parole dette*, ms, pp. 3-4.
[2] R. FALSINI, *Il Card. Antonelli*, cit., p. 174.
[3] F. ANTONELLI, *Commento alla riforma*, cit., p. 11.
[4] A. BUGNINI, *Parole dette*, ms, p. 4.
[5] F. ANTONELLI, *Note sulla Riforma*, cit., p. 21.
[6] R. FALSINI, *Il Card. Antonelli*, cit., p. 184.

Appendix A: On the origin of the Pontifical Commission for the Reform of the Sacred Liturgy and on its work from 1948 to 1960

Origin and Constitution of the Commission

1 With the publication of the Apostolic Constitution, *Divino afflatu,* on November 1, 1911, containing a new disposition of the Psalter, and of the *motu proprio, Abhinc duos annos,* of October 23, 1913, Blessed Pope Pius X explicitly promised that the Holy See would proceed with a general reform of the liturgy. This, however, would demand "*labores cum magnos, tum diuturnos*"; and thence, "*longa annorum series intercedat necesse est, antequam hoc quasi aedificium liturgicum*" might be constructed.

2 Unfortunately, such labors which required such a long time to bring to completion, did not begin immediately. With the outbreak of the War, the reform remained merely a desire cherished by liturgists. In 1930 Pius XI established the Historical Section of the Congregation of Rites. It was, in the first place, charged with the historical-critical examination of the causes of Saints, as well as with the emendation of the liturgical books. This event rekindled the hope of the liturgical reform nurtured by the liturgists.

3. Meanwhile, during these decades historical studies made great advances. The liturgical-pastoral movement took on increasingly wider proportions, which resulted in the movement's exerting an increasing influence, nearly everywhere, which recommended that the long desired reform be taken in hand.

4. In this context, the Historical Section prepared the *Promemoria intorno alla Riforma liturgica* in 1946. Cardinal Salotti, Prefect of the Congregation of Rites, referred it to the Pope at the audience of May 10, 1946. The Holy Father ordered the preparation of a concrete proposal for a general reform of the liturgy.

5. The Historical Section was asked to prepare a proposal since it was the competent organism to compile documented material and to prepare the basis for the discussions that would necessarily have to take place so as to

establish the criteria and specific terms for such a reform.

6.   While this work was in progress, the Lord called Cardinal Salotti to himself on October 24, 1947. He was succeeded as Prefect of the Congregation of Rites by Cardinal Micara.

7.   Having been informed with the progress of the work, Cardinal Micara referred the matter again to the Pope in an Audience on May 28, 1948. The Holy Father decided to institute a Pontifical Commission with the specific task of examining the proposed reform in detail.

8.   By a *biglietto di nomina* signed by Cardinal Micara, Prefect, the following persons were called to form the Commission, with Micara presiding:

1. His Excellency Msgr. Carinci, Secretary of the Sacred Congregation of Rites;

2.   The Very Reverend Father Ferdinando Antonelli, *Relator-Generalis* of the Historical Section of the S.R.C.;

3. The Very Reverend Father Joseph Löw, *Vice Relator-Generalis* of the same Historical Section;

4. The Very Reverend Father Anselmo M. Albareda, OSB, Prefect of the Apostolic Library in the Vatican;

5. The Very Reverend Father Agostino Bea, SJ, Rector of the Pontifical Biblical Institute;

6. The Very Reverend Father Annibale Bugnini of the Congregation of the Mission, editor of *Ephemerides Liturgicae*.

9.   Shortly afterwards, so as to have available the views of a number of people who represented, on a wider scale, scientific developments and the current demands of pastoral liturgy, a further three eminent liturgists were nominated Consulators of the Liturgical Section of the Sacred Congregation of Rites: Father Josef Jungmann, SJ, of the University of Innsbruck, the French speaking Dom Capelle, Abbot of Mont César and Professor of liturgy of the University of Louvain, and Msgr. Mario Righetti of Genoa, who recently published an excellent manual on the History of the Liturgy. These would be available to assist with the more important questions that would arise.

10.   At the Audience of April 3, 1951 the Holy Father nominated as a member of the Commission the Very Reverend Msgr. Enrico Dante, *Sostituto* of the S. Congregation of Rites and Prefect of Pontifical Ceremonies.

11.   The Pontifical Commission for the Reform of the Liturgy as presently constituted, is composed of the following:

1. His Eminence Card. G. Cicognani, Prefect of the Sacred Congregation of Rites;

2. His Excellency Msgr. Carinci, Secretary of the S.C.R.;

Appendix A: On the origin of the Pontifical Commission for the Reform of the Sacred Liturgyand on its work from 1948 to 1960

3. The Very Reverend Ferdinando Antonelli; *Relator-Generalis* of the Historical Section;

4. The Very Reverend Msgr. Enrico Dante, *Sostituto* of the S.C.R.;

5. The Very Reverend Joseph Löw, *Vice Relator-Generalis* of the Historical Section;

6. The Very Reverend Father Albareda, Prefect of the Apostolic Library in the Vatican;

7. The Very Reverend Father Agostino Bea, SJ, of the Pontifical Biblical Institute;

8. The Very Reverend Father Annibale Bugnini, of *Ephemerides Liturgicae*, who from the outset acted as secretary.

12.   For important questions, the Commission then had the following specialist consultors:

Dom Capelle, Abbot of Mont César in Louvain, Father Josef Jungmann, SJ, of the University of Innsbruck, and Msgr. Mario Righetti of Genoa.

13.   It should be noted that from the beginning the members of the Commission were required to observe a strict religious silence about the work of the Commission, and its publications were to be regarded as absolutely reserved.

Work Done by the Commission

14.   The Commission, which had been nominated on May 28, 1948, meet for the first time on June 22, 1948 at Cardinal Micara's residence. There was an initial exchange of ideas and it was decided to await the publication of the *Memoria sulla Riforma Liturgica*, prepared by the Historical Section, which had already been sent to the printers.

15.   The *Memoria*, a volume of 342 pages printed on *octavo* paper, had been prepared by Father Joseph Löw, *Vice Relator-Generalis* of the Historical Section, in collaboration with Father Ferdinando Antonelli. It appeared early in 1949 and was presented to the Pope by Cardinal Micara, Prefect of the Congregation of Rites, and by Father Antonelli, *Relator-Generalis* of the Historical Section in an Audience on July 22, 1949.

The meetings of the Commission began in the Autumn of 1949.

16.   Thirty meetings were held between November 17, 1949 and November 27, 1953.

17.   Of these thirty meetings, 19 were spent examining the *Memoria*. The first section of the *Memoria,* concerning the calendar and its constituent parts, was discussed (articles 1-180, pp. 1-168). Five meetings were devoted to an examination of the new *Ordo Sabbati Sancti*, which had been drawn up at the request of some bishops and on the Holy Father's instructions. It was

promulgated by decree on February 9, 1951. A further 5 meetings were spent discussing a proposal for the restoration of the rites of Good Friday and Holy Thursday. This project, when completed, was sent for printing but has not yet been published.

18. During these undertakings, it gradually became more clear that material would have to be prepared so as to be able to undertake any indepth study of several important questions.

19. Thus, the Supplements to the *Memoria* began to appear. So far, the following have been published:

Supplementum I (1950) on the gradation of the liturgy;

Supplementum II (1950) containing replies and notes on various questions posed by the *Memoria*. These were prepared by Dom Capelle, Father Jungmann, and Msgr. Righetti;

Supplementum III (1951) containing historical, biographical, and liturgical material for the reform of the calendar.

Work Remaining to be Done by the Commission

20. At the present state of its work, the Commission has to do two things:

First, continue with the examination of the *Memoria*, especially the section on the Breviary (articles 181-311, pp. 169-304).

21. Secondly, discuss and approve a specific draft for the reformed calendar. The proposal for such a calendar, drawn upon the basis of specific criteria, is ready. The copies for the Commission are being printed.

22. There is also an incidental question, which is somewhat urgent, namely the possible institution of the feast *Maria Regina*. Some bishops have proposed it, and the Holy Father has asked for an opinion from the Congregation. It was spoken of during the last meeting, which was held on November 27, 1953. Opinion was divided on the question, and it was decided to seek a *Votum* from these three Consulters: Dom Capelle, Father Jungmann, and Msgr. Righetti. These *Vota* have arrived and will now be communicated to the Commission.

Commission for the Reform of the Liturgy

Minutes of the 1ˢᵗ Meeting

23. The following members of the Commission gathered on Tuesday, June 22, 1948 at 6 p.m. in the *Accademia Ecclesiastica, Piazza della Minerva*, residence of Cardinal Clemente Micara, Prefect of the Sacred Congregation of Rites:

    1. His Excellency Msgr. Alfonso Carinci, Secretary of the S.R.C.;

    2. The Very Reverend Father Ferdinando Antonelli, the *Relator-Generalis*, Historical Section of the S.R.C.;

    3. The Very Reverend Father Joseph Löw, CSSR, *Vice Relator-Generalis*, Historical Section of the S.R.C.;

    4. The Very Reverend Father Agostino Bea, SJ, of the Pontifical Biblical Institute;

    5. The Very Reverend Dom Anselmo Albareda, OSB, Prefect of the Apostolic Library in the Vatican.

24. Father Annibale Bugnini, editor of *Ephemerides Liturgicae* was absent because he was travelling abroad.

25. The Cardinal explained the Commission's purpose, which was to deal with the important question of the general liturgical reform.

26. In this respect, he mentioned one element of the reform, which was nearing completion, namely, the new version of the Bible, a distinguished production of the Biblical Institute.

27. Father Bea declared that this was too much to hope for. Work still continued on the version of the pericopes used in the liturgy. At least six years' work would be required to bring it to completion.

28. In reply to a question from the Cardinal, Father Bea reckoned that while it would be possible to expedite the undertaking, it would still take at least a further five years.

29. The Cardinal asked a fundamental question: What was to be proposed to the Holy Father, merely a reform of the Breviary or an authentic general reform of the liturgy?

30. All replied that the liturgy did not admit of partial reform, since it was a self-contained whole. Indeed, the actual state of the liturgy was such that

it required a complete and authentic reform.

31. His Eminence mentioned the need to form Sub-commissions to prepare specific material on various questions. It would be necessary to have specialists for the Sub-commissions.

32. All agreed with His Eminence on this need. At present, however, the matter was not yet urgent.

33. Following this initial meeting, His Eminence proposed deferring further meetings of the Commission until the *Memoria sulla Riforma Liturgica* was printed. It had been prepared by the Historical Section, and Father Antonelli presented the first drafts that had arrived from the printers in those days.

34. All agreed that it would be best to await the printing and distribution of this text so as to have a basis for discussion.

35. The Very Reverend Father Albareda then spoke, and he said that he was very conscious of the grave responsibility before the Church which lay upon the Commission. Thus, he insisted that the Commission's work should necessarily require a rather long period of time if it were to be carried out well.

36. The Very Reverend Father Bea insisted on one important point, that is, the Sacred Scripture "*occurrens*", and he had conducted some special studies in this area and he rapidly indicated the conclusions at which he had arrived.

37. The Very Reverend Father Löw presented some tables that he had drawn up and said that he too had reached similar conclusions. This confirmed the accuracy of the results, which had been arrived at independently.

38. Father Antonelli presented the drafts of the first part of the *Memoria*. He quickly explained its contents and the way in which it had tried to facilitate the Commission's work by repeatedly posing questions so that the Commission would be able to reply to them and become more precise.

39. His Eminence closed the meeting and expressed his thanks for the various explanations that had been made, and he announced that the following meeting would take place after the distribution of the *Memoria*. In the meantime the Holy Father would have to be informed of everything.

40. The meeting was closed at 7 p.m..

Minutes of the 2nd Meeting

41. [The second meeting] took place at 4 p.m. on Thursday, November 17, 1949 at the *Palazzo della Cancelleria* in the apartments of His Eminence Cardinal Clemente Micara, Prefect of the Sacred Congregation of Rites.

42. All members of the Commission were present.

43. The Cardinal opened the meeting with the *Actiones nostras*. He thanked

all present for having accepted the invitation to be part of the Commission
and for having come to the meeting. He gave a brief resumé of the history
leading up to the decision to undertake the reform and to prepare the
Memoria, which, he said, would serve as "the basis for all discussion".
He proposed Father Bugnini as Secretary of the Commission, and
the proposal was unanimously accepted. He announced that, having
completed the *Memoria*, the Historical Section had prepared a fascicle of
historical/hagiographical material which would be useful for drawing up
the calendar. He asked Father Antonelli to have it printed and distributed
to the members of the Commission.

44. He said that various Sub-commissions, which would handle the various
parts of its work, would assist the Commission in due course and that
he had already spoken to the Holy Father, and *Sub secreto* he announced
that it had been sent to Dom Bernardo Capelle, OSB, Abbot of Mont
César (Louvain), to Professor Josef Jungmann, SJ (Innsbruck), and to
Msgr. Mario Righetti (Genoa) who would examine it within two months.
These people could be invited to Rome from time to time, and if necessary,
some extraordinary meetings of the Commission could be held. With that
said, His Eminence invited Father Antonelli, as *Relator-Generalis* of the
Historical Section, to begin his exposition and discussion of the *Memoria*.

45. Father Antonelli briefly recounted the history of this initiative, and he
pointed to the reasons which lay behind it, all of which were set out in
Chapter I of the *Memoria*. There was no need to dwell on them. He moved
on to Chapter II and read out the basic principles for the direction of
the reform contained therein. In general these were accepted by all as
adequate to meet the demands of a good and serious reform.

46. Father Albareda declared that it was necessary to avoid all forms of
extremism, be it of too conservative a kind, or one which favored
innovations. This was agreed upon without discussion. He expressed his
wish that the Commission would quickly and better decide what direction
it intended to take – whether perfectly in the middle, or rigidly firm, or
slightly indulging into current positions.

47. Father Antonelli, summing up again what Fathers Löw and Bea had said,
insisted that it would be difficult to make such a decision for the moment.
The discussion of the *Temporale* would assist greatly in developing a
particular line, which could be employed when it came to discussions of
the *Santorale*. While that line would have to be somewhat severe, at the
same time, it would always have to follow the just mean *ex principio*.

48. Finally, His Eminence announced that the Commission would meet every
fortnight, preferably on Fridays at 4:30 p.m.. After praying the *Agimus*, he
closed the meeting at 5 p.m..

Minutes of the 3rd Meeting

49. [The meeting was held] at 4:30 p.m. on Tuesday, December 5, 1949 at the *Palazzo della Cancelleria* in the apartments of His Eminence Cardinal Clemente Micara, Prefect of the Sacred Congregation of Rites.

50. All members of the Commission were present.

51. After the usual prayer, His Eminence said that he had informed the Holy Father of the previous meeting, and he blessed the work of the Commission. The Cardinal then asked Father Antonelli to continue his report on the *Memoria*.

52. Father Antonelli drew attention to the headings for the various questions contained in Chapter III, *Programma organico della Riforma* (articles 20 ff.). Each point was then examined.

53. Article 28 – Whether it is convenient to ascribe the five principal feasts of redemption to a single supreme category; and

54. Article 29 – Whether it is convenient to divide all other feasts of the year into three general categories: solemn, ordinary, and minimal. All are in agreement.

55. Article 30 – Whether it is convenient to subdivide each of these three categories into solemn, ordinary, and minimal, and into major and minor. Father Albareda regarded this latter subdivision as unsatisfactory because it would complicate the gradation again, and it would not reflect what was needed. Psychologically the minus would satisfy nobody. He proposed retaining a gradation of 7 or 6 classes, more simply formulated, possibly expressed with one single word, stating the gradation positively, comparatively, or superlatively e.g. *solemne, solemnius, solemnissimum*. Also *officium feriale cum commemoratione* or *cum memoria* could all be changed to *in festum commemoratum* or *memoratum*.

Indeed, this distinction could be abolished altogether by adding the simplest elements found in the Saints biography in the antiphon *ad Benedictus* of the *memoria*. The *commemoratio* could then be suppressed. A succinct and concise terminology must be formed containing the peculiarities by which a feast is classified.

56. Father Bea believed that the term *solemnitas* should be reserved to 5 major feasts. The remaining fests could be classed as *festa communia*, and he believed, moreover, that 6 classes should be sufficient.

57. To this, Father Löw observed that in fact 6 grades were proposed since the "*summum festum*" was in a class of its own. Accepting the common opinion [of the Commission], the *Relator-Generalis* proposed bringing the question up to day so that it might be examined more closely at the next meeting. All agreed.

Appendix A: On the origin of the Pontifical Commission for the Reform of the Sacred Liturgy and on its work from 1948 to 1960

58. *Il Calendario.*

59. Article 39 a) *Convenienza di dare alle dominiche d'Avvento un grado eguale e solenne, in modo che l'ufficiatura non manchi mai.* This was unanimously accepted.

60. Article 39 b) *Esclusione di ogni eccezione al principio precedente, compresa la festa dell'Immacolata, che, nel caso, dovrebbe passare al 9 dicembre.*

61. In general terms, the principle of emphasizing the Sundays of Advent was acceptable. It was noted, however, that since the people, *de facto*, would continue to celebrate the Immaculate Conception on December 8, the celebration of the Mass of Our Lady, either sung or solemn, could be conceded in the parishes. The office, however, should be removed to December 9.

62. His Eminence also observed that in order to make December 8 more solemn recourse could be made to other means, including extra liturgical functions, preaching, processions, etc..

63. Article 40 – *Vigilie ed ottave in Avvento.*

There was an unanimous consensus recommending their suppression. After all, noted Father Bea, such would not be displeasing since we were already accustomed to celebrating the most solemn feasts, such as Christ the King, without vigils and octaves.

64. Articles 42-44 – *Preparazione prossima al Natale, 17-23 dicembre.*

65. The proposal to give Advent, and in general, to the period of preparation for Christmas an ascensional character, just as Lent has in relation to Easter, was generally accepted. Father Bea believed that this might offer an opportunity to emphasize the Blessed Virgin, by the restoration, for example, of the Mass "*in exspectatione partus*". This would mean that the office for this period would have to reflect a Marian and a messianic theme. The versicle: *Prope est iam Dominus* of the Invitatory for the third Sunday of Advent should be exclusively assigned to this period. It was also generally agreed that proper Masses should be assigned to each day of this week of intensive preparation for Christmas – as indicated in the *Memoria* (p. 38), and to assign proper Prefaces to Advent, one for the Sundays and another for the period from December 16-23. Concerning the formularies to be used in these Masses, there was a common desire that they should be taken from the ancient liturgical books so as to avoid new compositions as much as possible.

66. Article 43 – *La festa di San Tommaso* [The feast of St. Thomas].

There was unanimous agreement that this fest should be transferred out of the Advent period preferably to October 6 – as in the Oriental Churches.

67. Saying the prayer "*Agimus*" they concluded the meeting at 6 p.m.. The next meeting was arranged for December 16 at the same time.

Minutes of the 4ᵗʰ Meeting

68.   [The meeting] was held at 4:30 p.m. on December 16, 1949 at the *Palazzo della Cancelleria* in the apartments of Cardinal Clemente Micara, Prefect of the Congregation for Rites.

69.   All members were present.

70.   After the prayer and the reading of the minutes, His Eminence asked Father Antonelli to speak, as arranged, on Article 32 of the *Memoria* concerning the gradation of feast days. Father Bea presented a schedule reducing the classification of feasts to six, divided into two groups: *festa novem lectionum* and *festa trium lectionum*. He proposed the following terminology: *festum memoratum, festum simplex, minus, ordinarium, secundae classis, primae classis, sollemnitas*.

71.   Father Albareda drew attention to the substance of the question, before which matters of terminology were secondary. For any terminology to be objective and adequate, it had to have a theological basis in the purest liturgical tradition. Seven grades could thus be proposed:

1. The cycle of the Redemption whose feasts could be called *festa sacratissima*;

2. *Cultus latriae* and *cultus hyperduliae*;

3. The summit of holiness;

4. Persons associated with the life of our Saviour and the principal martyrs of the Church's first three centuries;

5. Saints of major influence on the universal Church;

6. Saints of lesser influence or of personal sanctity;

7. Saints who are venerated but about whom little is known.

The terminology, therefore, should be based on this classification, on the basis of these [7] grades.

72.   All agreed with the proposal. Given the importance and gravity of the subject, the *Relator-Generalis* asked the secretary to have copies of the proposal drawn up and circulated to the members of the Commission so that it might be carefully studied before being discussed at future meetings. Given that the solution to this problem did not jeopardize the remainder of the *Memoria*, at least as far as the *temporale* was concerned, he proposed that its examination continue.

73.   Article 45 a) *Nome di Natale* [The Title of Christmas]: *Natale or Nativitas?*

74.   Father Bugnini suggested that the ancient denomination of *Natalis Domini* should be reintroduced. In the liturgy, he observed there were two instances of nativity days, in the modern sense of the term, that of Saint John the Baptist and of the Blessed Virgin Mary. Both are signaled by the

term *Nativitas*. He asked if the three instances should use a common form of denomination or simply use the term *Natalis* for the Birth of our Lord, leaving the other two instances unchanged.

75.   All favored the restoration of the term *Natalis* in all three cases.

76.   Article 45 b) – *Ultimo Vangelo della 3ʳᵈ Messa di Natale* [The Last Gospel of the 3rd Mass of Christmas]

Msgr. Carinci thought that the present pericope should either be suppressed or retained. In the event of retaining the Gospel, Father Bugnini proposed Luke 2:33-35. Father Bea proposed Mt 1:20 ff. (the genealogy of our Lord) because the temporal birth of our Lord should be meditated on, having already meditated on his elevated birth (*In principio*). While conceptually the proposal was extremely suggestive, in practical terms it might not be so because of the dryness of the text.

His Eminence proposed Luke 1:18-21, which is read at the Vigil of Christmas. Father Albareda was decidedly in favor of the abolition of the last Gospel at the 3ʳᵈ Mass, which should end with the *Ite Missa est* and the blessing.

77.   This proposal received a majority consensus. However, a definitive decision on the matter was postponed until the Mass would be studied *ex professo*.

78.   Article 46 – *Feste nell'ottava di Natale* [Feasts in the Christmas Octave].

All agreed that no other feasts should be celebrated during the octave apart from the *Comites Christi*.

79.   Article 47 – *Ottava di Natale* [The Christmas Octave].

It was unanimously agreed that the Marian character of January 1 should be restored, and all agreed that it would be a suitable day to celebrate the feast of the Motherhood of the Blessed Virgin Mary. From a spiritual and pastoral perspective the Motherhood of the Blessed Virgin Mary on New Year's day would lend itself to an appropriate application.

80.   Thus, the definitive denomination should read: *Octava Domini. Festum Maternitatis B.M.V., Nome di Gesù:* The Commission took the view that the feast should not be suppressed. It should be celebrated on a fixed day between January 1 and 5 (a priori its present mobility had to be excluded), and preferably on January 2.

81.   January 3 was proposed as a date for the celebration of the Holy Family. This would have the advantage of freeing the Sundays from the additional feasts of Saints and of filling up the period between January 1 and 5, which are part of Christmas tide, with the mysteries and persons connected with the birth of our Redeemer.

82.   Disposing of this as outlined in the foregoing, January 4 would still remain free. This would have to be provided with a proper Mass corresponding to Christmastide. Alternatively a Saint's feast day could be assigned to it.

83.   Article 48, 1 – The Octave of the *Comites Christi*. All agreed on its suppression.

84.   Article 48, 2 – *Sistemazione delle domeniche tra l'ottava del Natale e tra il 1 and il 5 gennaio* [The Organization of the Sundays between the Christmas Octave and the 1st and 5th of January].

The proposals made in the *Memoria* were unanimously accepted.

85.   The meeting closed at 6 p.m. with the usual prayer. The next meeting would be held after the Christmas period, on a day to be decided at a later date.

Minutes of the 5th meeting

86.   [The meeting] took place at 4:30 p.m. on Tuesday, January 17, 1950 at the *Palazzo della Cancelleria* in the apartments of Cardinal Clemente Micara, Prefect of the Sacred Congregation of Rites.

87.   All members were present.

88.   The meeting began with the *Actiones nostras*. His Eminence thanked Father Albareda for his "precise and perfect project" on article 32 of the *Memoria*. He then asked the Very Rev. *Relator-Generalis* to speak. [Father Antonelli] said that he thought he spoke for all when he expressed his thanks to Father Albareda for his "well thought out" proposal, and he asked the members of the Commission to study it carefully so that it might be useful when it came to examining the *Sanctorale* that is under article 124. The *Relator-Generalis* announced that Father Jungmann, SJ, had returned his copy of the *Memoria,* which he had annotated. Generally on the whole, and with regard to the individual questions, his judgment on the project was very favorable. He expressly states in a letter to His Eminence: *Ceterum magno cum gaudio vidi iam iis quae in Memoriali continentur reformationem liturgicam optima ratione conceptam et fundamentum solidum iactum esse"*.

89.   Examinations of the *Memoria* then resumed.

90.   Article 48, 3 – *Vigilia dell'Epifania*. Father Bea said that he would be agreeable to the inclusion of the pericope Mt 2:1-6, and he proposed that a proper Mass be prepared and other less suitable texts be changed; for example, *Dum medium silentium* was well adapted to Christmas but not for the Epiphany – for the epistle, a text from St. Paul or from Isaiah could be chosen in which the conversion of the Gentiles is foretold.

91.   Both proposals were unanimously accepted by the Commission.

92.   Article 49 – *Ottava dell' Epifania*. In a supplement to the *Memoria* it was proposed that the Octave be suppressed and the eighth day alone be celebrated. The Gospel texts were arranged as follows: January 6, coming of the Magi: *Dom. infra. Oct*: the Baptism of Jesus; January 13 the Wedding feast at Cana.

93. The proposal left the Commission perplexed. Father Albareda again raised the need for the Commission to have a clear line when examining the *Memoria*. He also raised the question of the "classes" according to which the feasts would be properly classified since this would clearly determine the rest. As a purely working hypothesis, he suggested transferring the feast of Christ the King to this period. Conceptually it would harmonize well with the Epiphany. Father Bea observed that the feast had been fixed for the last Sunday of October because of its proximity to all Saints, so as to glorify both King and court at the same time.

94. *Quas Primas* (December 11, 1925) of Pius XI, explicitly emphasizes this idea.

95. Father Antonelli underlined the difference between the transcendental meaning of the present feast of the Kingship of Christ, and the Regality of Christ manifested in the mystery of the Epiphany. However, it was concluded that since it was a recent institution, the question of the date [for the feast of Christ the King] could he reconsidered.

96. Article 49 a) – All agreed that the Octave of the Epiphany should be suppressed, and that the octave day only should be retained.

97. Article 49 b) – With regard to the Gospel pericopes, the aforementioned proposal was accepted, in general terms: January 6, coming of the Magi; *Dom. Infra Oct.* Baptism of Jesus; Octave day, the Wedding feast at Cana.

98. Article 52 – *Prequaresima.*

     After a short discussion, all agreed that the three Sundays in the pre-Lent period should be elevated to the level of the Sundays of Lent.

99. Article 54 – *I Quattro giorni dopo le Ceneri* [The four days after Ash Wednesday].

     Father Bugnini tended toward the idea of starting the Lenten Office with Ash Wednesday. Father Albareda could not find a plausible reason for changing the actual state of things. He would leave them unchanged. Against this, Father Bea found it more logical to begin the Lenten office with Ash Wednesday. It appeared to him that the reasons advanced for maintaining the office as it is at present were not valid.

     Father Albareda demonstrated the usefulness of having a clearer line [with regard to the principles to be applied by the Commission]. A change should only be made if unanimously approved by a vote of the Commission. A serene discussion on this point followed, at the end of which the *Relator-Generalis* asked the members of the Commission to reflect on the matter in preparation for a discussion on it, which would take place in the next meeting. That discussion could consider two points:

     1. should the principle of unanimity be adopted for the resolution of controversial issues;

2. Should the present state of affairs be changed or not in the current circumstances.

100. Articles 56 – *Riportare la quaresima alla sua integrità con esclusione dei Santi, ad eccezione di S. Giuseppe e dell'Annunciazione* [To Recover the integrity of Lent by excluding the Saints with the exception of St. Joseph and the Annunciation].

When it had been explained that this project, perhaps so very clear in its formulation, proposed transferring the celebration of the feast days of the principal Saints to more convenient dates outside of Lent, all [the members of the Commission] were in agreement. They noted, however, that the choices of suitable dates outside of Lent should be based on the venerable liturgical traditions of both the East and West, with particular regard to the Ambrosian tradition which had maintained the principle of excluding the celebration of feast days during Lent.

101. Article 57 – *Prefazi in Quaresima.*

It appeared excessive to have a preface for every day in Lent and consequently, by unanimous vote, the proposal was excluded. The proposal of introducing daily prefaces for said Masses, leaving sung Masses with the present preface, was not accepted either. Someone suggested a preface for each Sunday that could be said throughout the entire week. Father Albareda would not oppose this proposal; provided that they did not constantly emphasize fasting and penance. Father Bea agreed with the proposal for Lent as agreed, and proposed the following suggestions:

1. A preface from Ash Wednesday to the second Sunday of Lent;

2. A second preface from the Second Sunday to the fourth Sunday of Lent (*Laetare*);

3. A third preface for Palm Sunday.

Finally, Father Albareda made the proposal of retaining the present beautiful preface for the ferials of Lent and of introducing new prefaces reflecting the character of the Mass only for the Sundays. These prefaces could be taken from ancient formularies. All agreed with the proposal.

102. Article 58 – *Scrittura Corrente.*

The proposal of reforming the current reading of Sacred Scripture and of the Fathers was acceptable to all.

103. Article 59 – *Stazioni quaresimali nella 6° lezione del Breviario* [The Lenten Stations in the 6th Lesson of the Breviary].

104. The proposal, for the most part, was not well received and was consequently rejected. Father Bea underlined the importance of the "stations" during Lent and proposed that an appropriate clause be inserted in the future

Codex iuris liturgici prescribing special instruction on this point in the teaching of liturgy in the seminaries.

105.   The meeting ended at 6:30 p.m. and the next meeting will be held on January 27 should nothing unexpected arise.

Minutes of the 6th Meeting

106.   [The meeting] was held on Friday, January 27, [1950] at 4:30 p.m. at the *Palazzo della Cancelleria* in the apartments of Cardinal Clemente Micara, Prefect of the Sacred Congregation of Rites.

107.   All members of the Commission were present.

108.   The meeting opened with the usual prayer, and the minutes were read. His Eminence asked the *Relator-Generalis* to speak. He proposed clarifying the problems that had arisen during the examination of article 54. These had been studied so as to allow for a more careful examination [of the article]. The questions were this:

1. Should the principle of unanimity be adopted for the resolution of controversial questions?

2. Should the office for Lent begin with Ash Wednesday?

109.   With regard to the first, His Eminence observed that the principle of unanimity should not be insisted on, no more than having to return to check each point individually for coordination once a debate had been concluded. It seemed, therefore, simpler to continue and to gather the various opinions [on the *Memoria*] and note in the minutes (as had been done up to then) whether they had been accepted unanimously or whether someone had dissented together with the reasons [for his position].

110.   On the second point, a further examination produced no new elements. In conclusion, the majority view was that it would be more logical to begin the Lenten formularies with Ash Wednesday. His Excellency, Msgr. Carinci and Msgr. Albareda, remained convinced that there was no need for this change. They held that the Lenten formularies should continue to be used from the first Sunday of Lent as a token to the historical development [of Lent].

111.   Article 61 – *Rito nella Settimana Santa.*

Three rites seemed excessive and all agreed that two would be sufficient.

112.   Article 62 – *Messa e Comunione nel Giovedì Santo.*

The following points were agreed:

1. Both a consecrating and a merely ceremonial concelebration are to be excluded.

2. Reduce to a minimum privileges of private Masses;

3. The convenience of priests assisting at the Holy Thursday Mass being in a distinct place (the Sanctuary) vested in surplice and stole.

113. Article 63 – *Duplicazione delle formole.*

   The proposal contained in the *Memoria* recommending that the formulae not be duplicated was unanimously accepted.

114. Article 64 – *Messa dei presantificandi.*

   It was agreed not to change the strictly indispensable, for example, the *Orate Fratres.*

115. Article 65 – *Preci per i governi civili.*

   All agreed that the prayer for the [holy] Roman Emperor should be suppressed and replaced by one for governments in general, not only in the solemn prayers of Good Friday, but throughout the entire liturgy.

116. Article 74 – *Sabato Santo. Ripristino della celebrazione vigiliare: la notte.*

   All agreed with the proposal. It was added that the best means would be to begin the Office at an hour that would permit the Mass to begin at midnight, like it is at the Vigil of Christmas.

117. Article 74, 2 – *Rinnovazione delle promesse battesimali.*

   [The proposal] was favorably accepted and its implementation will be accelerated by drawing up a fixed Latin formula based on the exhortations given at Ordinations. Subsequently, each nation would be asked to produce an official translation for use in the rite.

118. The meeting closed at 6:15 p.m..

Minutes of 7th Meeting

119. [The meeting took place] at 4:45 p.m. on February 14, 1950 at the *Palazzo della Cancelleria* in the apartments of Cardinal Clemente Micara, Prefect of the Sacred Congregation of Rites.

120. All members of the Commission were present.

121. After the reading and approval of the minutes of the previous meeting, His Eminence invited the *Relator-Generalis* to speak. He announced that Dom Capelle had written a good letter in which he promised to forward his observations as soon as possible to the Cardinal Prefect.

122. Article 75 –The *tempus paschale.*

   [The Commission] agreed unanimously to restore the primitive character of joy to the Paschal season as proposed in the *Memoria.* [This required] the suppression of ferial and penitential elements, such as intercessions and suffrage, including the *commemoratio de cruce* and daily Masses for the dead.

123. Article 76 – *Ottava dell' Ascensione.*

The Commission agreed to a proposal of Father Albareda deferring consideration [of this question] to a general examination of octaves where it might be more profitably considered in the context of octaves *ex professo*.

124. As to the Friday after the Octave, on which the office of the preceding Sunday is repeated, Father Bea observed that this is explainable in that after the Octave of the Ascension, the ferial office, which is that of the preceeding Sunday, resumes. This matter, however, should also be examined in connection with the general question of Octaves.

125. Article 79 – *Ottava di Pentecoste*.

Here too the question of the Octave has to be examined in the light of the problem of the classification of feasts and that of the octaves in general. The suppression *sic et simpliciter* of the Octave of Pentecost seemed somewhat excessive, according to Father Bea, since it would have negative practical implications. For example, in the German-speaking lands Whit Monday is a most important feast. By ancient tradition it is a *festiva de praecepto*. When Pius X abolished [the obligation] for the universal church, the German Bishops obtained [an indult, so] that it would remain an obligatory feast day in Germany. Father Albareda favored Father Jungmann's proposal of retaining the first two days of the octave.

126. Article 80 – *Benedizione del Fonte*.

Rather than regarding it as an adaptation of the rite, the Commission called for the complete suppression of this ceremony since it no longer had a *raison d'etre* [reason for existing]. Father Bea took the opportunity to emphasize the fact that all of the major ceremonies of the liturgical year, for example the blessing of the font on Holy Saturday, always took place at the high altar, *coram populo*, and not, as presently is the case, in a side chapel. The proposal was approved.

127. Article 83 – *Corpus Domini*.

All agreed that this feast should be classified as "*summum festum*".

128. Article 84 – *Ottava del Corpus Domini*.

The question would have to be examined in the context of the general consideration of octaves.

129. Article 85 – *Prefazio e Hanc igitur per il Corpus Domini*.

A proper preface was desired by all, provided it was well done. The proposal of a *Hanc igitur* was rejected for the reasons advanced by Father Jungmann. The *Hanc igitur* is used to celebrate something concrete and not a mystery of Our Lord.

130. Article 86 – *Festa del Sacro Cuore*.

The feast is to be conserved and at the highest grade. With regard to an octave, the question will be discussed in the context of the general considerations of octaves.

131.   Article 87 – *Festa di Cristo Re.*

The Commission agreed to accord the highest grade to this feast. With regard to the day of its celebration, the suggestion emerged of moving it to the last Sunday of the liturgical year, which would require moving the Gospel on the last judgment, currently read on the 24th Sunday after Pentecost, to the 23rd Sunday after Pentecost. It was unanimously requested that the Office of the Kingship [of Christ] be revised, so as to emphasize the concepts of glory, majesty, power, joy, and exaltation of the royal power of Christ over all creation, avoiding texts, which refer to the cross, passion, death, etc.

132.   The central text inspiring the whole office should be Mt 28:18: *Data est mihi omnis potestas in coelo et in terra.*

133.   Article 88 – *Celebrazione della Domenica.*

All concurred that the "day of the Lord" should be better valued. The contemporary liturgical movement stressed this point in various countries. Sunday must always be celebrated. The Sunday offices are doctrinally very rich and are very helpful for preaching, as His Eminence observed.

134.   Article 89 – *Soppressione nelle domeniche di quanto non ha carattere festivo* [The Suppression on Sundays of all elements without festive character].

Approved.

135.   Article 90 – *Simbolo Atanasiano* [Athanasian Creed].

It was requested that it be conserved for use only on the feast of the Most Blessed Trinity.

136.   Article 92 – *Festa della SS. Trinità.*

It should be retained and classified at the highest grade.

137.   The meeting ended at 6:15 p.m..

Minutes of the 8th Meeting

138.   [The meeting took place] at 5 p.m. on Friday, April 21, 1950 at the *Palazzo della Cancelleria* in the apartments of His Most Reverend Eminence the Lord Cardinal Clemente Micara, Prefect of the Sacred Congregation of Rites.

139.   All members of the Commission were present.

140.   The session opened in the usual manner. His Eminence announced that the "Annotations" to the *Memoria* requested from Father Jungmann, Dom Capelle, and Msgr. Righetti had come to hand. He asked Father Antonelli to have them printed as a supplement to the *Memoria*. Examination of the question began.

141.   The *Relator-Generalis* began by saying that the meeting had been delayed

until today so as to allow time for a concrete project to be prepared on a theological basis that would provide a general direction [for the Commission]. The proposal had been made by Father Albareda and accepted by all present at the meeting of February 14. The project had already been circulated as *Supplement I* to the *Memoria*: Since the members of the Commission had already received and studied the proposal with regards to liturgical gradation, there was no need to make a special presentation. The examination of the individual questions, therefore, resumed.

142. Article 11 – Is it convenient to adopt as a general principle the theological basis proposed by Father Albareda?

143. Unanimously agreed.

144. Article 18 – Is it convenient to divide *cultus latriae* into two classes?

145. Father Albareda asked to speak firstly. Having explained some aspects of his *votum* as reproduced in the *Memoria*, he insisted principally on two points:

1. The proposed theological division should not be taken too much by the letter, since in this case theology was at the service of liturgy;

2. The classification to be drawn up should be a genuinely liturgical classification, that is, each succeeding class should liturgically have something more than the preceding class and something less than the subsequent class.

Moreover, for the Saints, the principle already accepted of emphasizing their importance for the life of the Church should be retained.

146. Father Löw stressed that these principles had inspired the present proposals; that certain liturgical peculiarities had been indicated on p 23; that it had not been possible to list all the discriminating elements that occurred in the liturgy, since some of them that still remained had to be examined by the Commission [i.e. the *orationes de tempore*, occurrence and concurrence, suffrage, intercessions etc]. Their organization depended on whether or not they would be retained.

147. Father Bea agreed, in general terms, with the idea proposed by Father Albareda but underlined the need to reduce the number classes, e.g. class 7 and class 8 could be unified, especially where no great differences occurred. Indeed, class 6 could also be added to 7 and 8. The choice of names in every class being limited to a merely representative number, would not always seem justified, since some Saints or martyrs who had an equal or better right to be mentioned would be overlooked, e.g. among the Martyrs (p. 24) some, like Sts. Gervasius and Protasius, who are mentioned in the Canon or in the Litanies of the Saints, would certainly have to be included.

148. All in all, Father Bea thought that 6 or 7 categories should suffice. Other members of the Commission agreed.

149.   Concretizing what had been said and approved by all, in general terms, the following classification was arrived at:

   1st grade: *Festa Suprema Redemptionis*;

   2nd grade: *Alia festa Christi Domini*;

   3rd grade: *Festa B.V.M.*;

   4th grade: *Angeli, Apostoli, Santi cum Christo speciali coniuncti*;

   5th grade: *Sancti insigniores*;

   6th grade: *Sancti insignes*;

   7th grade: *Sancti commemorati*;

   (8th) grade: *Officium feriale*.

150.   To these grades were then attributed the liturgical characteristics which rendered them truly liturgical grades.

151.   The meeting was dissolved at 6:30 p.m..

Minutes of the 9th Meeting

152.   [This meeting was held] at 5 p.m. on Tuesday, January 23, 1951, at the *Palazzo della Cancelleria* in the apartments of His Eminence Cardinal Clemente Micara, Prefect of the Sacred Congregation of Rites.

153.   All members of the Commission were present.

154.   This meeting was convoked because of an urgent need to examine a special question: "the return of the liturgy of Holy Saturday to its ancient form", which was desired and requested by "dignitaries and Catholics from various countries". Some days previously, a "plan" had been distributed to the members of the Commission that was accompanied by a letter from His Eminence the Cardinal Prefect.

155.   Having opened the meeting, His Eminence asked Father Antonelli to present and explain the aforementioned "plan". Before moving to an examination of its individual parts, the *Relator-Generalis* asked whether the proposed project, in general terms, was acceptable to all. The reply was an affirmative and unanimous. Father Bea, however, added that in the event of the concessions being granted, it should be explicitly stated that the innovation was optional and "*ad experimentum*", so as not to prejudice the work of the Sub-commission that would examine the Sacred Triduum in the context of the general reform. The proposal was unanimously accepted.

156.   [The meeting] then moved to an examination of each point.

157.   p. 3; Minor Hours.

   The relevant rubric was approved as stated in the text.

158.   p. 4; Vespers

The rubric was acceptable, and of the two antiphons proposed as substitutes for *Calicem salutaris* of the first Psalm, the second, *Hodie*, was preferable, but with the text according to the new version of the Psalms.

159.   In the *Oratio* the expression "*gratiam et*" was to be deleted from the final sentence, so as to maintain the flow of the *cursus*.

160.   p. 5; Compline

Its abolition was not accepted. As with Vespers, a simplification was proposed.

161.   p. 6; The Solemn Easter Vigil

Father Albareda noted that with Holy Saturday becoming "liturgical" again, it would be good if Matins was restored to its original time. Thus, its anticipation on the evening of Good Friday, *in choro*, should be abolished. Good Friday is already encumbered by enough various pious practices. The proposal was commonly accepted. It was decided to draw up an appropriate rubric.

162.   p. 7; *Benedictio novi ignis.*

Rubric. Father Albareda insisted that the time for the vigil office should coincide with mid-night, at least for Easter, which began with the singing of the Alleluia. This opportune proposal might experience some practical difficulties, however, it was substantially accepted. Consequently, the rubric would have to be modified to read: "*versus mediam noctem*". Father Bea was unhappy with the expressed prohibition of the "*quattuor ceroferarii cum candelis accensis*". The text would have to be abolished. Equally undesirable was the expression: "*ante portam ecclesiae, vel in ipso aditu ecclesiae*". He desired that it be more clearly stated and that the ceremony should take place where it could be followed by all the people. He proposed the expression: "*vel in ipso aditu ecclesiae, i.e. eo loco ubi fidelibus melius pateat aspectus*" or something similar. Finally, he thought that the expression: "*diende / celebrans / dicit unam ex tribus orationibus vel omnes tres*" would have to be modified, and the second part of the phase should be abolished so as to simplify the rite and to preserve it as much as possible from the arbitrary judgment of the individual. Both proposals were accepted.

163.   p. 9; *Incisio crucis.*

The rubric was approved *prout iacet*.

164.   p. 11; *Insertio granorum incensi.*

The proposed rubric was acceptable.

165.   *Ibidem*; *Accensio cerei.*

Both the rubric and the new text were favorably received.

166.   *bidem*; *Benedictio cerei.*

The restoration of the original text in the *Veniat* received unanimous approval.

167.   p. 13; *Processio.*

Rubric. Unanimously approved but for a minor emendation to the part saying that the deacon carries the Paschal candle, "*adiuvantibus, si opus sit, acolythis*", which was not acceptable. This insertion was struck out.

168.   p. 14; *Laus Cerei.*

The rubric was approved without difficulty.

169.   *Ibidem; Testo dell'Exsultet.*

Father Bea suggested that the direct association of the name of civil rulers with those of the Pope and the Bishop did not seem appropriate. While the prayer "for the Roman Emperor" would retain its actual position, its text would have to be composed *ex novo*. It should express the idea that the people, subject to their respective civil rulers may enjoy material prosperity and supernatural happiness. The proposal was accepted and Father Löw was asked to draft a new text.

180.   Towards the end of the meeting, and to the satisfaction of all, His Eminence announced that he would tell the Pope of the progress [of the Commission's] work at the next Audience which would take place on January 26. He said that he would hope to conclude its work at the next session which was fixed for the following Tuesday, January 30 at the same time.

171..   The meeting ended with the recitation of the *Agimus* at 6:45 p.m..

Minutes of the 10th Meeting

172.   [The meeting] was held at 6 p.m. on Tuesday, January 30 at the *Palazzo dell Cancelleria* in the apartments of Cardinal Clemente Micara, Prefect of the Sacred Congregation of Rites.

173.   All members of the Commission were present.

174.   After the usual prayer, the meeting opened, and Father Bea spoke. He asked for some further information concerning the proceedings of the previous meetings;

1. On the antiphon for the *Magnificat* at Vespers for which he suggested the entire text of Mt 27:66;

2. Concerning the prayer for civil rulers in the *Praeconium paschale*, [he said] that with the necessary adaptations it would be entirely based on the present prayer for the Roman Emperor.

175.   Both proposals were accepted.

176.   Examination of the "project" [for the liturgy of Holy Saturday] was resumed.

177.   p. 15; *Nocturnus.*

Father Albareda was of the view that Matins was not involved in this since it belonged, not to the liturgy of Holy Saturday, but to that of Easter Sunday. The *Relator-Generalis* observed that the Matins of Easter had been introduced here to solve the problem of the *pro vesperis* in whose place it was necessary to substitute something. A *pro laudibus* had been suggested, and this, in turn, supposes Matins.

Father Albareda would resolve the problem by suppressing Matins and by celebrating None before the Solemn Mass, and by leaving the *pro vesperis* where it was. Father Löw believed that it was inadmissible to suggest celebrating None at eleven o'clock at night or at midnight and Vespers at one or two o'clock on the morning of the following day. Father Albareda put forward another idea: transform the *pro vesperis* into a Marian Lauds. Father Bea proposed simply to drop the *pro vesperis*. The present antiphon at the Magnificat could be used as a communion antiphon. The post-communion, *Spiritum nobis Domine* and all the rest would follow as usual.

178.   p. 18; *Le profezie.*

All were in agreement that:

1. The number of prophecies should be reduced;

2. As little as possible should be left to the arbitrary judgment of individuals.

It was established, therefore, that the simplest schema of 4 prophecies should be adopted. The Canticles, however, were to be retained so as to avoid pauperizing the Missal and Gradual by the loss of these musical pieces. Father Bea suggested the following choice of prophecies: the 1st, the creation; the 4th, the fulfillment of the Messianic kingdom; the 8th, the happiness of the Messianic kingdom; the 11th, the exhortation of Moses to the People of God.

179.   p. 21; *Lingua.*

Father Albareda suggested that the question of language should not be raised. He stressed the great advantage for the Church in using a single language for worship. Father Bea agreed with this idea, as did all the other members, more or less, while acknowledging that the reason put forward in the "*progetto*" as well as of those who asked for its use in some rites merited careful consideration. On the other hand, Father Löw observed that in some countries [an indult for the use] of a bilingual ritual for some of the sacramentals had been obtained.

In view of the particular concession that had been made and of the fact that the renewal of baptismal promises was completely new, but corresponded to those parts of the bilingual rituals that could be administered in the vernacular, Father Bea asked that the rubric should state explicitly that the renewal of baptismal promises could be done in the language of the proper rituals.

180. p. 23; *Benedizione del fonte.*

It is appropriate for the rite to be done in the sanctuary, *Coram populo*, whether it involves the actual blessing of the font or only the renewal of baptismal promises. This would avoid a procession, which would be reduced merely to the stationing of the clergy around the Paschal candle, before which could be placed the receptacle for the blessing of the Easter water.

181. p. 26; *Rinnovazione delle promesse battesimali.*

Father Albareda asked that the initial exhortation should not be left to the free choice of the celebrant. It should be specified in a set formula. Father Bea was of the same idea. He suggested that the formula for the renewal of promises should closely follow the baptismal rite found in the ritual. Father Löw stated that this was the first intention behind the "*progetto*", but the absence of any "promises" in the actual text necessitated the preparation of a completely new text. The conclusion was that the proposed text should be revised so that it followed the ritual as closely as possible.

182. With regard to the use of the vernacular for the promises, the observations already made in relation to the prophecies also hold here.

183. Although *Christus Vincit* is a very beautiful hymn, the Commission did not favor its use at the moment of Baptism during the rite.

184. p. 28; *Messa Solemne.*

The relative rubrics were approved as well as the points raised at the beginning of the meeting concerning the *pro vesperis*.

185. Having completed the examination of the proposal [reform on Holy Saturday], it was agreed that the entire text of the rubrics would be drawn up, together with the proposed variants, and that it would be sent to the members of the Commission so that they might be able to express their *placet* with regard to the final text. His Eminence announced that he would present the final draft to the Holy Father in the Audience of February 9.

186. The prayer *Agimus tibi gratias* concluded the meeting at 7:25 p.m..

Minutes of the 11th Meeting

187. [The meeting was held] at 5 p.m. on Tuesday, June 26 at *the Palazzo della Cancelleria* in the apartments of Cardinal Clemente Micara, Prefect of the Congregation of Rites.

188. All of the usual members were present, as was Msgr. Enrico Dante, Prefect of the Pontifical Ceremonies, and *Sostituto* of the Sacred Congregation of

Rites, who had been appointed to the Commission by the Holy Father on April 13, 1951.

189. The prayer was said and the minutes were read. His Eminence asked the *Relator-Generalis* to speak. He gave an account of the outcome of the restored Easter Vigil, on the basis of the reports, which had been received from the [diocesan] Ordinaries, private institutions, abbeys, and from persons both lay and clerical.

190. Thus far, 125 official reports had been received; 63 were Italian, 24 were French, and the remainder coming from elsewhere. The five continents were represented, and none of the reports was contrary. The success was most consoling since the experiment had been a complete success.

191. Someone noted that those who were opposed would not have celebrated the vigil since it was merely optional. On the other hand, the fact that all those who had celebrated it or permitted its celebration were happy with the outcome was worthy of note. Some secondary and local difficulties had been encountered, and these would be studied so as to arrive at an appropriate solution. These included confessions, blessing of homes, the ringing of bells, and the Eucharistic fast, etc..

192. One point which all of the reports were in agreement on and that merited attention was the pastoral and spiritual advantages of the restored vigil. The great participation of the faithful at the Vigil rites and at the sacraments was emphasized which was very pleasing to the pastors of souls. Many expressly requested that the experiment be made definitive and others asked that the work of restoration be extended to Holy Thursday and Good Friday.

193. In conclusion Father Antonelli suggested four possible solutions that could be taken into consideration:

194. 1. Return to the *statu quo antea*: this would not seem [justified].

195. 2. Continue the experiment for a further year *sic et simpliciter*: This is a possible solution, but given some of the matters raised and the suggestions made, it would not seem the best solution. Some practical modification would have to be made.

196. 3. Issue some *Ordinationes* to the *Ordo*, incorporating the required emendations and finding some means of enabling the sacred functions to be celebrated by the priest even in the more remote parishes.

197. 4. Revise and restore the Sacred Triduum as suggested in the *Memoria* so that it would constitute a single "liturgical unit".

198. His Eminence observed that this last proposal seemed premature. He believed that the experiment should continue for a further year and that the *Ordinationes* for the regulation of problematic points should be issued.

199. After a fruitful exchange of views, all agreed to the prolongation of the

experiment and the following conclusions were approved.

200.   1. Continue the Easter Vigil for another year "*ad experimentum*".

201.   2. Prepare a series of *Ordinationes* issuing specific directions for the resolution of the various difficulties that had been encountered and reported to the Sacred Congregation during the celebrations of the vigil.

202.   3. Examine the *Ordinationes* before October in order to publish them at the beginning of December.

203.   The meeting ended at 6:10 p.m. with the *Agimus*.

Minutes of 12th Meeting

204.   [The meeting took place] at 6 p.m. on Tuesday, November 13, 1951 at the *Palazzo della Cancelleria* in the apartments of Cardinal Clemente Micara, Prefect of the Sacred Congregation of Rites.

205.   All the members of the Commission were present.

206.   After the *Actiones nostras* and the reading of the minutes, His Eminence announced that this meeting would only be concerned with questions arising out of the new experimental *Ordo Sabbati Sancti*, so as to draw *Instructiones et Ordinationes* for 1952.

207.   A *pro-memoria* on the desires of the bishops with regard to the new *Ordo* had been distributed in advance before the meeting. It gave particular attention to the time of celebration, the possibility of a reduced rite for one priest, the vernacular, the Divine Office, the Eucharistic fast, and other minor difficulties.

208.   The *Relator-Generalis* began by communicating some statistics on the favorable reception of the new *Ordo* that had been gathered from the reports (over 200) sent by the diocesan Ordinaries.

1. *Ora della Celebrazione*

209.   The "proper" time for the celebration [of the Vigil] is that fixed by the *Ordo*, i.e. in the middle of the night; the "Vigil" therefore unties both Saturday and Sunday and naturally participates in the historicity of the event. A certain number of bishops asked that the time be moved to the late evening. Others, fewer in number, asked that it be moved forward to the early hours of Easter Sunday morning.

210.   Father Löw held that the principle of the *Hora competens*, already established, had to be maintained. In extremely rare circumstances, however, a certain anticipation might be left to the bishops' discretion. [The vigil should not, however, begin] before 8 p.m.. The other members of the Commission accepted the proposal.

2. *Rito semplice quando vi è un solo sacerdote*

211.   Approval was given to adapt the present rubrics for cases in which only one

priest celebrates the rite. The simplified rubrics could be inserted into the text with typographical adjustments. Instead of the expression *pueri ministrantes*, another term providing for older servers was considered desirable.

3. Lingua Volgare

212. Father Löw was of the opinion that both the renewal of baptismal promises and the reading of the four prophecies could be done in the vernacular since such was desired by many and impinged on a part of the rite outside of the Eucharistic sacrifice. Father Albareda warmly emphasized the moral value of a single language in the Church's official worship. [He also emphasized] the grave precedent which would be set by the abandonment of Latin in such a solemn rite. He thought that the vernacular might be conceded for the renewal of baptismal promises but never for the readings. Msgr. Dante and Father Bea were of the same mind. Father Bea suggested that the question should be studied calmly and thoroughly by a Sub-commission. Hence, it would not now seem opportune to limit the deliberations of such a Sub-commission.

213. The conclusion was that the vernacular might be conceded only for the renewal of baptismal promises.

4. Sistemazione dell'ufficio divino (Compieta del Sabato, Mattutino e Lodi del giorno di Pasqua)

214. While no unanimous agreement was reached, the Commission finally arrived at the decision to maintain Compline. The Matins of Easter could be substituted with the Vigil rites. A simplified Lauds could be placed at the end of Mass to take the place of the *pro vesperis* of the old rite with everything ending with the singing of the antiphon *Regina Coeli* (Father Albareda) instead of the Gospel of St. John (Father Bea).

5. Digiuno eucaristico

215. The Commission was of the opinion that a fast of at least two hours prior to the Vigil Mass should be established. A single norm applicable to both clergy and laity would be desirable. [The Commission, however, was not competent] to deal with this question.

6. Difficoltà minori

216. The late hour did not allow [the Commission] to examine this question in detail. An appropriate solution could be expected with the drafting of the *Ordinationes et Instructiones*.

217. The *Agimus* concluded the meeting at 7:15 p.m..

Minutes of 13ᵗʰ Meeting

218. [The meeting took place] at 5 p.m. on Tuesday, December 11, 1951 at the

Palazzo della Cancelleria in the apartments of Cardinal Clemente Micara, Prefect of the Sacred Congregation of Rites.

219. All members of the Commission were in attendance.

220. The entire session was devoted to an examination of the text of the *Ordinationes*, which would be published together with a decree proroging the new *Ordo Sabbati Sancti ad triennium*.

221. The text of the *Ordinationes* had been distributed to the members of the Commission a few days before the meeting together with a copy of the *Ordo* which had simplified rubrics for a single priest inserted. The necessary changes had also been made [to the text].

222. Each article of the *Ordinationes* was read, discussed, and approved with some minor emendations.

223. The rubrics of the *Ordo*, however, were only in part examined. The remainder was postponed to the following meeting which would take place as soon as possible.

224. As the meeting opened as usual with a prayer, so it was concluded by a prayer at 7:15 p.m..

Minutes of the 14th Meeting

225. [The meeting took place] at 5 p.m. on Tuesday, January 8, 1952 at the *Palazzo della Cancelleria* in the apartments of Cardinal Clemente Micara, Prefect of the Sacred Congregation of Rites.

226. All members were present, except for Father Albareda, who was indisposed.

227. The meeting began with the *Actiones nostras*, and His Eminence asked the *Relator-Generalis* to speak. He proposed that the Commission examine three questions that arose at the previous meeting and seemed to need further clarification.

228. First, should the priests receive Holy Communion at the Easter Vigil when he had to celebrate on the following morning.

229. Father Albareda had let it be known that he was opposed to this. Msgr. Dante was of the same view. The other members were, more or less, perplexed. Hence, it was decided to leave the matter unchanged.

230. Secondly, should the proposal of abolishing the blessing of the font on the vigil of Pentecost, since it had been blessed at the Easter Vigil, be reconsidered.

231. All were in favor of the abolition.

232. Should the antiphon that was currently used for the *Benedictus* in the Lauds of Easter Sunday be adopted for the *Benedictus* in the *pro laudibus*

at the end of the Vigil Mass (proposed by Father Albareda).

233. The Commission unanimously accepted the proposal.

234. The examination of the modifications to the rubrics of the *Ordo Sabbati Sancti* was resumed and completed.

235. Finally, a schema by Msgr. Dante on the question of gradation was distributed to the members.

236. The next meeting will take place on January 22, [1952], at 5 p.m.. Examination of the *Memoria* will resume at Article 93 (feriale), the point at which its consideration had been interrupted on February 14, 1950.

237. The meeting concluded with a prayer at 6 p.m..

Minutes of the 15ᵗʰ Meeting

238. [The meeting took place] at 5 p.m. on Tuesday, January 22, 1952 at the *Palazzo della Cancelleria* in the apartment of Cardinal Clemente Micara, Prefect of the Sacred Congregation of Rites.

239. All members of the Commission were present.

240. Father Antonelli gave a brief resumé regarding the Commission's discussion of the *Memoria* up to the point at which it had been interrupted for a long period by the consideration of the [*Ordo*] *Sabbati Sancti*.

Discussion of the *Memoria* had reached Article 92, and an earlier question (liturgical gradation Articles 22-32) also remained open since no definite conclusion had been reached.

241. Discussion of this latter point would now have to be resumed since it was central to the reform of the calendar, which was the primary object of the Commission's next task.

242. While the *Memoria* was being examined, Father Albareda proposed and then commented upon a fundamental idea with regard to gradation, and it made an excellent impression on all present. He suggested that the triple theological division of worship should be employed for the liturgical gradation: *cultus latriae, cultus hyperduliae,* and *cultus duliae.* A special fascicle had been prepared on the basis of this proposal [*Supplementum I*], which was then discussed.

[The Commission] arrived at 7 grades (8 with the feria). Several important points concerning the practical application [of this system] remained in suspense.

243. Recently, Msgr. Dante, who had joined the Commission in April 1951, presented a new proposal (April 15, 1951) for liturgical gradation. It attempted maximum possible simplication, while maintaining the basic triple division proposed by Father Albareda (*Festa Domini, festa B.V. M.,*

festa Sanctorum) it also retained the proposal, contained in the *Memoria*, of dividing each grade into two classes (*festum maius* and *festus minus*).

244. After Father Antonelli's resumé, Msgr. Dante's proposal which had already been distributed at the previous meeting was read.

245. A lively discussion took place on the first part of the proposal. The point being that a *festum maius* of any grade, including those of the Saints, could take precedence over a *festum minus* of a Superior grade, including the minor feasts of Our Lord and of the Blessed Virgin Mary. Father Albareda insisted on an absolute separation of the categories. No other feast could take place of a feast of Our Lord or of the Blessed Virgin Mary because these always take precedence over every Saint's feast. The others (Msgr. Dante, Father Bea, and Father Löw) noted that in particular cases, such as that of a titular or Patron, [the feast of Saints] could assume enough significance to take precedence over the minor feasts of the Lord and of the Blessed Virgin Mary. This, for example, could happen in the case of the feast of the Holy Shroud or of Our Lady of Mount Carmel, and on the basis of the Church's constant tradition.

246. Father Albareda adhered firmly to the principle that for a liturgical reform to be a true reform, a basic logical principle was required and that principle had to be pursued logically in all of its consequences, without compromise with the actual [liturgical] situation. Since the Commission, however, did not favor this procedure in its entirety, Father Albareda felt constrained to say that he did not intend to pursue his proposal any further.

[The Commission] then moved to a consideration of Msgr. Dante's proposal, which was accepted in general terms. The meeting closed at 6 p.m. with the recitation of the *Agimus tibi gratias*.

Minutes of the 16th Meeting

247. [The meeting was held] at 5 p.m. on Tuesday, February 5, 1952 at the *Palazzo della Cancelleria* in the apartments of Cardinal Clemente Micara, Prefect of the Sacred Congregation of Rites.

248. All members of the Commission were present.

249. The minutes of the previous meeting were read. Father Albareda spoke on some new possibilities that arose with the Commission's adoption of the principle of festivity as the basis for classifying feasts.

250. The principle of a division *intuitu personae*, proposed by Father Albareda, logically implied the adoption of the triple theological sub-division of *cultus latriae, cultus hyperduliae,* and *cultus duliae,* as the basis for gradation. This principle, [was] now abandoned because it gave rise to many practical difficulties, a fact that Father Albareda did not deny. The Commission now

considered it convenient to use a better system for organizing feasts. Msgr. Dante's proposal tried to arrive at a compromise between the two principles but, it was not, however, all together certain of a real cohesion between the two possibilities of accommodation. The liturgical feasts, at present, present a gammit, which is much wider than any gradation. Account would also have to be taken of this [aspect of the question].

251. Father Albareda said that it was a matter of two irreconcilable principles, with diametrically opposing consequences. To simplify matters, it would be better to progressively number the classes I, II, III, etc.. The liturgical feasts could then be inserted into the relevant class as deemed appropriate (dominical feasts, feasts of Our Lady, feasts of the Saints, ferials, vigils, and octaves).

252. A lively debate ensued on this proposal of Father Albareda. Msgr. Dante maintained that no opposition existed between the two principles and that both could be reconciled since they both complemented each other. With the subdivision of feasts into *maius* and *minor*, the gradation would be greatly simplified and there would be no conflict between the feasts of the general calendar. These were fixed so as [to be celebrated] only once, thereby avoiding a situation in which two feasts of the same grade occurred on the same day. Conflicts could only happen between the general calendar and particular calendars. In such cases, the more "proper" feast had precedence.

253. Father Löw maintained that a real opposition existed between the two systems and that they could not be reconciled. The system of gradation based on the triple theological distinction of cult, on *intuitu personae*, which had been taken up again, even if in a mitigated form by Msgr. Dante, necessarily creates closed categories. Inevitably, such categories will necessarily relegate certain great feasts of Our Lady and of the Saints to significantly lower classes, in opposition to the Church's constant tradition and the *sensus commune* of the faithful. [This system lends itself] to too strong of a tendency to level [out the differences between the feasts], even if it could be justified from a purely theoretical theological perspective.

254. The Church's traditional system [of gradation] is based on *external solemnity* or *festività* in the context of the community celebrating the feast. It has a greater ductibility and adapts perfectly to man's natural sentiment, which relates all things directly to the given circumstances of time. It is, therefore, much less rigid and exclusive.

255. Father Bea made the same observation. He emphasized that the [Commission's] objective was to simplify [the system of gradation]. Father Albareda's proposal to construct a system of perhaps five classes, excluding the commemorations, seemed to meet that objective and was preferable because it provided a general solution for the problem.

256. It was finally decided to prepare a new schema of gradation based on what had been proposed by Father Albareda and generally accepted by the Commission. It would be sent to the members of the Commission in the coming days so that they might be able to discuss it and come to a final decision about it at the next meeting.

257. At this point, it should be noted that the problem of liturgical gradation was one of the most sensitive points raised in connection with the liturgical reform and was also one of the important factors for the success of that reform. The toil generated by this question was not in vain for [the Commission began to realize] that an acceptable way forward had been found which, above all, was compatible with the Church's tradition.

259. Article 93 – *Feriale.*
    The division of the *ferials,* as proposed [in the *Memoria,*] was accepted by all. It would be finally settled once the new system of gradation had been drawn up.

260. Articles 95-96 – *Quattrotempi.*
    All were agreed that the days in the quarter tenses should be upgraded and that their celebration should be really observed.

261. Article 97 and *Supplementum* II; p. 27.
    Father Löw's proposal to introduce an official prayer for the clergy and for vocations on the Saturdays of Quartertense was acceptable, but the problem was to find ways of implementing it without changing the present system of liturgical texts.

262. Articles 98-250 – *Spostamente della tempora.*
    This is a complex question and could be more conveniently discussed when [the Commission] deals with the question of organization of the Quartertenses.

263. The meeting ended at 6:20 p.m.. The next meeting will be held on February 19.

Minutes of the 17th Meeting

264. [The meeting was held] at 5 p.m. on Tuesday, February 19, 1952 at the *Palazzo della Cancelleria* in the apartments of Cardinal Clemente Micara, Prefect of the Sacred Congregation of Rites.

265. All members were present.

266. Having read and approved the minutes of the previous meeting, an examination of the *Memoria* was resumed.

267. Article 101
    a. Is it convenient to grant canonical character to the litany of the Saints

236

used in public processions, even when recited in the vernacular?

268. All opinions agreed in the affirmative.

269. Article 101

b. Is it convenient to transfer the feast of St. Mark to another day and to provide for the integral celebration of the *litania maior*?

270. All agreed.

271. Article 101

c. Is it convenient to entrust the study of the litanies to a special Sub-commission?

272. The general opinion recommended that this Sub-commission be comprised of members of the Commission.

273. A specimen draft of a gradation was then examined that had been drawn up on the basis of the conclusions of the previous meeting. It had already been circulated to the members of the Commission, and it was a schema for the first three classes in which an attempt had been made to establish criteria for assigning the feasts to the various classes.

274. The principle feasts of the redemption were placed under the heading of *maximae solemnitates* (Christmas, Epiphany, Easter, Ascension, Pentecost, and the Sacred Triduum) and were regarded as extraneous to every class.

275. His Excellency, Msgr. *Segretario*, asked why the feast of the Divine conception of Jesus (the Annunciation) had not been listed among these feasts. Father Albareda, who had made the proposal the previous year, noted that while the proposal was fine in theory, practically it would be too arid and depart from the traditional line. The liturgical year begins with Advent, the preparation for the birth of Our Savior, and not with the Annunciation. Father Löw noted that the Annunciation had never had much external celebration given that the feast fell in Lent.

276. Father Albareda suggested a clear distinction between these "*fuori classe*" feasts. He said that some should be called *solemnitates*, and all the others should be given the title of *festa per annum*.

277. Msgr. Dante believed that such represented a return to a classification based on *persona* rather than *festività*. Father Löw observed that some reference to the *persona* was inevitable and that it would be indispensable in arriving at some criteria to assume objectivity in assigning the feasts to the various classes and to avoid a subjective adscription of the feasts to the various classes in the future, which would inevitably tended towards a higher gradation.

278. Father Bea favored both the system [of classification] and the criteria in which he saw a favorable combination of the two tendencies that had emerged at the previous meeting. It was agreed that the *solemnitates* and

the first class feasts would remain as they were presented in the "*progetto*". As with the other feasts, some observations were made which would be taken into account when the "*progetto*" was being finalized.

279.   The meeting concluded at 6:20 p.m. with the recitation of the *Agimus*.

Minutes of the 18th Meeting

280.   [The meeting was held] at 5 p.m. on Tuesday, March 11, 1952 at the *Palazzo della Cancelleria* in the apartments of Cardinal Clemente Micara, Prefect of the Congregation of Rites.

281.   All members were present except for Father Bea.

282.   After the usual prayer, the Cardinal asked the *Relator-Generalis* to speak. He raised the question of the Rogation days, referring to a study prepared by Father Löw that had been distributed prior to the meeting. This study foresaw the transferal of the feast of Saint Mark to September 23, thereby leaving April 25 free for the celebration of the minor litany.

283.   Father Albareda noted that:

1. Were the feast of St. Mark transferred to the September 23, then the feast of two apostles would be celebrated close to each other.

2. Not infrequently, either one or the other feast would be impeded by the Quarertense of September. Given these difficulties, and the objective of simplifying matters, he suggested a new idea: the *litania maior* was an invocation of God's blessing on the fruits of the earth. Twelve days in the year are dedicated to that purpose: the Quartertenses. Ultimately, the *litania maior* is a duplication. To simplify matters could [the Commission] not think of combining the *litania maior* which nobody wishes to suppress because of its antiquity, with a day in the Quartertense of Spring, preferably with the Friday [in the Quartertense]? The idea was favorably received. On this basis, it was agreed that consideration would be given to finding a better solution for the problem.

284.   Father Antonelli authorized the reading of the problems encountered with regard to the 3rd class of gradation. This proved especially [difficult] for the classification of founders and doctors. He asked the Commission to reflect carefully on the following points in order to discuss them at the following meeting:

285.   1. Should there be only one collective feast for all doctors and another one for founders?

286.   2. Should founder-patriarchs and the great doctors be treated separately?

287.   3. Should several doctors be grouped together; and should several

founders be grouped together, if so on what criteria?

288. 4. What criteria should be laid down for the reception of new saint founders into the calendar of the universal Church?

289. A preliminary exchange of ideas tended to the following solution: the eight great doctors and the great founders should retain their proper feasts. No serious difficulties were foreseeable in grouping together, according to specific criteria, the remaining doctors and the more conspicuous founders. The scheme for the 3rd and 4th classes would therefore be worked out along these general lines. Consideration would also be given to the 4th point, namely, the introduction of new founders into the universal calendar.

290. The session ended at 6 p.m..

Minutes of the 19th Meeting

291. [The meeting was held] at 5 p.m. on Tuesday, April 29, 1952 at the *Palazzo della Cancelleria* in the apartments of Cardinal Clemente Micara, Prefect of the Sacred Congregation of Rites.

292. All members were present.

293. The meeting began with the *Actiones nostras*. His Eminence asked Father Antonelli to speak. He gave a brief synopsis of the position that had been prepared and circulated on the Rogation days, of the *litania minor*, and proposed some solutions for the problems encountered with regard to the litanies. The following unanimous conclusions were reached:

294. 1. The *litania minor*, or the three Rogation days, which was of Gallican origin and was not, as all acknowledged, in harmony with the spirit of Easter, should be eliminated.

295. 2. As was already decided, the *litania maior* should be retained, and detached from the feast of Saint Mark (April 25) which should not be transferred. [The litany] should then be moved to the Saturday of the nearest Quartertense, which would be that of Spring.

296. Discussion returned to the gradation of feasts. A proposal had been prepared and distributed for the 3rd and 4th classes of liturgical feasts. Time, however, only allowed for the examination of the third class.

297. The discussion had a general character. Only incidentally were particular questions raised, for example, the question of the dedication of churches – a matter that would have to be examined separately. Again, it was noted that every system of gradation would encounter practical difficulties in defining accurately the vast amount of material necessarily contained in the lower grades. In any event, Father Bea observed that some system would have to be adopted and thoroughly applied. No system was without its difficulties and complications, especially when dealing with such complex

material as the feasts and the calendar. The first two classes were, thus, approved as it was appropriate to follow through in the same line.

298.	The meeting ended at 6:20 p.m. with the *Agimus*.

Minutes of the 20ᵗʰ Meeting

299.	[The meeting took place] at 5 p.m. on Tuesday, May 13, 1952 at the *Palazzo della Cancelleria* in the apartments of Cardinal Clemente Micara, Prefect of the Sacred Congregation of Rites.

300.	All members of the Commission attended.

301.	The meeting opened. His Eminence asked Father Antonelli to speak and he resumed discussion of the *litania maior*. He suggested that were it possible to find a suitable date, it might be more conveniently united with the Quartertense of Pentecost, rather then with that of Spring, as had been proposed at the previous meeting, bearing in mind all the transferals caused by the mobility of Easter. Also, the distance of time between the original date (April 25) and the Quartertese of Pentecost is shorter than that between [April 25] and the Quartertense of Spring.

302.	Father Bea, however, noted that the formularies for the Quartertense of Pentecost did not lend themselves very well to the *litania maior*, since they speak of harvest rather than flowering. The matter should be examined again in order to arrive at a satisfactory solution.

303.	A proposal for the 4ᵗʰ class of gradation, which had been circulated previously, was then discussed. All agreed with regard to the criteria to be followed in the formulation [of this class]. Msgr. Dante observed that it would not be appropriate to insert the feasts of Our Lady into this class since it corresponded to the present *simplex*.

304.	He regarded two series of feasts in this class as exaggerated. Father Bea agreed with both observations, and he proposed that the list of ferias be inserted as number 1 in the 3ʳᵈ class.

305.	Finally, Father Antonelli outlined tentatively, the criteria to be adopted for the distribution of the Popes, Doctors, and founders. In general, the Commission agreed with the principles, which were outlined by Father Antonelli, the *Relator-Generalis*. Concrete proposals regarding this matter would soon be communicated.

306.	The meeting closed at 6 p.m..

Minutes of 21ˢᵗ Meeting

307.	[The meeting was held] at 5 p.m. on Tuesday, June 10, 1952 at the *Palazzo della Cancelleria* in the apartments of Cardinal Micara, Prefect of the Sacred Congregation of Rites.

308. All members of the Commission were present.

309. The meeting began and the minutes were read. Then commenced the examination of the rubrical part [of the *Memoria*] concerning the liturgical day, the law of precedence, and translation. Discussion was based on a *pro-memoria* that had been previously circulated.

310. With some marginal observations, the proposal was favorably received by the Commission.

311. [The Commission] then moved on to examine the proposed distribution of the Doctors of the Church.

312. Father Albareda prefaced his comments by expressing some of his ideas concerning the criteria for the grouping [of the feasts of Doctors and founders].

According to what had been agreed, the eight great Doctors would continue [to have feast days] allotted to them, possibly on their mortuary days or on some other justifiable significant day. The Commission unanimously accepted this argument.

314. Various criteria would guide the grouping of the other doctors. The first four groups presented no difficulties. The foundation of the fifth group, which included St. Isidore and Bede, gave rise to some comments. In this arrangement, a group of Doctors would be created, all of whom belonged to the Benedictine Order.

315. With regard to St. Isidore, it would have to be seen whether to unite him with another group, or with another Holy Doctor, or to leave him with a separate feast. The ninth group also gave rise to some difficulties because of the great differences between figures such as St. Bernard and St. John of the Cross. No decision was taken in the matter. The other groups were unanimously accepted.

316. After the usual prayer, the meeting closed at 6:20 p.m..

Minutes of the 22nd Meeting

317. [The 22nd meeting] was held at 5 p.m. on Wednesday, June 25, 1952 at the *Palazzo della Cancelleria* in the apartments of Cardinal Clemente Micara, Prefect of the Sacred Congregation of Rites.

318. All members attended, except His Excellency Msgr. Carinci.

319. As usual, the meeting began with a prayer and the reading of the minutes. Father Antonelli reported that various requests had reached the Sacred Congregation of Rites for the concession of celebrating Holy Thursday and Good Friday in the evening. In those regions, which had an indult for the celebration of the evening Mass, the practice had been highly successful and drew a great number of the faithful. The Holy Father might be asked

to study the question.

320. All agreed. His Eminence said that he would propose the matter to the Holy Father in the next Audience.

321. The *Relator-Generalis* returned to the question of the Doctors, which had remained in suspense.

1. St. Isidore; he proposed uniting him with St. Hilary and St. Peter Chrysologus. Thus, three Doctors, relatively close in time, would represent the three great Latin nations (France, Italy and Spain);

2. While St. Bernard and St. John of the Cross were distinct from each other in time and in culture, they converged in the series of Doctors because they represent the most eminent spiritual and mystical theologians. One belonged to the pre-scholastic period, while the other belonged to a period full theological development. Given that they could not otherwise be united, and it was inconvenient to assign separate feasts to them, it seemed opportune to combine them and set one feast for both of them (August 20).

322. The Commission unanimously accepted both solutions.

323. An examination of the groupings of founders then commenced.

324. The first group (*Fondatori che entrano in altra categoria*) and the second group (*Fondatori patriarchi*) encountered no difficulties. The third group (*Monaci orientali*) appeared too well stocked to some members, since some names which did not occur in the general calendar had been inserted. Msgr. Dante, Father Albareda, and Father Bea thought that new feasts should be avoided, given that the Orientals had proper calendars and proper liturgies in which the oriental Saints were duly commemorated. Father Bea thought that the feast of St. Hilarion could be abolished, as well as that of St. Saba, whose ancient titular Church in Rome would, however, require a *memoria*. With regard to the group including St. John [*Climaco*], St. Maximus the Confessor, and St. Theodore the [*Studite*], with whom a certain doubt existed, one memorial could be made while Sts. Macarius and Nilus should be omitted. The Commission accepted the proposals of the *memoria* with regard to the others, and resolved the remaining problems as follows:

Sts. Columba and Columbanus: *memoria;*

St. William: eliminated;

Sts. Benedict of Aniane, Ugo, Maiolo, Odilone, and Odone: omitted from the universal calendar;

St. Albert, Patriarch of Jerusalem: omitted;

St. André Fournet: omitted;

St. Paul of the Cross: united to St. Jean Eudes and St. Louis M.

Grignion de Montfort;

St. Michael Garicoïts: omitted;

St. Mary of St. Euphrasia Pelletier: *memoria* on April 24;

St. Jeanne Franciose Frémiot de Chantal: *memoria* on August 1;

St. Giuliana Falconieri: omitted;

St. Joan of France: omitted.

325. The session ended after the usual prayer at 6:15 p.m..

Minutes of the 23rd Meeting

326. [The meeting took place] at 5 p.m. on Tuesday, July 8, 1952 at the *Palazzo della Cancelleria* in the apartments of His Most Reverend Eminence Clement the Lord Cardinal Micara, Prefect of the Sacred Congregation of Rites.

327. All members were present.

328. The meeting began with the *Actiones nostras* and the reading of the minutes.

329. The *Relator-Generalis* began to explain the proposal for a group of Popes. A detailed *pro-memoria* had previously been circulated to the Commission that had been prepared by Father Löw in collaboration with Father Antonelli.

330. All the members approved the general principles.

331. All the rules governing the proposed insersion or omission [of Popes] from the universal calendar were favorably received by the Commission.

332. The proposal to institute a single feast of *Omnium Sanctorum Summorum Pontificum* encountered serious difficulty.

333. Father Albareda noted that:

1. All the Popes who had really attained sanctity or who had suffered martyrdom should be inserted in the universal calendar because the Pope is Bishop of the entire Church;

2. As a criterion we cannot say what the state of a Pope is before God, but of that which emerges from historical evidence;

3. Consequently, a feast of "*Omnium Summorum Pontificum*" is inadmissible because if all Popes are individually inserted into the calendar, such a feast would lack all purpose, or constitute a duplication. On the same basis, a feast would have to be instituted for all Martyrs, and Confessors and so on.

334. Father Antonelli explained that the purpose of such a feast was:

1. to venerate and do homage to the Papacy;

2. that some excluded Saints, while not having an ancient cult, would not fulfill the criteria for insertion in the universal calendar that had

been drawn up in reference to historical data. While these had a certain cult, over the course of the centuries, it would be sufficient to continue it with a collective feast. There are also some Popes whose cult has been confirmed (Gregory X and Innocent V), or who had been beatified and had not been inserted in the calendar (Pius X), because they had not yet been canonized.

335.   Father Löw expressed a similar view. Msgr. Dante tended towards the positions held by Father Albareda. Father Bea supported the introduction of the feast because:

1. while the criteria for the selection of the Popes were objective and sound, at the same time, they were not absolute but relative: They had been in force since the 4th century. It is possible that other Popes have had a cult but we cannot prove it because of the absence of documentary evidence;

2. an act of particular devotion for the Papacy was a duty.

336.   Msgr. Carinci and His Eminence supported the introduction of the feast. A feast of *Omnium Summorum Pontificum* could be inserted into the universal calendar during the Octave of the Apostles Peter and Paul, on July 3, as a II class rite.

337.   The specific proposals to assign days for the feasts of the holy Popes did not encounter any special difficulty. Father Albareda expressed the view that a higher grade should be assigned to the major figures such as St. Gregory and St. Leo and a lesser grade to minor figures. Others also supported this view. Canonized Popes and Doctors would be assigned to the III class while the others would be counted as IV class. This would also facilitate the compilation of the historical readings for these Popes, about whom little is often known.

338.   This was the final meeting before the summer vacation of the series covering the years 1951-1952. There had been 12 in all. The work accomplished by the Commission, especially during the last number of meetings, had been extremely constructive. It had been greatly facilitated by material prepared for the discussions by the Historical Section of the Sacred Congregation of Rites. This work opened up the possibility for the reform now to progress quickly and securely so as to satisfy the many desires daily reiterated by various parts of the Catholic world.

339.   The meeting closed with the *Agimus* at 6:20 p.m.. The next meeting will be held at beginning of October. In the interim material pertinent to the examination and discussion of Holy Thursday and Good Friday would be prepared since the Holy Father had authorized the relevant study.

Minutes of the 24th Meeting

340. [The meeting took place] at 5 p.m. on Tuesday, October 18, 1952 at the *Palazzo della Cancelleria* in the apartments of His Eminence Clemente the Lord Cardinal Micara, Prefect of the Sacred Congregation of Rites.

341. All members were present except Father Albareda who was in Spain.

342. The session began with the usual prayer and the reading of the minutes.

343. Father Antonelli, *Relator-Generalis*, explained the topic for the meeting: the restoration of the rite of Holy Thursday and Good Friday to the evening. A scheme had been prepared by Father Löw in collaboration with Father Antonelli and circulated prior to the meeting. It was divided into two points: the *Ordinationes* which prefaced the rite (to be examined during the meeting), and the *Ordo* with texts and rubrics. The drafts of the *Ordo* would also be presented to the meeting.

344. Father Antonelli mentioned that the Holy Father had authorized the Commission to study the question of the Reform of Holy Thursday and Good Friday the previous July which had been solicited by various bishops. The examination of the text of the *Ordinationes* then commenced.

345. Generally, the scheme was favorably received. The matters raised related more to the form of election then to the substance of the scheme.

    Giovedì Santo [Holy Thursday]

346. Article 9 – *Ora*.

    An ample space of time (3 p.m. to 9 p.m). was conceded so as to allow the faithful to participate at the rites, especially in the mountains where many places were distant from the Church. Father Bea thought it sufficient to establish the time between 3 p.m. and 9 p.m.. The Commission accepted the proposal.

347. Article 11 – *Modi di assistenza alla Messa* [Ways of assisting at Mass].

    This paragraph had been inserted into the *Ordinationes* to clarify the terminology that would subsequently be used throughout the *Ordinationes* and in the *Ordo*. It presented some difficulty as it differed in some respects from the terminology employed in the liturgical books. Some changes need to be made to remove all ambiguity.

348. Articles 16-17 – *Digiuno eucaristico* [Eucharistic fast].

    The norms established were to be regarded as transitory, until the Holy See should regulate the question of the Eucharistic fast by a general law.

349. Article 18 – *Mandato* [The washing of the feet]

    The comments in the scheme were pleasing [to the Commission]. They were amended in such a way that the decision whether or not to have these rites was vested in the Rector of the Church, "*de licentia Ordinarii*".

350. *Venerdì Santo* [Good Friday]

351. The respective *Ordinationes* were approved, with the sole modifications that the same *horarium* and the same norms for the Eucharistic fast be adopted both on Holy Thursday and on Good Friday.

352. The meeting ended at 6:50 p.m.. At the end, His Eminence announced that he would report, in general terms, on the meeting to the Holy Father in the next audience.

Minutes of the 25th Meeting

353. Meeting held at 5 p.m. on Friday, December 12, 1952 at the *Palazzo della Cancelleria* in the apartments of His Eminence Clemente the Lord Cardinal Micara, Prefect of the Sacred Congregation of Rites.

354. All members were present.

355. After the *Actiones nostras* and the reading of the minutes, the 25th meeting opened. Father Antonelli addressed the subject of the *Ordo Feriae V in Cena Domini,* the drafts of which had previously been circulated to the members of the Commission.

356. *De Officio divino.*

The proposal of moving Matins from Wednesday night to Thursday morning (as had happened with Holy Saturday) drew Msgr. Dante to observe that the recitation of Matins, Lauds, and the minor hours, together with the *Missa chrismatis,* would constitute a grave burden. Msgr. Carinci observed that the Matins of *Tenebre* was much beloved of the faithful, with many of them participating at it. Other members agreed that the observations were well founded. Holding to the principle of restoring Matins and Lauds to the mornings of the Sacred Triduum, the question was raised of the convenience of granting a faculty only to Cathedrals so as to anticipate it on Wednesday evening, in view of the solemn ceremonies of the following morning.

357. *De Missa chrismatis.*

Father Albareda made a general observation on the entire *Ordo:* he thought that the formulation of the rubrics echoed a certain prolixity. He would prefer that the rubrics only mention what is absolutely indispensable, leaving the rest to the missal and to the breviary. This was also motivated by economic reasons. The impression of changing everything should not be given.

358. Father Löw observed:

1. The reform had a directly pastoral objective. It was therefore thought appropriate to add parts of the rubrics that refer to the spiritual preparation of the faithful and to their participation in the rite;

2. The inclusion of the fixed parts of the Mass, the Canon and Ordinary

which are reproduced in the *Ordo*, was deemed necessary to avoid having the celebrant going from the missal to the Ordo and vice versa.

359. Article 4 and following

The texts for the *Missa chrismatis*, including those composed *ex novo*, were accepted by the Commission, except for the *Introit*. Father Bea thought that a better text might be chosen, preferably from St. Paul. It would also be preferable were the *Communio* taken from the Gospel of the day which speaks of anointing with oil.

360. *De Missa Solemni vespertina.*

The most controversial point is that of ceremonial concelebration.

361. Msgr. Dante recalled that at a previous meeting he had not favored "ceremonial concelebration", since, properly speaking, assistance at a Solemn Mass was proper to bishops. Moreover, he did not see why the clergy should be made to recite the prayers while remaining at their stalls in the choir.

362. Father Albareda, who had been absent from the previous meeting, said that he did not favor ceremonial concelebration for the following reasons:

1. It would not be easy to harmonize the recitation of the prayers, especially if the numbers present were great;

2. The diversity of liturgical colors would make a poor impression since in most cases it would be impossible to provide vestments of the same color;

3. This would be a particularly striking innovation foreign to the line of moderation and restraint thus far followed by the Commission;

4. Finally, the question did not seem completely mature and thus it would be opportune to seek the views of some specialists.

363. Father Löw emphasized:

1. All the Popes, from the time of Pius X, had warmly recommended the participation of the laity in the Mass; how much more so then should priests participate in the Mass of Holy Thursday;

2. It would be the only case of priestly assistance at Mass and so as to honor the priesthood on the day of its institution;

3. If viewed in this manner, the rite sought to give visible representation to the scene of the Last Supper.

364. Father Bea observed:

1. That ceremonial concelebration had existed from the 10th – 11th centuries, because private Masses were relatively rare and concelebration died out with the growth of private Masses;

2. On the other hand, in some countries, such as Germany, a certain discrediting of private Masses was noticeable which served to promote

sacramental concelebration. Merely ceremonial concelebration could furnish the extremists with a pretext for the promotion of consecratory concelebration.

365. After a useful exchange of ideas, pro and contra, Father Antonelli was of the idea that:

1. A ceremonial concelebration, with participation of all the clergy present, on the day on which the institution of the Catholic priesthood is commemorated, seemed to him, in general terms, beautiful, desirable and possible;

2. Basically, this did not represent an innovation since it was a form of assistance already present in the primitive Roman liturgy that went into disuse during the Middle Ages because of the rise of private masses;

3. However, given the importance of the question, and the fact that the Commission could not reach agreement about it, it would seem best to defer discussion of the report until it could be considered in the general context of other problems arising with regard to the Mass. In the meanwhile, the advice of experts, already aware of the Commission's work, could be sought. Thus, Father Jungmann, Dom Capelle, and Msgr. Righetti might be consulted.

366. Finally, His Eminence said that he did not regard the proposed ceremonial concelebration as unattainable.

367. His experience of a large number of Sacred Ordinations demonstrated to him that from a practical point of view there would be no serious difficulties with ceremonial concelebration which would be greatly edifying for the faithful. His Eminence said that he would mention this to the Holy Father in the next audience.

368. Examination of the *Ordo* resumed and encountered no significant difficulty.

369. The meeting ended at 6:30 p.m. with the recitation of the *Agimus*.

Minutes of the 26th Meeting

370. [The meeting took place] at 5 p.m. on Friday, January 2, 1953 at the *Palazzo della Cancelleria* in the apartments of His Eminence Clemente the Lord Cardinal Micara, Prefect of the Sacred Congregation of Rites.

371. All the members were present.

372. Father Bea presented the narrative texts for the *Missa chrismatis* of Holy Thursday that he had been kind enough to select. To all, they seemed inspired.

373. The entire meeting was devoted to an examination of the *Ordo Feriae sextae in Passione et Morte Domini*. The members of the Commission had

already received printed drafts of the *Ordo*.

374. The initial articles encountered no difficulties.

375. Article 11 – *Canto del Passio*.

Father Albareda opposed the insertion in the text that the Passion could be sung or said in the vernacular for the same reasons already advanced in other circumstances, i.e. the unity of language in the liturgy is so great a treasure for the Church that no advantage could compensate for its demise. If the vernacular were to be introduced for the *Passio*, it would also have to be introduced for the other readings. Msgr. Dante agreed. The other members of the Commission were also of the same mind, more or less. The insertion was deleted.

376. Article 13 – *Oratio 48: Pro rei publicae gubernantibus*.

Father Bea proposed replacing the word *regnarum* with *populorum* in the *Oremus*. The proposal was accepted.

377. *Oratio 8: Pro conversione Iudaeorum*.

Father Bea believed that the practice of kneeling and praying in silence as with the other prayers should be reintroduced, otherwise the celebrant's invitation to prayer would be senseless. Kneeling exists since primitive times as is clear from the Gelasian [Sacramentary]. The Commission accepted the proposal.

378. Article 27 – *Sermo exhortatorius*.

Father Albareda opposed [the proposal], because after all the Lenten preaching it did not seem appropriate, especially on such a day when the sacred action spoke eloquently for itself.

379. The comment was well received. The proposed sermon was established at this point.

380. Article 33 – *Comunione dei fedeli*.

Father Albareda opposed the introduction of this innovation for the f ollowing reasons:

381. 1. Good Friday is dedicated to the cross, which the Church celebrates with the *cultus latriae*;

382. 2. It was an a-liturgical day, if there is no tree, there cannot be any fruit;

383. 3. This innovation would greatly separate us from the Greek liturgy which has neither Mass nor Communion;

384. 4. There is also a practical reason: we are human, and among men when the father dies one does not eat but rather remains silent and sorrowful;

385. 5. This would constitute the introduction of a devotional element into the liturgy on a day which has always remained close to the primitive liturgy.

386. Father Antonelli observed that:

387.   1. Communion had been administered in classical times and during the Middle Ages.

388.   2. Holy Communion on Good Friday has a profound theological significance: there is no Eucharistic sacrifice, but all share in the fruits of the redemption by Communion with the Divine Victim, having commemorated the bloody sacrifice of Christ in the adoration of the cross.

389.   Father Löw mentioned that communion [on Good Friday] ceased in 15th century when the communion of the faithful became less frequent. Pius X brought the people back to the Eucharist.

390.   Father Bea was very favorable to general communion on Good Friday for exegetical and theological reasons: the Eucharist is the special fruit of the Passion of Our Lord.

391.   Father Albareda asked whether it might at least be possible to relate the adoration of the cross more closely to communion. Provision would be made for this by simplifying the procession with the Blessed Sacrament from the altar of repose to the Mass altar.

392.   Article 37 – *Benedizione della Croce.*

Father Bea observed that it did not seem opportune to introduce this element *ex novo*. While in the Oriental liturgies such a blessing is very frequent at the end of a ceremony commemorating the mystery of the cross, it was completely unknown in the Roman liturgy. The Commission accepted this comment and agreed that it would not be opportune to introduce a blessing with the cross.

393.   The meeting ended at 7 p.m..

Minutes of the 27th Meeting

394.   [The meeting was held] at 4:30 p.m. on Tuesday, January 23, 1953 in the *Palazzo della Cancelleria* in the apartments of His Eminence Clemente the Lord Cardinal Micara, Prefect of the Sacred Congregation of Rites.

395.   All were present except His Excellency Msgr. Carinci and Father Löw who were indisposed.

396.   The meeting was devoted to the clarification of a number of points relating to Holy Thursday and Good Friday which had been raised during a discussion at previous meetings.

397.   *Mattutino delle tenebre.*

Since the people were accustomed to the singing of the Matins of *Tenebre* in many places, as a transitional measure, the *Relator-Generalis* proposed extending the faculty granted to Cathedrals to anticipate *Matins* to all who wished to have it.

398. The proposal was accepted and the rubric of the *Ordo* was accordingly modified.

399. *Sepolcri.*

Father Antonelli proposed that devotion to the [Easter] Sepulcher be permitted until the liturgical rites of the following day so as to avoid breaking too briskly with the present usage.

400. The Commission agreed. Article 18 of the *Ordo* would be modified accordingly. Article 19 would be suppressed. Father Albareda insisted that parish priests should be explicitly required to regulate devotion at the [Easter] Sepulcher so that all the parochial associations would take turns for adoration and gradually eliminate those pious practices which were profane or which gave rise to distractions.

401. *Oratio pro Judaeis.*

The *Relator-Generalis* returned to the question of the terms *perfidi* and *perfidia*. He asked if it might not be appropriate to change these to *increduli* and *incredulitas* because:

402. 1. The term sounds negative today in the vernacular, and the original meaning of "unbelief" or "infidelity" is no longer understood. The term [does not] mean "perfidy". Since this was the case, the Sacred Congregation of Rites had granted a faculty to use those terms in vernacular translations.

403. 2. It seemed opportune to remove this apparent contradiction when the *Ordo* would have to be reordered and revised.

404. Father Albareda did not favor any modification of the present text. He pointed out that Pius XI had already examined this question, and he had forbidden any changes. He also pointed out that a change of this kind could be seen as a concession with political overtones given the persecution of the Jews that was going on in Russia. Any decision in the matter would have to be left to the Holy Father. Msgr. Dante added that complaints had reached [the Sacred Congregation of Rites] because of the continued presence of those terms in the Missal. Notwithstanding that, he was of the opinion that nothing should be changed.

405. Father Bea favored a change because the principle applied in the new version of the Psalms should also be used here, that is avoid all expressions [or terms] which had acquired new meaning with the evolution of the vernacular languages. However, taking the political considerations into account, he too believed that the matter should be referred to the decision of the Holy Father. The Commission agreed on this point.

406. The *Relator-Generalis* announced that the next concern of the Commission would be the preparation of a decree of the Sacred Congregation of Rites to simplify the rubrics as much as possible taking as a principle the fact that

the liturgical books in use were not to be changed and that the task should be carried out without prejudice to the future work of the reform, e.g. [of the simplification, he mentioned] octaves, vigils, prayers, Athanasian creed, etc. This work was ardently desired by the Holy Father and had been communicated to his Eminence the previous year. The collection of material necessary for the project was well advanced and would be presented to the Commission.

407. The meeting ended at 5:20 p.m..

Minutes of the 28th Meeting

408. [The meeting was held] at 5 p.m. on Tuesday, March 11, 1953 in the *Palazzo della Cancelleria* in the apartments of His Eminence Clemente the Lord Cardinal Micara, Prefect of the Sacred Congregation of Rites.

409. All were present except Father Löw.

410. The Commission had been called to examine some questions concerning Holy Thursday and the Easter Vigil that had been raised by various bishops. His Eminence believed that it would be opportune to hear the views of the Commission before replying to them.

411. The questions concerned the following points:

412. *Ora della Veglia* [Time of the Vigil]. Some of the German speaking bishops had asked for a faculty to anticipate the Vigil at 7 p.m. or 8 p.m. or to celebrate it at 3 a.m. or 4 a.m. on Easter Sunday morning. The reply was negative. Father Albareda pointed out that existing usage had to be accommodated to the new rite and not *vice versa*. The Easter Vigil is the only liturgical celebration to commemorate the mystery of the "proper" time. This was historically certain.

413. This important fact had to be preserved.

414. The other members of the Commission were of the same mind. Exceptional cases could eventually be resolved by indult.

415. *Digunio Eucaristico* [Eucharistic fast].

The prescription of the Apostolic Constitution *Christus Dominus* of January 6, 1953 would have to apply to the Vigil.

416. *Suono delle campane* [Ringing of Bells].

Given that this was a period of transition, it would be appropriate for the Commission to abstain from making any decision in this matter, and to leave its regulations to the local bishops. No decision should be made either with regard to the proposal to broadcast the sound of bells on the radio.

417. *Giovedì Santo* [Holy Thursday].

The Commission decided to change nothing for the moment. The Sacred Congregation of Rites would give an official reply to the individuals who had asked about the matter.

418.   The session rose at 5:45 having recited the *Agimus*.

Minutes of the 29th Meeting

419.   [The meeting was held] at 5 p.m. on Friday, November 6, 1953 in the *Palazzo della Cancelleria* in the apartments of His Eminence Clemente the Lord Cardinal Micara, Prefect of the Sacred Congregation of Rites.

420.   All members attended.

421.   This was the first meeting of the Commission since the summer vacation. The 29th Meeting of the Commission opened another year of the Commission's work. According to the letter of convocation, the Commission would resume the discussion and examination of the *Memoria* from Article 139, the point at which the discussion had ceased on July 8, 1952 (23rd Meeting).

422.   Articles 139-142 – *Santi e apostoli "nazionali"* [National Saints and Apostles].

Msgr. Dante observed that the Commission would have to bear in mind constantly that it was concerned with the reform of the "Roman" calendar and not with the reform of the universal calendar. This aspect would have to be emphasized and the proper calendars left with all of their Saints. As the Oriental Church does not celebrate the Saints of the Latin Church, and likewise the Latin Church does not celebrate the Orientals.

423.   His Eminence observed that some Saints would have to be inserted into all the calendars because of their importance for the entire Church. Father Albareda reiterated the Cardinal's point adding that in the past the Church had added new non-Roman Saints to the calendar. Today she should have no hesitation in doing the same when good reasons suggested it. The inconvenience of having too many Saints could be avoided by introducing groups of "national" Saints. For example, all of the Apostles of the Nordic countries would be grouped together, as well as those of missionary countries headed, or course, by St. Francis Xavier. Commenting on the term "national" Saints, Father Bea believed that the expression "national" should be eliminated because:

1. Emphasizing nationality would create thousands of difficulties;

2. If a United States of Europe is ever arrived at, the idea of nationality must be attenuated. These Saints will have to be grouped on the basis of a higher and more universal criterion, for example, their charity, the service to the Church or to the apostolate, etc..

424.   The Commission accepted this idea and proposed that it be adopted as the

guiding principle for the definitive revision of the calendar.

425. Articles 143-147 – *Fondatori* [Founders].

The question had already been raised separately at the 22nd meeting, held on June 25, 1952: (Minutes p. 61). Therefore, it would not be revisited.

426. Article 148

With regard to the desire, expressed by some, to introduce a greater number of holy priests to the calendar, and especially more recent Saints (e.g. St. Giuseppe Cafasso, St. Benedetto Cottolengo), the principle of not excessively burdening the calendar would have to be insisted upon. Priests were already well represented in the calendar. The readings, however, would have to emphasize the various apostolates to which they had dedicated themselves to for the edification of our times.

427. With regard to martyrs and the comment that, although recent centuries had produced numerous martyrs, few were represented in the calendar; account would have to be taken of the fact that very few of the post-sixteenth century martyrs had been canonized. Also, martyrdom already had a preferential place in the entire liturgy.

428. Article 149: *Santuari.*

It was unanimously agreed to remove the feasts of sanctuaries from the universal calendar. They would be inserted in the national or diocesan propers.

429. Articles 150-157 – *Feste minori del Signore* [Minor feasts of the Lord].

[The Commission] unanimously agreed to retain the following feasts: Holy Cross on September 14, the Holy Name of Jesus between January 1 and 5 as had been agreed by the Commission when studying article 47 of the *Memoria* on December 16, 1950 (cf. Minutes p. 12), and all other feasts were to be eliminated. There was some hesitation with regard to the feast of the Most Precious Blood (July 1). Not for any intrinsic reasons, but merely because it had been raised to a "double of the first class" as recently as 1933 by Pius XI.

430. The meeting closed with the usual prayer at 6 p.m..

Minutes of the 30th Meeting

431. [The meeting was held] at 5 p.m. on November 27, 1953 in the *Palazzo della Cancelleria* in the apartments of His Eminence Clemente the Lord Cardinal Micara, Prefect of the Sacred Congregation of Rites.

432. All members [of the Commission] attended.

433. The minutes were read. Father Bea observed that the feast of the Transfiguration had been omitted from the list of the minor dominical

feasts. It was unanimously inserted because it commemorated an evangelical event and because it was celebrated in the entire Church, both in the East and the West.

434. The *Relator-Generalis* then represented the question of the feast of the Most Precious Blood of Our Lord Jesus Christ (Article 157) for the Commission consideration, given that some hesitation had arisen in its regards.

435. After an interesting exchange of views, all of the consulters agreed that, *per se*, the feast should be eliminated. Its abolition, however, was not regarded as opportune given that its elevation to a higher grade had been relatively recent. In conclusion, the Commission indicated that it tended towards its suppression but suspended a decision for the present moment. The question will again be discussed when the definitive draft of the calendar will be examined.

436. Article 159 – *Nome di Maria* [The Name of Mary].

All agreed to retain this feast since it corresponded to the feast of the Holy Name of Jesus and because of its popularity.

437. Article 160 – *I titoli della Mercede e del Carmine* [The Titles of Our Lady of Mercy and Our Lady of Mount Carmel].

Msgr. Dante would eliminate [the feast of Our Lady of Mercy and reduce that of [Our Lady of] Mount Carmel to a commemoration or to a *Memoria*. Father Löw agreed. Father Albareda thought that both titles should be retained or abandoned without making a distinction in deference to the two religious families linked to them. Ultimately, he would have no difficulty were both reduced to a simple commemoration. Father Bea would abolish the feast of [Our Lady of] Mercy whose object – the Redemption of Slaves – and since the Order itself no longer enjoyed their former popularity or importance. [Our Lady of] Mount Carmel he wished to conserve as a commemoration on July 16. The ferial office should be assigned to it so as to avoid the inconvenience of having the office of a Saint clash with the commemoration of Our Lady. The Commission tended towards the abandonment of the Feast of [Our Lady of] Mercy and reduction of that of [Our Lady of] Mount Carmel to a commemoration. A final decision was postponed pending the definitive formulation of the calendar.

439. Article 161 – *Il Rosario Mariano*.

All agreed that a feast commemorating the holy Rosary could not be omitted. The rosary itself should not be celebrated, but Our Lady under this title. It was agreed thus:

1. to abolish the name *sacratissimi* and to denominate the feast: *Festum B.M.V. de Rosario*;

2. the Office was to be revised.

440. Article 162 – *I dolori di Maria.*

   All agreed to abolish this feast in Lent and to retain the feast observed in September because it was deeply rooted in popular piety. A revision of the Office would be desirable as well as the restoration of the original [liturgical] color of violet.

441. Article 163 – *Apparizione di Lourdes.*

   The Commission, when discussing sanctuaries (cf. Minutes, 29th Meeting, November 6, 1953), had already expressed a negative view with regard to the date [of this feast].

442. Article 164 – *Maternità di Maria.*

   All agreed to the suppression of this feast on October 11 so as to resore it to its original date in the primitive Roman liturgy, January 1.

443. Article 165 – *Cuore Immacolate di Maria.*

   It should not be suppressed. After an exchange of views, it was agreed that the date for its observance should be that of Saturday after the Sacred Heart of Jesus.

444. Article 166 – *Inserzione delle feste in futuro.*

   In general terms, the following principle was agreed on so as to avoid the indiscriminate introduction of feasts into the universal calendar: evident use for the life or piety of the Church.

445. Article 168 – *Feste della Passione.*

   Unanimously agreed to eliminate them from the liturgy because the *tempus Passionis* and the feast of the Holy Cross already covered them.

446. Article 169 – *Cuore eucaristico di Gesù.*

   Corpus Christi and the feast of the Sacred Heart of Jesus seemed sufficient to honor this title.

447. Article 170 – *Sacerdozio di Cristo.*

   Sufficient provision had been made for this feast with the votive mass *DNIC Summi et Aeterni Sacerdotis.* On the other hand, devotion (or "piety") should not be confused with "liturgy". The feast of the priesthood of Christ seemed to belong more to the former than to the latter.

448. Article 448 – *Vita interiore di Gesù.*

   For the same reasons all agreed that it should be omitted.

449. Article 172 – *Triumphus catholicae Religionis.*

   Negative reply and for the same reasons.

450. Article 173 – *Festa Mariana mensile* [The monthly Marian feast].

   Already provided for with the Office *S. Mariae in sabbato* which, with the reduction of the feasts, would now be recited more frequently.

451.   Article 174 – *Maggio Mariano*.

The idea should not be favored since it would confuse liturgy and devotions. That there should be some Marian feasts in May was not opposed (at the present time it is one of the few with none in the universal calendar).

452.   Article 175 – *Maria Regina Mundi*.

The Secretariat of State of His Holiness had transmitted requests from two bishops asking that this feast be instituted. It indicted that the Holy Father would not be against [the idea]. Msgr. Carinci added that these two petitions should be [seen in the light] of a further two hundred requests that had come to the Sacred Congregation of Rites in recent times.

453.   A long discussion on the subject ensued. The positive reasons [for the institution of the feast are]:

1. Marian theology has clear and precise principles from which the regality of Mary can be demonstrated;

2. This is not merely a matter of moral precedence but of a true and real participation in the kinships of her Son, but subordinate to and relative to that kingship of her Son. It derives from and depends on the divine maternity and on the association of Mary with the work of Redemption;

3. The regality of Mary is an external effect of her prerogatives (Maternity, Immaculate Conception, Co-Redemptrix, and Mediatrix) in that although created, she is raised above all creation including the angels;

4. As a complement to the feast of Christ the King a feast of the Queenship of May would not be inappropriate, bearing in mind, however, the due distance between God-made-man and His mother;

5. Finally, pastorally, in this undeniable development of Marian piety, a feast of the Queenship of Mary, already admitted in the piety of the peoples, would present the Mother of God in the context of the fullness of her glory. It would not be confused with the Assumption in which the formal object is the bodily Assumption [of Our Lady].

454.   The negative reasons are:

1. The liturgy should not promote conceptual feasts, and the universal calendar already has an abundance of Marian feasts;

2. A feast of the "Queenship" of Mary lacked a proper, formal subject: it is something beautiful but vague and has no Biblical foundation;

3. The idea of Queenship is already contained and celebrated in the Feast of the Assumption. Hence a particular feast would be a duplication;

4. The parallel between the Feasts of Our Lord and those of Our Lady (Nativity, Name, Death, Passion, etc.) is only in part valid and only to a certain degree. Mary is not on the same level as Christ.

455. Having counted the votes, the following results were announced: 4 in favor (His Eminence, Father Antonelli, Father Löw, Father Bugnini); 4 against (Msgr. Carinci, Msgr. Dante, Father Albareda, Father Bea). Finally, it was decided to ask the consultators of the Sacred Congregation of Rites for a written *votum*: Dom Capelle, Msgr. Righetti, and Father Jungmann.

456. *Maria Mediatrice.*

    The title was acceptable as would be a such a feast. However, it was regarded as inopportune to introduce it or suggest it since there had been no definition of a doctrine concerning the mediation [of Mary], and a liturgical feast would influence a theological proposition.

457. Article 175 – *Festa del Papa.*

    The establishment on January 18 of a "liturgical" feast for the Pope was rejected. Father Albareda's suggestion of drawing up a new schema of *Ordinationes* making the anniversary of the Pope's election or Coronation obligatory for the entire Church found acceptance. Father Löw observed that the question could be examined again when the Commission returned to the question of the *collectae imperatae.*

458. Article 176 – *Giornata delle Missioni* [Day of the Missions].

    All agreed that it could not be set for January 6 for reasons of convenience, even though the idea is suitable. All things considered, it seemed that its present date and form were the best available solution.

459. This article concluded the examination of the first part of the *Memoria* on the calendar. The study of questions relating to the breviary would commence at the next meeting. Meanwhile, a draft of the reformed calendar would be drawn up and placed before the Commission.

460. The next meeting will take place on Friday, December 11.

461. The meeting ended at 7 p.m. with the usual prayer, *Agimus.*

Minutes of the 31st Meeting

**This is the first meeting under the Presidency
of the New Prefect of the Sacred Congregation of Rites
His Eminence Cardinal Gaetano Cicognani.**

462. [The meeting was held] at 5:30 p.m. on Tuesday, January 12, 1954 at the Pontifical Spanish College in the apartments of the Lord Cardinal Gaetano Cicognani, Prefect of the Sacred Congregation of Rites.

463. All members attended.

464. The minutes of the previous meeting were read and approved. The question of the institution of the feast of "*Maria Regina*" was again raised. A *pro-memoria* had previously been circulated to the members of the Commission containing a letter from the Secretariat of State to the Sacred

Congregation of Rites seeking an opinion on the institution of the feast. Copies of the replies of Father Jungmann, Dom Capelle, and Msgr. Righetti to a similar question addressed to them following the last meeting were also circulated.

465.   The *Relator-Generalis* communicated that the Holy Father had received fourteen petitions for the institution of this feast, including one from the Bishops of the Lucano. He mentioned that since 1933 a group called the "*Movimento pro regalitate Mariae*" had intensely promoted the institution of this feast. More than 950 bishops had supported the petition, which was contained in 11 volumes. These had recently been presented to the Holy Father. The *Relator-Generalis* noted that from the time of the Council of Ephesus (431) [Christian] art had constantly represented the Blessed Virgin as Queen. Patristic and Medieval literature also affirmed [her as Queen]. She is constantly invoked as such in the Liturgy.

466.   A liturgical feast would confirm this general sentiment which was very deeply rooted in the Christian people.

467.   Father Löw emphasized that the idea of Queenship of Mary is very common in the Church's tradition. It might be asked if the institution of a particular feast were justifiable, or if it were dangerous, since people could attempt to put Christ the King and Mary, Queen, on the same level.

468.   Msgr. Dante, as far as the feast was concerned, was favorable, but suggested that its title should be "*Regina Ecclesiae*", as proposed by Msgr. Righetti.

469.   Father Albareda placed the question in the context of the liturgical reform and associated himself with the likes of Abbot Capelle and Father Jungmann, even though in the end he would love, with all his heart, to see the feast instituted.

470.   On further reflection, Father Bea said that he now completely favored [the move]. All tradition, including liturgical tradition, concurred in proclaiming the Queenship of Mary. Hymns, antiphons, and responsories all celebrated Our Lady under this title. Theologically, her Regality could be proved from her maternity, her association with the Redemption, which continued in the mediation and distribution of graces. Her Regality is real and not merely poetic. For this reason, together with Our Lord, the title of "*Regina Universi*", and not merely "*Regina Ecclesiae*", is fittingly attributed to her. On this, all tradition concurs unanimously, as is the Church's constant teaching. It can be said that following the definition of the Immaculate Conception which is the last personal Marian privilege to have been defined, attention can be more "sociologically" focused with regard to the study of the privileges and prerogatives of the Blessed Virgin Mary in relation to her influence in the Church, that is, in the Kingdom of God. This is undoubtedly a development in Marian doctrine. It has been

471.   Msgr. Carinci also said that he now favored [the institution of the feast].

472.   In calling for the votes, His Eminence declared that, as far as he was concerned, a feast of the Queenship of Mary seemed completely justified from the perspective of dogma, liturgy, and tradition. He did not share the fears advanced by Dom Capelle and by Father Jungmann that the faithful would be led to place the Regality of Mary on the same level as that of Christ. The simplest of the faithful are well able to make distinctions when it comes to two different things. An appropriate report would be drawn up and presented to the Holy Father after the Commission should have approved it.

473.   Examination of the *Memoria* then resumed, commencing with the second part which concerns the Roman Breviary. Father Antonelli explained the doctrinal principles upon which the reform would have to be based. These were amply explicated in the *Memoria* (pp. 169-200).

474.   The following questions were then examined:

475.   Articles 209-211 – Should the present division of the Offices into seven hours be retained, and for every hour should the present number of Psalms be retained?

476.   The reply was unanimously affirmative.

477.   Article 212 – Should the continuous reading of the Psalms be retained in the ferial arrangement of the Psalms? All replied affirmatively.

478.   Article 213 – In the festive cycle of Psalms should the traditional principle of a specific progressive selection be maintained? Reply: affirmative.

479.   Article 214 – In the ancient festive cycles for the principal feasts, should the Psalms be shortened to those elements essentially relating to the feasts? All were in agreement. All agreed that the division of the Psalms into strophes, which was highlighted in the new version, would greatly facilitate the work [of the Commission].

480.   Articles 215-214 – Should the Psalter be distributed over two weeks?

481.   The reply was unanimously for the [adoption] of such a principle.

482.   The examination of the proposal contained in Article 217 was deferred to the next meeting.

483.   The meeting concluded with the usual prayer at 7 p.m..

Minutes of the 32nd Meeting

484.   [The meeting was held] at 5:30 p.m. on Friday, January 22, 1954 at the Pontifical Spanish College in the apartments of the Lord Cardinal Gaetano Cicognani, Prefect of the Sacred Congregation of Rites.

Appendix A: On the origin of the Pontifical Commission for the Reform of the Sacred Liturgy and on its work from 1948 to 1960

485. All members attended.

486. The *Relator-Generalis* put two questions to the Commission which had to be resolved before preparing the *pro-memoria* for the Holy Father on the institution of a Feast for "*Maria Regina*": the title and date of the feast. A few days previous to the meeting some notes [on the subject] had been circulated to the Commission.

487. *Title of the Feast.*

Father Löw tended towards the title "*Regina Mundi*", basing his argument on the positive fact that, as Leo XIII had consecrated the human race to the Sacred Heart of Jesus, Pius XII had officially consecrated mankind to the Immaculate Heart of Mary, confirming this act with a prayer, in which he refers to "*Maria Regina del Rosario*" as "*Regina del mondo*". This title dissipates any doubt about the difference between the Regality of Christ and that of Mary.

488. Msgr. Dante proposed a specification of the title and thought that of "*Regina coeli et terrae*" would cover everything.

489. Father Albareda said that the question of the title was connected with the theological basis of the feast.

490. If was the Regality of Mary is to be understood in relation to that of Jesus, there it would have to have the same extension [as His]. Hence, for Mary, the title of Queen, without limitation was appropriate. Were something added, it would limit the significance [of the title].

491. Father Bea shared Father Albareda's opinion. The title of Queen, without qualification, is more simple and more theologically grounded.

492. There was thus agreement with regard to the title of the Feast: *Festum B.V.M. Reginae*.

493. *Date of the Feast.*

May 1 was proposed and accepted unanimously.

494. Examination of the *Memoria* then reserved at Article 217: proposal for a biweekly distribution of the Psalms. Father Bea distributed a sheet on which he had made some observation with regard to this proposal.

495. 1. *Compline.* Psalms 4, 90, and 133 should be retained, possibly in their entirety, for both weeks.

496. 2. *Athanasian Creed.* This would be recited only on Trinity Sunday, at Prime, following the Psalms.

497. 3. *Psalm 118.* This would be retained at *Prime* for both weeks since it is particularly appropriate for this Hour, being a meditation on the law of God.

498. 4. *Vespers of Sunday.* It was decided to retain Psalms 109, 112, and 113, this last divided into three parts.

499. 5. A Psalm should never be divided between different hours, with the exception of Psalm 118.

500. 6. The Psalmody for Sunday should be reduced since the proposed project was too heavy.

501. 7. The question of the Canticles would have to be revisited. The Canticles of Moses and Abraham should be set aside and replaced by substitutes

502. 8. The festive Office should be conserved. It should differ from that of Sunday.

503. A draft of the reformed calendar was circulated. It would be examined during the coming meetings.

504. The meeting ended at 7 p.m..

Minutes of the 33rd Meeting

505. [The meeting took place] at 5:30 p.m. at the Pontifical Spanish College in the apartments of the Lord Cardinal Gaetano Cicognani, Prefect of the Sacred Congregation of Rites.

506. All members attended.

507. The draft of the *pro-memoria* on the institution of a feast of the Queenship of Mary from the Holy Father was examined. The draft that had been previously circulated was accepted in substance by the Commission. The only comments made can be reduced to the following:

508. 1. A better exposition of the theological basis for the feast would be desirable. Father Bea presented a new text on this subject, to be included on p. 3 [of the *pro-memoria* in place of the present [exposition]. All agreed to this.

509. 2. His Eminence thought that the simple list of the Fathers and ecclesiastical writers on p. 3 should be filled out by citing some passages emphasizing the title of Queen attributed to Mary. He desired that the triplet from Dante (*Paradise*, Cantos 23, 32, and 33) referring to Mary as Queen should also be mentioned. To his mind, it would also be good to include the *pro* and *contra* arguments that had emerged during the debate.

510. 3. The examples of *Maria Regina* taken from liturgical art, cited on p. 3, were practically all taken from Roman sources. Hence, it should be mentioned that such was the vastness of the available material that it had to be restricted to Rome.

511. 4. Father Bea said that the parallel with the feast of Christ the King, mentioned on p. 6, would have to be expressed in such a way as to avoid and suggestion that it constituted the theological basis of the feast.

512. 5. In addition to the title of *Maria Regina* chosen by the Commission, it would be opportune to mention other titles [that had been considered]: for

example: "*Regina Ecclesiae*", "*Regina Universi*", "*Regina coeli et terrae*".

513.   6. Father Bea believed that it should be explicitly stated that May 1 had been chosen [as an appropriate date for the Feast] because popular piety reserves the month of May for special Marian devotion. Hence, May would seem a suitable time for the feast. This needed to be said so as to avoid the idea that the Church, in giving prominence to this feast, had been influenced by the external factor of Workers' Day.

514.   7. Father Albareda suggested that the *pro-memoria* should not mention which consultors had favored or not favored the exertion of the feast.

515.   The Commission then began its examination of the revised calendar, which had already been distributed. Father Löw's observations on the variations had also been circulated.

516.   January.

517.   January 1-6. The proposed arrangement was accepted.

518.   January 7. The founders of the Trinitarians and Mercedarians. Four Saints seemed too many to group together. The founders of the Mercedarians would be left at this date: The founder of the Trinitarians would be assigned to the November 4, the closest date to *dies natalis* of St. Felix de Valois (November 3). Given the reduced significance of both religious families, both feasts would have to be reduced from III to IV class.

519.   January 8. It was decided to remove St. Andrea Corsini whose importance for the Universal Church did not seem so significant.

520.   January 9. Holy Family. It would have been desirable to celebrate this feast on January 13, Octave of the Epiphany, but this will depend on the arrangements for the Sunday and their reference to the various epiphanies of the Lord. The question had to be suspended.

521.   January 18. Chair of Peter. Several reasons support maintaining this feast on January 18, rather than on February 22. All agreed to the elimination of the commemoration of St. Paul.

522.   January 23. St. Polycarp could be united to St. Ignatius on October 17 without difficulty.

523.   January 25. The proposal to abolish the feast of the Conversion of St. Paul provoked a serious discussion. His Eminence asked the Commission to reflect again on the matter and postponed a decision until the following meeting.

524.   The meeting ended at 7:15 p.m..

Minutes of the 34th Meeting

525.   [The meeting was held] at 5:30 p.m. on Friday, February 19, 1954 at the Pontifical Spanish College in the apartments of the Lord Cardinal Gaetano Cicognani, Prefect of the Sacred Congregation of Rites.

526. All members of the Commission were in attendance.

527. The meeting began by examining the *pro-memoria* on the institution of the feast *Maria Regina* to be presented to the Holy Father. After some minor changes, the *pro-memoria* was approved.

528. The examination of the biweekly Psalter then resumed. It had been reworked by Father Löw and Father Bea, especially the parts pertaining to Vespers, Lauds, Prime and Compline. Father Bea proposed that the first Psalm in the festive Lauds, Psalm 66 (*Deus miseratur nostri et benedicat nobis*), be substituted with Psalm 46 of Wednesday.

529. Examination of the revised calendar was then resumed.

530. The *Relator-Generalis* again raised the question of the Conversion of St. Paul (January 25) about which no conclusion had been made at the last meeting.

531. Father Löw suggested combining the feast with that of the June 30. The Commission, however, decided to retain it. It proposed that it should be a *memoria* or a commemoration at most.

532. Msgr. Dante said that he was very uncertain about the matter and agreed with the proposal of uniting it with that of June 30.

533. Repeating the distinction to be made between piety and liturgy, and recalling the principles guiding the work of the Commission, Father Albareda doubted the appropriation of the feast of the Conversion: were it necessary to retain it, then it should be either a *memoria* or a commemoration.

534. Father Bea proposed uniting the feast with that of June 30, and giving greater emphasis to the Conversion in the liturgical formulas of that day.

535. Father Antonelli agreed to this proposal.

536. Msgr. Carinci underlined the fact that the Conversion of St. Paul had always been given such importance in the Church's history and that, to him, a liturgical feast [for this event] seems indispensable.

538. A long discussion ensued.

539. In the end, it was decided to reflect further on the question, given that opinion was divided. A decision would be postponed to the next meeting.

540. The *Agimus* closed the session at 7:10 p.m..

Minutes of the 35th Meeting

541. [The meeting was held] at 5:30 p.m. on Tuesday, March 9, 1954 at the Pontifical Spanish College in the apartments of the Lord Cardinal Gaetano Cicognani, Prefect of the Sacred Congregation of Rites.

542. All members were present.

543. Examination of the bi-weekly Psalter in relation to Matins, Terce, Sext,

and None resumed on the basis of a proposal made by Father Löw and
Father Bea. Special attention was given to the Canticles, three of which
were new, having been newly translated *ex novo* by Father Bea. Of those
already in use, three were retained, with many changes. A number of
words were shifted in the new translations, so as to facilitate the singing of
the versicle.

544. A question of principle was raised about the Canticle of Habakkuk, which
is presently used on Wednesday and which is retained for Wednesday
in the bi-weekly Psalter. The Canticle had been shortened by omitting
two intermediary passages, verses 9-12 and 17-27. This helped to lighten
the Canticle. The logical sequence of thought was not interrupted. The
liturgical use of the Psalm conserved the essence of the Canticle.

545. Father Albareda observed that such a procedure – of shortening and omitting
verses – was new to the liturgical tradition. It would leave the flank exposed
for the critics. He believed that it would be better to end the Canticle at a
certain point, and then add on the final two verses to bring it to a close.

546. Father Bea observed that the omitted verses were merely amplifications of
ideas expressed in the preceding verses. Their omission would not affect
the logical sequence of thought. This would not happen were the Canticle
divided in two.

547. The Commission tended towards accepting this solution.

548. The question of the antiphon for Matins was raised.

549. The adoption of a bi-weekly Psalter, the division of the Psalm into strophes
and their distinction, implied the composition of many antiphons *ex novo*.
It could be asked whether it is opportune to retain antiphons for every
Psalm. This would result in prolonging and burdening the Office. Perhaps
a single antiphon could be used for every Nocturn in the Ordinary
psalmody (Sunday and non-festive ferials).

550. The Commission unanimously accepted this last solution.

551. With regard to the existing antiphons Msgr. Dante observed that they
should all be conserved so as not to lose much of the Gregorian melodies.
This question had already been raised and resolved in this sense when the
question of introducing the new version of the Psalms with the Liturgy
was considered.

552. Father Bea commented that his had been a provisional solution. The
adaptation of the antiphon to the Psalm from which it was taken was
indispensable.

553. Father Albareda said that the Vatican Library received several requests
every day for photographs of musical codices, especially for Gregorian
chant. Many of those requests came from Protestant or Jewish sources in

America where there is a truly obsessive interest in research into Gregorian chant and poliphony. There would be grave damage done, he added, were the Church now to abandon this sacred patrimony, while so many others are displaying such interest in it.

554. Father Antonelli suggested seeking the advice of some experts on the subject. It should come from the different musical currents and schools, so as to have the broadest and most accurate picture possible of the present situation. This should be presented to the Commission together with a *pro-memoria*.

555. The *Relator-Generalis* announced that some bishops had requested that the sound of bells from Rome should not be transmitted by Radio on Holy Saturday morning.

556. The matter would be addressed directly by asking the directors of Vatican Radio and of the Italian Radio [RAI] to suspend such transmissions.

557. Finally, Msgr. Dante asked if a concession should be granted permitting evening Mass to be celebrated solemnly or in pontifical rite. Some bishops had made the request.

558. Various members of the Commission observed:

1. Evening Masses are permitted to satisfy the dominical precept, and not to transport the Sunday liturgy into the evening;

2. Care should be taken to ensure that among the faithful the idea that Sunday is the Lord's day is not forgotten, by passing the morning at work or at entertainment, and postponing until the evening the sacred rites that sanctify the feast.

559. The Commission took the view that all such changes on festive days should be firmly opposed. There should not be extension of the present discipline which, as a remedial exception, provided for the celebration of a read evening Mass.

560. The meeting concluded with the usual prayer at 7 p.m..

Minutes of the 36th Meeting

561. [The meeting was held] at 5:30 p.m. on Tuesday, March 23, 1954 at the Pontifical Spanish College in the apartments of the Lord Cardinal Gaetano Cicognani, Prefect of the Sacred Congregation of Rites.

562. All members attended.

563. The *Relator-Generalis* announced that the Sacred Congregation of Holy Office had asked for the opinion of the Sacred Congregation of Rites with regard to the results of the restored Easter Vigil. This had been requested with a view to clarifying the question of the Eucharistic fast for the clergy and laity who attended the Vigil.

564. Father Antonelli read the reply that had been prepared. It was unanimously accepted [by the Commission] following some minor emendations which were necessary in stating the Commission's view.

565. Examination of the reformed calendar was then resumed, beginning where it had been interrupted on February 19.

566. January 25. Conversion of St. Paul. This question, which had already been discussed and was now in suspense, would be taken up again when it came to consider the feast of St. Paul on the June 30.

567. January 28. St. Albert the Great and St. Thomas. Father Bugnini, Father Löw, and Msgr. Dante recommended that the proposal to group these Saints together on this date should not be changed.

568. Father Albareda was of the same mind. He stressed that what was required by the principles of reform, even if at times costly, obliged that the present situation be suspended, even if everybody was attached to it. The combination of two holy Doctors seemed perfectly legitimate, as was already noted and previously agreed. This [case] was not notably inconvenient, remembering although, that St. Thomas occupies an eminent position in the Church.

569. This was not an attempt to express the greater or lesser importance of the Saints. It was a matter of trying to find the correct place for them in the official prayer of the Church. Moreover, granting two feasts [for these two Saints] would not avoid offending the susceptibilities of other orders, whose Doctors feasts had been combined.

570. Father Bea agreed with the date of January 28. He retained, however, that St. Thomas should be celebrated on his own. After St. Augustine, he is the Church's most important Doctor. Moreover, all Catholic schools celebrate the Feast of St. Thomas, not that of St. Albert the Great. Should it not be possible to combine [St. Albert the Great] with some other Doctor, in the final analysis, Father Bea would not object to the feast being celebrated *a solo* given that he was the patron the sciences. Thus, two feasts could be erected, one celebrating the Patron of the Sacred Sciences, the other the Patron of the Profane Sciences. Msgr. Carinci believed that the feast of St. Thomas should remain separate.

572. His Eminence reminded [the Commission] that the liturgy should reflect and interpret the life of the Church. Consequently, the Saints would have to be given a place of due honor.

573. Father Antonelli proposed that there should be further reflection on the question to see what arrangement could be made for the feast St. Albert the Great.

574. S. Agnes "secundo". Some trace of this feast should be retained because of its uniqueness in the liturgy and because of its antiquity (it is already to be

found in the *Leonianum*). The Commission decided to sacrifice the feast since its origins are not entirely certain and because the Saint is already sufficiently commemorated on January 21.

575. February.

576. February 4. With regard to the Japanese Martyrs, Father Bea observed that in the lessons it should be stated that they belong to several religious families. He believed that some other modern martyr, not belonging to the Company of Jesus, should be added. However, it was noted that there were no other canonized martyrs from this period.

577. March.

578. March 4. St. Casimir. There would be no objection to his suppression. Some group of lay Saints, however, should be celebrated.

579. March 24. St. Gabriel, the Archangel. It was proposed to leave the feast as a *memoria* rather then having a feast between December 10-17. Father Bea suggested uniting the feast with that of St. Raphael on October 24. The formula for the Mass and Breviary could be chosen so that they referred to both. Father Löw observed that this would have the advantage of placing all the Holy Angels in the *"pars autumnalis"* of the Breviary. This would allow the formulation of the *"Commune Angelorum"* for this part alone.

580. The other dates in the reformed calendar presented no difficulties. Therefore, the next question for consideration was the month of April.

581. The meeting closed at 7 p.m..

Minutes of the 37th Meeting

582. [The meeting was held] at 5:30 p.m. on Friday, April 3, 1954 at the Pontifical Spanish College in the apartments of the Lord Cardinal Gaetano Cicognani, Prefect of the Sacred Congregation of Rites.

583. All members attended.

584. The minutes were read and approved. The Cardinal called the Commission's attention to the question of the feast of St. Gabriel, the Archangel.

585. The three holy Archangels occupy such an important place in the economy of salvation that it seemed opportune to assign three separate feasts to them. His Eminence tended towards retaining the feast of St. Gabriel on March 24, reducing it to a simple commemoration, so as to conserve its association with the feast of the Annunciation which is of primary importance for the redemption.

586. Father Bea thought that it could be transferred to the beginning of Advent for the same reason.

587. Father Löw remarked that since Advent did not have a fixed date it should become a movable feast set for the Monday after the first Sunday of Advent.

588. Father Bugnini proposed December 16, at the beginning of the period of immediate preparation for Christmas. This was given serious consideration.

589. The question of the great Doctors arose once again.

590. In order to find a convenient solution for the feast of St. Albert the Great, and to combine him with some non-Doctor, Father Löw had prepared and circulated a *pro-memoria* proposing a new arrangement for Doctors. In this scheme, St. Augustine and St. Thomas, exponents of the two great periods in the history of theology, would be assigned separate feasts. The other Doctors, including the four "minor" Doctors would be combined with St. Albert the Great and assigned a single feast. In the absence of other Doctors, St. Anthony of Florence could also be added.

591. From the discussions, it was immediately obvious that the combination of St. Albert the Great with St. Anthony of Florence would present no difficulties. Consequently, the remaining questions could be examined on the basis of the original proposal that is:

592. 1. It was not opportune to combine the great Doctors. This would create the difficulty of many minor Saints having separate feasts;

593. 2. St. Thomas should have a separate feast;

594. 3. Whatever solution was arrived at, it would be important that it have a plausible basis. It should also reflect the objective criteria applied by the Commission.

595. The conclusion was this: Combine St. Albert the Great with St. Anthony and leave the others as originally proposed: i.e. St. Thomas and the great Doctors of antiquity on their own, the remaining eight together.

596. The Commission thus moved to consider another unresolved question from the proceeding meeting: lay Saints, on which Father Löw had prepared a very useful note. It was suggest that a group of lay Saints should be chosen from among the following names: St. Casimir, St. Nicholas of Flues, St. Rocco, St. Omobono, St. Joseph Benedict Labre.

597. While the proposal was not unacceptable, but other lay Saints would have to be taken into account, who had been raised to the glory of the altar in recent times: St. Dominic Savio, Contardo Ferrini, Ludovico Necchi, Giuseppe Toniolo, Frederick Ozanam, Bartolo Longo, and others.

598. The Commission postponed a decision to another time, but proposed a *memoria* or a commemoration on the day proper to St. Rocco, St. Nicholas of Flues, St. Joseph Benedict Labre.

599. One final question arose concerning the Most Holy Forty Martyrs and St. Francesca Romana. Contrary to what had been decided, Father Löw proposed a commemoration for the forty martyrs on March 9 since their

deeds are certain and very ancient. A *memoria* was proposed for St. Francesca Romana because her cult is almost exclusively limited to Rome.

600.   The Commission accepted the proposal.

601.   Examination of the reformed calendar then resumed.

602.   April.

603.   April 2. St. Francesco de Paula. A commemoration rather than a simple *memoria* should be made.

604.   April 5. St. Vincent Ferreri. A *memoria* would be made.

605.   April 14. St. Justin. It would be preferable to combine him with St. Irenaeus on June 27.

606.   April 24. St. Mary of St. Euphrasia Pelletier. The Commission did not think it opportune to introduce this feast.

607.   April 25. St. Mark. The idea of combining St. Mark with St. Luke was not accepted. St. Mark would be moved to April 26 leaving April 25 free for the *litania maior,* as already agreed.

608.   April 30. St. Catherine of Siena. This would be transferred to the anniversary of her death which was free since the abolition of the feast of St. Peter Martyr.

609.   The meeting ended at 6:50 p.m. with the usual prayer.

Minutes of the 38ᵗʰ Meeting

610.   [The meeting was held] at 5:30 p.m. on Friday, April 9, 1954 at the Pontifical Spanish College in the apartments of the Lord Cardinal Gaetano Cicognani, Prefect of the Sacred Congregation of Rites.

611.   All members of the Commission attended except for Father Albareda who was excused.

612.   The minutes were read. His Eminence read out a letter from the Secretariat of State, in which Msgr. Montini communicated that the Holy Father had benignly accepted the *pro-memoria* presented last February by the Sacred Congregation of Rites on the possible institution of a Feast *Maria Regina*, and had approved the proposal to institute such a feast, as well as the proposed title and date. He requested the Sacred Congregation of Rites to prepare the formulae for the Mass and Breviary.

613.   Discussion of the date for the feast of St. Gabriel, the Archangel, then resumed. Father Löw, as usual, had circulated some comprehensive notes to the Commission examining the situation of the calendar, were the date [for this feast] fixed for the Monday following the First Sunday of Advent or for the December 16. In the first case, it would always be celebrated for the first seven years, except one, when it would be reduced to a *memoria*

because if would fall on November 30, the Feast of St. Andrew. In the second case, (December 16), in seven years it would be more or less impeded four times: on three occasions it would be reduced to a *memoria* since it coincides with the Quartertense, and then on one occasion it would be suppressed because it clashes with the 3rd Sunday of Advent.

614. The Commission agreed that the Feast of St. Gabriel, the Archangel, should be fixed as a tribute feast for the Monday following the First Sunday of Advent.

615. Examination of the calendar resumed.

616. May.

617. May 1. This would be taken up by the Feast *Maria Regina*. The feast of Saints Philip and James would be moved to May 4.

618. May 8. St. Mary Magdalen. The feast could not be omitted from the calendar. Father Bea would study the question of the various Marys and report to the next meeting of the Commission.

619. May 16. St. John of Nepomuk. If the question of his martyrdom can be clarified, then a commemoration can be proposed rather than a simple *memoria*.

620. May 17. Sts. Patrick, Augustine, and Colombanus. Concerning the celebrations of these three Irish Saints, some proposed that St. Patrick should be observed as a feast and the other two reduced to a commemoration. It was observed, however, that St. Augustine is the Apostle of England and St. Patrick is that of Ireland. Others opposed the reduction of the feast of St. Colombanus, who is the only truly Irish saint of the three, in whose favor there is a strong movement. Requests continually come to the Sacred Congregation of Rites for the extension of his feast to the universal calendar. Others wished to combine Patrick and Colombanus (as Irish) and to unite Augustine and Bede (as English), but this union was displeasing. It was decided to more attentively re-examine the question so as to find an appropriate solution.

621. May 29. St. Mary Magdalen de' Pazzi. It was decided to remove her from the universal calendar.

622. June.

623. June 13. Sts. Bonaventure and Anthony. His Eminence objected to this combination and proposed distinct feasts for both Saints because:

1. St. Bonaventure is a preeminent figure both as a Doctor and as an exponent of the ascetical-mystical movement of the Middle Ages. A separate feast would be completely justified. If St. Theresa of Avila is to be given a feast for her mystical doctrines it cannot be denied St. Bonaventure.

624. 2. Moreover, His Eminence pointed out that in St. Anthony's case the doctorate was a very secondary thing to the enromous devotion to him and

because of his thaumaturgery. It would therefore be entirely inappropriate to have St. Anthony with St. Bonaventure who would necessarily be left in shade and would ultimately not be celebrated at all.

625. Msgr. Dante observed that this would constitute a second break in the Commission's principles as far as Doctors were concerned. Father Löw held that it could be justified in addition to the 8 great doctors of antiquity. One would have the two great Doctors of the Middle Ages: St. Thomas and Saint Bonaventure.

626. For St. Albert the Great, he could be combined with some learned Saint, even if not a doctor. St. Anthony is a unique saint. He is known as a thaumaturg and not as a Doctor.

627. Also, the recent matter of the doctorate was no more than a confirmation of the cult of a Doctor.

628. June 19. As for Sts. Romualdo, Giovanni Gualberto, and Silvester, it was decided to remove this last figure because of his secondary importance and that of his order.

629. June 21. Sts. Luigi Gonzaga, John Berchmans, and Stanislaus Kostka. Msgr. Dante proposed making St. Luigi a feast and the other two a *memoria*. The proposal was accepted and approved, especially, as Father Bea, observed Saints John Berchmans and Stanislaus Kostka would now be introduced to the general calendar.

630. June 30. "*S. Pauli proprii*" [The Commemoration of St. Paul]. Father Antonelli returned to the very complex question of the feasts of Saints Peter and Paul noting that:

631. 1. The feast of June 30 is observed by nobody.

632. 2. The feast of January 25 could be retained, understanding St. Paul's "*conversio*" to be this vocation to the apostolate, that is a "*conversio*" from being a persecutor "*in apostolum*"?

633. 3. This would result in a logical and appropriate situation: two separate feasts for the Apostles. [These would be] January 18 for the "*Cathedra Petri*" (the feast of the Primacy); January 25 the "*Conversio S. Pauli*" (his assumption of the apostolate); and finally, a common feast for both Apostles on June 29.

634. The Commission unanimously accepted the proposal.

635. The session ended at 6:45 p.m. with the *Agimus tibi gratias*.

Minutes of the 39th Meeting

636. [The meeting was held] at 5:30 p.m. on Tuesday, April 27, 1954 at the Pontifical Spanish College in the apartments of the Lord Cardinal Gaetano Cicognani, Prefect of the Sacred Congregation of Rites.

637. All members of the Commission were present, except Msgr. Dante who was excused.

638. The minutes of the previous meeting were read. Father Albareda observed that further reflection was needed in relation to St. John of *Nepomuceno* (May 16), to verify if his were a true martyrdom or a violent death occasioned by a court intrigue. A recent article in the *Revue d'Histoire ecclésiastique* of Louvain seemed to suggest this latter possibility.

639. Father Antonelli said that since this was a case of a recently canonized Saint there existed a regular process in the archive of the Sacred Congregation of Rites. The matter would be studied on the basis of the acts of the process.

640. Discussion then returned to the Feast of St. Mary Magdalen (July 22). Father Bea had prepared a detailed study of this complex question, which caused to the following conclusions:

641. 1. Mary Magdalen is not to be identified with Mary of Bethany, the sister of Lazarus. This is currently regarded as certain.

642. 2. Mary Magdalen and the sinner are not identical. This would be admitted by most.

643. 3. The sinner is not identical with Mary of Bethany. Most would equally accept this.

644. Two feasts can safely be introduced: the one of Lazarus, Mary, and Martha, the other of Mary Magdalen.

645. Father Bea's exposition, as outlined in the aforementioned *pro-memoria*, was followed by a note of Father Löw, proposing the feast of the family of Bethany for July 22, and that of Mary Magdalen for May 8, during Eastertide.

646. Father Albareda noted that in the absence of a unanimous patristic, liturgical, or historical tradition in the entire matter, it did not seem opportune to change the "*status quo*". Thus he favored retaining the feast of July 22 as it was, and of not introducing the other [proposed feast].

647. From this diversity of opinions, a long and fruitful debate ensued in which all members participated. Father Antonelli suggested that since this was an historical question the Historical Section of the Sacred Congregation of Rites might be asked to study it. The conclusion was: the liturgical reform proposed to eliminate those elements that were certainly erroneous, and to leave the "*status quo*" in matters of doubt. In the present case, an uncertain situation would be exchanged for a certain one. Were the feast of the friends of Jesus at Bethany (Mary, Martha, Lazarus) introduced, as proposed, and were the feast of St. Mary Magdalen retained but limited to her presence under the cross and Christ's appearance to her, we would avoid a situation of uncertainty and enter one of certainty.

648. With regard to the date, it appeared opportune to celebrate the feast of

Mary, Martha, and Lazarus on July 29, presently the feast of St. Martha, and that of St. Mary Magdalen on May 8 during Eastertide.

649. With regard to the "sinner" which is an effective catechetical episode to illustrate divine mercy, the relevant pericope could be emphasized in a reordering of the Sunday pericopes.

650. The meeting ended at 7 p.m..

Minutes of the 40th Meeting

651. [The meeting was held] at 5:30 p.m. on Tuesday, May 11, 1954 at the Pontifical Spanish College in the apartments of the Lord Cardinal Gaetano Cicognani, Prefect of the Sacred Congregation of Rites.

652. After the reading of the minutes of the previous meeting, Father Albareda proposed that the Feast of St. Mary Magdalen (July 22) not be moved because of its popularity among the faithful.

653. Father Bea suggested that the gospel be taken from the account of her standing under the cross instead of the Risen Lord's appearance to her, which is read during the Easter Octave.

654. An examination of the proposals for the reform of the ceremonies of Palm Sunday then began. Father Löw, in collaboration with Father Antonelli, had prepared and circulated to the Commission, a *pro-memoria* containing an historical account [of the ceremonies] and the general lines for a reform which envisaged the simplification of the blessing of palms by emphasizing the original conception of the solemn rite as an act of homage to Christ the King. This aspect of the rite had been lost.

655. Two new "*Oremus*" [Collects] had been proposed and drafted: one for the blessing of palms, and the other to conclude the procession.

656. The structure of the Mass remains unchanged.

657. On the whole, the proposal was acceptable to the Commission.

658. Father Albareda made a clearer distinction between the blessings of palms and the Mass. He proposed that the former take place outside of the Church, as with the blessing of a fire on Holy Saturday. During the discussion, it grew increasingly clear that certain problems could not be resolved. Father Albareda proposed using rose for the blessing of palms and the procession. The liturgy uses this color on two occasions to indicate a window of joy during a period of sorrow. The Commission agreed that either rose or red could be used.

659. Msgr. Dante proposed a simplification of the first part [and suggested the following order]: singing of the Hosanna, blessing the palms with one of the present prayers, distribution of palms, readings of the Gospel, procession, and concluding prayer.

660. The suggestion was acceptable to all. The foregoing schema was generally accepted for the preparation of the relevant rubrics.

661. Of the proposed texts, the prayer for the blessing of the palms was discarded and the final prayer was retained since its homage to Christ the King was sufficiently evident. It would still have to be revised, though only from a stylistic point of view.

662. The meeting ended at 6:40 p.m..

Minutes of the 41ˢᵗ Meeting

663. [The meeting was held] at 5:30 p.m. on Tuesday, May 18, 1954 at the Pontifical Spanish College in the apartments of the Lord Cardinal Gaetano Cicognani, Prefect of the Sacred Congregation of Rites.

664. All members of the Commission were present except Father Albareda who was excused.

665. The minutes of the previous meeting were read. Examination of the proposed revised rubrics for Palm Sunday began. The text prepared and distributed in a fascicle was favorably received. The following modifications were proposed:

666. Article 3 – Concerning the vestments for the priest, the phrase "*vel manet sine casuala*" will be added after "*stola et pluviali*", as had been inserted in *Ordo Sabbati Sancti* for situations where no cope was available. Reference to vestments being "*solemniores*" for the "*ministrantes*" was revised.

667. Article 10 – The distribution of palms to the clergy should preferably be done at the altar rather than *in piano*

668. Article 14 – State explicitly that after the chanting of the Gospel the celebrant "*osculatur librum*", but [the book] is not incensed.

669. The versicle proposed for the procession ("*Procedamus in iubilo*") was not accepted. It was decided to retain the "*Procedamus in pace*" of the Missal.

670. Article 15 – It was accepted that a non-veiled cross be carried in procession, even if this creates a precedent for an eventual revision of the principle on the question of covering sacred images and crucifixes during Passiontide.

671. While this might be justified for sacred images, it could not be for the crucifix, upon which, especially in this time, both the eyes and the devotion of the faithful should be fixed.

672. Article 18 is to be amalgamated with Article 19.

673. Article 22 – The ministers change the vestments at the bench, and not in the sacristy.

674. In the section for the Mass, at Msgr. Dante's suggestion, it was decided to make an insertion to Article 4, omitting the last gospel not only for sung or Solemn Masses, but for all Masses on this day.

675.   The meeting concluded at 6:45 p.m..

Minutes of the 42nd Meeting

676.   [The meeting was held] at 5:30 p.m. on Tuesday, May 25, 1954 at the Pontifical Spanish College in the apartments of the Lord Cardinal Gaetano Cicognani, Prefect of the Sacred Congregation of Rites.

677.   All members of the Commission were present less Msgr. Dante who was excused.

678.   After the prayer and the reading of the minutes, examination of the reformed calendar resumed at the month of July, where the previous examination had ended at the 38th meeting held on April 19, 1954.

679.   The first 15 days of July, as proposed, were approved without difficulty.

680.   July 16. The feast of Mount Carmel would remain as commemoration since it was celebrated in many places with great solemnity, that of Our Lady of Mercy (September 24) as a *memoria*.

681.   July 20. St. Margaret, Martyr, would be eliminated.

682.   July 23. St. Bridget: transferred to July 24 so as to leave St. Apollinaris on July 23.

683.   St. Francis Borgia, to be moved to October 10 and celebrated as a commemoration.

684.   August 1. There should be a *memoria* for the SS. *Maccabei* [The Most Holy Maccabees] the only Saints of the Old Testament included in the universal calendar. Their feast could be transferred to August 2 so as to slightly free up August 1, already occupied by other Saints.

685.   August 5. "*Dedicatio Basilicae S. Mariae Maioris*". This question presented an opportunity to discuss the dedicational feasts of the four major patriarchal basilicas on the basis of supplemental information supplied by Father Löw. The following conclusions were made:

686.   1. Assign a solemn feast for St. John in Lateran as "*omnium ecclesiarum mater et caput*";

2. Assign a commemoration on November 18 for the Basilicas of St. Peter and of St. Paul, the two great basilicas which are dedicated to the two Apostles and universally known;

3. Assign a commemoration to the Basilica of St. Mary Major on August 5, the largest and oldest of the Marian Basilicas, and eliminate reference to the legend of the snow.

687.   August 11. Remove St. Susanna who is shrouded in legend.

688.   August 13. The three Oriental Saints (John Climaco, Maximus the Confessor, and Theodorus Studita) proposed for a commemoration are to be removed.

689. The meeting ended at 7 p.m..

Minutes of the 43rd Meeting

690. [The meeting was held] at 5:30 p.m. on Tuesday, June 8, 1954 at the Pontifical Spanish College in the apartments of the Lord Cardinal Gaetano Cicognani, Prefect of the Sacred Congregation of Rites.

691. All members of the Commission were present, except Father Albareda who was excused.

692. As usual, the meeting began with the *Actiones nostras* and the reading of the minutes. Examination of the reformed universal calendar then resumed at August 15, where the previous examination had ceased.

693. August 19. These important Saints seemed too many. It was decided to move St. Paul of the Cross to another date.

694. August 20. St. Robert, it did not seem opportune to include him in the universal calendar.

695. August 25. St. Louis of France to be retained as a commemoration.

696. August 27. The inclusion of St. Caesar of Arles was acceptable to all.

697. August 28. St. Monica, model of all Christian Mothers, required a special feast and not just a simple *memoria.*

698. The feast was therefore moved to the following day.

699. August 29. St. Sabina, a very uncertain [historical] figure, is to be removed.

700. It was decided to retain the feast of the decollation of St. John the Baptist since it commemorates an event taken from the Gospel.

701. August 30. St. Rose of Lima is the only Saint in the universal calendar from South America. All thought it convenient to retain the feast (IV class).

702. September.

703. September 8. The old title of *Nativitas B.V.M.* should be retained rather than that of *Natalis.*

704. September 11. Sts. Proto and Giacinto. Rather than a *memoria,* a commemoration would be preferable, bearing in mind for the readings that the relics of St. Giacinto have certainly been authenticated.

705. September 16. It was decided to have a *memoria* for St. Euphemia, who is a historical person.

706. September 22. A *memoria* for the soldier Saint Marnice seemed opportune.

707. September 23. St. Tecla is a martyr shrouded in legend. It was decided to remove her.

708. September 27. His Eminence thought that St. Vincent de Paul, a typical figure for Christian Charity, should be celebrated on his own. St. Joseph Benedict Cottolengo should be joined to another saint.

709. September 29. St. Michael the Archangel. It seemed more convenient that he be celebrated on his own without the "angelic choirs".

710. October.

711. October 8. St. Bridget. In the reformed calendar the feast would be observed on July 23, her mortuary day, but in the previous meeting it came to be considered an inconvenience to celebrate this Saint with St. Apollinaris. As a result, it was decided to restore her to October 8. But now, all things considered, [the Commission] believes that the Feast can remain on July 23 without difficulty and observed as a commemoration, while the feast (IV class) will be that of St. Apollinaris.

712. October 21. St. Hilarion and Saba: a commemoration is sufficient.

713. The meeting closed at 7 p.m..

Minutes of the 44th Meeting

714. [The meeting was held] at 5:30 p.m. on Tuesday, April 27, 1954 at the Pontifical Spanish College in the apartments of the Lord Cardinal Gaetano Cicognani, Prefect of the Sacred Congregation of Rites.

715. All members of the Commission attended.

716. The meeting opened with a prayer and the reading of the minutes.

717. Examination of the reformed calendar resumed at November 1, the point reached [at the previous meeting].

718. November.

719. November 3. St. Charles. It was more convenient to leave it on November 4, so as to avoid complications that would arise when the "*commemoratio omnium fidelium defunctorum*" is transferred from November 2 when this falls on a Sunday.

720. November 17. St. Gregory Thaumaturg. From a historical perspective, this person raises many difficulties. In the Latin Church, at least, he is of little importance. It was decided to remove him from the universal calendar. St. Gertrude could be moved to this day since it is the day of her death.

721. November 21. *Oblatio B.V.M.* Essentially, the Presentation of Our Lady. It is based on the apocryphal gospels. It was not considered opportune to remove the feast because of its many religious associations with the pious practices of the faithful, without mentioning the many religious institutions whose names derive from this mystery.

722. November 25. A *memoria* of St. Catharine of Alexandria seemed appropriate.

723. November 29. It was appropriate to retain the vigil of St. Andrew, since it is one of the most ancient vigils.

724.   December.

725.   December 3. St. Francis Solano is to be united to St. Peter Claver, thereby [constituting a feast for the] Apostles of the three most numerous races: the Chinese, the Indians and the blacks.

726.   December 7. A commemoration instead of a *memoria* for St. Francis Frémiot de Chantal. Thus concluded the examination of the reformed calendar. The calendar would be examined once again at the beginning of the new working year, i.e. in October. At that point, any imbalances or incongruence that arose during the revision could be eliminated, and, if possible, the *sanctorale* further reduced. In the meanwhile, the necessary material would be prepared.

727.   The working year 1953-1954 closed with this meeting.

728.   From November 6, 1953 to June 22, 1954, 16 meetings were held of which 14 were presided over by Cardinal Gaetano Cicognani. These meetings treated amply of the feast *Maria Regina*, the bi-weekly Psalter, the reform of the rite of Palm Sunday, and of the reformed calendar.

729.   The meeting ended at 6.40 p.m. with the usual *Agimus tibi gratias*.

Minutes of the 45th Meeting

730.   [The meeting took place] at 5 p.m. on Tuesday, October 19, 1954 at the Pontifical Spanish College in the apartments of the Lord Cardinal Gaetano Cicognani, Prefect of the Sacred Congregation of Rites.

731.   All members of the Commission attended.

732.   The meeting, the first of the new [working] year, began after the prayer. His Eminence communicated that he had reported to the Holy Father on the reform of Holy Week, at the Audience of August 18. He emphasized the two most important and controversial points; the question of the sepulcures of Holy Thursday, and the Communion of the faithful on Good Friday. Having read the *pro-memoria* prepared by the *Relator-Generalis* and Father Löw, the Holy Father let it be known that he did not consider these problems to be insuperable. It was his desire, however, that the questions be placed before the Cardinals of the Sacred Congregation of Rites. A *Ponenza* would therefore have to be prepared.

733.   Father Antonelli explained that the project was already well advanced and he briefly outlined the principal point of the *Positio* which would be presented as soon as possible at the Commission.

734.   The feast of *Maria Regina* was then examined.

735.   Through Msgr. Dante, the Holy Father let it be known that he preferred the May 31, so as to leave the May 1 free for an eventual Feast of Christ, the Worker.

736. Msgr. Dante had respectfully drawn the Holy Father's attention to the fact that May 31, because of the 35 possible dates for Easter, would be impeded 19 times, while the May 1 could be impeded only 4 times. Other dates, such as the Octave of the Assumption, a Sunday in May, etc., would cause various difficulties. All things considered the Commission continued in the opinion that the most suitable date would be May 1. His Eminence would communicate the mind of the Commission to Msgr. Montini.

737. The draft for the Mass was examined.

738. Introit. *Signum Magnum* (Rv 12:1) was proposed, however it did not seem appropriate since it is already used for the Assumption. A different [antiphon] would be preferable. Msgr. Dante proposed Eccl 45:12, *Corona aurea super caput eius.*

739. Oratio. Pleasing on the whole. Father Bea suggested *"eius potenti praesidio suffulti"*, rather than *"eius intercessione muniti"*. Others proposed *"muniti"* for *"suffulti"* and the elimination of *"saeculo"* after *"praesenti"*. The expression *"eius praesidio muniti"* was accepted as was the second proposal.

740. Gradual. Father Antonelli suggested Ps 44:7, *"Thronus tuus"* instead of Rv 19:6. It seemed well suited [to the feast] and, since it was taken from a Psalm, it was more consonant with the best liturgical tradition. For the *Alleluia* versicle, it was proposed to use a simplification of the original opening of the *Salve Regina* rendering it: *Salve Regina misericordiae.*

741. Msgr. Dante observed that in the Gradual, it would be necessary to include firstly the text for Eastertide and then *"per annum"* since the feast would be mostly observed during Eastertide. Moreover, the first verse of the text for Eastertide would have to be the same as that for the Alleluia for the *"per annum"* period. Both emendations were happily received.

742. Offertory. Raises great difficulties. The time proposed seemed too heavy while the corrections and emendations were not satisfactory. Father Bea would suggest the following: *Ave Maria, Christi Mater, passionis socia, consors regni et gloriae.* We will have to think it over some more. It was agreed by all that it would be well to accentuate the maternity of Mary as one of the foundations of her glory.

743. Secret (from Leonine Sacramentary). Acceptable. The world *"nostrae"* after *"Reginae"* in the second line is to be removed.

744. Postcommunion. In the second line the word *"solemnitate"* to be replaced by *"festivitate"* so as to avoid the cacophony with *"solemniter"* in the first line.

745. The next meeting will take place on next Friday, October 22. It will examine the new Mass and Office for the feast of *Maria Regina*. The relative texts were distributed at the meeting.

746. The usual prayers concluded the meeting at 6 p.m..

Appendix A: On the origin of the Pontifical Commission for the Reform of the Sacred Liturgy and on its work from 1948 to 1960

Minutes of the 46th Meeting

747. [The meeting was held] at 5 p.m. on Friday, October 22, 1954 at the Pontifical Spanish College in the apartments of the Lord Cardinal Gaetano Cicognani, Prefect of the Sacred Congregation of Rites.

748. All members of the Commission were present except Msgr. Dante who was excused.

749. At the opening of the meeting, His Eminence read a letter from Msgr. Montini communicating in the name of the Holy Father that the Feast of *Maria Regina* had been fixed for August 22 in the Octave of the Assumption, and that the feast of the Immaculate Heart of Mary had been moved to May 31.

750. Those texts of the Mass which had given rise to difficulties were then re-examined.

751. Introit. It was decided to use the *Gaudeamus*. It had been the original *Introit* for the Assumption (from the 8th century on) and had the advantage of having a well-known solemn melody.

752. Gradual. Those [texts] proposed in the first draft were preferable.

753. Offertory. Father Albareda proposed the third antiphon of the Nativity of the Blessed Virgin Mary: *Regali ex progenie*. The Proposal was accepted.

754. Examination of the Office then ensued.

755. Antiphons. Some were amended, others substituted with texts from the Common.

756. Hymn for Matins by Father Genovesi. It was acceptable but some slight changes were recommended for 2nd and 4th strophes.

757. Responsories. Father Antonelli presented a new draft which was accepted with slight changes.

758. Lessons. All were acceptable to the Commission, including those from the third Nocturn taken from an unpublished sermon of St. Bonaventure.

759. Hymn for *Lauds* is taken from a 13th century sequence. It was very simple, but devout and easily understood. It was accepted by all.

760. Antiphon for the *Benedictus*. This will adopt that which is found in the *Schema* as recommended for II Vespers: *Regina mundi dignissima.*

761. Antiphon for the *Magnificat* for II Vespers. All agreed that that of II Vespers of the Assumption would be very suitable.

762. Using these modifications, drafts of the both the Mass and the Office will be prepared. Once printed, they will again be submitted to the Commission for examination, but this time, for final revisions.

763. The meeting ended at 6:45 p.m..

Minutes of the 47ᵗʰ Meeting

764.   [The meeting was held] at 5:30 p.m. on Tuesday, December 21, 1954 at the Pontifical Spanish College in the apartments of the Lord Cardinal Gaetano Cicognani, Prefect of the Sacred Congregation of Rites.

765.   All members of the Commission were present except Fathers Löw and Albareda.

766.   As agreed at the previous meeting, the Mass and Office for the feast of *Maria Regina* were again examined, the printed drafts having been circulated to the Commission.

767.   Only very slight modifications were made:

a) some changes to the Antiphons for the *Magnificat* at both Vespers, and to the *Oremus*;

b) the versicles for the Nocturns and the responsories were more logically disposed so as to correspond to the theological concept underpinning the feast: Father Bea had made the suggestion;

c) the proper Antiphons for Vespers and Lauds were abolished. These had been taken from the Psalms of Vespers, and they should not be added to the Psalms of Lauds. Neither was it opportune to have new antiphons for Lauds;

d) Father Genovesi's hymn for Matins was slightly adjusted.

768.   Father Antonelli reported on the *Positio* regarding the reform of Holy Week to be proposed to the Cardinal members of the Sacred Congregation of Rites.

769.   With regard to Holy Saturday, it was regarded as opportune to propose to the Holy Father a further prorogation, for another year of optional celebration, and to communicate the same [to the Ordinaries].

770.   The meeting closed at 6:15 p.m. by presenting Christmas greetings to His Eminence, the Cardinal Prefect.

Minutes of the 48ᵗʰ Meeting

771.   [The meeting was held] at 5:30 p.m. on Tuesday, February 1, 1955 at the Pontifical Spanish College in the apartments of the Lord Cardinal Gaetano Cicognani, Prefect of the Sacred Congregation of Rites.

772.   All members of the Commission were present.

773.   Examination of the proposal for the *De rubricis simplificandis* began.

774.   The prayer was said and the minutes read. Father Antonelli gave a brief resumé of the history of this project. Many years ago, in two audiences, the Holy Father had expressed to Cardinal Micara, the Prefect of the S.R.C., his desire to do something to render the saying of the Office easier, especially for

those priests with the *cura animarum*. Father Löw prepared a draft proposal in 1953, which was ready by June of that same year. Several reasons, both then and now, had prevented discussion of the proposals. Now seemed an opportune time to do it. Hence it was presented to the Commission.

775. Msgr. Dante moves to a question of principle: there are already two series of general rubrics in the Breviary and Missal, those of St. Pius V (*Additiones et Variationes*) and those of St. Pius X. It is necessary to produce a third series? Or would it perhaps be more fitting to fuse all three, producing one definitive series?

776. Msgr. Dante's question was given serious consideration by all. The Commission, however, came to the view that it was opportune to draw up a simplification [of the rubrics] and to leave the *status quo* for the moment. The reasons being:

1. this is a transitional measure between the present situation which had become very complex and the general reform which would still take some years;

2. the simplification had to be done in such a way that the present liturgical books remained unchanged;

3. some relief from the present rubric was desired by all, because even a specialist can easily lose himself in the current labyrinth;

4. the object of the simplification is to make prayer more easy, not to reduce it. Even if it had to be reduced quantitively, by omitting the repetitious formulae, this would be some advantage to the clergy, especially the pastoral clergy.

777 The Commission, for these reasons, unanimously decided to proceed with the examination of the project. Titles and articles, with slight modifications, were approved. The [examination] then arrived at title III: *De commemorationibus*.

778. The next meeting will be held on February 11.

779. The meeting ended at 7 p.m..

Minutes of the 49th Meeting

780. [The meeting was held] at 5:30 p.m. on Friday, February 11, 1955 at the Pontifical Spanish College in the apartments of the Lord Cardinal Gaetano Cicognani, Prefect of the Sacred Congregation of Rites.

781. All members of the Commission except Father Löw were present.

782. The minutes were read. His Eminence observed that a further reason would have to be added to the four, adopted in the previous meeting, in favor of a simplification of the rubrics. The present simplification is designed in such a way that it can be assumed into the general reform

without noticeable changes. This will further indicate the principles on which it is based.

783. Examination of the *pro-memoria* resumed. The complex material in the title III, *De commemorationibus,* caused much discussion. Various proposals were advanced. The general tendency is to reduce the commemorations even further, greatly simplifying what has been proposed in the project.

784. The other titles were accepted without essential modifications.

785. Finally, it was agreed to invite a rubricist, who is both capable and competent, so that, on the basis of the principles outlined already, he might examine the rubrics minutely for possible practical implications for the formulation of the calendar.

786. Father Pizzoni's name was mentioned and all agreed.

787. The next meeting would convene when this basic work has been completed.

788. The meeting ended at 7 p.m..

Minutes of the 50th Meeting

789. [The meeting was held] at 5:30 p.m. on Tuesday, March 1, 1955 at the Pontifical Spanish College in the apartments of the Lord Cardinal Gaetano Cicognani, Prefect of the Sacred Congregation of Rites.

790. All members of the Commission except Father Löw attended.

791. His Eminence communicated that he had, that morning, reported to the Holy Father on the matter of the simplification.

792. The project, corrected and revised, was again examined taking into account the observations of the previous meeting. It was approved with some slight modifications.

793. The meeting concluded at 7 p.m..

Minutes of the 51st Meeting

794. [The meeting was held] at 5:30 p.m. on Friday, June 24, 1955 at the Pontifical Spanish College in the apartments of the Lord Cardinal Gaetano Cicognani, Prefect of the Sacred Congregation of Rites.

795. All members of the Commission attended.

796. The meeting was entirely devoted to a revision of the *Positio "De instauratione liturgica Maioris Hebdomadae",* prepared by the *Relator-Generalis* and the Historical Section. It was due to be circulated to the Cardinal members of the Sacred Congregation of Rites who would discuss it on July 19.

797. His Eminence wished that it should be emphasized that this was not

restoration for the sake of restoration, but a restoration demanded and impelled by pastoral circumstances.

798. Father Bea thought that reference could be made to the positive reception given to the evening Mass.

799. Msgr. Dante wished that the *Positio* should explicitly state that the Matins of *Tenebre* are to be said in the morning and that Holy Communion may not be received at the *Missa Chrismalis*.

800. Others suggested that it might be better to distribute the liturgical text for Holy Week together with the *Positio*.

801. With some minor changes, the *Positio* was unanimously approved for printing and distribution to the Most Eminent [Cardinals].

802. Father Antonelli then mentioned the work that awaited [the Commission] after the holidays: examination of the Office of St. Joseph "*Artigiano*"; the "*Ordinationes*" for Holy Week; and a complement to the decree of March 23 which would make important clarifications regarding votive Masses, conventual and commemorative Masses, the calendar, the Sub-commissions, etc..

803. The meeting closed at 6:30 p.m..

804. This was the final meeting of the work year 1954-1955.

805. Seven meetings were held during this year (the 45th through the 51st) compared to the 16 which were held during the previous year. During these meetings, three questions were examined and concluded: the Office for the feast of *Maria Regina*; the Decree *De Rubrics ad simpliciorem formam redigendis* of March 25, 1955; and the *Positio* for the reform of Holy Week, whose preparation had absorbed most of the Commission's time.

Minutes of the 52nd Meeting

806. [The meeting was held] at 5:30 p.m. on Friday, October 7, 1955 at the Pontifical Spanish College in the apartments of the Lord Cardinal Gaetano Cicognani, Prefect of the Sacred Congregation of Rites.

807. All members of the Commission except His Excellency, Msgr. Carinci.

808. The prayer was said and the minutes read. Examination of the Office and Mass of St. Joseph the Worker began. A draft had been prepared by Father Löw in collaboration with Father Antonelli which had been sent to the members of the Commission some days prior to the meeting.

809. The examination began with the Mass. Father Bea had prepared and distributed a new draft. Both drafts were studied. Following a detailed discussion, the general outline of the individual texts was agreed. A third draft would be drawn up for presentation at the next meeting of the

Commission. The Office was then examined. The general idea guiding [the texts] was accepted to all. The texts for Vespers were considered and, following some modifications, approved.

810. The meeting ended at 6:50 p.m.. The next meeting will take place on October 11, at the same time. The *Ordinationes* for the restored Holy Week will be examined.

Minutes of the 53rd Meeting

811. [The meeting was held] at 5:30 p.m. on Tuesday, October 11, 1955 at the Pontifical Spanish College in the apartments of the Lord Cardinal Gaetano Cicognani, Prefect of the Sacred Congregation of Rites.

812. All members of the Commission were present.

813. The agenda for the meeting proposed the examination of the *Ordinationes* for the restored Holy Week. Father Antonelli prefaced his remarks by saying that many requests had been made to vary the texts of the readings, or to replace them altogether. Some had asked for three readings, and others for four, but different from those proposed, others again asked that the celebrant be allowed to choose from the 12 readings in the Missal. The Commission decided not to alter the decision previously made with the regard to the *Ordo Sabbati Sancti*.

814. Msgr. Dante asked whether the "*Passio*" from St. Matthew's Gospel for Palm Sunday, should not be moved to the Monday of Holy Week, so as to lighten the ceremony. The proposal was not excluded but, the reasons for and against such a change indicated that the matter would have to be carefully considered and a decision taken at a later date.

815. The *Ordinationes* for Holy Week were then read. His Eminence proposed calling [the document] an "*Instructio*". The various articles were then discussed one by one and were generally approved pending another examination of the definitive text.

816. Finally, [the Commission] considered a proposal, from various groups, to reduce the text of the *Exsultet*. The Commission, however, decided to conserve the traditional text since the passages that could be eliminated were few and of slight importance.

817. The meeting concluded at 7:15 p.m..

Minutes of the 54th Meeting

818. [The meeting was held] at 5:30 p.m. on Friday, October 21, 1955 at the Pontifical Spanish College in the apartments of the Lord Cardinal Gaetano Cicognani, Prefect of the Sacred Congregation of Rites.

819. All members of the Commission attended.

Appendix A: On the origin of the Pontifical Commission for the Reform of the Sacred Liturgy and on its work from 1948 to 1960

820. Two questions were on the agenda:

1. examination of the "*Instructio de ordine Hebdomadae Sanctae iuxta instauratum ritum peragendo*";

2. The proposal to transfer the "*Passio*" of St. Matthew's Gospel from Palm Sunday to the Monday of Holy Week.

821. After the usual prayer, examination of the *Instructio* began.

822. The greater part of the Commission took the view that the decree would only contain binding norms, while the *Instructio* should contain directional norms. On this basis, the various articles were examined and checked one by one, and assigned either to the Decree or to the *Instructio*.

823. As to the second point, the Commission unanimously rejected transferring the "*Passio*" of St. Matthew from Palm Sunday given the antiquity of this tradition. It did, however, accept a proposal advanced by Father Bea to reduce the length of the text by 40 verses. Thus the readings would begin at Mt 26:36 and end at Mt 27:61.

824: The meeting ended with the *Agimus* at 7 p.m..

Minutes of the 55th Meeting

825. [The meeting was held] at 5 p.m. on Friday, October 28, 1955 at the Pontifical Spanish College in the apartments of the Lord Cardinal Gaetano Cicognani, Prefect of the Sacred Congregation of Rites.

826. All members of the Commission attended.

827. The prayer was said and the minutes read. Father Antonelli introduced both items posted in the agenda: the ordering of the "*Passio*" in Holy Week, and the examination of the draft of the dispositive part of the decree on the "*Ordo Hebdomandae Sanctae Instrauratus*".

828. As to the first point, all agreed with the reduction from four readings of the "*Passio*" proposed by the *Relator-Generalis*. The reduction slimmed down the pericopes and gave them a certain uniformity. In conclusion, the four narrations of the passion would be reduced as follows: Palm Sunday, Matthew, 93 verses instead of 111; Tuesday of Holy Week, Mark, 86 verses instead of 118; Wednesday of Holy Week, Luke, 85 verses instead of 124; Good Friday, John, 82 verses (unchanged).

829. The dispositive section of the decree was minutely examined, checked, and approved, with due modifications, article by article.

830. On the suggestion of Father Albareda, it was agreed not to mention the *Instructio* in the decree, so that it was clear that it was a document of the Congregation.

831. The meeting concluded at 6:10 p.m..

The Development of the Liturgical Reform

Minutes of the 56th meeting

832. The meeting was held at 5 p.m. on Friday, November 11, 1955 at the Pontifical Spanish College in the apartments of Cardinal Gaetano Cicognani, Prefect of the Sacred Congregation of Rites.

833. Absent: Msgr. Carinci, indisposed, and Father Löw.

834. After the usual prayer the general decree *"quo liturgicus sanctae hebdomadae ordo instauratur"* and the appended *Instructio* were read and approved. Both documents were accepted by the Commission with much satisfaction.

835. The *Relator-Generalis* then read a *pro-memoria* of Cardinal Lercaro addressing: Palm Sunday; the fast; and bell ringing on Holy Saturday. Cardinal Lercaro desired that the blessing of olive branches and the relative Mass on Palm Sunday take place in the evening. His request was justified by pastoral circumstances in that more people would be able to take part in the ceremony on Sunday evening.

836. With regard to the fast, His Eminence wished that it would end at mid-day, as established in the Code. He also proposed that bells cease at this time and that the rite of the Easter Vigil take place in the evening.

837. All things considered, the Commission was of a mind to retain that which had already been established: i.e. all ceremonies on Palm Sunday should take place in the morning, thereby emphasizing for the faithful that the entire day of the Lord should be sanctified. The pastoral inconveniences of moving the ceremonies to the evening would not differ greatly from those occasioned by the morning celebration of the ceremonies.

838. Likewise, the Commission retained that the fast on Holy Saturday should end at midnight, as in the time before the Code. The purpose of the fast was to instill a more severe discipline in the faithful, and to conserve the morning for the Lord's death which characterized this day. The *Instructio* to the decree (article 25) makes sufficient provision for the time and manner of bell ringing.

839. Examination of the *Ordo* for Holy Week began and proceeded as far as *Feria II*. The various observations that were made mainly concerned points of detail.

840. The meeting ended at 7:15 p.m..

Minutes of the 57th Meeting

841. (The meeting was held) at 5 p.m. on Friday, November 25, 1955, at the Pontifical Spanish College in the apartments of Cardinal Gaetano Cicogni, Prefect of the Sacred Congregation of Rites.

842. All members were present.

843. The prayer was said and the minutes read. Examination of the *Ordo* for

Holy Week resumed from *Feria II*. On Holy Thursday at the *Cena Domini* Mass, it was agreed that the confession at the foot of the altar, even at solemn evening Mass, should be retained.

845. The remainder of the examination consisted of minor emendations.

846. At the end of the meeting, His Eminence announced that in the future, the Commission would consult, in general terms, the Metropolitans, so as to ascertain the views of the Episcopate in such an important matter and to have practical suggestions that might prove useful.

847. The meeting ended at 7:15 p.m..

Minutes of the 58ᵗʰ meeting

848. The meeting was held at 5 p.m. on Tuesday, November 29, 1955 at the Pontifical Spanish College in the apartments of Cardinal Gaetano Cicogni, Prefect of the Sacred Congregation of Rites.

849. Absent and excused: Msgr. Carinci and Msgr. Dante.

850. The minutes were read and examination of the *Ordo Hebdomadae Sanctae Instauratus* resumes at Good Friday (*Feria VI*) *in passione et morte Domini*, from the point where the previous meeting has stopped, to the end. The modifications were slight. Msgr. Carinci and Msgr. Dante had consigned written observations to the *Relator-Generalis*. These were mentioned during the examination.

851. After the usual prayer, the session rose at 6:15 p.m..

Minutes of the 59ᵗʰ Meeting

852. [The Commission met] at 5 p.m. on Tuesday, January 17, 1956 at the Pontifical Spanish College in the apartments of Cardinal Gaetano Cicognani, Prefect of the Sacred Congregation of Rites.

853. All members were attended.

854. Examination of the Mass and the Office of St. Joseph the Worker resumed, having been partially concluded at the meeting October 7. The following modifications were made to the draft circulated at that time:

855. Mass.

856. Introit. Wisdom 10:17, *Sapientia reddidit*, was accepted instead Psalm 127:1-2, *Beatus qui ambulat*, which had the disadvantage of coming from two different Psalms – something extremely rare in the liturgical tradition.

857. *Oratio*: A new one, presented by the *Relator-Generalis* was accepted instead of the one proposed at the meeting of October 7.

858. Epistle, Gradual, and Gospel. These remain as approved.

859. Offertory: Psalm 89:17, *Bonitas*, was proposed and accepted.

860. Secret, Communion, and Postcommunion. These remain as previously approved.

861. The Office.

862. Antiphons, Chapter, Versicle, Hymn. "*Te Joseph, celebrent*" of Vespers remain unchanged.

863. Two new hymns, composed by Fr. Evaristo d'Anversa of Tivoli, were proposed and accepted for Matins and Lauds.

864. Lessons: those already chosen for the first Nocturn remain but in a shortened form. An extract from the tract "*De Maria Deipara Virgine incomparabili*" was accepted as a second reading. The readings taken from St. Albert the Great, commenting on the corresponding extract form the Gospel, were approved for the third Nocturn.

865. Following examination of the Office for the feast of St. Joseph, some questions relating to the restored Holy Week were raised.

866. I. His Excellency Msgr. Montini made two proposals:

867. His first proposal was that the time for the Good Friday liturgical ceremonies be postponed until 8 p.m., so as to allow all, including workers and employees, to participate.

868. R. Having carefully considered this proposal, the Commission took the view that changes with regard to the time of celebration could be conceded to individuals who requested them: after some experimental years, the Sacred Congregation of Rites will decide whether the concession should be generalized.

869. Montini's second proposal was that participation at the celebration of Mass at the Solemn Easter Vigil, even if held before midnight, should also satisfy the obligation to attend Mass on Easter Sunday.

870. R. The Commission unanimously rejected the proposal.

871. II. Father Bevilaqua, of the Oratory of Bergamo, proposed that the procession of palms should be detached from the Mass and conducted in the evening.

872. R. While the Commission appreciated the proposal, it did not, however, regard it opportune for the present, to modify the *Ordo*.

873. III. In virtue of the recent decree, have those religious communities which have a faculty for a read Mass on Holy Thursday lost this privilege?

874. R. The matter will be referred to the canonists.

875. IV. When inserting the text of the new *Ordo* in the Missals, must the entire text of the *Decree* and the *Instructio* be included or only those parts explicitly cited?

876. R. The passages cited are to be included [in the Missals] together with

the necessary modifications to the rubrics which will be prepared by the Commission.

877. The session rose at 7 p.m.

Minutes of the 60ᵗʰ Meeting

878. [The Commission met] at 5:30 p.m. on Tuesday, February 14, 1956 at the Pontifical Spanish College in the apartments of Cardinal Gaetano Cicognani, Prefect of the Sacred Congregation of Rites.

879. All members attended except Father Albareda who was excused.

880. At the opening of the meeting, His Eminence communicated that, from various parts, requests had arrived, for adaptations of new *Ordo* for Holy Week, especially with regard to Holy Thursday.

881. In particular, the following had written:

882. His Eminence Cardinal Pla y Deniel, Primate of Spain, on behalf of the majority of the Spanish Episcopate; Cardinal D'Alton, on behalf of the Irish Bishops; the Episcopate of Venezuela; Cardinal Mooney of Detroit and Cardinal Stritch of Chicago; and some of the Australian Bishops through Msgr. Carboni, the Nuncio.

883. In order to facilitate a greater participation of the faithful at the Eucharistic table, the above mentioned desired that a faculty be conceded to permit the celebration of a read Mass and the Communion of the faithful on Holy Thursday morning, or at least the distribution of Holy Communion *extra Missam* to the faithful.

884. After careful and mature consideration, the Commission, in an effort to meet the needs of considerable numbers of the faithful and facilitate a gradual introduction of the new dispositions, suggested that a faculty be conceded to celebrate a read Mass on Holy Thursday morning on the following conditions:

885. 1. The concession was to be made for the parish churches only;

886. 2. Holy Communion was to be distributed only at Mass or "*continuo ac statim a Missa expleta*".

887. 3. The faculty was to be granted *ad annum* as a transitional measure, and the Most Excellent Ordinaries were asked to persuade the clergy and faithful to accept the entire new rite as quickly as possible;

888. 4. The faithful are to be instructed so that they do not receive Holy Communion twice, on the morning and evening of Holy Thursday, at the *Cena Domini* Mass;

889. 5. The solemn *Cena Domini* Mass is to be celebrated everywhere in the evening;

890. 6. In the cathedrals, only the *Missa Chrismatis* is to be celebrated during which it will be licit to distribute Holy Communion;

891. 7. The indult will be communicated individually to those concerned, remitting its application to the prudence of the bishops. Other questions, coming from diverse parts, were then raised.

892. In the name of the Lombard Bishops, Msgr. Montini insisted that a faculty be conceded permitting the celebration of the Good Friday ceremonies at a time later than that established in the decree. The Commission agreed that it could begin at 7 p.m.. Finally, His Eminence communicated that the ACLI were taking practical steps to ask the various companies to suspend work on the afternoon of Good Friday. This initiative was proceeding well and should it have a positive outcome, the need for the foregoing concession would be obviated.

893. Questions of minor import had been sent by the Archbishop of Lyons, the Bishop of Versailles, the Bishop of Troyes, etc..

894. His Eminence then read the [letters] of support which had arrived and spoke of the enthusiastic reception of the New *Ordo* in many dioceses.

895. Finally, he communicated that the Holy Father approved, in general terms, a consultation of the Metropolitans with regard to the reform of the Breviary so as to ascertain their desires and to give them a sense of confidence.

896. The session closed after the usual prayer at 7 p.m..

Minutes of the 61st Meeting

897. [The Commission met] at 5:30 p.m. on March 9, 1956 at the office of the Cardinal Prefect of the Sacred Congregation of Rites, in the Palazzo of St. Callisto.

898. All members attended.

899. After the opening of the meeting, His Eminence presented some questions relating to the restored Holy Week.

900. I. The Secretariat of the State thought that opportune indications concerning the celebration of Holy Week could be broadcast by Vatican Radio. It had sent a text to the Sacred Congregation of Rites comparing the adaptations and changes made to old and new rites. His Eminence read the text to the Commission. The essential points were retained, including that of changing the time to the evening or at night. The Commission expressed a favorable view [on the text].

901. II. Msgr. Carboni, Apostolic Delegate in Australia, requests that the ceremony for the palms be permitted in the evening in Australia, because it would interfere with the normal celebration of Mass on successive hours.

[902. R. The Commission did not believe that the change was necessary, because the new rite had shortened rather than lengthened the ceremonies. Consequently, inconveniences should not be greater now than they had been in the past.

903. Equally, some Australian Bishops foresaw that the numbers of people (attending the ceremonies) could not be contained in the churches. They asked, consequently, permission to hold the liturgical action *sub diu*.

904. R. The Commission favored this concession.

905. The *Declaratio* concerning the churches in which the sacred Triduum could be celebrated was then examined. Once the *Declaratio* has been read, discussed, and approved, it will be submitted to the Holy Father with the proposal that it be published in the *Osservatore Romano* as soon as possible.

906. The *Relator-Generalis* gave an excursus on the ancient tradition in the Latin Church which prohibits "private" Masses on Holy Thursday and which provides for the clergy assisting at a single festive Mass to receive Holy Communion [at that Mass].

907. The excursus was based on the fact that the decree *Maxima Redemptoris Nostrae Mysteria*, referring to Canon 862, insists on the traditional practice of the Church. The Sacred Congregations for Religious and for Sacraments, however, even at present, continue to grant a significant number of privileges for the celebration of private Masses, *et quidem*, on Holy Thursday morning. Requests for the privilege are encouraged by the idea that every priest should be able to celebrate Mass individually on Holy Thursday, the day on which the priesthood was instituted.

908. It seems opportune to draw the Holy Father's attention to this important point, so as to limit the aforementioned concessions.

909. The Commission examined the problem minutely and agreed that a note be prepared on the subject and presented to the Holy Father.

910. The text of a letter to Metropolitans asking for their views on the reform of the Breviary, which had been desired by the Holy Father, was read and approved.

911. The *Relator-Generalis* announced that [the publishing house] Desclée had printed a booklet containing the chant for Holy Week. The old version of the Psalms, however, had been used. This would have to be reproved because it was in direct contravention of the *editio typica* of the *Ordo*.

912. The Commission agreed that the Sacred Congregation should officially remind the publishers of their duty to reproduce the liturgical texts according to the *editiones typicae*, and ask them to withdraw the booklet from sale.

913. The meeting ended at 6:45 p.m..

Minutes of the 62nd Meeting

914. [The Commission met] at 5:30 p.m. on Friday, April 6, 1956 at the office of

the Cardinal Prefect of the Congregation of Rites in the Palazzo St. Calisto.

915. All members attended.

916. The Cardinal opened the meeting by announcing that several bishops had reported much success with the celebrations of the restored Holy Week. He had received favorable reports from Tarragona, Valencia, Catania, Texas, and from the [Superior] General of the Clarissians.

917. Examination of the Mass and Office of St. Joseph the Worker then resumed. Some texts giving too much emphasis to manual labor were revised, modified, or replaced.

918. The Epistle for Mass, which had already been approved, was replaced with that of Col 3:14-15, 17, 23-24 which seemed more appropriate. The Introit Psalm was also changed.

919. Some of the antiphons in the Office were attenuated, and the 5th and 6th responsories were changed. The readings for the second Nocturn were to be based on the discourse of the Holy Father for May 1, 1955.

920. The meeting ended at 7 p.m..

Minutes of the 63rd Meeting

921. [The meeting was held] on Friday, April 20, 1956 at the offices of the Sacred Congregation of Rites in the Palazzo St. Calisto.

922. All members of the Commission were present. The minutes were read. The *Relator-Generalis* distributed a draft of the letter to the Metropolitans concerning the reform of the Breviary. It was decided to have it revised by the Latinists of the Congregation and to present it to the Holy Father. It would then be sent to all Metropolitans and to those bishops immediately subject to the Holy See.

924. Secondly, Father Antonelli read a letter from Msgr. Martin, Archbishop of Rouen, and President of the French Episcopal Commission for the Liturgy. On behalf of the French Cardinals and Bishops he asked that on Sundays and feast days, at least for an experimental period, that the readings at Mass be read directly in the vernacular by the celebrant, and that the Latin text be omitted when it was too long.

925. Some pointed out that this was a grave question and that it would have to be broached at some stage. The Commission took the view that the question should be submitted to the Holy Father, asking him to clarify the question of competence in the matter. In recent years, various dicasteries had made concessions and emanated dispositions [on the use of the vernacular]. Such would avoid a situation, previously experienced, of one dicastery making a concession and and another refusing it.

926. Finally, the *Relator-Generalis* presented a plan for the Commission's next

work on the general reform of the liturgy.

927. As was known, the matter of the calendar reached its final stage: Father Antonelli noted, though, that all recognized, and recognize, that the proposed (reform of the calendar) is a compromise, with which we are happy. It seemed, therefore, opportune to delay consideration of the *Sanctorale*, and to tackle the reorganization of the Sunday series. The proposal was accepted. It was agreed that a detailed plan for the first Nocturn would be drawn up on the basis of article 225 of the *Memoria*.

928. The meeting ended with the usual prayer at 6:45 p.m..

Minutes of the 64th Meeting

929. [The meeting took place] at 5:30 p.m. on Tuesday, May 22, 1956 at the offices of the Sacred Congregation of Rites in the Palazzo St. Calisto.

930. All members of the Commission attended.

931. The minutes were read. The Commission began the examination of the proposed organization of the occurring scriptural readings. Prior to the meeting, an *"Esposto intorno alla 'Scriptura occurrens'"* (compiled by Father Löw and revised by Father Antonelli) had been distributed. It outlined the *"status quaestionis"* and presented complicated situations with regard to its matter. In so far as is possible, it proposed the elimination of present inconveniences about which complaint had been made. It suggested the abandonment of the present three systems of division and distribution of the scriptural readings and proposed that a single system be adopted in which the scripture [readings] would be arranged according to the weeks. [It also proposed] certain shortenings [of the readings] and the conservation of certain traditional elements.

932. The various parts of the *Esposto* relative to the various parts of the liturgical year were then examined.

933. Paschal Segment (p. 10). In order to spare time, it was agreed to reorganize the Biblical readings, even in Lent, increasing the daily Office from one Nocturn to three. With regard to the distribution of the Biblical books, the proposal of the *Esposto* was accepted, with some slight modifications, suggested by Father Bea, which made greater use of the Acts of the Apostles, both letters of St. Peter, and the letters of St. John and St. James.

934. Advent-Epiphany Segment (p. 11). More room should be made for the letter to the Romans. After several proposals, however, it was decided to maintain the *status quo* in the end, since any changes would involve major difficulties.

935. *"Tempus per Annum"* Segment (p. 13). The [proposals of] the *Esposto* were substantially accepted with the following modifications: 4 weeks rather than 6 were assigned to the Book of Kings; 5 weeks rather than 4 were

assigned to the *Sapiential Books*; and 4 weeks instead of 3 were given over to the (Prophets) Ezekiel and Daniel.

936. The meeting ended at 6:45 p.m.

Minutes of the 65th Meeting

937. [The Commission met] at 5:30 p.m. on Friday, June 8, [1956] at the Sacred Congregation of Rites in the Palazzo St. Callisto.

938. All members of the Commission attended.

939. Examination of the *Esposto* on the question of the "*Scriptura occurrens*" resumed at p. 18, which had been reached at the last meeting.

940. Some provisions resulting from the new order of the "*Scriptura occurrens*" had to be made.

941. The *Esposto* proposed the following, so as to safeguard as much as possible the Biblical readings:

942. 1. on the great feasts, the proper scripture readings were to be retained;

943. 2. historical Biblical readings narrating an account of a saint or a mystery were to be moved to the 2nd Nocturn;

944. 3. a 4th historical reading was to be introduced for the feasts reduced to the rank of simplex, so as not to lose or combine the 3rd Biblical reading.

945. The Commission, following a long discussion, established the following:

946. 1. proper Biblical readings were to be retained for the great feasts only. The *occurrens* readings would be used for the other [feasts].

947. 2. Biblical reading must always be included in the 1st Nocturn and never moved to the 2nd, for the following reasons:

948. a. it would reduce the Biblical readings to the level of the historical readings in the 2nd Nocturn, which from a historical perspective, generally lack any organization;

b. it is contrary to tradition;

c. it would give rise to an admiration, any provision for it would be unjustified.

949. 3. The 2nd and 3rd readings on simple feasts, are to be united, so as to conserve integrally the "*Scriptura occurrens*". For the 3rd reading, a historical passage is read, as at present;

950. 4. (p. 20) Three readings with proper responsories or one reading with one responsory? Again, [should it be] three antiphons and three Psalms, or a single antiphon and three Psalms for each Nocturn?

951. The question arose because reviews and publication from various parts of the world, as well as liturgical congresses and study weeks, had a certain tendency to favor the latter solution. They emphasized that the frequent

interruption caused by the readings' being broken up into short passages did not help the continuity of thought or the concentration [of the reader]. The responsories, which were perfectly adapted to the sung Office, seemed incongruous in the read Office which is more typical of most cases.

952.   The Commission decided to retain the traditional basis of three readings with their respective responsories. The abandonment of this system would not be justified by the foreseeable advantages of another system. Father Bea observed that the Biblical readings often did not correspond to the spirit of the liturgical times, which was to be found in the reponsories.

953.   The second part of the proposed question (three antiphons or a single antiphon with three Psalms) would be treated *ex professo* during discussions on the bi-weekly Psalter.

954.   5. On the adaptation of the tenses (p. 23). It was agreed to move the Quartertense of Pentecost to the 2nd week [after Pentecost] and that of September to the 16th week after Pentecost.

955.   The meeting ended with the *Agimus* at 6:30 p.m..

Minutes of the 66th Meeting

956.   [The Commission met] at 5:30 p.m. on Friday, July 6, 1956 at the Sacred Congregation of Rites, His Eminence Cardinal Gaetano Cicognoni, Prefect, presiding.

957.   All members of the Commission attended.

958.   The Commission had been convoked to examine two proposals, which had been circulated during the preceding day:

1. a presentation of a plan for a new "*Capitulare lectionum et evangeliorum*" for the Roman Missal;

2. proposed scripture readings for the pre-Lenten and Lenten periods.

959.   Father Löw had proposed the first project and Father Bea the second.

960.   1. *Nuovo Ordinamento delle pericopi scrittuorali del Missale*

961.   Father Albareda raised a prejudicial matter: were the powers of the Commission limited to the reform of the Breviary, or did they also extend to the Missal? Father Antonelli, referring to the *Memoria*, stated that the Commission had been nominated [to study] the general reform of the liturgy. Hence, that also included the Missal.

962.   The *Relator-Generalis* gave a brief explanation of the lengthy introduction to the project and read its conclusions. The following question was then discussed: "In general terms, should a system of three Biblical readings for the week be adopted in such a way as to have a triennial cycle of readings".

963.   Msgr. Dante saw no reason to expand the present system, both for the

practical difficulties, and because priests often take a single theme for their homilies, on which they preach throughout the year.

964.   Father Bea observed that thematic preaching was not congruent with the tradition. From the preaching of the Gospel up to the 7th century at least, there was a constant tradition of homiletical preaching, i.e. an examination of the Gospel of the Mass. For this reason, and because of the great pastoral advantages deriving from a more varied reading of Scripture, he [Father Bea] welcomed the project.

965.   While Father Albareda recognized the validity of Father Bea's argument, he believed that the project had not sufficiently matured, and since there was no strict bond of interdependence between the Breviary and the Missal, he believed that it would be better to finish the reform of the Breviary before beginning that of the Missal.

966.   His Eminence noted that this involved a plurality of *schemata*, similar to that made by modern commentators on the same pericope used in the Sunday Gospels. Hence, in principle, he would not be unfavorable to a study of the proposal.

967.   After a number of other marginal comments made by other members of the Commission, His Eminence framed the question in the following manner: "In general terms, should the scriptural pericopes of the Mass be expanded?"

968.   The Commission unanimously accepted the proposal.

969.   2. *Lettura scritturistica corrente per la Prequaresima e Quaresima.*

970.   This subject was already known to the Commission since it had been raised at its last meeting. Father Bea had distributed the scriptural readings for all the days of both periods, having applied the criteria [for selection] already approved.

971.   Questions (p. 3):

972.   a. Should the proposed extracts be accepted? Reply: Affirmative.

973.   b. Should the Book of Ruth be omitted?

974.   Almost all members of the Commission expressed a desire that this book should be read (three readings) on one day, because the new arrangement [of scripture readings] uses something from all the books of Sacred Scripture.

975.   c. Should one Nocturn be maintained during the pre-Lenten period or should three Nocturns be introduced?

976.   All favored [maintaining] one Nocturn.

977.   The meeting ended at 6:40 p.m..

Minutes of the 67th Meeting

978.   [The Commission met] at 5 p.m. on Tuesday, December 11, 1956 (feast of

St. Damasus) at the Sacred Congregation of Rites with Cardinal Gaetano Cicognoni, the Prefect, presiding.

979. All members of the Commission attended.

980. The prayer was said and the minutes of the previous meeting (July 6, 1956) were read. An examination of some proposed "*Ordinationes et declarationes*" began. [These attempted] to resolve some difficulties concerning the celebration of Holy Week.

981. Prior to the meeting a *pro-memoria* had been circulated to the members of the Commission.

982. I. Palm Sunday.

983. 1. *Processione anche nelle ore pomeridiane.*

984. Some bishops had requested a concession to hold the solemn procession of palms in the evening in certain circumstances.

985. Msgr. Dante observed that this matter was connected with the more general question of the discipline for evening Mass and would have to be resolved in that context. Evening Mass had been permitted merely to facilitate the satisfaction of the obligation to attend Mass. The solemnities had been excluded. Such Masses had to be read Masses. Increasingly, however, requests had been made for sung or Solemn Masses, or for Masses connected with other events.

986. Were this concession made (and the matter would have to be referred to the Holy Father), the Commission would have no difficulty in conceding a faculty to the bishop permitting the solemn procession to be held in the evening "*Rationabili et gravi causa*".

987. 2. *Benedizione delle Palme senza Processione.*

The Commission took a negative view. The blessing of palms is closely connected with the procession which is [the main] characteristic of this Sunday. A blessing [of palms], without a procession would reduce it to a simple sacramental. This would be to the detriment of the rite which would lose much of its forcefulness.

988. II. Holy Thursday.

989. 1. *Ora della Messa in Cena Domini.*

In response to very many request, the Commission took a favorable view, with regard to extending the time at which the *Cena Domini* Mass could be celebrated, and fixed it thus: 4 p.m. – 9 p.m..

990. 2. *Una Messa letta al mattino.*

The following was noted with regard to the pastoral reasons advanced by some bishops to encourage the faithful to receive Holy Communion on the day on which the Holy Eucharist was instituted:

    1. it would be difficult to discipline the matter;

    2. there is the danger that the older practice would be gradually reintroduced;

    3. the matter would have to be referred to the bishops who could permit it *"gravi de causa"* in particular cases, especially for teaching or nursing sisters.

991.   The Commission agreed to this disposition and approved the concession of the faculty.

992.   3. *Comunione dei ministri e dei chierici che assistono alla Missa Chrismatis.*

993.   The unanimous decision of the Commission was negative.

994.   4. *Comunione degli ammalati nel Giovedì Santo.*

995.   The Commission agreed on this.

996.   III. Good Friday.

997.   1. *Se permettere che l'Azione liturgica possa essere repetuta.*

998.   Monsignor Dante completely opposed [the suggestion] because the practical difficulties would be considerable and not easily resolved. Father Albareda also opposed it, noting that a single celebration of this ceremony on Good Friday was a very important element which, it could be said, was integrally connected to the entire rite.

999.   Father Bea said that in theory he would not be unfavorable to the repetition of the *Actio Liturgica* of Good Friday. It could be repeated for grave pastoral reasons. Insufficient space [for a congregation] might require a repetition of the ceremony. He observed that *"Sacramenta sunt propter homines"*. The participation of the faithful at the sacred ceremonies had to be facilitated as much as possible.

1000. After an exhaustive discussion during which the question was considered in all its aspects, the Commission agreed not to mention the subject in the *Declarationes*. The Sacred Congregation of Rites would study the question, case by case, as the bishops asked for such a concession, and concede particular indults as required.

1001. 2. *Ora della celebrazione.*

1002. As in the case of Holy Thursday, the Commission agreed to concede moving the *Actio Liturgica* to a time between midday and 9 p.m..

1003. 3. *Adorazione della croce.*

1004. Of the four proposals (p. 6) made to facilitate the adoration of the cross in the bigger and more crowded churches, the Commission favored the 3rd proposal. Following the adoration of the cross by the clergy, the cross should be shown to the people from the altar, on the pulpit, or the altar rails, while the celebrant would invite the faithful to recollect themselves in adoration, during a minute's silence.

1005. IV. Easter Vigil.

1006. 1. *Ora della celebrazione.*

1007. Some of the German speaking countries requested the German practice of celebrating the Vigil in the early hours of Easter Sunday morning. Since this was a local practice, there was no great danger that it would spread. The Commission agreed not to mention this in the *Ordinationes*. Particular indults could be conceded to those who requested them.

1008. 2. *Ordinazioni durante la Veglia.*

All agreed that dispositions would have to be made prohibiting any further ordinations to Sacred Orders during the Vigil.

1009. The meeting ended with the usual prayer at 7:10 p.m..

Minutes of the 68th Meeting

1010. [The meeting was held] on Tuesday, December 16, 1957 at 5 p.m. in the Sacred Congregation of Rites, Cardinal Gaetano Cicognoni, Prefect, presiding.

1011. All members of the Commission attended except Father Albareda, who was excused.

1012. Having said the usual prayer, Father Antonelli, *Relator-Generalis*, briefly introduced a fascicle entitled, "*Dubia circa novam editionem Pontificalis romani*", which was to be presented to the Cardinal members of the Sacred Congregation of Rites at the next ordinary meeting of the Dicastary.

1013. The Roman Pontifical was no longer commercially available. Before reprinting the Pontifical, the publishers had asked the Sacred Congregation of Rites whether a new edition should be printed as rumor had it that the Pontifical was about to be reformed. In the event of a reprinting of the Pontifical, they asked if they might not omit some parts no longer in use.

1014. Having referred the matter to the Holy Father, he decided that the matter should be placed before the Cardinal members of the Sacred Congregation of Rites. A brief *posizione* had been drawn up about which His Eminence, the Cardinal Prefect, wished to have the Commission's opinion.

1015. The questions and the proposed replies were favorably received by all. The publication of an "*Excerptum*" from the Pontifical could easily be produced as a fascicle. This seemed to be the best solution. His Eminence observed that it would be good to draw up a precise list of the rites to be retained in the new *Pontificale*. The Secretary of the Commission was asked to propose the list.

1016. Examination of the *Instructio Musicae Sacrae* then began. It was the second document on the agenda of the meeting. The new draft, officially prepared by the Historical Section, taking account of the four previous drafts, was more or less unanimously approved by the Commission. The first 20 articles were examined. Only marginal comments of little significance were made.

1017. The next meeting of the Commission, to be held on December 20, would resume examination of the *Instructio* at Chapter III: *Normae speciales*.

1018. The meeting ended with the *Agimus* at 6:30 p.m..

Minutes of the 69th Meeting

1019. [The Commission met] at 5 p.m. on Tuesday, January 7, 1958 at the Sacred Congregation of Rites, Cardinal Gaetano Cicognoni, Prefect, presiding.

1020. All members of the Commission attended.

1021. After the usual prayer, examination of the Instruction on Sacred Music resumed from articles 21-59.

1022. Slight changes were made to articles 33 and 45; as for the rest, the Commission unanimously approved the proposed text.

1023. The meeting ended with the *Agimus* at 6:15 p.m..

Minutes of the 70th Meeting

1024. [The meeting met] at 5 p.m. on January 28, 1958 in the *Sala del Congresso* of the Sacred Congregation of Rites, ·Cardinal Gaetano Cicognani, Prefect, presiding.

1025. All members of the Commission attended.

1026. The prayer was said, and the meeting opened. Two items were on the agenda: the blessing of ashes; and the examination of the remaining articles of the Instruction on Sacred Music.

1027. 1. *Blessing of Ashes.*
Some bishops asked [for the concession] to bless ashes on the *"Feria IV in capite ieiunii"* at an evening Mass, as well as at morning Mass.

1028. The Historical Section took this opportunity to revise the whole rite in accordance with the principles of the liturgical reform, and to model this rite on the blessings of palms [on Palm Sunday].

1029. Discussion of the project was prefaced by a study of the question of principle asking:
could the blessing of ashes be repeated several times on the same day;
should this concession be granted for evening Masses;
and, should the entire rite in the Missal be revised?

1030. Views differed [on these questions]. It was observed that:

1031. 1. it did not seem opportune to change either the formulae or the rite in the Missal. It [was opportune] to await the general reform to do it;

1032. 2. *di per sé* it did not appear indispensable to repeat the blessing of ashes, if they were to be imposed throughout the entire day.

1033. These and other reasons, led the Commission to propose a concession permitting the blessing of ashes at the evening Mass, but without any variation of the rite. This decision would be placed before the Holy Father, and, if approved, it would be published in the *Osservatore Romano*.

1034. 2. *Instruction on Sacred Music.*

Examination of articles 60-97 resumed. They were unanimously acceptable and fully satisfactory to the Commission.

1035. The meeting ended, with the usual prayer at 6:30 p.m..

Minutes of the 71st Meeting

1036. [The Commission met] at 5 p.m. on Friday, February 28, 1958 in the Sacred Congregation of Rites, His Eminence Cardinal Gaetano Cicognoni, presiding.

1037. All members of the Commission were present.

1038. Following the usual prayer, examination of the *Instructio* on Sacred Music, from article 96 to the end, resumed.

1039. No notable comments were made.

1040. The meeting closed with the *Agimus* at 6:15 p.m..

Minutes of the 72nd Meeting

1041. [The meeting took place] at 5 p.m. on Friday, May 3, [1958] at the Sacred Congregation of Rites, His Eminence Cardinal Gaetano Cicognoni, presiding.

1042. All members of the Commission were present, except Msgr. Albareda, and Msgr. Carinci who was ill.

1043. A final revision of the *"Istruzione sulla Musica Sacra e la Sacra Liturgia"* was done. It concentrated on a number of points, which had to be re-done *ex novo*, especially articles 2, and 22 to 38.

1044. The Commission approved the corrections. Some doubts persisted with regard to articles 13, 14, and 16, which required greater accuracy.

1045. The meeting ended with the *Agimus* at 7 p.m..

Minutes of the 73rd Meeting

1046. [The Commission met] at 5 p.m. on Tuesday, November 18, 1958 in the *Sala del Congresso* of the Sacred Congregation of Rites, the Prefect, His Eminence Cardinal Gaetano Cicognani presided.

1047. All members of the Commission attended except Father Albareda, absent from Rome, and Father Löw, indisposed.

1048. The Commission had been convoked to examine the reformed rite for the consecration of churches.

1049. The simplified rite, as usual, had been drawn up by the Historical Section. The draft had been examined by a dozen "*periti*" and finalized on the basis of their observations.

1050. The new rite, together with a printed copy of the old rite of dedication, for comparitive purposes, had been circulated to the Commission in July 1958.

1051. On October 30 a brief explanation, which served to orient the work of the Commission, had also been [sent to the members].

1052. Following the prayers, the meeting opened. The *Relator-Generalis* explained the criteria guiding the reform. The individual articles of the text were then examined.

1053. Article 2 – Msgr. Dante believed that the consecration of churches should not be permitted in the afternoon. It was observed that the Holy Office had given a faculty to the local Ordinary to determine the opportunity of having Mass in the afternoon when such is necessary. The Commission retained the concession for an evening Mass for the dedication rite, in accordance with the terms established by the Holy Office: "*quando bonum notabilis partis fidelium id postulet*" (S. Ufficio 404/46-236, June 11, 1957).

1054. This limitation eliminated the third line, "*Licet*", and the fourth, "*Hoc in casa*".

1055. Article 5 – The fourth line which permitted the omission of the hours of the Office corresponding to the time for the consecration of the church was deemed inopportune and thus deleted.

1056. Article 6 – The term "*Prelati*" (here and elsewhere) seemed too general. It was to be replaced by "*Episcopi*". The second paraparph was to be suppressed as it was best to retain [current] usage, recently introduced for the co-consecrators at Episcopal consecrations, whereby all consecrating bishops say the formulae.

1057. Article 7 (15) – Father Bea observed that it would be necessary to specify the use of violet vestments here.

1058. Article 9 – Msgr. Dante observed that the term "*Possessio*" did not seem quite accurate. The church had already taken possession of the ground with the laying of the foundation stone. Hence, some difference in their significance had to be admitted.

1059. With the laying of the foundation the ground is set apart from profane use and designated [as a place] destined for the building of a church. With the dedication of a church, it is the sacred edifice, together with the ground, in their totality, which are designated as the House of God.

1060. In the second paragraph, Msgr. Dante found the ceremony for the relics too hurried. It was reduced merely to putting on vestments and seemed more suitable for a sacristy than a chapel. He suggested the introduction of an antiphon and an "*oratio*".

1061. The Commission accepted the emendation.

1062. The examination reached article 13. The next meeting would take place on the following Tuesday, November 25.

1063. The meeting ended at 6:30 p.m..

Minutes of the 74th Meeting

1064. [The Commission met] at 5 p.m. on Tuesday, November 25, 1958 in the *Sala del Congresso* of the Sacred Congregation of Rites, the Prefect, Cardinal Gaetano Cicognani, presiding.

1065. All members attended except Father Löw, who was indisposed.

1066. The examination of the proposed reform of the rite of consecration of a church resumed at article 13 and continued to article 25.

1067. Article 13 – [The Commission] wished to reduce to one, the triple "*Aperite*" declaimed by all present.

1068. Article 14 – In the litany of the Saints, it was well to restore the invocation of St. Anastasia, so as to have a representative of the Holy Widows. It would also justify the invocation "*Omnes Sanctae Virgines et Viduae*".

1069. As in the past, it was asked that the invocation "*Ut ecclesiam et altare hoc*" be repeated three times since this was a solemn moment.

1070. Article 24 – The verb "*occupamus*" in the formula "*Ad honorem...*" should be omitted. The text was slightly modified.

1071. It was suggested that Psalm 47 be omitted since it was not "functional".

1072. The session rose at 6 p.m.. The next meeting would be held on December 9, 1958.

Minutes of the 75th Meeting

1073. [The Commission met] at 5 p.m. on Tuesday, December 9, 1958 in the *Sala del Congresso* of the Sacred Congregation of Rites, the Prefect, His Eminence Cardinal Gaetano Cicognoni, presiding.

1074. All members of the Commission were present except for Father Löw who was indiposed.

1075. Article 35 – The "*oratio*": "*Deus qui ex omni coaptatione Sanctorum*" should read according to its original text as found in the Gelesian Sacramentary.

1076. Article 36 – In the formula for the consecration of the church and the altar, it was desirable that the Saint to whom the church is dedicated should be named with the following formula: "*In honorem Dei te in memoriam sancti*".

1077. Article 39 – The formula: "*Porta sis benedicta*" should be simplified to: "*Porta sis consecrata et Domino Deo commendata; Porta sis ostium, etc.*".

1078. Article 46 – With regard to the three antiphons it was determined: "*dicuntur una vel plures*".

1079. Article 51 – The rubric had to be changed so as to commemorate the titular Saint "*sub unica conclusione*" in the "*oratio*" of the dedication. All other commemoration of whatever kind were to be excluded.

1080. Article 55 – This article was to be suppressed.

1081. The meeting ended at 6:30 p.m. with the usual prayers.

Minutes of the 76th Meeting

1082. [The Commission met] at 5 p.m. on Friday, February 20, 1959 in the *Sala del Congresso* of the Sacred Congregation of Rites, the Prefect, Cardinal Gaetano Cicognoni, presiding.

1083. All members of the Commission attended except Father Albareda, OSB, who was excused.

1084. The Commission had met in special session to consider two urgent matters relating to Holy Week: the question of whether large readings of Holy Week could be done in the vernacular was raised by Cardinal Frings, in the name of the German Episcopate, and several other bishops; [and the other matter to consider was] the question of whether the liturgical action of Good Friday could be repeated once or twice.

1085. A *pro-memoria* outlining the "*status quaestionis*" had been circulated to the members of the Commission some days prior to the meeting.

1086. 1st Question: *Le grandi letture della Settimana Santa in volgare.*

His Eminence explained the problem and announced that the matter had been submitted to the Holy Father for his consideration. His Holiness did not oppose [the proposal]. The votes of the members of the Commission were then collected. The Secretary of the Commission favored the concession because:

1. it was part of the nature of a reading that its hearers should understand something of it;

2. since there is no common policy existing among the various Dicasteries, even if the Sacred Congregation of Rites refused the concession, other [Dicasteries] would grant it anyway, just as it had happened in similar cases in the past.

1087. Father Löw emphasized the point that a speaker had to be understood. Matters had advanced to such a degree on the subject that if the Sacred

Congregation of Rites did not make the concession, it would be done of their own accord (without reference to the Congregation). Thus he also favored granting the concession.

1088. Father Bea observed:

1. historically, the principle of understanding the readings has always been vivid in the Church. The writings of Eteria, St. Augustine, and others reflecting Roman usage, make this clear;

2. it is expedient and justifiable to concede the use of the vernacular for those parts [of the ceremonies] which are long, in order salvage the rest;

3. no concession should ever be made for the singing of the *Exultet*, in whole or part, in the vernacular;

4. study and resolve the the question of the competence of language. Father Bea voted in favor.

1089. Msgr. Carinci was favorable and vindicated the competence of the Sacred Congregation of Rites in the matter.

1090. Father Antonelli was also favorable to the proposal. The growing participation of the faithful in the liturgy justified the concession. Fifty years previously, this would not have been the case. For that reason, the need which is increasingly felt now, had not been as noticeable. On the other hand, it is already accepted that the readings, often the singing or reading of the texts in Latin, could be read in the vernacular. While that is possible on ordinary festive days, it is impossible when readings such as the *Passio* are so long. He therefore favored reading the *Passio* on Palm Sunday, and Good Friday, and the four readings of the Easter Vigil directly in the vernacular.

1091. Following a serene and ample discussion, the Commission decided to propose to the Holy Father the granting of a concession for the entire Church for the Passio on Palm Sunday and Good Friday to be read in the vernacular, according to terms to be established by the Sacred Congregation of Rites, and [also to grant a similar concession] for the four readings at the Easter Vigil.

1092. 2nd Question: *Ripetizione dell'Azione liturgica al Venerdì Santo*.

1093. All agreed to the concession in view of the great numbers of the faithful being able to attend the ceremony in the evening and because of a rediscovered sense of the liturgy among the people.

1094. The meeting ended, after the usual prayer, at 6:30 p.m..

Minutes of the 77th Meeting

1095. [The Commission met] at 5 p.m. on Friday, May 15, 1959 in the *Sala del Congresso* of the Sacred Congregation of Rites, the Prefect, Cardinal Gaetano Cicognani, presided.

1096.   All members attended.

1097.   The letter convoking the Commission contained the agenda for the meeting: Examination of a reformed rite of some consecrations and blessings contained in the second part of the Roman Pontifical, i.e.

1098.   consecration of a church (definitive draft);

1099.   consecration of an altar without the consecration of a church;

1100.   blessing of a foundation stone for a new church;

1101.   blessing of churches;

1102.   blessing of a portable altar;

1103.   consecration of bells;

1104.   blessing of a cemetery;

1105.   reconciliation of churches;

1106.   reconciliation of cemeteries;

1107.   *examination of the definitive drafts for the consecration of a church.*

1108.   Article 2 – Msgr. Dante observed that any reference to a bishop permitting, for pastoral reasons, the consecration of a church in the evening should be removed. A prolonged discussion ensued. The members of the Commission were divided as to whether to permit the concession or not.

1109.   Since a question of principle was involved in this matter, it should be referred to the Holy Father for a decision.

1110.   Article 14 – Msgr. Dante noted that in the litany of the Saints, St. Agatha followed St. Cecilia, while she preceded St. Agnes in the old text.

1111.   Article 19 – Msgr. Dante also observed that the order of the ceremony for the aspersion of the altar should be inverted. The aspersion of the altar should take place before tracing the crosses on the mensa.

1112.   Both emendations were accepted.

1113.   Article 53 – Msgr. Dante took the view that the prayers at the foot of the altar should be omitted. It should be noted that the rite of consecration of a church was almost exclusively penitential in character. It was designed to evoke those sentiments of purification and penance in both the celebrant and people which were expressed in the prayer of the "Confession". The omission (of the prayers at the foot of the altar) was both logical and justified. An analogous precedent had been established in the revised liturgy of the Easter Vigil. The majority of the members of the Commission took this view.

1114.   *Consecration of an altar.*

1115.   Father Antonelli expressed the view that the title should be united with others: e.g. "*Ordo Consecrationis altaris sine Ecclesiae dedicatione*". The proposal was accepted.

1116. Article 9 – Father Bea observed that the rubric ("*Hic Pontifex...*") had been taken directly from the rite of consecration of a church. Since it did not read well as it was, it would have to be adjusted.

1117. The proposal was accepted.

1118. Article 10 – Father Bea observed that the prayer *Magnificare*, while suitable for the consecration of a church, was not suitable in this context and should be changed. This amendment was accepted by all.

1119. Article 11 – As already noted in the case of the consecration of a church, the order of the ceremony would have to be changed with regard to the aspersion.

1120. *Blessing of a foundation stone for a new church.*

1121. Article 12 – Restore the old rubric which gave better expression to the bishop's function of "laying" the foundation stone.

1122. The meeting ended at 6:15 p.m. with the usual prayers.

Minutes of the 78th Meeting

1123. [The Commission met] at 5:30 p.m. on Friday, July 10, 1959 in the *Sala del Congresso* of the Sacred Congregation of Rites, the Prefect, Cardinal Gaetano Cicognani, presided.

1124. All members of the Commission were present.

1125. The Commission met to examine the final draft of the Roman Pontifical.

1126. p. 71 – Consecration of the paten before the chalice was rejected. The title also had to be changed.

1127. p. 73 – The blessing of incense was better left in its own place (p. 25) in the rite for the consecration of a church.

1128. p. 74 – The blessing of the [altar] linen was best left in its proper place [in the rite] for the consecration of a church (p. 25). The word "*consecratiorum*" should be omitted from the title; and the expressions "*sanctificare et consecrare*" suppressed in the "*Oremus*".

1129. p. 75 – This blessing follows the consecration of the altar.

1130. p. 76 – Omit "*sanctificare*" and leave only one prayer, preferably the second.

1131. p. 78 – Retain the first prayer only. Add the blessing for the purificators and the palls, and adapt the second "*Oremus*".

1132. p. 80 – Omit the second and third "*Oremus*".

1133. p. 82 – The initial rubric must be adjusted.

1134. p. 85 – The "*sub tuum praesidium*" is to be the final hymn.

1135. p. 87 – Insert the *Salve Regina* for the "*Extra tempus paschale*". Check the entire formulary against that used by the Sacred Congregation of Rites.

1136. p. 89 – Omit "sanctificare".

1137. p. 90 – Omit the second "*Oremus*".

1138. p. 95 – The blessing for "Gregorian" water is to be restored to the rite for the consecration of a church.

1139. The meeting ended at 6:30 p.m..

Minutes of the 79ᵗʰ Meeting

1140. [The Commission met] at 5 p.m. on Friday, May 27, 1960 in the *Sala del Congresso* of the Sacred Congregation of Rites with the Prefect, Cardinal Gaetano Cicognani, presiding.

1141. A reorganization of the Pontifical Commission for the Reform of the Liturgy, instituted by His late Holiness, Pope Pius XII in 1948, became necessary following the elevation of His Eminence Cardinal Bea, SJ to the Sacred Purple, the promotion of Msgr. Carinci to Secretary Emeritus of the Sacred Congregation of Rites, the nomination of Msgr. Dante as Secretary (of the same Congregaiton), the nomination of Father Antonelli, OFM as *Promoter Fidei*, of Msgr. Frutaz as *Relator-Generalis*, and of Father Löw as Adjunct *Relator-Generalis*. Following these recent nominations, the Commission was constituted as follows: President – the Prefect of the Sacred Congregation of Rites, Cardinal Gaetano Cicognani.

1142. Original members:

1143. His Excellency, Msgr. Dante, Secretary of the Sacred Congregation of Rites;

1144. The Most Reverend Father Antonelli, OFM, *Promotor Generalis Fidei*;

1145. The Right Rev. Abbot Albareda, OSB, Prefect of the Apostolic Library of the Vatican and Consultor of the Sacred Congregation of Rites;

1146. The Most Reverend Father Löw, CSSR, Vice *Relator-Generalis*, now Adjunct *Relator-Generalis*;

1147. The Most Reverend Father Bugnini, CM, Consultor of the Sacred Congregation of Rites and Secretary of the Commission.

1148. Recently appointed members:

1149. His Excellency Msgr. Cesario D'Amato, OSB, Abbot of St. Paul's;

1150. Msgr. Amato Pietro Frutaz, *Relator-Generalis* of the Historical Section;

1151. The Reverend L. Rovigatti, Parish Priest (of the Parish of the Nativity, Rome);

1152. The Most Reverend Father Braga, CM, *Attaché* for the liturgical reform.

1153. The Commission met to examine the proposed second simplification of the rubrics, following that of 1955. The following documents had been distributed to the members of the Commission prior to the meeting:

1154. 1. *Calendarium Breviarii et Missalis Romani* in printed draft form, accompanied by 6 pages of "*Note esplicative*" [Explanatory notes];

1155. 2. *Rubricae Breviarii et Missalis Romani, Prima Pars: Rubricae Generalis*, accompanied by 9 pages of "*Note esplicative*".

1156. Following a brief introduction of the subject by the Cardinal Prefect, Father Löw, Adjunct *Relator-Generalis* of the Historical Section, explained the general lines of the project, and outlined its structure, objective, advantages and the criteria on which it had been based.

1157. Discussion began.

1158. Msgr. Dante remarked:

1. The Commission should firstly draw up a general plan for such an important undertaking and outline all the directives to be followed, so as to avoid wasting time and work.

2. The 4th class of feasts seemed superfluous and could be amalgamated with the third.

1159. Monsignor continued by making some remarks about the calendar which, with the abolition of some feasts (e.g. St. Peter in Chains), would have to be radically modified.

1160. Father Antonelli regarded the proposed project as good. The abolition of some of the doubly celebrated feasts was completely justified and would not substantially modify the calendar.

1161. Each article of the plan was then examined and approved unanimously by the Commission after some minor comments.

1162. The two proposals mentioned at the end of the "*Note esplicative*", concerning the liturgical colors in missionary territories and some of the pontifical vestments, were also approved in accordance with the proposals set out in the project.

1163. The meeting ended with the *Agimus* at 6:45 p.m..

Minutes of the 80th Meeting

1164. [The Commission met] at 3:30 p.m. on Tuesday, June 14, 1960 in the *Sala del Congresso* of the Sacred Congregation of Rites, the Prefect, Cardinal Gaetano Cicognani, presiding.

1165. All members were present except Father Albareda who was excused.

1166. The Commission met to continue its examination of the "*Rubricae Breviarii et Missalis Romani*". Prior to the meeting the following had been circulated to the members:

1167. 1. a printed draft of the "*Pars Secunda, Rubricae Generalis Breviarii Romani*";

1168. 2. 12 pages of "*Note esplicative*" [Explanatory notes] attached to the "*Pars Secunda*".

1169. The usual prayer was said and the minutes read. Father Löw spoke on the question of four classes [of feasts]. Was it opportune to have three or four classes? Father Löw noted that the third and fourth classes could be amalgamated for feasts, and kept distinct for ferials, votive Masses, and for Masses for the dead.

1170. The *Rubricae generalis Breviarii* were then examined.

1171. Article 139 – A faculty to omit Terce, Sext, and None on Sundays, so as to facilitate the clergy with the *cura animarum*, caused perplexity among the numbers of the Commission. Father Antonelli opposed the idea because:

1. such a measure, in his view, would bring no appreciable relief [to the clergy];

2. reduction of the present discipline would create a dangerous precedent;

3. no reason could be seen for reducing Sundays in this manner and not the other days of the week which were equally demanding for the priestly ministry, e.g. the first Friday of the month.

1172. With regard to Prime, Father Antonelli favored simplifying it, by eliminating or moving the *officium capituli* in whole or part. In an effort to meet the needs of the pastoral clergy, Father Antonelli made the counter suggestion that consideration be given to the adoption of a bi-weekly Psalter. This would represent a tangible reduction of the entire Office and avoid the inconveniences and complaints caused by the proposal of article 139.

1173. The Commission, thus, concentrated its attention on the bi-weekly Psalter. The following favored [its introduction]: Father Braga, the Secretary of the Commission, Don Rovigatti, Father Löw, Father Antonelli, Msgr. D'Amato. Msgr. Frutaz opposed [its introduction] for it would effectively create a new Breviary. Msgr. Dante did not oppose the proposal, but thought it better not to activate it until after the Ecumenical Council. In conclusion, parts 2 and 3 of article 139 were abolished. The proposal to introduce a bi-weekly Psalter should be referred to the Holy Father as soon as possible.

1174. Article 144 – The possibility of anticipating Matins from 2 p.m. was to be retained.

1175. Article 147 – The insertion "*flexis genibus*" was to be eliminated as it did not correspond to reality. In choir, Compline was recited standing up.

1176. The proposal of abolishing the absolutions and blessings when the office was said "*a solo*" was acceptable to no one. This would incurr the loss of further choral elements from the Office. Since the Commission had previously decided to avoid creating distinctions between the choral Office and the Office recited "*a solo*", these formularies had to be retained.

1177. Article 235 – It was necessary to state explicitly that the *Te Deum* was to be said during the vigil of Pentecost.

1178. Articles 241 and 242 – A proposal to omit the Chapters and short responsories from the minor hours when the office was said "*a solo*" was opposed by those who emphasized the unity of the Office. In consequence of its previous decision, the Commission decided to leave these parts [of the Office] unchanged.

1179. Article 247 – The replacement of the *Dominus vobiscum* with the *Domine exaude* was approved for the recitation of the Office "*a solo*". A good precedent was to be had in the Office recited by a subdeacon.

1180. Article 257c. – Msgr. Frutaz suggested that this part of the article be modified. It should be specified that when the Office of a Confessor Pontiff at Lauds also has the commemoration of a non-Pope Confessor, the antiphon should be taken from Vespers and not from Lauds, so as to avoid repeating the identical antiphon.

1181. The meeting ended at 7:15 p.m.. The next meeting to be held on July 1. It would examine the "*Tertia pars, Rubricae, Generalis Missalis*".

Minutes of the 81ˢᵗ Meeting

1182. [The Commission met] at 5:30 p.m. on Tuesday, July 1, [1960] in the *Sala del Congresso* of the Sacred Congregation of Rites, the Prefect, Cardinal Gaetano Cicognani, presiding.

1183. All members of the Commission were present except Father Albareda who was excused.

1184. The examination of the second simplification of the rubrics resumed. Prior to the meeting, the following had been distributed [to the members of the Commission]:

1185. 1. A printed fascicle containing the *pars tertia* of the rubrics: *Rubricae generalis Missalis Romani*;

1186. 2. A folder of 29 pages containing: the "*Note esplicative*" (pp. 1-16) for the previously mentioned document; some questions and proposals to be submitted to the Commission (pp. 17-29). The meeting began with an examination of the latter section.

1187. 1. *Concerning the appropriations of reducing the Sunday Office.*

At the meeting of the June 14, the Commission had accepted a proposal to introduce a bi-weekly Psalter so as to reduce the Office as a whole. On further reflection, implementation of the proposal did not seem opportune. Consequently, the question of reducing the Sunday Office was reintroduced. The [Sunday Office], as a result of the new simplification of the rubrics, would [still] end up longer than the other days. It was proposed to reduce this Office to nine psalms and three readings. In this case, there were two possibilities with regard to the readings: either retain the scripture readings for the first two readings and for the third, add one of the three lessons which provided commentary on the Gospel; or, revise the readings on the basis of the vigil scheme, admitting the three commentaries on the Gospel. The majority of the Commission favored the first solution: two scripture readings and a homeletical reading.

1188. 2. *Document for the promulgation of the second simplification.*

After careful study, it was generally agreed that the second simplification of the rubrics would be most opportunely promulgated by means of a general decree of the Sacred Congregation of Rites. At most, the proposal could be made to the Holy Father to have it promulgated as a *motu proprio*.

1189. 3. *Concerning the appropriations of modifying the plan for the "Communio Sanctorum".*

The Commission decided that it was more convenient to leave the plan unchanged for the present.

1190. 4. *Extension of the concessions already granted for Holy Week:*

1191. a. Incensation during a *Missa Cantata*. The Commission took the view that (the concessions) should be extended to all sung Masses of the year as a general law.

1192. b. Silent prayer at the "*Flectamus genua*". Approved.

1193. c. Omission of the *Confiteor* at the Communion "*infra Missam*". Approved.

1194. d. Permission for the celebrant to omit silent reading of those parts which are sung by the [various] ministers "*vi proprii officii*". The concession was unanimously approved.

1195. e. Omission of the last Gospel. The Commission did not regard this as opportune.

1196. f. Permission for the celebrant to omit reading silently those parts sung by the "*schola*".

1197. The Commission did not regard this as opportune.

1198. 5. *Other possible concessions.*

1199. a. *Genuflection at the final doxology of the Canon.*

The Commission decided not to make any changes for the moment.

1200. b. Prefaces of Advent, of the Most Holy Eucharist, and of the dedication [of a church].

1201. The proposed texts were not very satisfactory. While the majority of the Commission believed that it was necessary to introduce proper Prefaces for the aforementioned Masses, it recognized that such was not possible for the present.

1202. Examination of the *Rubricae generalis Missalis Romani* then began.

1203. Article 282 – It was necessary to state explicitly that [female] religious are bound to follow the diocesan calendar—possibly by inserting the phrase "*utriusque sexus*".

1204. Article 296 – Msgr. Dante wished to make the second Mass of Christmas a conventual obligation. On reflection, it was agreed to leave things as is, so as to ease the obligations of the Office on [Christmas] day.

1205. Article 307 – Msgr. Dante desired the elimination of the part referring to a votive Mass for the *Beati* [Beatified], because the *Beati* cannot have a votive Mass. The amendment was accepted. Consequently, all other articles mentioning the subject would be corrected.

1206. Article 333 – Msgr. Dante observed that it would be good always to permit the *Missa Dedicationis* on the day of the consecration of a church. [It should, however, be] explicitly stated that such was a special case. The amendment was accepted.

1207. Article 349 – Msgr. Dante desired that the *Missa Pro Pace* should be retained on the second day of the *Quarantore* [Forty Hours]. However, he accepted the majority view which considered it more convenient to leave a freedom of choice based on local circumstances in this matter.

1208. At this late stage (7:30 p.m.) the meeting was suspended. Father Löw distributed a further dossier containing:

   1. the second edition of the *Calendarium Brevarii et Missalis Romani*;

   2. 26 typed pages, containing the *Variationes in Brevario et Missali Romano ad normam novae Redationis Rubricarum* (pp. 1-13) and the *Annotazioni* to the calendar (2nd edition) and to the *Variationes* (pp. 14-26).

1209. After which, the prayer was said, the date of the next meeting announced [Friday, July 8 at 5:30 p.m.], and the meeting closed.

Minutes of the 82nd Meeting

1210. [The Commission] met at 5:30 p.m. on Friday, July 8, [1960] in the *Sala del Congresso* of the Sacred Congregation of Rites, the Prefect, Cardinal Gaetano Cicognoni, presiding.

1211. All members of the Commission were present except Father Albareda who was excused.

1212. Examination of the *Rubricae generalis Missalis Romani* resumed at article 373, which had been reached at the previous meeting.

1213. Article 373 – Msgr. Dante asked that legislation with regard to Masses in sanctuaries be better regulated and adapted to all sanctuaries.

1214. The remaining articles were approved with minor observations.

1215. Examination of the revised calendar began. It had been distributed prior to the meeting. Msgr. Frutaz proposed reducing the feasts of St. Alexius, St. George, and St. Eustace to commemorations because their "historical" sections were completely fictitious. The proposal was accepted. Monsignor also asked that the feast of St. Irenaeus be transferred to the July 3, which was free, because in Rome it would coincide with the feast of the Roman proto-martyrs. This emendation was also accepted.

1216. Msgr. Dante was of the view that that commemoration of St. Paul on the feast of St. Peter, and vice-versa, be retained.

1217. After careful consideration, this request was approved.

1218. Finally, a draft for the *Decretum generale* (changed later to a *motu proprio* by disposition of the Holy Father) was examined and approved with some stylistic emendations.

1219. This concluded the examination of the second simplification of the rubrics, and practically brought to a close the work of the Pontifical Commission for the Reform of the Liturgy before [the opening] of the Ecumenical Council.

1220. Having recited the *Agimus*, the meeting ended at 7:30 p.m..

Bibliography

Introductory Note

This study and exploration of the thought of Fr. Ferdinando Giuseppe Antonelli began with the collection and classification of his papers. In the present work, we are interested only in his liturgical writings. Antonelli's papers also contain material on hagiography, Franciscan themes, the religious life, the *Opera della Regalità*, and many other topics. His importance as a liturgist emerged gradually as we sorted through his papers all of which are annotated by him. Our research into his work and thought is restricted to the liturgy – that delicate sector of the Church's life.

It was necessary to take into consideration Antonelli's diaries. These extend from 1915 (*Memorie sulla vita militare*) to 1993, the year in which he died. They afford an insight into the heart of his thought, reveal the extent of his energy, his impressions, his emotions, and his transparency.

In view of what we discovered, we have been able to compile a new and fuller bibliography of material relating to Antonelli, integrating it with previous bibliographies. Every work was carefully examined. From this, new things emerged concerning Antonelli's lectures, conferences, conventions, meetings, and publications. Although we have not undertaken a specific study of the articles published by Antonelli, we have examined all of the manuscripts deposited in the archives at *La Verna* and in the Sacred Congregation for the Causes of Saints. We have also used manuscripts in order to clarify particular aspects of Antonelli's work and life, as well as to reconstruct specific incidents in the history of the liturgical reform (1948-1970). Among these, mention should be made of the three notebooks containing the chronicle of the all the meetings of the "*Consilium*".

With regard to Antonelli's literary output in the area of liturgy, it has to be said that it does not consist of research in theoretical subjects, nor is it very voluminous. His primary concern was for the revision and updating of the rites based on a more adequate understanding of the liturgy and its sensibility to contemporary man, marked by a constant effort to balance traditional elements with innovative proposals. This required accurate historical, biblico-theological, liturgical, and pastoral knowledge and an ability to work with a team which was not always the easiest.

Antonelli's role was decisional but ultimate responsibility did not lay with him.

It is thus easy to understand the prudence and wisdom necessary while exercising such a delicate office which affected the entire Church.

When his proposals and those of his collaborators were accepted and made official, he carefully followed their application both normatively and in promoting a wider knowledge of the new rites. He explained the ideas behind them and the objectives sought by these new rites through television appearances, radio broadcasts, lectures, conferences, and by a series of articles published in the *Osservatore Romano* and other specialist publications.

Bibliography of Antonelli's Works

Unpublished Writings

1 9 4 3

1. *Conferenze sulla Santa Messa,* 1943, to April 3, 1971, in *ALV,* pp. 1-106.

1 9 4 4

2. *L'anno Liturgico.* Lectures on the Liturgy, October 30, 1944 to 8 June 1967, in *ALV,* pp. 1-226.

1 9 4 5

3. *La Liturgia dei Sacramenti.* Lectures on the Liturgy, November 4, 1945 to 4 May 1958, in *ALV,* pp. 1-221.

1 9 4 7

4. *La Liturgia e l'Archeologia a servizio della formazione spirituale.* Course for Italian Franciscan teachers, August 22 - September 22, 1947, in *ALV,* pp. 1-18.

5. *Pietà popolare e Liturgia,* Lecture notes from a course for Italian Franciscan teachers, September 1947, in *ALV,* pp. 1-91.

1 9 4 8

6. *Studi fatti dalla Sezione Storica. Memoria del 1948,* in *SCCS,* 1-343.

1 9 5 1

7. *Progetto per la revisione dei riti del Sabato Santo nella eventualità di un ripristino della vigilia di Pasqua,* 1951, SRC Sect. Hist., in *SCCS,* pp. 1-30.

8. *Il ripristino della Solenne Veglia Pasquale,* March 14, 1951, in *ALV,* pp. 1-20.

1 9 5 2

9. *Per l'adunanza del June 10, 1952,* in *SCCS,* pp. 1-4.

10. *Liturgia del tempo di Avvento e ciclo natalizio,* December 3, 1952, in *ALV,* pp. 1-15.

11. *Il "Triduum Sacrum", l'Eucaristia e la pace di Cristo,* Lecture manuscript, Barcelona 1952, in *ALV,* pp. 1-15.

1 9 5 3

12. *Questioni intorno alla Veglia pasquale,* for the meeting of March 10, 1953, in *SCCS,* pp. 1-4.

1 9 5 4

13. *Conferenze sulla S. Messa.* Lectures on the Liturgy, March 4, 1954 to April 3, 1957, in *ALV*, pp. 1- 44.

14. *Annotazioni intorno alla riforma della domenica delle Palme,* May 15, 1954, in *SCCS*, pp. 1-20.

15. *Promemoria sulla riforma della Settimana Santa. Stato della questione,* August 1954, in *SCCS*, pp. 1-16.

16. *Intorno alla Settimana Santa,* April 30, 1954, in *SCCS*, pp. 1-2.

17. *La Madonna nella liturgia occidentale,* Lecture delivered at S. Marcello al Corso, Rome May 8, 1954, in *ALV*, pp. 1-6.

1 9 5 5

18. *Sull'aggiornamento della Settimana Santa,* 1955, in *SCCS*, pp. 17- 45.

19. *Sulla sistemazione del Giovedì e Venerdì Santo,* 1955, in *SCCS*, pp. 1-8.

20. *Annotazioni intorno alla riforma della liturgia della Domenica delle Palme,* 1955, in *SCCS*, pp. 1-15.

21. *Sulla riforma della Liturgia del Giovedì Santo e Venerdì Santo,* 1955, in *SCCS*, pp. 1-5.

22. *La Quaresima,* Lecture delivered to the students of the *Antonianum,* February 24, 1955, in *ALV*, pp. 1-9.

1 9 5 6

23. *La Riforma della Settimana Santa,* February 21, 1956, in *ALV*, pp. 1-14.

24. *Storia dei Riti del Triduo Sacro,* Conversation broadcast on RAI March 26, 1956, in SCCS, pp. 1-9.

25. *La Riforma dell'Ordo Liturgico della Settimana santa,* Conversation broadcast on RAI March 27, 1956, in *SCCS*, pp. 1-7.

26. *La Messa,* Weekly conference delivered at S. Sebastiano al Palatino, Rome November 24, 1956, in *ALV*, pp. 1-15.

1 9 5 7

27. *La Riforma liturgica della Settimana Santa,* April 7, 1957, in *ALV*, pp. 1-10.

1 9 5 8

28. *La Santa Messa.* Religious instruction delivered at "*Convivio*" about 1958, in *ALV*, pp. 1-29.

29. *Il Breviario.* Liturgical lectures delivered in March 1958 up to October 10, 1971, in *ALV*, pp. 1-118.

30. *Liturgia e vita cristiana.* Lecture delivered to GFAC, February 20, 1958, in *ALV*, pp. 1-9.

1 9 6 3

31. *La Costituzione della Sacra Liturgia,* Notes released to the press agency,

ANSA, November 30, 1963, in *SCCS*, pp. 1-3.

32. *Note P. Antonelli. 2ª Sessione Vat. II*, September 29 – December 4, 1963, in *SCCS*, pp. 1-81.

33. *Promemoria sulla revisione dei libri liturgici in esecuzione della Costituzione Conc. della S. Liturgia*, December 19, 1963, in *SCCS*, pp. 1-8, 1-9.

1 9 6 4

34. *La Costituzione de S.Liturgia*, January 25, 1964, in *ALV*, pp.1-29.

35. *La Costituzione de Sacra Liturgia, Convention* OR, February 4 - 7, 1964, in *ALV*, pp. 1-15.

36. *Note sulle Adunanze del "Consilium" 1964, n. 1*, from March 11 to October 1, 1964, in *SCCS*, pp. 1-130.

37. *La Costituzione liturgica nella lettera e nello spirito*, October 8, 1964, in *ALV*, pp. 1-11.

38. *Il nuovo "Ordo Missae"*, November 22, 1964, in *ALV*, pp. 1-35.

39. *La Costituzione Conciliare sulla S. Liturgia. Antecedenti e grandi principi*, December 26, 1964, in *ALV*, pp. 1-18.

40. *La "Instructio" del 26 sett. 1964. Indole, scopo, principi e prescrizioni concernenti la Messa*, December 27, 1964, in ALV, pp. 1-20.

1 9 6 5

41. *Ragioni storiche e prospettive pastorali del rinnovamento liturgico*, January 12, 1965, in *ALV*, pp. 1-5.

42. *Note sulle Adunanze del "Consilium" 1965 n. 2*, April 26 to December 1, 1965, in *SCCS*, pp. 1-170.

1 9 6 6

43. *Bilancio sommario del 1° anno della Riforma Liturgica*, at a parish in Rome, February 10, 1966, in *ALV*, pp.1-5.

44. *Note sulle adunanze del "Consilium" 1966 n. 3*, from October 6 to October 14, 1966, in *SCCS*, pp. 1-89.

45. *Congregazione Plenaria mista delle SS. Congregazioni: Riti, Seminari, Religiosi e del "Consilium", sulla questione della Concelebrazione nei Seminari*, October 22, 1966, in *SCCS*, pp. 1-6.

1 9 6 7

46. *Prospettive e riflessioni intorno alla riforma liturgica postconciliare*, January 9, 1967, in *ALV*, pp. 1-7.

47. *Adunanza speciale sulle questioni d'Olanda*, January 17, 1967, in *SCCS*, pp. 1-7.

48. *Note sulle adunanze del "Consilium" 1967 nn. 3-4*, from April 10 to November 28, 1967, in *SCCS*, pp. 1-98.

49.   *Intorno allo "Statuto" del "Consilium"*, July 15, 1967, in *SCCS*, pp. 1-5.

1968

50.   *Note sulla Riforma liturgica 1968-1971*, in *SCCS*, pp. 1-31.

1969

51.   *Breve appunto compilato su richiesta di S. E. Mons. G. Benelli sostituto della Segreteria di Stato intorno all'Ordo Missae e alla annessa Institutio generalis Missalis Romani*, November 12, 1969, in *SCCS*, pp. 1-3.

1970

52.   *Ultima Sessione del "Consilium ad exsequendam Constitutionem de Sacra Liturgia", che ora è denominata Speciale Commissione per la riforma dei libri liturgici. Inaugurazione S.C. Culto Divino*, April 9 – 10, 1970, in *SCCS*, pp. 1-53.

Published Writings

1 9 2 7

53. *De re monastica in Dialogis S. Gregorii Magni*, in *Antonianum*, 2 (1927), pp. 401-436.

1 9 2 8

54. *I primi monasteri di monaci orientali in Roma*, in *RAC*, 5 (1928), pp. 105-121.

1 9 4 7

55. *L'elemento liturgico nel dottorato di S. Antonio.* Atti delle settimane Antoniane, Rome 1947, pp. 249-260. The article was translated into German by Fr. Sofronio Closen: *Die Erhebung des hl. Antonius von Padua zum Kirchenlehrer. Eine liturgie-geschichtliche Unterwenung von P. Fernand Antonelli*, in Franziskanische Studien, 31 (1949), pp. 304-314.

1 9 4 8

56. *La festa dell'Assunzione nella liturgia romana.* Atti del Congresso nazionale mariano dei FF.MM. d'Italia, Rome 1948, pp. 223-239.

57. SRC, *Memoria sulla Riforma Liturgica*, Historical Section n. 71, Vatican City 1948, pp. 343.

1 9 5 1

58. *Considerazioni sulla santa Messa.* Circolare, in *Istituto secolare delle Missionarie della Regalità di N. S. Gesù Cristo*, pro manuscripto, Rome 1951, pp.1-7.

59. *Il ripristino della solenne Veglia Pasquale*, in *L'Osservatore Romano* March 4, 1951, p. 1. The article was reproduced in its entirety in French: *La Liturgie du Samedi Saint retrouve sa place dans la nuit de Pâques. Un commentaire du T.R.P. Ferdinando Antonelli*, in *La Croix* March 7, 1951.

60. *De solemni vigilia paschali instauranda. Decretum et Rubricae sabbato sancto servandae si vigilia paschalis instaurata peragitur,* in *AAS*, 33 (1951), pp. 128-137. The Decree was drawn up by Fr. Ferdinando Antonelli. The Rubrics were produced by Fr. J. Löw, and revised by Fr. F. Antonelli and discussed in the Liturgical Commission, in which Antonelli acted as *Relator.*

61. *Ordo Sabbati Sancti quando vigilia paschalis instaurata peragitur.* Typis Polyglottis Vaticanis 1951, pp. 40 March 3, 1951.

62. SRC, *Memoria sulla Riforma Liturgica* Historical Section n. 79, Supplement II (Historical and hagiographical material for the reform of the Liturgical Calendar), Vatican City 1951, pp. 203. In collaboration with Fr. Joseph Löw.

1 9 5 2

63. *Monachesimo occidentale*, in *Enciclopedia Cattolica Italiana*, VIII (1952), col. 1246-1256.

64. *Continuazione della Veglia Pasquale.* Article published in *L'Osservatore Romano,* February 13, 1952. The article was published in the French edition of *L'Osservatore Romano* February 22, 1952; an ample account of the article also appeared in *La Croix,* February 19, 1952.

65. *De facultativa celebratione instauratae Vigiliae paschalis ad triennium prorogata additis ordinationibus et rubricarum variationibus,* in *AAS,* 44 (1952), pp. 53-63. The Decree and *Ordinationes* were drawn up by Fr. F. Antonelli and revised with G. Löw. Both were reproduced in *Ordo Sabbati Sancti,* ed. altera, Typis Polyglottis Vaticanis 1952, edited by Fr. J. Löw, Fr. A. Bugnini and Fr. F. Antonelli.

66. *Liturgia Mariana.* Article published under the title "Maria" in *Enciclopedia Cattolica,* VIII (1952), col. 92-97.

67. *Adnotationes ad Decretum S.R. Congregationis de facultativa celebratione instauratae vigiliae paschalis* 11 Aprile 1952, in *Monitor Ecclesiasticus,* 77 (1952), pp. 24-30.

68. *Ritorno alla Veglia Pasquale,* in *Ecclesia,* XI (1952), pp. 161-163.

69. *La santità di Pio X,* in *Rivista di vita spirituale,* 6 (1952), pp. 120-132. Published also in *Studium,* 50 (1954), pp. 381- 385.

1954

70. *Il Triduum Sacrum, l'Eucarestia e la pace di Cristo,* in *XXXV Congresso eucaristico internazionale,* Sessiones de Estudio, Barcellona 1954, Tomo I (1954), pp. 764-768.

1955

71. *La Regalità di Maria nella Liturgia,* in *Rivista Liturgica,* 41 (1954), p. 14.

72. *De instauratione liturgica Maioris Hebdomadae.* Positio (Sectio historica n. 90), Vatican City 1955, pp. 110.

73. *Prefazione* al volume di A. BUGNINI, *La semplificazione delle Rubriche,* Rome 1955, pp. 7-8.

74. *Importanza e carattere pastorale della riforma liturgica della Settimana Santa,* in *L'Osservatore Romano,* November 27, 1955. The *Decretum Generale* of the Sacred Congregation for Rites published here was also drafted by Fr. F. Antonelli. The same article was reproduced in several languages. Here we limit ourselves to the French edition and to a number of reviews.

    Reprinted in: *Ecclesia,* X (1956), pp. 8-11; in *Iniziativa,* IX (1956), n. 3, p. 4; in *Il nuovo Rito della Settimana Santa,* Milan 1956, pp. 3-9.

    Versions: *Importance et caractère pastoral de la réforme liturgique de la Semaine Sainte,* in *L'Osservatore Romano,* ed. French, December 9, 1955; *Monumentum et character pastoralis instaurationis liturgicae Hebdomadae Sanctae,* in *Ephemerides Liturgicae,* LXX (1956), pp. 15-19;

Bedeutung und Charakter der Liturgiereform der Karuwte: Kölner Pastoralblatt, (1955), pp. 35-39; *Die Bedeutung und der pastorelle Charakter der liturgischen Wiedererneurung der heiligen Wocte* in *Heiliger Dienst*, X (1956), pp. 13-17; *De Reform der Liturgie der heiligen Woche, ihre Bedeutung und ihr Pastoraler Charakter*, in *Die Feier der heiligen Woche*, (1956), pp. 28-36; [*sub eodem titulo*] in *Liturgisches Jahrbuck*, (1955), pp. 199-203.

1956

75. *Pio XII maestro e riformatore della Sacra Liturgia*, in *Il Quotidiano*, March 11, 1956.

76. *La riforma della Settimana Santa*. Account of a conference delivered to the Circolo S. Pietro March 17, in *L'Osservatore Romano* 22 March 22, 1956.

77. *La riforma liturgica della Settimana Santa*, in *VeP*, 39 (1956), pp. 151-161.

78. *I motivi storici delle riforme nella liturgia della Settimana Santa*, in *Il Giornale d'Italia* March 30, 1956, p. 3.

79. *La riforma liturgica della Settimana Santa: importanza, attuazione, prospettive*, in *La Restaurazione liturgica dell'opera di Pio XII. Atti Primo Congresso Internazionale di Liturgia Pastorale* (Assisi 1956), Genova 1957, pp. 179-197.

80. *Reforma liturgiczna Wielkiego Iyzodnia* in *Homo Dei*, 26 (1957), pp. 262-277.

81. *Die liturgishe Erneurung der hl. Woche: ihre Wichtigkeit, Verwirklichung und ihre Aufgaben*, in *Anima*, II (1956), pp. 373-388.

82. *La restaurazione liturgica nell'opera di Pio XII*, Genova 1957, pp. 179-197.

1957

83. *Rivivere il grande mistero della Redenzione*, in *L'Osservatore Romano*, February 15, 1957. The article was published in *Il Quotidiano* e *L'Avvenire* ; da *Rivista liturgica*, 44 (1957), pp. 8-10; da *Les Questions liturgiques et paroissiales*, 39 (1958), pp. 29-32.

84. *Prefazione* a AA.VV., *La nuova liturgia della Settimana Santa*, Milan 1957, 3ª ed., pp. 5-6.

1958

85. *Recensione* all'opera di H.A. SCHMIDT, S.J., *Hebdomada Sancta*, 2 vol., Rome 1956-1957, in *Ephemerides Liturgicae*, 72 (1958), pp. 150-157.

86. *L'istruzione della S. Congregazione dei Riti sulla Musica sacra e la sacra Liturgia*, in *L'Osservatore Romano*, October 2, 1958. The article was published in *Il Quotidiano* e *L'Avvenire*; an English version in *The Furrow*, 9 (1958), pp. 700-709 and in *Worship*, 32 (1958), pp. 626-637.

87. *Introduzione* a *Istruzione della S. Congregazione dei Riti sulla Musica Sacra*

e sacra Liturgia, Opera della Regalità, Milan 1959, pp. 7-20.

1 9 5 9

88. *Presentazione* al libro di M. FARINA - R. FALSINI, *La liturgia spiegata ai fedeli*, Milan 1959, pp. 11-12.

89. *La spiritualità di P. Gemelli*, in *VeP*, 42 (1959), pp. 561-572.

1 9 6 0

90. *Il movimento liturgico*, in *Itinerari Catechistici* (1959-60), n. 4, pp. 9-14.

1 9 6 1

91. *Valorizzazione della Domenica nel nuovo Codice delle Rubriche*, in *Sussidi liturgico-pastorali*, 3 (1961), pp. 20-29

92. *La Domenica. Aspetti storici, liturgici e pastorali*, Milan 1961, pp. 23-30.

93. *Presentazione* a R. FALSINI, *Padre Gemelli e la rinascita liturgica in Italia*, Milan 1961, pp. 5-6.

1 9 6 2

94. *Presentazione* a Dom B. CAPELLE, *Commento delle Collette domenicali del Messale Romano*, Milan 1962, pp. 7-9.

95. *Introduzione* a *La Pastorale dell'Anno liturgico. I misteri della Redenzione* (Sussidi liturgico-pastorali n. 5), Milan 1962, pp. 11-16.

1 9 6 3

96. *Antecedenti, importanza, prospettive della Costituzione della Sacra Liturgia*, in *L'Osservatore Romano*, December 8, 1963. Reproduced in P.C. MORETTI (a cura di), *Costituzione sulla Sacra Liturgia*, Torino 1967, pp. 11-23.

97. *Presentazione* all'edizione italiana di G.A. MARTIMORT (editor), *La Chiesa in preghiera*, Rome 1963, pp. 9-10.

1 9 6 4

98. *Introduzione* a F. ANTONELLI - R. FALSINI (editor), *Costituzione conciliare sulla Sacra Liturgia.*, Milan 1964, pp. 9-21.

99. *La Magna Charta della Liturgia*, in *Il Maestro*, 11 (1964), pp. 1-5.

1 9 6 5

100. *Costituire un'assemblea sacra*, in *Le Missioni Francescane*, 3 (1965), pp. 8-9.

101. *Ragioni storiche e prospettive pastorali del rinnovamento liturgico*, in *L'assistente ecclesiastico*, 35 (1965), pp. 97-105.

102. *Riforma Liturgica* in *La Costituzione liturgica e la formazione seminaristica*. Acts of from the Natational Convention of Franciscan Educators of Italy (*Convegno Nazionale Educatori Francescani d'Italia*) (Rome July 26 – 29, 1965), Bologna 1966, pp. 17-23.

103. *Introduzione* a *Il culto eucaristico nel rinnovamento liturgico*. Acts of the

IX pastoral liturgical Convention (*Convegno liturgico-pastorale*), Rome February 7 - 10, 1966, pp. 9-13.

104. SRC, *Urbis et Orbis. Super concelebratione Missae in Seminariis. Stato della questione*, Rome 1966, pp. 3-4.

1 9 6 7

105. *Presentazione* a R. FALSINI, *Commento alle Orazioni dopo la Comunione delle domeniche e feste*, Milan 1967, pp. 5-7.

106. *Costituzione sulla Sacra Liturgia* (edited by C. MORETTI), Turin 1967. Fr. Antonelli's article published in *L'Osservatore Romano*, December 8, 1963 is reprinted on pp. 11-23.

1 9 6 8

107. *Introduzione* a *Il Canone della Messa. Per una valorizzazione pastorale della preghiera eucaristica*. Acts of the XI *Convegno pastorale-liturgico*, Rome 19-22 Febbraio 1968, pp. 9-11.

1 9 7 0

108. *Introductio seu Relatio ad schema de S. Liturgia in Concilio Vaticano II propositum*, in *Acta Synodalia Sacrosancti Concilii Vaticani II* (Periodus prima. Pars I. Sessio Publica I. Congrega tionis Generalis I-IX), vol. I, Vatican City 1970, pp. 304-308.

1 9 7 1

109. *Introduzione* a *Messaggio biblico per il nostro tempo. Per l'uso pastorale del Lezionario festivo*, Milan 1971, pp. 12-16.

1 9 7 2

110. *Introduzione* a R. FALSINI, *Il dono dello Spirito Santo per la pastorale della cresima*, Milan 1972, pp. 8-10.

1 9 7 4

111. *Conclusione* of the XVI *Convegno liturgico-pastorale* OR, in *Liturgia*, 168 (1974), pp. 194-195.

112. *Presentazione* a A.G. MARTIMORT, *Bilancio della Riforma liturgica: a dieci anni dalla Costituzione Conciliare sulla Sacra Liturgia*, Milan 1974, pp. 5-7.

113. *Introduzione* e *Conclusione* a *Il "nuovo" Messale*, Milan 1974, pp. 7-8; 205-207.

1 9 7 7

114. *Introduzione* a AA.VV., *L'ultima Pasqua del cristiano. Dalla morte alla vita. Problemi pastorali delle esequie cristiane*, Milan 1977, pp. 7-9.

1 9 7 8

115. F. ANTONELLI, *Communication au Cinquantenaire de l'Institut d'archéologie chrétienne*, in Atti *del IX Congresso Internazionale di Archeologia cristiana*, vol I, Vatican City 1978 (*Studi di antichità cristiana*, 32), pp. 87-89.

1979

116. *Consacrazione e Missione negli Istituti Secolari,* Milan 1979, pp. 144.

1980

117. *Discorso del card. Antonelli sulla Musica Sacra,* in *Bollettino Ceciliano. Rivista di Musica Sacra,* 75 (1979), nn. 10-11; 31-33.

118. *Sulla Musica Sacra,* Discorso del Card. Antonelli, in *Atti del XXIII Congresso Nazionale di Musica Sacra,* Rome 1980, pp. 31-33.

1984

119. *Introduzione* a R. FALSINI, *Concilio e Riforma liturgica,* Milan 1984, pp. 7-10.

120. *Introduzione* a R. FALSINI, *La Parola di Dio nella celebrazione,* Milan 1984, pp. 7-8.

121. *Pio XII e la Riforma liturgica,* in *Pius XII, in memoriam,* Rome 1984, pp. 139-142.

122. *Prefazione* a *Mens concertat voci,* for Msgr. A.G. Martimort on the occasiion of his 40 years of teaching and the 20th anniversy of the Constitution *"Sacrosanctum Concilium",* Rome 1983, pp. 9-12.

1988

123. *A quarantanove anni dalla morte di Pio XI. Ogni incontro una lezione di cultura e di bontà,* in *L'Osservatore Romano,* February 10, 1988, p. 4.

Works on Antonelli

[ANONYMOUS], *La scomparsa del Cardinale Ferdinando Giuseppe Antonelli*, in *L'Osservatore Romano*, July 18, 1993, p. 7.

CESCHI J. R., *"Hacia una liturgia totalmente renovada"*, in *Corresponsal especial de ESQUIU en Roma*, pp. 14-26.

FALSINI R., *La Riforma della Veglia Pasquale (1951-1991)*, in *RPL*, 29 (1991), pp. 74-78.

– *Il Cardinale Antonelli e la riforma liturgica*, in *RPL*, 180 (1993-5), pp. 72-76.

– *Una pagina di storia. Il Card. Antonelli e la Riforma Liturgica*, in AA.VV. *Il mistero cristiano e la sua celebrazione*, Milan 1994, pp. 173-184.

LARRAÑAGA T., *Omaggio a S. Em. Card. Ferdinando Giuseppe Antonelli*, in *Antonianum*, 61 (1986), pp. 507-519.

MARTIMORT A. G., *"In memoriam". Le cardinal Ferdinando Antonelli (1896-1993)*, in *Notitiae*, 324 (1993), pp. 432-437.

PONZI M., *L'estremo omaggio ad un uomo di pace*, in *Notitiae*, July 15, 1993, p. 5.

SODANO Card. A., *Servì generosamente la Chiesa nel solco della spiritualità francescana*, in *L'Osservatore Romano*, July 15, 1993, p. 5.

SIRBONI S., *Il mistero cristiano*, in *Vita Pastorale*, 4 (1994), pp. 123-125.

VARIOUS AUTHORS, *Adveniat*, 12 (1993), pp. 1-17.

VARIOUS AUTHORS, *Una pagina di storia. Il Card. Antonelli e la Riforma Liturgica*, Milan 1994, pp. 173-184.

General Bibliography

Magisterial and Conciliar Documents

PIUS Pp. X, Constitutio Apostolica *Divino afflatu,* November 1, 1911, in *AAS,* 3 (1911), pp. 633-638.

– *motu proprio, Abhinc duos annos,* October 23, 1913, in *AAS,* 5 (1913), pp. 449-51.

PIUS Pp. XI, Constitutio Apostolica *Divini cultus,* December 1928, in *AAS,* 21 (1929), pp. 6-14.

– *motu proprio, Già da qualche tempo,* February 6, 1930, in *AAS,* 22 (1930), pp. 87-88.

PIUS Pp. XII, Motu Proprio *In cotidianis precibus,* March 25, 1945, in *AAS,* 37 (1945), pp. 65-67.

– *Litterae Encyclicae, Mediator Dei,* November 20, 1947, in *AAS,* 39 (1947), pp. 521-600.

– *Constitutio Apostolica, Christus Dominus et* Instructio S. Officii, *de nova displina servanda quoad ieiunium eucharisticum* January 6, 1953, in *AAS,* 45 (1953), pp. 15-24.

ENCHIRIDION VATICANUM, *Documenti ufficiali della Santa Sede,* voll. 1-13, Bologna 1966-1993.

– *Acta synodalia sacrosancti Concilii oecumenici Vaticani II,* vol. I, Periodus prima. Pars II, Vatican City 1970, p. 305.

– *Insegnamenti di Paolo VI,* II, Vatican City 1964.

IOANNES PAULUS Pp. II, Litterae Apostolicae *Vicesimus quintus annus* quinto iam lustro expleto conciliari ab promulgata de sacra liturgia constitutione "*Sacrosanctum Concilium*", December 4, 1988, in *AAS,* 81 (1989), pp. 898-918.

SACRA RITUUM CONGREGATIO, *Memoria sulla riforma liturgica,* Vatican City 1948.

– *Memoria sulla riforma liturgica.* Supplemento I, *Intorno alla graduazione liturgica,* Vatican City 1950, pp. 38.

– Supplemento II. *Annotazioni alla "Memoria", presentate su richiesta dai Rev.mi*

> *Dom Capelle OSB, P. Jungmann SJ, Mons. Righetti,* Vatican City 1950, pp. 64.

– Supplemento III. *Materiale storico, agiografico, liturgico per la riforma del Calendario,* Vatican City 1951, pp. 204.

– *Ordo Sabbati Sancti,* Vatican City 1951.

– *De Instauratione liturgica maioris hebdomadae,* Vatican City 1955, pp. 110

– *Simplificatio Rubricarum,* Vatican City 1955, pp. 218-224.

– *Maxima Redemptionis Mysteria,* in *AAS,* 47 (1955), pp. 838-847.

– Supplemento IV. *Consultazione dell'Episcopato intorno alla Riforma del Breviario Romano (1956-1957). Risultati e deduzioni,* Vatican City 1957, pp. 140.

– *Instructio de Musica Sacra et Sacra Liturgia ad mentem litterarum encyclicarum Pii Papae XII "Musicae sacrae disciplina" et "Mediator Dei",* a SRC emanata, September 3, 1953, in *AAS,* 50 (1958), pp. 630-663.

Studies

ADRIANOPOLI L., *Liturgia e pastoralità nella figura di Mons. Moglia* in *L'Osservatore Romano* August 19, 1966.

AUF DER MAUR H., *Le celebrazioni nel ritmo del tempo: I. Feste del Signore nella settimana e nell'anno.* The Liturgy of the Church, a manual of liturgical science, Turin 1990.

BATIFFOL P., *Leçons sur la Messe,* Paris 1923.

BAUDOT G., *Il Breviario Romano. Origini e storia,* Rome 1909.

BERTI G., *La Settimana Santa. Commento storico, dogmatico e pastorale al nuovo Ordo,* Milan 1957.

BOTTE B., *Le mouvement liturgique. Témoignages et souvenirs,* Lovanio-Parigi 1973.

BOUYER L., *Architecture et Liturgie,* Paris 1967.

BROVELLI F., *Le celebrazioni del Triduo pasquale,* in AA.VV., *Il Messale Romano del Vaticano II, Orazionale e Lezionario, vol. I* (Quaderni di Rivista Liturgica, Nuova serie, n. 6), Leumann-Turin 1984. pp. 351-397.

BRUYLANTS P., *Les oraisons du Missel Romain. Tabulae synopticae fontium Missalis Romani,* Indices Tomorum I-II, Louvain 1952.

BUGNINI A., *La riforma liturgica (1948-1975),* Rome 1980.

– *Il primo esperimento della Veglia pasquale restaurata. Sguardo di insieme sulla stampa,* in *Ephemerides Liturgicae,* 66 (1952) pp. 90-98.

– *Documenta Pontificia ad instaurationem liturgicam spectantia (1903-1953),* Rome 1953.

CABROL F. – LECLERCQ H., *Dictionnaire d'archéologie chrétienne et de liturgie*, vol. 1.13, Paris 1909, 1953.

CATTANEO E., *Il culto cristiano in Occidente. Note storiche*, Rome 1984, pp. 486-487.

DE PUNIET P., *Le Pontifical Romain*, I-II, Lovanio 1930.

DUSCHESNE L., *Origines du culte chrétien. Etude sur la liturgie latine avant Charlemagne*, Paris 1925.

EISENHOFER L., *Compendio di liturgia*, Torino 1944.

FALSINI R., *Il Cardinale Antonelli e la riforma liturgica*, in *RPL* 180 (1993), pp. 72-76.

– *La riforma della Veglia pasquale (1951-1991)*, in *RPL*, 29 (1991), pp. 74-78.

– *Padre Gemelli e la rinascita liturgica in Italia*, Milan 1961, p. 15.

– *Padre Agostino Gemelli*, in AA.VV. *Profili di liturgisti*, Rome 1970, pp. 175-178.

– *Una pagina di storia. Il card. Antonelli e la riforma liturgica* in Idem *Il mistero cristiano e la sua celebrazione*, Milan 1994.

– *I convegni liturgico-pastorali dell'Opera della Regalità di NSGC*, in *Notitiae*, 270-271 (1989), pp. 195-202.

FRISÓN B., *Cardenal Larraona*, Madrid 1979.

GEMELLI A., *Liturgia e "liturgismo"* in *RdC*, 14 (1933), pp. 491-494.

GRISAR H., *Roma alla fine del mondo antico*, Rome 1930.

HANSSENS J. M., *Amalarii Episcopi opera liturgica omnia*, tomi I III, Città del Vaticano 1948.

HOLWECK F.G., *Calendarium liturgicum festorum Dei et Matris Dei*, Philadelphia 1925.

JOSI E., *Istituto Pontificio di Archeologia cristiana*, in *Enciclopedia Cattolica*, vol. VII, Rome 1951, Col. 351-352.

JUNG V. H. E., *Die vorarbeiten zu einer liturgiereform unter Pius XII*, in *LJ*, 26 (1976), pp. 165-182.

K. A. H., *L'Anno ecclesiastico e le feste dei santi nel loro svolgimento storico*, versione dal tedesco di A. Mercati, Rome 1914.

LAMERI A., *L'attività di promozione liturgica dell'Opera della Regalità (1931-1945)*, Milan 1992.

LARRAÑAGA T., *Omaggio a S. Em. Card. Ferdinando Giuseppe Antonelli*, in *Antonianum*, 61 (1986), p. 510.

LÖW J., *La Settimana Santa restaurata e la pastorale liturgica*, in *RL*, 44 (1957), pp. 79-92.

The Development of the Liturgical Reform

MARAVAL P., *Égérie, Journal de voyage*, SCH 296, Paris 1982.

MARTIMORT A.G., *Bilancio della riforma liturgica. A dieci anni dalla Costituzione Conciliare sulla Sacra Liturgia*, Milan 1974.

– *In Memoriam: le Cardinal Ferdinando Antonelli (1896-1993)*, in *Notitiae*, 324 (1993), pp. 432-437.

– *La Constitution sur la liturgie de Vatican II. Esquisse historique*, in *Bulletin de Littérature Ecclésiastique*, 85 (1984), pp. 60-74, ripresa da *LMD*, 157 (1984), pp. 33-52.

– *La riforma conciliare nel cammino storico del movimento liturgico e nella vita della Chiesa*, in AA.VV., *Assisi 1956-1986. Il movimento liturgico tra riforma conciliare e attese del popolo di Dio*, Assisi 1987, pp. 75-93.

NEUNHEUSER B., *Storia della liturgia attraverso le epoche culturali*, Rome 1977.

NOÈ V., *La storia della Costituzione Liturgica. Punti di riferimento*, in SACRA CONGREGAZIONE PER IL CULTO DIVINO, *La Costituzione Liturgica "Sacrosanctum Concilium"*, Rome 1986, pp. 9-24.

RIGHETTI M., *Manuale di storia liturgica*, vol. I-IV, Milan 1946.

ROUSSEAU O., *Histoire du mouvement liturgique*, Paris 1945.

SCAGLIA SYXTO P., *Notiones archaeologiae christianae disciplinis theologicis coordinatae*, vol. I-II, Rome 1909-1911.

SCHMIDT H., *Hebdomada Sancta*, 2 vol., Rome 1956.

SCHUSTER A. I., *Liber Sacramentorum. Note storiche liturgiche sul Messale Romano*, Turin 1933.

SORCI P., *Una pagina di storia del movimento liturgico in Italia: i trenta convegni nazionali di Liturgia dell'Opera della Regalità*, in *RPL*, 150 (1988), pp. 69-76.

VARIOUS AUTHORS, *La restaurazione liturgica nell'opera di Pio XII*. Atti Primo Congresso di Liturgia pastorale (Assisi 1956), Genova 1957.

VARIOUS AUTHORS, *La Sacra Liturgia rinnovata dal Concilio. Studi e commenti intorno alla Costituzione Liturgica del Concilio Ecumenico Vaticano II*, Torino-Leumann 1965.

WILPERT G., *La fede della Chiesa nascente secondo i monumenti dell'arte funeraria antica*, Vatican City 1938.

Index

and, 146
need for, 22, 57–58, 143–146
negative reactions to, 150
Ordo Sabbati Sancti (1952), 49
pastoral character of, 58–59
Pius XII's role in, 16–18
preparatory factors, 145–148
problems addressed (list), 50
*See also Consilium ad exsequendam
   Constitutionem de Sacra Liturgia;
   Memoria sulla Riforma Liturgica;*
   Pontifical Commission for the
   Reform of the Liturgy
Liturgical year. *See* Calendar
Löw, Joseph, 9, 29, 59, 226
on ceremonial concelebration, 247
on classes of feasts, 312
on the Divine Office, 227, 264, 265,
   312
on the Easter Vigil, 230
*Esposto intorno alla 'Scriptura
   ocurrens'*, 295
friendship with Antonelli, 74–75
on Holy Week rites, 228, 246–247,
   250, 274
on the liturgical calendar, 236, 238,
   243, 244, 263, 264, 267, 268,
   269, 269–270, 270–271, 273
on liturgical gradation, 234, 237
on *Maria Regina* feast, 258, 259, 261
on Mass of St. Joseph the Worker,
   285
Memoria sulla Riforma Liturgica and,
   19, 20, 21, 207
on missal lectionary, 297
on papal feast, 258
Pontifical Commission for
   the Reform of the Liturgy,
   appointment, 18, 26, 206, 207,
   310
on rubrics simplification, 311
on scriptural readings, 295
on vernacular language use, 231,
   306–307
mentioned, 250, 252, 282, 283, 284,
   288, 303, 305
Lutz, Wilhelm, 29

M
Maccarone (Msgr.), 85, 89

Malula(Msgr.), 78, 80, 95
on Confirmation, 97
on sacred music, 106
mentioned, 111, 117, 118, 119
Marian feasts, 23, 25, 255–257, 258
Annunciation, 237
during Christmas Octave, 215
Immaculate Conception celebration
   date and, 213
Maria Regina, 25, 208, 257–258,
   259–260, 261, 262–263, 270,
   279–280, 281, 282
See also Feast day classification
Marriage. *See* Matrimony
Martimort, Aimé Georges
on Anointing of the Sick, 97
Antonelli's friendship with, 9, 77
on application of the Constitution,
   124
on Baptism, 96
on the Divine Office, 100, 101, 102,
   103, 120
on Extreme Unction, 97
on the liturgical calendar, 108, 110
on religious professions, 115
on sacred music, 105, 106
on vernacular usage, 98, 122
viii, ix-x, 9, 74, 75, 77, 78, 82, 83,
   91, 92, 93, 94, 95, 99, 104, 112,
   116, 119, 123, 158, 164
Martin (Archbishop of Rouen), 294
Martin (Bishop), 80, 81, 82, 86, 156
on application of the Constitution,
   124
on Chapter I *modi*, 119
on the Divine Office, 99, 101, 102,
   103, 104, 111, 113, 118, 120
on sacred music, 106, 114
mentioned, 121, 122
Martin (Msgr. from Trier), 156
Martini, Urbano, 2
Masi (Msgr.), 78
Masses, 170
active participation by laity, 76, 145,
   148
binated, 64
changes proposed for, 280–281
concelebration, 93–94, 117, 123
Divine Office relationship to,
   101–102

Z

Zama, Antonio, 29

Zauner (Bishop), 93, 106, 156
   on the liturgical calendar, 109, 110,
      111, 113, 120
   on vernacular usage, 123
   mentioned, 117, 118